Keeping Fires Night and Day

Keeping Fires Night and Day

Selected Letters of Dorothy Canfield Fisher

Edited with an Introduction by
Mark J. Madigan

Foreword by
Clifton Fadiman

University of Missouri Press
COLUMBIA AND LONDON

5   4   3   2   1   97   96   95   94   93

Library of Congress Cataloging-in-Publication Data

Fisher, Dorothy Canfield, 1879–1958.
   Keeping fires night and day : selected letters of Dorothy Canfield Fisher / edited
with an introduction by Mark J. Madigan ; foreword by Clifton Fadiman.
       p.   cm.
   Includes bibliographical references and index.
   ISBN 0-8262-0884-3 (alk. paper)
   1. Fisher, Dorothy Canfield, 1879–1958—Correspondence.
2. Authors, American—20th century—Correspondence.   I. Madigan,
Mark J., 1961–   .   II. Title.
PS3511.I7416Z48   1993
813′.52—dc20
   [B]   92-43128
                                                                                                           CIP

∞™ This paper meets the requirements of the
American National Standard for Permanence of Paper
for Printed Library Materials, Z39.48, 1984.

Designer: Elizabeth Fett
Typesetter: Connell-Zeko Type & Graphics
Printer and Binder: Thomson-Shore, Inc.
Typefaces: Baskerville and Signet Roundhand

For my mother
and father
and brother, David

Contents

Foreword by Clifton Fadiman   ix

Acknowledgments   xi

Editorial Practice   xiii

Chronology   xvii

Introduction   1

Part 1: Letters, 1900–1908   23

Part 2: Letters, 1912–1919   37

Part 3: Letters, 1920–1929   83

Part 4: Letters, 1930–1939   149

Part 5: Letters, 1940–1949   207

Part 6: Letters, 1950–1958   285

Bibliography   327

Calendar of Letters   333

Notable Recipients   341

Index   351

Foreword

$\mathcal{A}$lmost half a century has passed since, relatively young and absolutely terrified, I sat down at Dorothy's right, attending my first meeting of the Book-of-the-Month Club Editorial Board. I have never forgotten that day, or her, or the many years of the friendship that, with a flashing smile and warm words of welcome, she at once initiated.

For comfort Dorothy used a footstool. She was a smidgen sensitive about her height. She had little need to be, for she never gave the least impression of frailty and remained to almost the end of her long life an extraordinarily attractive woman.

As the reader will discover from this splendid collection of her letters, she wanted, like most professional writers, to be remembered for her books. I hope she will be. Time, tireless winnower, will make the final judgment. For all its copiousness and fineness of feeling, her work may lack the trail-blazing energy that confers survival value on some of her younger contemporaries such as Hemingway, Faulkner, Fitzgerald, and Richard Wright. Nevertheless, her contribution is apparent: she helped twentieth-century American literature to come of age. Perhaps she is only of her period, but whatever distinction that period had it owed in part to her labors.

But I prefer to think of her in a different way.

Today, when we are all engaged in selling each other something, character and personality tend not to be congruent: image is all. With Dorothy they were one: she was incapable of deceiving anyone, including herself. She was, quite literally, an individual, an integer. That integrity was old-fashioned, rooted in her family background, in Puritanism's finer elements, in Quaker influences. It was rooted also in her tacit conviction that the cultivation of the mind took on meaning only if it helped the burgeoning of the moral sense, helping one to live well, as Socrates would have us live well. In consequence she spent much of her life doing good deeds, but without the least self-consciousness, just as great athletes perform well almost because they cannot help it.

Do-gooders sometimes make us feel uneasy, partly because they seem to fly in the face of realism. Dorothy glowed with humor and common sense. Concerning Henry James's fear that some of the characters in *The Bostonians* might be destroying "the sentiment of sex," she remarks tartly, "as if anything could." It was this intelligent New England pawkiness that made it impossible for her nobility of character to make the rest of us feel inferior. Somewhere in these pages she writes, "I feel sure that I am much like everybody else." Untrue, but also true, for she was that rare thing in a political democracy, a genuine, a spontaneous democrat.

As I think back on it, remembering the many monthly meetings of our board as we discussed hundreds of books, trying hard to be fair, to be honest, to be unbiased, it now becomes clear to me that it was Dorothy who, quite unaware of it, educated the four of us. It was her moral example that was at work, her constant reminder that books, good books, were not "products" but the laborious issue of human intelligences, acts of life-affirmation that might actually influence other minds. She made us feel that, however trivial our work might be as compared with graver economic or political issues, it was nonetheless serious.

And that is how and why I remember Dorothy Canfield Fisher.

CLIFTON FADIMAN

Acknowledgments

$\mathcal{I}$ am profoundly indebted to many people for whatever success this volume may claim. Its deficiencies, however, must rightly be attributed to me alone. My professional debt to Arthur F. Kinney is paramount. He has been an astute critic and advisor from the start. David Porter and Connell Gallagher also read the manuscript at an early stage and generously gave of their time in many ways. Ralph H. Orth introduced me to the multiplicitous joys—and frustrations—of literary research and set an example for editorial excellence which I hope to achieve someday. The late Marie Hénault was an inspirational teacher and friend.

Librarians who should be accorded special mention for their efforts on my behalf are Alice L. Birney of the Library of Congress, Donald Gallup of Yale University (emeritus), Sylvia Knight, Jeffrey Marshall and Nadia Smith of the University of Vermont, Eva Moseley of Radcliffe College, Linda Seidman of the University of Massachusetts, Mary Lou Thomas of the Russell Vermontiana Collection, and Robert A. Tibbetts of Ohio State University. I owe thanks to Mme. Eugene Arnaud, the late Mildred Bennett, Clifton Fadiman, Louise Forscher, Elizabeth Hovinen, Arnold Gates, Mary C. Jane, and Helen Cather Southwick for graciously allowing me to examine letters in their private collections.

Clifton Fadiman also answered my questions as I worked on the annotations. Vivian S. Hixson, too, responded to my queries about her grandmother Dorothy Canfield Fisher, and offered full cooperation as executrix of her estate. Fisher's former secretary, Helen Congdon, provided information about the author's epistolary habits. Charlene Sexton located an important collection of letters to Louise Pound at the Nebraska State Historical Society, and Judith Thurman told me of the existence of the Dinesen correspondence in the Royal Library, Copenhagen. Joan Schroeder and Richard Sweterlitsch helped with the annotation of letters to Sarah Cleghorn. Ida H. Washington, Joseph Lovering, and Elizabeth Yates McGreal offered their invaluable insights as pioneering Fisher scholars. Fisher's letters to Céline Sibut were translated from the French by Malcolm Daggett.

For opening their homes to me during my research travels, I am grateful to Patricia and John Duffy Gallagher, Steven Keough, Ksenya Kiebuzinski, Elena Nugent, Dr. C. Q. Pratt, John Remy, Rich Steckler, Boo, and Ned

Strianese. Their hospitality and good cheer made the work all the more enjoyable. One could not ask for better friends.

To the University of Massachusetts I am grateful for a fellowship, which came at a crucial juncture. I am also thankful for the support of the University of Vermont English Department, especially that of Chairperson Anthony S. Bradley. The expertise of those at the University of Missouri Press, particularly Jane Lago and Sara Fefer, was of inestimable value to this first-time author.

Finally, I am most grateful to my parents for their unfailing support and encouragement and love.

Editorial Practice

Criteria for Selection and Scope of Search

$\mathcal{T}$he primary focus of this collection is literary, although not exclusively so. Letters have been chosen according to their relevance to Fisher's career and development as a writer. Relevance is broadly defined to include both direct discussion of literary topics and reflections of the personality, interests, background, and spirit which inform the author's approach to literature. The inclusion of only whole letters (no excerpts) has been a major criterion in the selection process, as has the aim of preserving the author's own words (with the exception of Letters 8 and 10, which have been translated from the French). My intent has been to honor both the art of letter writing and Fisher's epistolary voice. However, some otherwise excellent letters have been excluded due to their length. Fisher's "round-robin" letters from France during World War I, meant for circulation among friends and family, fall into this category, as many run ten single-spaced, typed pages. In this case, one of the shorter "round-robins" (Letter 34) has been included as an example.

The letters presented here were chosen from over twenty-five hundred items, of which I examined either the originals or photoduplications. This edition is, thus, but a highly selective sample of Fisher's correspondence. The search included private collections (8) and all known institutional repositories of Fisher letters (59, listed in the Calendar of Letters), the largest collections being housed at the University of Vermont and Columbia University. Calls for letters were published in the *Willa Cather Newsletter* (Summer 1989), *Documentary Editing* (September 1989), *New York Times Book Review* (November 12, 1989), and *American Notes & Queries* (July 1990).

Format and Arrangement

Each letter is preceded by a three-line heading, which lists on the first line the entry number and recipient, on the second line the date, and on the third line the place from which the letter was written.

The letters are arranged chronologically. Undated letters are assigned dates in brackets based on internal or circumstantial evidence. Letters for which a complete date could not be established are listed at their earliest possible place in the Calendar of Letters. For instance, Letter 69 [1927] precedes all other letters of that year. Conjectural elements in dates are followed by a question mark as dictated by the strength of supporting evidence. Unsupported dates appended to copy-texts *ex post facto* by the author or other persons are followed by a question mark.

Copy-Texts

The majority of Fisher's letters survive in either typescript or manuscript, and these have been used as the copy-texts whenever possible. However, a significant number exist only in less authoritative versions, such as carbon copies (which do not contain alterations that may have been made on the original) or published letters for which the original has not been located, and these were then used as copy-texts. The state, length, and location of the copy-text is noted in the Calendar of Letters.

Emendations

The objective of this edition is to print Fisher's letters in a form that is clear and faithful to the copy-text. Some letters have required editorial intervention to emend distractions to the reader.

A. Emendation of Substantives
1. Place is appended in brackets when not included in the copy-text.
2. Words or phrases necessary to the readibility of a passage are added in brackets.
3. Cancellations are not reproduced. Routine typographical and dittographical errors and slips of the pen are emended silently. There are no concealed editorial deletions or omissions.
4. Handwritten additions to typed letters are preceded by a notation in brackets: [Handwritten].

B. Emendation of Accidentals
1. Date and place information is printed against the left margin as part of the uniform three-line heading, regardless of manuscript location. The dateline format has been normalized to indicate month, day, and year, in that order. Place information written in Fisher's hand is listed fully. Letterhead information is recorded in the notes. The salutation is printed below the place and date, again regardless of the copy-text location, and is followed uniformly by a colon. Signatures are printed below the body

of each letter against the left margin. No signature appears on Fisher's carbon copy letters.

2. The first line of each paragraph is indented five spaces wherever the copy-text clearly indicates a new paragraph is intended.

3. Missing punctuation is added silently to titles or abbreviations (such as Mrs., St. or mss.) and the ends of sentences.

4. All ellipses are Fisher's and have been normalized to three periods (. . .).

5. Dashes are indicated by a double dash (—) regardless of length in the copy-text.

6. Missing elements in pairs of quotation marks and parentheses are supplied silently.

7. Misuse of the apostrophe (Fisher often omitted the apostrophe from the contraction "it's," for example) and punctuation with quotation marks (she sometimes placed her periods and commas after rather than inside a closing quotation mark) have been corrected silently.

8. Fisher was an excellent speller. Her rare spelling errors have been emended silently except when variations of spelling allow the reader to observe the evolution of Fisher's epistolary style over time.

9. Foreign terms, names of ships, and titles of periodicals and books have been italicized. Quotation marks have been added around the titles of essays, short stories, and manuscripts.

Undeciphered Words and Conjectural Readings

An undeciphered word or words is noted by an x or an appropriate number of x's in brackets, so that [x] would indicate that one word has not been deciphered, and [xxxx] would indicate four words. Conjectural readings are also printed in brackets followed by a question mark, such as [Zephine ?].

Textual Notes

Numbered annotations to the letters follow the letters as notes. Allusions and references to persons, places, and events are identified upon their first appearance in the text; readers are cross-referred to the original annotation thereafter. Birth and death dates are listed for all persons mentioned in the text whenever possible. Full bibliographical information is listed for all works mentioned in the text. Information on recipients of Fisher's letters may be found under Notable Recipients rather than numbered annotations. Annotations which may be found in standard reference works have been kept brief.

Chronology

1873   (June) Flavia A. Camp and James Hulme Canfield marry.

1879   (February 17) DCF born in Lawrence, Kansas; father is professor of Political Economy and Sociology at University of Kansas, mother is artist; DCF spends summers at Canfield relatives' house in Arlington, Vermont.

1890   (Winter) DCF makes first trip to Europe, accompanies mother to Paris; later attends French schools.

1891   Fishers move to Lincoln, Nebraska; father becomes chancellor of the state university where Willa Cather is a student.

1894   Publishes "The Fear That Walks by Noonday" (collaboration with Willa Cather) in University of Nebraska yearbook.

1895   Fishers move to Columbus, Ohio; father becomes president of Ohio State University, where DCF enrolls as student.

1899   (Spring) DCF graduates from OSU. Father resigns presidency, becomes librarian of Columbia University, New York. (Fall) DCF begins graduate work in French at the Sorbonne in Paris.

1902   (March) First professional publication, *New York Times* article on Holy Week in Spain; (Fall) Travels with Willa Cather in Europe.

1903   Turns down assistant professorship at Western Reserve University, Cleveland, Ohio.

1904   (Spring) Receives Ph.D. from Columbia; (May) dissertation, *Corneille and Racine in England,* is published by Columbia University Press. (May) Meets John Fisher. (Fall) Accepts job as "secretary" at Horace Mann School, New York City. (Winter) Quarrels with Willa Cather over "The Profile." Publishes stories in magazines.

1905   (Summer) Travels in Germany, Norway, and France.

1906   *Elementary Composition* (with George R. Carpenter) published by Macmillan.

1907   (May) Marries John Fisher, moves to Arlington, Vermont. *Gunhild* (novel) published by Henry Holt.

1908   (June) Meets Sarah Cleghorn and Zephine Humphrey.

1909   (March 29) Father dies; (July 30) daughter, Sally, born.

1911   (Winter) Meets Maria Montessori in Rome.

1912   *A Montessori Mother* published by Henry Holt; *The Squirrel-Cage* (novel) published by Henry Holt. (November) Hires Paul Reynolds as literary agent.

1913   (December) Son, James (Jimmy), born. *A Montessori Manual* published by Richardson Co.

1914   *Mothers and Children* published by Henry Holt.

1915   *Hillsboro People* (stories) published by Henry Holt; *The Bent Twig* (novel) published by Henry Holt. (December) Meets Robert Frost in Boston.

1916   *The Real Motive* (stories) published by Henry Holt; *Fellow Captains* (misc. prose, with Sarah N. Cleghorn) published by Henry Holt; *Self-Reliance* published by Bobbs-Merrill. (April) John Fisher leaves for France to aid in war relief; (August) DCF travels with children to join her husband in relief work in France.

1917   *Understood Betsy* (young adult novel) published by Henry Holt. (Spring) DCF loses hearing in one ear

1918   Fishers return to Arlington. *Home Fires in France* (stories) published by Henry Holt.

1919   *The Day of Glory* (stories) published by Henry Holt.

1921   Honorary Ph.D., Middlebury College. *The Brimming Cup* (novel) published by Harcourt, Brace. Becomes first woman elected to the Vermont State Board of Education.

1922   Honorary Ph.D., Dartmouth College; Honorary Ph.D., University of Vermont. *Rough-Hewn* (novel) published by Harcourt, Brace. Reconciles quarrel with Willa Cather.

1923   *Raw Material* (stories) published by Harcourt, Brace; *Life of Christ* (translated from the Italian of Giovanni Papini) published by Harcourt, Brace.

1924   *The Home-Maker* (novel) published by Harcourt, Brace.

1925   *Made-to-Order Stories* (stories) published by Harcourt, Brace.

1926   Accepts position on Book-of-the-Month Club Committee of Selection; eyesight steadily diminishes as a result of professional reading. *Her Son's Wife* (novel) published by Harcourt, Brace.

1927   *Why Stop Learning?* published by Harcourt, Brace.

1929   Honorary Ph.D., Columbia University.

1930   (August 15) Mother dies. *The Deepening Stream* (novel) published by Harcourt, Brace.

1931   (Spring) Anzia Yezierska begins year-and-a-half stay in Arlington. Honorary Ph.D., Northwestern University; elected to the National Institute of Arts and Letters. Recommends *The Good Earth* as a B-O-M; begins friendship with Pearl Buck. *Basque People* (stories) published by Harcourt, Brace.

1932   (December) Recommends Isak Dinesen's (Karen Blixen's) stories to agent Paul Reynolds. *Tourists Accomodated* (play) published by Harcourt, Brace; *Work: What It Has Meant to Men through the Ages* (translated from the Italian of Adriano Tilgher) published by Harcourt, Brace.

1933   Daughter, Sally, marries John Paul Scott. *Bonfire* (novel) published by Harcourt, Brace.

1934   Honorary Ph.D., Rockford College.

1935   Honorary Ph.D., Ohio State; Honorary Ph.D., Swarthmore College; Honorary Ph.D., Williams College. (June) Son, Jimmy, marries Eleanor Bodine.

1939   Honorary Ph.D., Mt. Holyoke College; Honorary Ph.D., University of Nebraska. *Seasoned Timber* (novel) published by Harcourt, Brace.

1939–
1940   (September-April) Organizes Children's Crusade for Children.

1940   *Nothing Ever Happens and How It Does* (children's stories, with Sarah N. Cleghorn) published by Beacon Press; *Tell Me a Story* (children's stories) published by University Publishing Co.

1943   "The Knot-Hole" wins second prize among the O. Henry Prize Stories. *Our Young Folks* published by Harcourt, Brace. (March) John Fisher suffers heart attack.

1944   (July) Advises Richard Wright on *Black Boy*.

1945   (January 31) Son, Jimmy, dies in Philippines.

1946   *American Portraits* published by Henry Holt.

1949   *Four-Square* (anthology) published by Harcourt, Brace.

1950   *Our Independence and the Constitution* (children's history) published by Random House; *Paul Revere and the Minute Men* (children's history) published by Random House.

1951   Retires from Book-of-the-Month Club. (February) Receives Constance Lindsay Skinner Award from Women's National Book Association; Honorary Ph.D., Marlboro College.

1952   *A Fair World for All* (children's history) published by Whittlesey House.

1953   Donates papers to the University of Vermont. (December 1) Suffers stroke. *Vermont Tradition* published by Little, Brown.

1954   Honorary Ph.D., Smith College.

1956   *A Harvest of Stories* (anthology) published by Harcourt Brace.

1957   *Memories of Arlington, Vermont* published by Duell, Sloan, Pearce.

1958   (November 9) Dorothy Canfield Fisher dies of stroke.

1959   *And Long Remember* (children's history) published (posthumously) by Whittlesey House; (June 1) Husband, John, dies of complications from influenza.

Keeping Fires
Night and Day

Introduction

— *I* —

$\mathcal{I}$n 1948 Dorothy Canfield Fisher (1879–1958) wrote to literary critic Albert L. Guerard about the University of Vermont's proposal to establish a collection of her papers at their Burlington campus:

> Their idea is not a bad one I think, not to wait until an author has been dead twenty or thirty years, and his children and grandchildren have lost most of his papers—for who nowadays with families moving around all the time could possibly keep a mass of papers together?—but to collect them while the author is still alive. Most of them will not be of any interest to anybody, perhaps none of them will be. But no harm is done in placing them in a fire-proof building instead of in a trunk under the eaves in the attic. (Letter 154)

These remarks reveal much about Fisher: her interest in public education, her foresight, her modesty, and her common sense. They also raise an important question: Of what interest and significance could Fisher's letters possibly be? The letters themselves present the best argument for their publication: set against the American historical and cultural landscape from 1900 to 1958, they are the firsthand account of a singularly gifted, intelligent, and spirited woman who, among many other accomplishments, became one of America's most popular novelists.

Named after the heroine of *Middlemarch,* Dorothea Francis Canfield was born on February 17, 1879, in Lawrence, Kansas. She and her older brother, James, were the children of James Hulme Canfield, a university professor, and Flavia Camp Canfield, an artist. Dorothy grew up in a cultured home and traveled widely while still a child. She moved from Lincoln, Nebraska, to Columbus, Ohio, and then to New York City as her father relocated for academic appointments, and she paid frequent visits to the Arlington, Vermont, home of her father's relatives, and to Paris, where her mother kept a studio. Her early homelife was loving and supportive, but it was not without difficulty. Biographer Ida H. Washington notes that young Dorothy was sensitive to a strain of incompatibility between her parents—a conflict Fisher described in a fictional guise in *The Deepening Stream.* About the relationship of James, an idealistic, ambitious teacher and school administrator, and Flavia, an equally

1

fervent devotee of the arts, Washington writes, "Her quickness of speech and action were, however, to make problems for him as great as those his sense of social responsibility created for her. The differences in temperament created a home in which a sensitive little daughter grew into a deeply perceptive novelist."[1]

Fisher received her bachelor's degree from Ohio State University, where she had concentrated on languages and literature, particularly French. She pursued her scholarly interests at the graduate level, and her academic career culminated in 1904 when she received the Ph.D. in French from Columbia University with a dissertation on Corneille and Racine. Although her training qualified her for a university teaching career, Fisher turned down an offer of a professorship at Case Western Reserve University for family reasons and became secretary at the Horace Mann School in New York. In 1907 she married John Redwood Fisher. A fellow graduate of Columbia, he had been captain of the football team and roommate of Alfred Harcourt, who would later become Dorothy's publisher. They soon moved to Arlington, where she had inherited her great-grandfather's farm. From that Vermont home base she pursued one of the most productive careers in all of American literature.

In all, Fisher published twenty-two works of fiction (for business purposes under her maiden name, Dorothy Canfield) and eighteen works of nonfiction covering a remarkably wide range of subjects. She introduced the child-rearing methods of Dr. Maria Montessori to the United States in *A Montessori Mother* (1912), was a pioneering advocate of adult education in *Why Stop Learning?* (1927), translated Giovanni Papini's *Life of Christ* (1923) and Adriano Tilgher's *Work: What It Has Meant to Men through the Ages* (1931) from the Italian, chronicled the history of Vermont (her adopted home state and the setting for much of her fiction) in *Vermont Tradition* (1953), and wrote several highly regarded books for children (now commemorated by the children's book award that bears her name).

A woman of manifold talents, Fisher's achievements were hardly limited to the literary world. She spoke five languages, founded a Braille press and a children's hospital in France during World War I, organized the Children's Crusade for Children during World War II, was the first president of the Adult Education Association, and was the first woman to serve on the Vermont State Board of Education. Shortly before Fisher's death, Eleanor Roosevelt referred to her as one of the ten most influential women in America.

The variety of her activities notwithstanding, it was primarily as a fiction writer that Fisher was best known and as which she wanted to be remembered.[2] She said in 1944 that writing fiction was "like falling in love" (Letter

---

1. Ida H. Washington, *Dorothy Canfield Fisher: A Biography,* 14.
2. Ibid., x.

134) and worried a year before her death that a biography in progress was "saying too much about actual material actions and activities of mine, and giving too little space to the novels and short stories" (Letter 185). To Fisher, writing was the chief means for making a decisive difference in the world, for educating her fellow citizens, for promulgating moral principles, for initiating social change. Her novels *The Brimming Cup* and *The Home-Maker,* for instance, critique the evils of racism, sexism, and materialism while promoting the virtues of equal access to education and employment.

Yet she did not view her fiction as merely ideological. She was an accomplished critic and was ever-conscious of the flaws in her own work. A tireless reviser, she often felt a sense of artistic inadequacy upon finishing a story or novel. In 1925, she wrote to the author of a soon-to-be-published rhetoric: "I can dimly remember a happy time when I could look at a page of mine and think 'Well, I don't see what more I can do to that.' Never any more! Any page of mine, taken at random, throws me into an acute fever of remorse for the mistakes in it, and an ardent desire to sit down and wrestle with it. This does not increase the joy of authorship, of course, but I hope it increases the quality of the product" (Letter 64).

What emerges clearly from the correspondence is that Fisher lived her life as one piece, drawing together many interests and concerns, so that it is virtually impossible to separate the literary from the biographical, the private from the public. Indeed, to understand the primacy of writing to Fisher is to appreciate its interrelation with the other elements of her life.

—— *II* ——

Fisher's literary career began, like that of many American authors of the early twentieth century, by way of publication in popular magazines—especially women's magazines—such as the *American, Everybody's,* and *Harper's Bazaar.* She had little trouble placing her work and was publishing a steady flow of stories and articles within a few years. Her first novel, *Gunhild,* was published by Holt in 1907, sold only six hundred copies, and received little critical attention.[3] *The Squirrel Cage* appeared five years later to far more favorable reviews. For example, a notice in the *San Francisco Call* read, "We do not quarrel any more about 'The' great American novel, but no reader will deny that this is 'A' great American novel," while the reviewer for the *Progressive Woman* unabashedly stated, "*The Squirrel Cage* deserves to rank as one of the best American novels yet written."

As a result of the novel's reception and the burgeoning market for her maga-

3. Sarah Cleghorn, *Threescore,* 130.

zine work, Fisher attracted the attention of Paul Reynolds, the first literary agent in America. Although reluctant to employ an agent at first (Letter 11), Fisher prospered from her association with him. Through his connections in the publishing world, Reynolds brought Fisher's name to a wider readership, and she soon expressed surprise at the prices he was able to secure for her stories.

Such business considerations were vital to her since she supported a husband and two young children (a daughter, Sally, was born in 1909 and a son, James, in 1913). When Dorothy and John married, they planned to support themselves as professional writers. However, when Dorothy's literary career blossomed and outgrew his own, John assumed the role of secretary and editor of her work. Since they were rarely separated, John Fisher remains a background figure in the letters. (One exception is Letter 8 to Céline Sibut, in which DCF writes at length about her impending marriage.) All indications are that he was deeply loved by Dorothy and that he provided her with invaluable support. Biographer Ida H. Washington has called their home life "harmonious but unconventional." Washington writes, "Dorothy was the chief breadwinner, and John assumed an editorial, consultative relationship to her work. Dorothy thus played the major role in the outside world; at home, however, her respect and affection for her husband were constant, and she sought his judgment on matters practical and literary and submitted to his direction in the details of everyday life."[4] John also tended to the demanding physical chores of rural Vermont life and became involved in local and state politics, serving on the Vermont State Board of Education for many years.

Fisher's popular reputation continued to grow with publication of *The Bent Twig* (1915), a novel, and *Home Fires in France* (1918) and *The Day of Glory* (1919), collected stories based on her experiences in France during World War I. But she could hardly have imagined the success *The Brimming Cup* would encounter upon publication in 1921. Characterized by William Allen White as an "antidote" to the negative portrayal of small-town life in *Main Street*,[5] *The Brimming Cup* finished the year just behind Lewis's novel, as the second most purchased novel in the country. The work brought Fisher to her highest prominence so far; with that attention came the various honors and distractions attendant upon fame: requests for interviews and speeches; invitations to dinner receptions and university commencements; appeals to join committees, support worthy causes, and read the manuscripts of fledgling writers; and a flood of mail from readers across the country.

Nor did Fisher's reputation diminish. Her translation of Papini's *Life of Christ* was second on the best-seller list for nonfiction in 1923, and *The Home-*

---

4. Washington, *Biography,* 64.
5. William Allen White, "The Other Side of Main Street," 7.

Maker was among the ten best-selling novels of 1924. *Her Son's Wife* (1926) also sold well and received considerable critical acclaim. William Lyon Phelps wrote to publisher Alfred Harcourt: " 'Her Son's Wife' is Dorothy Canfield's masterpiece and it is also *a* masterpiece. It is a profound, subtle analysis of human character and human life and a very remarkable book. I predict that it will win the Pulitzer Prize for 1926. It deserves it" (August 25, 1926). Not surprisingly, the comment was featured in the novel's advertising. Although Sinclair Lewis won (and declined) the Pulitzer for *Arrowsmith* that year, Fisher remained one of America's best-known writers for decades.

The thirties brought three more popular novels, *The Deepening Stream* (1930), *Bonfire* (1933), and *Seasoned Timber* (1939), and two collections of stories, *Basque People* (1931) and *Fables for Parents* (1937). A Dorothy Canfield Club was established in 1934, but there is perhaps no more impressive testament to Fisher's popularity than the fact that the serial rights to *Bonfire* were under contract for thirty thousand dollars at the lowest ebb of the depression. The end of the decade was marked by the publication of Fisher's last novel, *Seasoned Timber* (1939). "The Knot-Hole" was published in the *Yale Review* in 1944 and won second prize among the stories in the O. Henry volume that year. Fisher revised earlier stories for *Four-Square* (1949), oversaw the publication of an anthology, *A Harvest of Stories* (1956), and continued to write children's books and magazine articles until near the time of her death in 1958. A letter to Mary C. Jane reveals that Fisher was at work on a history book for children in 1957, which was published posthumously (1959) as *And Long Remember* (Letter 187).

Yet even if she had published none of these works, Fisher would be a notable figure in American letters for her role as a Book-of-the-Month Club (BOMC) judge. She was one of the members on the Board of Selection from its inception in 1926 until 1951 (serving on the original Board with Henry Seidel Canby, William Allen White, Heywood Broun, and Christopher Morley, and later with Clifton Fadiman and John P. Marquand). The board chose the "book-of-the-month," which was regularly bought by more than half of the club's subscribers, and Fisher has been called one of the two "most influential" members of the board and its "most conscientious reader."[6] In fact, she read to the point of near-blindness, averaging fifteen books a month over her twenty-five-year tenure. Since by 1950 a million Americans belonged to the club and read the selections, it would be modest, but not incorrect, to say that she helped determine popular literary taste in America for nearly three decades. She did more: she shaped authors' careers. Pearl Buck, Isak Dinesen (Karen Blixen), and

6. Al Silverman, ed., *The Book-of-the-Month: Sixty Years of Books in American Life,* xviii.

Richard Wright were among the many writers Fisher introduced to the American public through the BOMC.

During her lifetime, Fisher was awarded the honorary degrees and prizes reserved for famous writers, and her works were anthologized and translated into several foreign languages. Yet lasting recognition has eluded Fisher. Her fiction was popular with the reading public, but not subsequently favored by those modernist critics who instead championed Faulkner, Fitzgerald, and Hemingway from the same period. Fisher's authentic narratives of everyday American life were deemed unfashionable, her narrative technique was considered too conventional, and she was relegated to a marginal position in the literary pantheon. She was not entirely ignored, though. In 1952, Edward Wagenknecht offered a dissenting estimation in *The Cavalcade of the American Novel*:

> She is often regarded as a merely "popular" writer, and criticism has done little with her work. Yet few novelists have had a richer intellectual background or enjoyed wider or more fructifying contacts with life. It is her great virtue that she has refused to shut her eyes to the horror and terror of human experience, at the same time declining to close her mind against the conviction that life is shot through with spiritual significance.

But the damning appraisal of F. Scott Fitzgerald held sway: "Dorothy Canfield as a novelist is certainly of no possible significance."[7] The first doctoral dissertation on Fisher, Joseph P. Lovering's *The Contribution of Dorothy Canfield Fisher to the Development of Realism in the American Novel,* appeared in 1956, and Elizabeth Yates's biography, *Pebble in a Pool,* was published in 1958, but without a solid base of critical support for the subject, a long period of silence followed.

However, interest in Fisher was revived again in the eighties, due in part to a re-evaluation of neglected women writers. Ida H. Washington's biography was published in 1982, scholarship on the BOMC grew, Fisher's friendship with Willa Cather received increased attention, paperback editions of *The Brimming Cup, The Home-Maker,* and *Her Son's Wife* were reissued, and Fisher's name began to appear once more in the *MLA Bibliography*. Given the current reappraisal of the American literary canon in terms of race, class, and gender, the time for a re-evaluation of Fisher's work is clearly at hand. Although her *ouevre* is uneven, she did write much that is of enduring value and interest. Fisher's stories based on her World War I experiences in Europe, for instance, provide a valuable and well-crafted counterpoint to the handling of similar subject matter by such male contemporaries as Hemingway. *The Brimming*

7. Edward Wagenknecht, *Cavalcade of the American Novel,* 294; Andrew Turnbull, ed., *The Letters of F. Scott Fitzgerald,* 571.

Cup, too, is as rich in material detail as Sinclair Lewis's fiction, yet written from the woman's perspective, which Lewis's work lacks. *The Home-Maker,* finally, is a story of role-reversal in a marriage and has contemporary relevance to issues of child-rearing and women's rights. Fisher's letters collected here thus document the life of one of the twentieth century's most remarkable women in a way that no biography nor even the most autobiographical of her own works can. Here, in her own words, is the story of her life and literary career as told in correspondence spanning nearly six decades.

—— *III* ——

Dorothy Canfield Fisher was a prolific letter-writer. Her former secretary, Helen Congdon, recalls that she wrote several letters in her study nearly every day, usually in the afternoon or evening after finishing her professional writing. She wrote to friends, relatives, fellow authors, politicians, publishers, and readers. During a period in the mid-twenties, the quantity of Fisher's mail necessitated the use of a card that explained that she was unable to answer all of her letters. But she did respond to many of them, with letters to readers whom she had never met often running several pages. In 1943 her housekeeper, Elizabeth Cullinan, said, "Characteristically, she answers letters promptly, handles her own correspondence. It's enormous." Soon after Fisher's death, Bradford Smith also noted the volume of correspondence: "Into the house, as Dorothy's audience widened, poured a great tide of correspondence. Her writing made readers think of her as a friend. The mail literally came by the basketful. After it had come in, the small study often looked as if a whirlwind had struck it, with letters piled here and there according to the way they were to be handled. . . ."[8] The list of recipients in even a selected edition such as this bears evidence of the diversity of Fisher's correspondents. The eye may light on the famous names, but some of the most interesting letters are to common folk. There are also the names of the once famous, but now lesser-known, much like Fisher herself: Cleghorn, Suckow, Webster, and Yezierska. Lamentably, there are few extant letters to Fisher's immediate family—John, James, and Sally—as she was rarely apart from them.

Fisher's letters were usually typed on letterhead stationery, although occasionally she wrote by hand, during short trips away from Arlington, Vermont. Her typing could be erratic, but Fisher was generally attentive to details of spelling and grammar. Even though her eyesight began to fail in the mid-forties, Helen Congdon reports, Fisher continued to correspond by dictating

8. Helen W. Congdon, letter to the author; Nanette Kutner, "If You Worked for Dorothy Canfield Fisher," 196; Bradford Smith, "Dorothy Canfield Fisher," 73.

her letters into a tape recorder.[9] She registered her dissatisfaction with "the remoteness of that way of answering letters" in 1955, but found no better alternative (Letter 181). Fisher once told Paul Reynolds that the process of writing a novel "usually ends by carrying me off my feet so that I can't think of anything else" (Letter 60), and she was absorbed by her letter writing in similar fashion. The enthusiasm she felt for crafting the language, for communicating her thoughts, feelings, and ideas is evident in both the quantity and quality of her correspondence. In many cases, what were intended to be polite notes turned into full-length epistles. Nearing the end of such letters would often come a sheepish apology like that offered to William Lyon Phelps—"I oughtn't to bother you with such a long rambling letter. I didn't mean, when I began, to do more than to thank you" (Letter 44)—or some wry acknowledgment of the letter's generous length, such as her closing line to Harry and Bernardine Scherman, "Hastily—though you'd hardly believe it!" (Letter 101).

There is an immediacy to these letters, as though Fisher is conversing with her correspondent in person. They are peppered with colorful expressions of speech: "get-up-and-git" (Letter 29), "honest injun" (Letter 39), "a durn sight worse" (Letter 41), "wrestling like Jacob" (Letter 63), "a calorific meal" (Letter 104), and "a real Jenny-welcome" (Letter 174). Fisher's opening sentence to Pearl Buck, "How you and I always feel the impulse to put our heads together, to clasp hands closely, to share what is in our hearts, in grave moments of crisis!" (Letter 126), and poignant closing paragraph to Christopher Morley, "There, that's my news bulletin—of what's going on within. Little, really nothing—to report of what is visible physically—a quiet old country woman, deaf, with dimmed eyes, partially paralyzed, going slowly along the paths where she used to outrace her own children" (Letter 179), are but two examples of the intimacy she shared with her correspondents.

—— *IV* ——

The letters say a good deal about Fisher on a personal level. The complexity of the individual they reveal is commensurate with Fisher's wide interests, learning, and activities. What becomes immediately apparent is that Fisher lived in two worlds, one literary, one domestic. As a woman, wife, and mother of two children, she was expected to fulfill several roles. From the birth of Fisher's first child, Sally (who would also become a children's book author), in 1909 through her child-rearing years, Fisher's letters bear witness to the competing forces of art and domesticity in her daily life.

According to her mother, Fisher used to hold her son, Jimmy, to her breast

9. Congdon, letter.

with one hand and write with the other.[10] In 1912, she told Paul Reynolds that her daughter was growing older and needed "more time and attention" and that her literary output was "very limited" because she had "a great deal to do besides being an author" (Letter 11). Subsequent letters refer to the increased demands, which now included her elderly mother. She wrote to Alfred Harcourt in 1920: "We have been having a real siege here, with John in bed with a badly infected knee and a high temperature and us in quarantine with both children whooping it up with chicken-pox, and the thermometer at twenty below and me keeping fires night and day and tending to my sick-a-beds," (Letter 39). After spending a summer abroad to concentrate on the writing of *Rough-Hewn,* Fisher told Julia Collier Harris of the conditions under which she normally worked: "As a rule I work in the midst of a very stirring family and neighborhood life, with a thousand interruptions of all sorts. This is the first time I've been separated from the children for more than a day, since they were born, and the first time I've not kept house, the regular three-meals-a-day-routine, since I was a young girl. It seemed so strange to get up in the morning with nothing to do *except write!*" (Letter 49). Virginia Woolf's *A Room of One's Own* comes to mind when reading of how often the silence of Fisher's study was broken by her children, neighbors, and other visitors. The challenge Fisher faced was the same she articulated for women readers of *Mothers and Children:* to be a good wife and mother *and* to maintain interests outside of the home. As she told Henry Kitchell Webster, she did not believe that giving her children "orange-juice at the right hour" should be the sole concern of any woman (Letter 21). Fisher sought to define herself not only in relation to the needs of her family—which were paramount—but also as a writer. Her record of publication testifies to her success at finding time to write, but her letters show that the work was not produced without great effort and many distractions.

The same strong will that enabled Fisher to write amidst divergent responsibilities evinces itself elsewhere in the letters. In fact, Fisher was willing to risk her life for her beliefs, as illustrated by her participation in the World War I relief effort. In 1916, she made a perilous trip across the Atlantic with her two children to join her husband, who was working for the American Ambulance Corps in France. Before the war's end, she had founded a Braille press for blinded soldiers and a hospital for refugee children. Her readiness to volunteer is discussed in a letter to Sally Cleghorn:

> As you say, *now* is the time to stick to our principles . . . and it has made me sick to hear such crowds and crowds of Americans all writing vociferously to the papers that the Allies are fighting the cause of civilization for us, while we stand off in safety and profit by their blood and suffering . . . and yet nobody has done any-

10. Zephine Humphrey, "Dorothy Canfield," 36.

thing! Even John and I who have felt so keenly that France was standing between our world and all that threatened its permanence, have done nothing but send money, we haven't been willing to sacrifice our comfort and convenience . . . for that is practically all we are thinking of sacrificing now. There will be some danger of course, but not more than there always is in doing something worth doing. . . . (Letter 18)

Further evidence of this fiery side of Fisher's character is displayed in her description of a debate about modern literature with critic John Aldridge in 1949: "So by and by, I took an axe in one hand, a hatchet in the other and a knife between my teeth and sailed in. No courtesy is needed between an old woman and a young man, and my foot was on my native heath, and I wasn't under obligation to anybody—quite the contrary—for having invited me to Vermont" (Letter 162). The *Burlington Free Press* called the discussion, which was part of a literary symposium sponsored by the University of Vermont, a "slugfest." And Fisher was not one to couch her opinions in euphemisms. Commenting on Henry James's satire of Boston reform women and his charge that they were destroying "the sentiment of sex," she wrote: "Is *that* a joke! As if anything could! And this fear lest the 'sentiment of sex' be diminished, from a man who, as far as the eye can see, never had a bit of it. Something like the Pope telling the world in all the modern languages about what the relations between husband and wife should be" (Letter 173).

Although she was at various times a social crusader, a campaigner for moral improvement, and a famous author, Fisher had a modest sense of self-importance and did not lack a sense of humor. A small woman, she often expressed her self-consciousness about her size through humor. In a 1916 letter to Louise Pound, she enclosed a photograph of herself standing next to a donkey and joked, "Now if you know how big a donkey is, you can see how tall I am" (see Letter 19 and photograph). In the same letter, she referred to a published photograph of herself with an upraised hand as being "ridiculously like the hand of a bishop, bestowing the episcopal blessing." Later, she wrote to Pound about publicity photographs in general, "The less people know how I look, the more they'll think of me" (Letter 22). This despite the fact that Fisher was, by all accounts, an attractive woman.

The letters also portray a woman of great generosity. That Fisher gave of her time and money to numerous worthy causes is a matter of public record. But the letters show her magnanimity in other ways. There is praise and support for her friends' work, as exemplified in the letters to Pearl Buck and Ruth Suckow. There are the offers to lend her name to the publicity of worthy books, such as James Weldon Johnson's *God's Trombones* (Letter 69). There are the efforts to get good books published, as in the case of Isak Dinesen's *Seven Gothic Tales;* and the careful readings of works-in-progress, as in the case of Anzia

Yezierska's *All I Could Never Be*. There are also the more modest kindnesses, such as Fisher's response to an invitation to read: she suggested to the club woman that she also invite Sarah Cleghorn and pay her the honorarium in full (Letter 106).

One of the most intriguing episodes in the letters in regard to Fisher's character involves Willa Cather. The story of the Fisher-Cather friendship is chronicled in the 104 letters (all but five from Cather to Fisher), written during the years 1899 to 1947, that constitute the Cather file of the Fisher papers at the University of Vermont. Included in this collection are twenty-five letters (twenty by Cather, three by Fisher, one by Cather's mother, and one by Cather's friend Isabelle McClung) that had remained unread by anyone save the correspondents themselves until July 1987, when they were found in a barn on the Fisher homestead in Arlington. Along with assorted manuscripts and related material, they had been inadvertently left behind when Fisher's letters were donated to the university. These letters, like all of Cather's, may be neither published nor directly quoted, as specified by provisions in the author's will. Cather drew up these restrictions to protect her privacy and professional reputation; for the same reason she destroyed nearly all the letters she received.

Cather and Fisher were first drawn to each other by their mutual interests in French literature, painting, and music. Their friendship began in 1891 when Dorothy's father became chancellor of the University of Nebraska, where Cather was a student. Cather was then publishing stories and reviews in local and campus papers; Fisher was her younger admirer and protégée. Fisher felt most honored at the time to collaborate with Cather on a short story, "The Fear That Walks by Noonday," which appeared in the university's literary magazine (and was reprinted in 1931, see Letters 84 and 88). Soon after Cather's death in 1947, Fisher remarked upon the regard in which she held her older friend: "Later on, of course, as we both grew into the twenties and the thirties, this difference in years [six] dwindled to nothing at all, as differences do to adults, so far as any barrier to our close comradeship went. But my lifelong admiring affection for Willa was, at first, tinctured with the respectful deference due from a younger person to a successful member of the older generation."[11]

Cather and Fisher stayed in touch after leaving Nebraska, as they would for most of their lives. Yet long gaps in the correspondence from 1905 to 1921 remained a mystery to Cather and Fisher scholars and occasioned a good deal of conjecture; it is only recently, with information from the newly found Cather-Fisher letters, that the rift may be understood. The dispute had its basis in Cather's first trip to Europe in 1902, when she met Evelyn Osborne, a friend

11. Dorothy Canfield Fisher, "Novelist Remembers Blue-and-Gold Christmas in Pittsburgh," 42.

and fellow graduate student of Fisher's. Although only passing reference is made to Osborne—a young woman with a prominent facial scar and a taste for extravagant clothes—in Cather's letters at the time of the trip, it was she who would later stand at the center of the disagreement over "The Profile"— significantly, the story of a young woman with a grotesque facial scar and an interest in extravagant clothes.

More specifically, "The Profile" is set in Paris, where portraitist Aaron Dunlap is commissioned to paint Virginia Gilbert, whose face bears a jagged scar on one side. Throughout their ensuing courtship the scar is never mentioned between the two, although Dunlap desperately wants to share the burden of Virginia's disfigurement. Even after their marriage and the birth of a daughter, Virginia's vanity prevents her from discussing the scar with Dunlap, which creates a gap between the husband and wife. When Dunlap becomes attracted to Virginia's cousin Eleanor, who is their houseguest, his wife leaves him. On the night of her departure, she arranges for a dressing table lamp to explode in Eleanor's face, so that she, too, is permanently disfigured. The story closes as Dunlap, mercifully divorced from Virginia, marries Eleanor.

Fisher first expressed concern about the story, which was to be included in *The Troll Garden*, Cather's first collection of short fiction, in a telegram sent a few days before Christmas 1904. Writing from Arlington to Cather in Pittsburgh, Fisher said she had just heard of "The Profile" and that she would "suspend judgment" until hearing from Cather, whom she implored to reply immediately. Cather did so, claiming that the story was not really cause for concern since, in her opinion, Virginia Gilbert did not resemble Osborne except for the scar on her face. She pointed out that the protagonist was married, unlike Osborne; that Osborne's taste in clothes was not nearly so bad; and that the story focused on the character's domestic infelicities, which could not possibly be traced to Fisher's friend. Scars were not so uncommon, Cather said, that one would link the character to Osborne specifically.

Fisher next asked Cather for a copy of the story, which reached Arlington on December 30. She wrote to Cather just two days later, pleading that it not be published for fear of the damage it would do to Osborne's delicate psyche: "I am quite sure you don't realize how exact and faithful a portrait you have drawn of her—her beautiful hair, her pretty hands, her fondness of dress and pathetic lapses of taste in wearing what other girls may, her unconsciousness— oh Willa don't do this thing. . . . I don't believe she would ever recover from the blow of your description of her affliction" (Letter 3; ellipsis mine).

Fisher's letter was answered promptly, not by Cather but by Isabelle McClung, to whom Cather had turned for advice. McClung firmly supported Cather's right to publish the story. Cather followed up McClung's letter with one of her own in which she said that the page proofs of *The Troll Garden* had already been returned to the press and that to omit "The Profile" would make an already slim volume too small to publish. She asked for Fisher's understanding and hoped that their friendship would remain intact.

Fisher, though, persisted in her efforts to protect Osborne. She told Cather that she had consulted with her parents about the affair and that they had recommended the matter be referred to *The Troll Garden*'s publisher, S. S. McClure, if Cather did not withdraw the story herself. When Cather failed to respond, Fisher wrote her final, uncharacteristically terse, letter on the matter, threatening "further action" (Letter 5). In "Autobiography in the Shape of a Book Review," the poet Witter Bynner, once Cather's editorial colleague, mentions a dispute over "The Profile" that took place at McClure's office. He describes the meeting between the two parties as "tense" and claims that Cather insisted on publication, even though it was suggested that Osborne might commit suicide if she read the story (253). Bynner did not name those who objected, but we can now be sure Fisher was among them. Finally, neither side could claim victory, for although the story did not appear in the 1905 edition of *The Troll Garden*—which was dedicated to Isabelle McClung—it was published two years later (June 1907) in *McClure's*. There is no evidence of whether Osborne ever read the work and no further mention of her in the Cather-Fisher correspondence.

The rift between the two authors was not bridged until nearly fifteen years later, when Cather enlisted Fisher's help in authenticating the details of the French setting of her Pulitzer Prize–winning novel, *One of Ours* (1922). They maintained a faithful correspondence thereafter, with Fisher paying Cather occasional visits at her New York apartment. Fisher's letter to Cather recollecting their 1902 visit to A. E. Housman was among the last Cather read before her death in 1947 (Letter 148).

The disagreement over "The Profile" is instructive for what it says about Fisher as an artist and person. While she was at the time of the dispute a published writer who had devoted a major part of her life to the formal study of literature, Fisher valued Osborne's feelings over Cather's story. She was also willing to risk Cather's longtime friendship for what she believed to be an issue of personal privacy and moral decency. As to the propriety of Fisher's actions, there is much to be said on both sides, but what is indisputable is her passion and resolve in defending Osborne. Some years later, Fisher took issue with Anzia Yezierska over modeling fictional characters after real people. In 1932, she objected to Yezierska's use of Arlington citizens as the basis for characters in her novel *All I Could Never Be* (Letter 91) and voiced her concern to the book's publisher, G. P. Putnam (Letter 89). Other letters document the care Fisher took to mask the identities of real people represented in her own work, including *The Deepening Stream* (Letter 81), *Seasoned Timber* (Letter 107), and "The Bedquilt" (Letter 138).

—— *V* ——

Readers will find these letters to be filled with information on American literature in general and Fisher's writing in particular. They deepen our knowledge of Fisher's sources and influences, her method of composition, and her authorial intentions. They offer the perspective of an author who was otherwise reluctant to "explain" her own works. They portray a serious artist who was concerned with the formal qualities of her writing, one who would not produce stories and novels carelessly for the high prices they commanded. At the same time, even as she wrote for traditional women's magazines, she could be experimental. A 1920 letter to William Lyon Phelps, for example, speaks about Fisher's use of point of view in *The Brimming Cup:*

> I have tried to make a glass door through which the reader looks into the heart and mind of one and another of the men, women, or children in the story, so that, once and for all, he knows what sort of human being is there. From that time on, it has been my intention to leave the reader to interpret for himself the meaning of the actions of that character, without the traditional explanations and re-iterated indications from the author. (Letter 44)

Among the broad patterns we observe in the letters is the growth and maturation of Fisher as a writer. Her progression from literary neophyte to self-assured professional manifests itself in several ways, one of which is a shift in tone in her correspondence with her agent and publishers. The earliest letter in this collection, to Louis Wiley of the *New York Times,* and a later one to Curtis Hidden Page are strikingly deferential in their phrasing. The nascent author informs Wiley that she would be willing to write an article on Spain "wholly subject" to his specifications and approval (Letter 1), and tells Page that "I handle my pen as I do my tongue and that is alas, quite without art" (Letter 3).

By 1924, however, Fisher's voice had grown more sure and authoritative. When pressed by her agent Reynolds to begin work on *Her Son's Wife* that year, she spoke her mind in no uncertain terms: "I do protest against being lumped in with the loafing authors who don't work unless they're hurried into it. No sir, by gracious, that is not me. Nobody *can* hurry me" (Letter 60). As she became a more experienced author, her letters to people in publishing took on a brisk and executive air. As far as the actual writing was concerned, though, she never lost the excitement and anxiety felt by a beginner. After almost fifty years as a professional author, Fisher told Bennett Cerf that she still never began work on a book "without butterflies in the stomach, like a singer going out on the platform for a solo" (Letter 163).

Fisher was assertive as far as the artistic integrity of her works was concerned. By all evidence, her business relationships were amicable—as long as the business people did not interfere with her creative talent. For instance, she refused to alter a story line dealing with anti-Semitism in *Seasoned Timber* that drew criticism from an editor considering the book for serialization. She wrote to Paul Reynolds:

> The story would lose its point if that strong element were left out. . . . I think race prejudice is creeping in insidiously to American life (for instance I bet you a nickel that the Country Club of your own town of Scarsdale is closed to Jews—without regard to their individual refinement or desirability). I'm ashamed of it, and I think most decent Americans would be ashamed of it, if they stopped to think about it. (Letter 105, ellipsis mine)

While nonfiction articles and serialized versions of novels were primarily a source of income, Fisher saw her books as her contribution to the world of letters. From romantic, often sentimental, magazine stories, she turned to novel-length examinations of human relationships and sought to portray them with depth and skill. As she once told William Lyon Phelps, "the richness and endless variety of human relationships . . . that's what authors, even the finest and greatest, only succeed in hinting at. It's a hopeless business, like trying to dip up the ocean with a tea-spoon" (Letter 44). Even in the case of serials, she could be reticent to compromise. After a meeting with a magazine editor concerning the possible serialization of *The Brimming Cup*, she objected to the suggestion that each installment end with a "big crisis": "I said earnestly that I wouldn't guarantee her that, nor even that I would in any degree try for that, and I wanted her to understand that fully, before she thought any more about the matter. In fact that I wouldn't guarantee her *any*thing in the way of style or 'action' etc." (Letter 41). And in the case of *Bonfire,* Fisher wrote two versions: a streamlined one, which was less risque in certain details of setting and plot for serialization, and another, "doing it as I want to do it" for book publication (Letter 87). While she habitually expressed doubt about the finished product, her commitment to the craft of writing is clear.

Fisher's letters also add a wealth of new information and insight to what we know of her literary taste and aesthetics. The breadth of her reading is immediately apparent. Trained as a scholar of French literature and foreign languages, her reading interests were far-ranging. She knew the classics and read widely in contemporary literature for the BOMC. The letters make plain her affection for Shakespeare, for the great Russian novelists, especially Tolstoy, and for the French, including Balzac and the fabulist LaFontaine. More modern preferences are also indicated for Buck, Cather, Dinesen, Frost, and Wright. In addition, she wrote to Julia Collier Harris in admiration of Harry Stillwell Edwards's and Joel Chandler Harris's stories featuring African-Americans (Letter 70), and a 1948 letter notes an early appreciation of Eudora Welty (Letter 152).

Fisher freely acknowledged the distinguished efforts of her peers in her published reviews, but restricted most negative criticism to her letters. In them we find some of her most lively, engaging literary commentary. She clearly had little taste for works containing rough language, explicit sex, or graphic violence. (John O'Hara, whose *Appointment in Samarra* Fisher criticized for an overabundance of those very elements, once referred to her as "Dorothy, I can field—no great pleasure, Mrs. Fisher"). Nor was she enamored of what she perceived to be a preoccupation with alienation, corruption, and meaninglessness in modern literature. Yet she did not care for escapist fiction either, as she explained to a Book-of-the-Month Club subscriber, who complained that the judges' choices were unsuitable for young people:

> No good is ever done, I think, by pretending that anything is different from what it really is, either in our explicit statement, or by implication. The prettifying of human relations in conventional old-fashioned, mid-nineteenth-century fiction, was responsible for some ghastly shocks when the readers of those pleasant books came up, in real life, against something which the novels they had read had led them to assume did not exist. (Letter 141)

At a time when moral values and meaning and even human communication were considered outmoded, Fisher held fast to her belief that the true artist wrote with a desire to express, in a helpful way, some new understanding about human life. She summarized her view in a 1945 letter: "The impulse of the writing person is to share this new understanding with the rest of humanity. He feels its importance as a help to understanding what takes place around us, and can hardly wait until he has put it into some form in which, he hopes, others may see the significance of events in human life which they have been taking perhaps callously, perhaps just with dull or slow lack of understanding" (Letter 138). Thus, Fisher did not reject modern literature per se, but bristled at many of its salient tendencies. In the modern tradition, she believed that literature should reflect the reality of the human condition. In her judgment of fiction for the BOMC, she was said to exercise "exacting standards" and to focus on "the accuracy of image, the unity of plot, the depth of characterization."[12] Her optimistic world view and belief in moral values, though, set her apart from the literary mainstream.

The correspondence also affords an opportunity to observe the application of Fisher's literary principles to specific works. An admirer of the tales of Hans Christian Andersen (see Letter 6), she did not hesitate to suggest that highly praised books of both past and present wore no finery. Such was the case with James Boswell's *Life of Samuel Johnson, LL.D.* Prior to a 1950 BOMC meeting

---

12. Matthew J. Bruccoli, ed., *Selected Letters of John O'Hara,* 237; Silverman, *Book-of-the-Month,* xviii.

in which *Boswell's London Journal, 1762–1763* was to be considered as a selection, she wrote to Harry Scherman to vent her dislike of Boswell and eighteenth-century literature as a whole. Her purpose in writing to Scherman in advance of the meeting was to avoid offending her colleague and friend Christopher Morley, who had written an adulatory "Introduction" to the newly discovered journal. "I have felt all my life, that Boswell's *Life of Johnson* is enormously over-estimated by professors of English Literature, and really is a bore to most people (as it certainly was to me)," she wrote (Letter 167). Fisher found the *Life* overly long and saw no need for the further elaboration in the London journal. She held nothing back in her letter to Scherman: "To add to that, *more* Boswell saying tiresomelessly over and over what has already been told to us in other books, about a period of no importance anyhow, and about a shallow-natured, trivial-minded man—." The journal was, finally, not chosen as a book-of-the-month but sent to subscribers as a dividend.

A striking example of Fisher's disdain for a more contemporary work is found in her letter concerning the Detroit ban against the sale and library circulation of Ernest Hemingway's *To Have and Have Not* (Letter 109). In reaction to complaints by the Detroit Council of Catholic Organizations, the novel was ruled to be obscene by city authorities in 1938. The League of American Writers protested the censorship, and Archibald MacLeish drafted a letter of protest, which was signed by Van Wyck Brooks and Thornton Wilder and published in the *Nation*. The letter charged that the real reason for the censure of the book was that the Catholic Church objected to Hemingway's involvement in the war in Spain. "Only a prurient mind could possibly find the book offensive," MacLeish wrote.[13] When Fisher, an otherwise ardent supporter of public libraries and free speech, was asked to add her signature to the letter, she replied, "I don't feel like signing it myself." She argued that MacLeish's reasoning was weak, but she also let it be known that she and several of her peers found the book to be "offensive."

Other notable figures who are subject to pointed criticism in the letters include George Santayana (a "heartless" man, Letter 122), John Steinbeck (*The Wayward Bus* was "false to human probability," Letter 146), Norman Mailer (*The Naked and the Dead* was vulgar, Letter 153), Sinclair Lewis (Fisher picked up his books "as with the tongs," Letter 156), John Dos Passos (the characters in *The Grand Design* were "nothing but names on the page, floating in and out of the interminable cocktail drinking, gossiping *talk* which fills the book," Letter 157), Arthur Miller (*Death of a Salesman* evinced an "odd lack of connection with reality," Letter 160), and D. H. Lawrence (whose works presented Indi-

---

13. Van Wyck Brooks, Archibald MacLeish, and Thornton Wilder, "Letter to the Editor on Detroit's Ban of *To Have and Have Not*," 96.

ans as "demi-gods," not real people, Letter 165). The list goes on, but even this brief catalogue illustrates Fisher's distaste for some of the most eminent American writers. Her reading for the BOMC kept her in touch with the current of modern literature, but she obviously felt little affection for much of what now constitutes the canon of the period.

Fisher's correspondence also sheds new light on her activities and influence as a member of the BOMC Board of Selection. Created by advertising executive Harry Scherman and publisher Robert Haas in 1926, the BOMC claimed more than sixty thousand subscribers within a year. The operating principles were straightforward: members agreed to buy a newly published book chosen monthly by the five-member Board. They paid full price with an option to exchange the book, upon inspection, for an "alternate" choice. Soon after, readers were asked to buy only four books a year and allowed to substitute the alternate selection before shipping. Fisher at first hesitated joining the group, but after observing the emptiness of Brentano's bookstore in New York in contrast to other stores, she decided there must be a better method of "getting books into the hands of American readers."[14]

Although Fisher de-emphasized the significance of her position with the BOMC, remarking in a 1941 letter that she was "surprised and somewhat daunted" by the influence one subscriber attributed to the monthly choice (Letter 115), she did play a key role in the careers of at least three well-known authors: Pearl Buck, Isak Dinesen (Karen Blixen), and Richard Wright. Fisher nominated Buck's *The Good Earth* for special consideration by the board after a first reader's report underestimated it, and then recommended the eventual Pulitzer Prize winner strongly at the judges' monthly meeting.[15] The result was that *The Good Earth* was the book-of-the-month for March 1931, the first of six works by Buck selected during Fisher's time on the board.

Dinesen owed no less than her first American book publication to Fisher, who was sent the manuscript of *Seven Gothic Tales* by the author's brother. As her letters from 1932 to 1933 indicate, Fisher put the book in the hands of its eventual publisher, and she wrote a "Preface" introducing Dinesen to the American public. *Seven Gothic Tales* was a book-of-the-month (April 1934), as were four subsequent titles by Dinesen.

Wright's association with the BOMC was important to his early success as well. His *Native Son* and *Black Boy,* now ranked among American classics, were distributed by the BOMC as monthly choices, and Fisher not only wrote reviews and introductions, but also suggested important revisions for both. Fisher's role in the textual history of *Black Boy*—documented in her correspondence here—is

14. Louis M. Starr, "An Interview with Dorothy Canfield Fisher," 6.
15. Ibid., 20.

discussed by Janice Thaddeus in her 1985 essay "The Metamorphosis of Richard Wright's *Black Boy,*" while Arnold Rampersad's notes to his Library of America edition of Wright's works explicate the *Native Son* connection.

—— *VI* ——

Ancillary to the explicitly personal and literary letters are those dealing with the social concerns that underpin much of Fisher's fiction. Three subjects are most prominent: the importance of education, women's rights, and the African-American struggle for racial equality.

Fisher's interest in education can be traced back to her upbringing as the daughter of an academic: her father was (in chronological order) a professor at the University of Kansas, chancellor of the University of Nebraska, president of Ohio State University, and librarian of Columbia University. In a letter to the president of Middlebury College in support of coeducation there, Fisher noted that she knew both sides of the issue because she had been "brought up on the discussion of it all my life" (Letter 52). She viewed education as the means by which American citizens could best develop their individual potential and contribute to society, and she made two major contributions to the field. First, she introduced the Montessori method of childhood education to America. Her explication of the system appears in *A Montessori Mother* (1912), published after her visit to Maria Montessori's Casa dei Bambini in Rome, *A Montessori Manual* (1913), and *Mothers and Children* (1914). Montessori principles are also present in the novel *The Bent Twig* (1915) and her well-known children's book *Understood Betsy* (1917), the story of a pampered city girl who learns the value of hard work and responsibility when she moves to a Vermont farm. The book highlights, in a fictional framework, Fisher's conviction that both boys *and* girls should be raised to be independent and self-reliant.[16] Secondly, Fisher helped establish the Adult Education Association, the first organization of its kind in the U.S. Her belief that education is a lifelong enterprise is expressed in *Why Stop Learning?* (1927). The enduring significance of the book to Fisher is evident in a later letter (1929) to Alfred Harcourt in which she wrote, "I'd like not to have people forget that book. I've said some things in it I'm glad to have said" (Letter 75).

Closely related to Fisher's commitment to education was her active support of women's rights. Surprisingly, Fisher once wrote that she "was never a feminist." She explained, "It was my older generation, my father and mother, who were. I was rather (as it often goes in generations) in reaction from their extreme zeal for 'women's rights' " (DCF to Helen K. Taylor, no date). Her de-

16. Washington, *Biography,* 70.

votion to the cause of equal opportunity for women, though, is unmistakable. Both Fisher's fiction (most notably *The Home-Maker,* in which the protagonist, Evangeline Knapp, is a wife, mother, and the family breadwinner) and her letters speak to her strong belief that women should not be limited in their access to education and job training, nor should they be bound by societal conventions. Characteristically, in a 1946 letter to Margaret Mead, she lamented "the social pressure, invisible and tyrannical, which the United States puts upon its women and girls" (Letter 142). The restriction of women's roles—and men's too: in *The Home-Maker,* the husband, Lester Knapp, draws great satisfaction from staying at home and caring for his children—seemed, quite simply, impractical to Fisher. She reasoned that since everyone is born with unique abilities, limitations, and temperaments, one's place should not be determined by gender. It was only when each person was in a role he or she was suited for that society could function productively, and Fisher lectured and wrote in support of that principle. As she remarked to Julia Collier Harris:

> So large a majority of fathers of our girls are heart-and-soul business men, it stands to reason that the girls themselves might do better if they were not automatically shoved off into being cultured teachers . . . although goodness knows our country needs cultured teachers enough sight more than business-people. Still, folks have to do what they are best fit for, and every opportunity for women means one less chance of a square peg living miserably in a round hole all its life. (Letter 68)

Nearly thirty years later, Fisher still worried over the obstacles women faced:

> I'm very much struck by the fact that although America offers us a life astonishingly safe from most physical dangers, it plunges us into another danger which is devilishly insidious because it falls so imperceptibly about us as we live—and that is the danger of becoming held and mastered by triviality. The little things of life, of no real importance, but which have to be "seen to" by American home makers, is like a blanket smothering out the fine and great potential qualities in every one of us. (Letter 181)

Lastly, a deep vein of concern for the problem of racial prejudice against African-Americans runs throughout Fisher's letters. The issue certainly was not foreign to her forbears. In a letter to Pearl Buck, Fisher proudly explained that her great-grandmother kept the bell of her Vermont village church tolling "from dawn to dark" on the day of John Brown's execution, that her grandfather had accompanied Henry Ward Beecher on his trip to England to influence British public opinion in favor of the abolitionists, and that her father, when he was president of Ohio State University, had created considerable controversy by inviting Booker T. Washington to lunch at their home. Fisher herself carried on the family tradition: she lectured against racial prejudice and wrote for the *Crisis;* she befriended African-American writers such as James

Weldon Johnson and Richard Wright; and she was a trustee of Howard University (1945–1951). Fisher, who counted African-Americans among her childhood friends (see Letter 47), also voiced her opposition to racism in her stories "An American Citizen" and "Fairfax Hunter" and in her novel *The Brimming Cup,* the first best-seller to contain such opinions. In that book, Ormsby Welles, a retired business executive, forsakes his comfortable life in Vermont to aid in the struggle against racial oppression in the South. In a letter to W. E. B. Du Bois, Fisher explained her reason for including the subplot in her popular novel about the married life of a Vermont couple:

> I wish never to lose a chance to remind Americans of what their relations to the Negro race are, and might be, and so into this story of Northern life and white people, I have managed to weave a strand of remembrance of the dark question. It is a sort of indirect, side-approach, a backing-up of your campaign from someone not vitally concerned in it personally, except as every American must be, which I hope may be of use exactly because it is not a straight-on attack, but one of a slightly different manner. (Letter 45)

The very idea of racism was antithetical to Fisher's democratic principles and she minced no words when discussing the subject. To Paul Reynolds she wrote:

> After seeing what idiots the Germans made of themselves for two long generations over that fantastic and so far, entirely unproved idea of Count Gobineau's, and what a well-deserved punishment they got for it, it does seem as though Americans might leave it alone. . . . The Ku Klux Klan (which of course has nothing but this Gobineau idea of inherent racial superiority at the bottom of its imbecilities) may make it odious enough to shorten its stay with us. (Letter 56, ellipsis mine)

Given her efforts on behalf of racial equality, it is appropriate that the last letter in this collection, written less than two months before Fisher's death, is an inquiry about the opportunities available to African-Americans at the U.S. Naval Academy (Letter 189).

—— *VII* ——

Fruits of further investigation will belong to the readers of these letters, who will develop further what is revealed so explicitly and, at times, so wittily or so poignantly. Fisher's personal trials—the wars in Europe, the loss of her son, who died while serving as a doctor in World War II, her later physical disabilities—are revealed here, often with startling and painful clarity. Her personal enthusiasms and interests—including classical music (see references to Bach and Beethoven, Letters 113 and 179), art, history, sports (see the numerous references to hiking, skiing, skating, and tennis), and current events (see

Letter 177 on apartheid)—help fill in the biographical record and suggest new approaches to her writing. The range of historical and cultural subjects discussed—the "New Woman" and the suffrage movement, racial discrimination and the emergence of the NAACP, the development of the national education system, both world wars, the depression, book clubs, and the literary marketplace among them—should encourage not only literary approaches to the use and interpretation of her work and her correspondence, but interdisciplinary ones as well.

Dorothy Canfield Fisher was well born—into a distinguished and cultivated family that gave her a fine education and a sense of self-worth. Her strong principles underpin her beliefs and writing; that she was to extend these concerns to independent women, to new forms of education, and to issues of racial oppression and respect for individual merit was the core of her achievement. Her letters amply display her own recognition of these facts, of this achievement.

— *Part 1* —

Letters, 1900–1908

1. To Louis Wiley
March 10 [1900][1]
[New York, New York][2]

My dear Mr. Wiley:

The approach of the end of Lent makes me think of the way in which I spent Holy Week of last year. My mother and I were travelling in Spain and saw the great celebrations during Holy Week at Madrid Toledo [x] and Seville. My recollections of these brilliant and unusual festivities are very vivid and my father has suggested that perhaps you might find a description of them interesting for the Magazine edition of the *Times* for Holy Week. Of course any such article would be prepared wholly subject to your approval but I would be extremely obliged if you would be kind enough to give me some idea if you could use such an article and also about how long you would like to have it.[3]

Hoping that this is not asking too much of your good-nature.

Very sincerely
Dorothy Canfield

---

1. Date: reference to having been in Spain the previous year. DCF was there with her mother in 1899.

2. Place: DCF was studying for the Ph.D. in French at Columbia University in New York City. She received the degree in spring 1904.

3. The article, "Holy Week in Spain," appeared in the *New York Times,* Mar. 23, 1902. In a note now housed among her papers at the University of Vermont, DCF recalled the circumstances of the article's publication differently than the letter indicates: "This was, I think, the first writing of mine to be published—and it was not intended, when written, for publication. I was studying at Columbia for my Ph.D. without the slightest idea that I might ever be an author. Someone in the editorial office of the *Times* had, by chance, seen some family letters written from Spain three years before this date, when I was there with my mother. . . . He suggested that they might be published if I ran two or three of the letters together. I did this and was astonished to the limit and beyond, when they were printed and I was paid for this casual nineteen-year-old home letter."

2. To Curtis Hidden Page
December 31, 1903
Columbus, Ohio

My dear Dr. Page:

Your note from Cambridge has just reached me after the usual amount of holiday travelling about. I'm very much pleased to know that Housman is in Cambridge where, I feel with you, he doubtless seems quite at home. You'll be interested to know that I've just heard from one of the *McClure* editors that they

are to have another Housman poem in the February number.[1] I'm so surprised to find that there *is* someone else who cares for him—although I notice
with pain that you refrain studiously from saying whether you do or not! It
only whets my curiosity, however that same silence on your part. We shall have
that out sometime! As to the *Kansas City Star* review—my word, no, I never
wrote it, I didn't dare to—after I had read the Ronsard[2] through. What am I
to undertake a task that would require such subtle handling and sureness of
touch. In spite of your astonishingly kind words about a hitherto unheard of
style, I handle my pen as I do my tongue and that is alas, quite without art.

I wish now that I'd tried my hand—no matter how clumsily—on the review, because, for one thing I'm not quite so daunted by the author of the book
as I was! I may do it yet. In the meantime the best of good wishes for a Happy
New Year to that same author!

Sincerely yours
Dorothy Canfield

---

1. A. E. Housman (1859–1936), English poet and scholar. Housman's "Song" ("Far in a
western brookland") and "Song" ("Into my heart an air that kills") from *A Shropshire Lad*
(1896) were published in *McClure's Magazine* 22 (Dec. 1903): 203; and 24 (Feb. 1904): 365.
2. *Songs and Sonnets of Pierre de Ronsard,* selected and translated with an "Introduction" by
Curtis Hidden Page (Boston: Houghton, Mifflin, 1903).

3. To Willa Cather
Sunday [January 1, 1905][1]
Arlington, Vermont

Dear Willa:
I have read the story and just as you thought I do ask that you do not publish it—not for my own sake but so that you will not have done a cruel thing.[2] I
take for granted that you don't realize what this will be if you do print this
story for if you did it would be unbelievable that you should do it. And I beg
you with all my heart—with *all* of me, and I have your best intents at heart, not
to strike a cruel and overwhelming blow to one who has not deserved it, who
has already lost her life's happiness through her deformity, and who was kind
to you. I am quite sure you don't realize how exact and faithful a portrait you
have drawn of her—her beautiful hair, her pretty hands, her fondness for dress
and pathetic lapses of taste in wearing what other girls may, her unconsciousness—oh Willa don't do this thing. You will be striking her just such a blow as
Dunlap does Virginia[3]—only that was from a man to a woman who had bitterly disappointed him, who was ruining his life and who had so wrought on

his nerves as to make him scarcely conscious of what he did. With you it would be from one woman to another who had tried to be kind to her, who was proud of knowing her, and who thought she had made a friend—and in cold blood. You can't see how it is—though you did in London when you first spoke of it. You said then "Of course it would be out of the question under the circumstances." I can hear your voice as you said it, and I have heard it ever since Edith[4] told me. Oh Willa, this is some dreadful dream—for Heaven's sake write me you are not going to do it.

Believe me, who have thought with such sick intensity about it that it will injure you in the end—in every way—and I think it would crush Evelyn—I don't believe she would ever recover from the blow of your description of her affliction—"It drew the left eye, the left corner of the mouth seemed to have shrunken the maxillary bone, made of her smile a grinning distortion like the shameful conception of some despairing medieval imagination." She doesn't know—she has always been so sheltered—I have come to be sure that she doesn't [x] what could be worth her anguish in knowing. I am too wildly agitated about it to write coherently but I can't wait to send back the tale to you and to beg you—to implore you not to publish it.

Dorothy

---

1. Date: Sunday stated, numerical date appended. On an index card attached to the letter, DCF wrote, "On Friday—December 23—I wrote a short letter asking to see the story and it was sent to Arlington reaching me on Dec. 30—Saturday." DCF's recollection of when she received Cather's response is apparently in error, as Dec. 30, 1904, was a Friday.

2. DCF and Cather were close friends from their years in Lincoln, Nebraska (1891–1895), where James Hulme Canfield was chancellor of the state university, and Cather was a student. They remained in touch with each other until Cather's death in 1947 (see Letter 148) save for the years between 1905 and 1921. The cause of their rift was a short story, "The Profile," which Cather based upon Evelyn Osborne, a friend of DCF's with a prominent facial scar. Cather wanted to include "The Profile" in *The Troll Garden* (1905), her first collection of short stories, but DCF protested on the grounds that Osborne would be deeply hurt by the vivid description of the scar in the story. When Cather refused to pull the story, DCF threatened to take legal action against her publishers and effectively blocked publication. The story was published in *McClure's Magazine* two years later (June 1907), however, and the dispute between Cather and Fisher continued. See the Introduction for further discussion.

3. Protagonists of "The Profile."

4. Edith Lewis (1882–1972), Cather's housemate in New York City (1908–1947), author of *Willa Cather Living: A Personal Record* (1953).

4. To Willa Cather
January 9, 1905
[Arlington, Vermont][1]

Dear Willa:

Your letter just received and although I thought I could not feel more hopelessly wretched over this misery than before, I am feeling as though a new calamity had overwhelmed me. I could not believe that after my letter to you your first point of view would not be modified. I am like one in a walking nightmare—it all seems so incredible to me—that I should be disputing with you thus, hurting you, spoiling your pleasure in what has been a long-looked-for pleasure, and that I should be forced to continue doing so. Isabelle's[2] fierce little letter is also here—tell her I do not resent her writing it as she thought I would, I think it fine of her to thus resent your worry in the matter. You never can sufficiently appreciate Isabelle! It is one of the cruel features of all this gloom that it strikes her so. You speak in your letter of asking the opinion of outside people on the point of issue between us. Feeling that I was in too desperately deep waters to go longer without advice, I have done the same. Father, Mother, and a member of Columbia faculty connected with one of the big publishing houses in New York have been taken into my confidence. I have told them the story very plainly without explanations (they all know Evelyn) and have read through your letters *and Isabelle's*. They see the matter quite as I do and quite as strongly. They think however that we—neither you nor I nor any of those whom you mention—are not the ones to judge in the matter as we all are too closely concerned to see clearly. Certainly if Isabelle and Francis Hill[3] are so deeply interested as you say, they cannot take an impartial standpoint anymore than I can, torn equally between two loyalties and two duties. Father, Mother, and the man of whom I spoke, think and I agree with them, that the matter ought to be laid before your publishers—these not only have more experience and good judgment than we, but they have actually as a matter of business more at stake. I think they should know, for your sake and theirs the facts of this affair and that the matter has been thus urgently brought to your attention; and they have opportunity to judge as to what they think best to do. I write therefore to tell you of the result of my conference with others and their suggestion that you at once lay the facts of the case before your publishers.

Dorothy Canfield

---

1. Place: implied.
2. Isabelle McClung (1877–1938), friend and housemate of Cather's in Pittsburgh.
3. Friend of Cather's in Pittsburgh.

5. To Willa Cather
January 19, 1905
[Arlington, Vermont][1]

Dear Willa:

Will you please wire me at once an answer to these questions. Have you written to your publishers about "The Profile" since the beginning of our correspondence about it, with a definite statement that friends of the original subject of the story object strongly to its publication! If you have not so written since our correspondence began is it your intention to do so immediately? Further action on my part will be determined by your reply.

Truly yours
Dorothy Canfield

---

1. Place: no reason to doubt Arlington.

6. To Family
July 30, 1905—Sunday
Vik, [x], Norway

Dear Family:

I'm sitting up in bed to write after a lazy day spent on my back with a hot-water bottle. I really haven't needed to stay in bed but there's so little else to do here that I thought I'd just be lazy. I've had a lovely time renewing the joys of my childhood with reading Hans Christian Andersen. I find that simple Danish like this I can now read about as easily as German but the same cannot be said of Ibsen—my word, he's a tough nut! I've just finished *An Enemy to Society*[1] which I've read aloud to Froken [Hapstock ?] to my great delight and her patient endurance. It's great! Father do you remember how delighted we were with it several winters ago? I still think it would be a success on the stage. I had forgotten what simple masterpieces Andersen's tales are—or else they don't come out so well in English—for I've really been absolutely enchanted by them. They have a fine edition here with the original old-fashioned pictures and I've lain here and devoured the entire volume in this one day—interrupted by frequent visits from the family who cannot do enough for me. The old great-aunt came in and regaled me with the most interesting reminiscences of Norway in *her* day—before the time of posts and telegraphs and telephones—and the isolation of people must have been something unthinkable. One of her uncles living in Nordland (as they call the country around Trondhjem) died and his family in Bergen did not hear of it for six months! Then Froken Nico has brought in a succession of tempting lunches (and you know I never want to eat) and Froken Julia has filled the room with roses from the garden. Fru Hopstostat has visited me with offers of hot plates and the like, and [Fru Rygge ?] brought in the best of all—jolly laughing little six-months-old Christian— who exhibited all of his graces for my delectation with his most toothless and merry grin. That makes me homesick for my family all together in lovely [Linsherlock ?]. That and Mother's letter from there describing the life so vividly that I longed to be there. That's no fair, Mother, to break up my lovely tranquility with eagerness to see you all. That's what I'm trying to forget— and that's the one fleck on the clear horizon of my sky here in Vik. I leave a week from next Tuesday—the 8th of August. I shall have been here four weeks to a day—and upon my word, I can't now remember that I ever spent four happier ones. Father sends a warning note in his last letter "not to keep too much company with yourself—It is dangerous." Well, it must be dangerous on the Puritan principle that whatever you enjoy you shouldn't have too much of—for I've enjoyed my own company immensely. Don't laugh—too hard, that is, I expect you to laugh some—I honestly have. I never knew there were so many lovely things to think about if one only had time. I take long walks, or I clamber over the mountains towering above the fjord, or I lie on a peak of rock in the sun and I think such interesting and lovely things and imagine such moving scenes that I am never ready to stop. I haven't written much—(one story "The Poet and the Scullery Maid" which is sad but somewhere near what I meant to say) but I've thought a lot more about my Norwegian story.[2] If I could write that as I now conceive it, it would be something I'd not be ashamed of. But of course I can't. I expect a fearful set-back when I begin work on it— the method will have to be so different from my written-at-one-spurt short stories. I have it pretty well planned—fourteen chapters, scenes here and in Christianssand but oh, my hero is so frightfully complicated a person. It wears me out to follow him in and out of the labyrinth of [motives] he gets himself tied up in. The old aunt is Aunt Phebe[3] with a sense of humor added. She's the only one from life—every scrap of the rest is pure make-up— "made out of my own head" as the young wife told the old professor of the pudding. I'm afraid I've set myself too hard a task in managing so many people: but it won't do any harm to be thinking about it. Did I tell you I had a long letter from Mr. Sedgwick[4] (*Leslie's* Editor you know) very warm and friendly and unexpectedly serious. He says that my "talent, heaven be praised, lies outside the ordinary channels of magazine literature. Don't try to make it run in those shallow ways. You can write stories with big ideas and true ones, back of them. *Do* it! Don't be willing to be amusing when you can do more" etc. etc. He winds up by saying he doesn't want to spoil my holiday with over-earnest exhortation but I am to bear in mind that "we in the office are following your work with the greatest interest and belief"— something like. I've mislaid the letter somewhere as I'd send it to you. I was pleased because you know I think a lot more of Mr. Sedgwick's opinion than that gushing Mr. Hall on *Every-body's*! I wrote Mr. Sedgwick that his letter came most opportunely when I was just getting up the nerve to take my writing more seriously. I said "big ideas" as he put it weren't exactly in my line but I did mean to try honestly to have the ideas I was trying to express true ones, and to try and move people to more than a passing interest in a certain verbal dexterity. I was ashamed to send the letter for a while after I'd written it. It's all very well to say to my family whatever "biggity" idea is in my head, but I was afraid to him it might sound pretentious. I sent it all the same. I'm getting up a fine strong variety of "literary nerve" if you know what I mean by that.

I haven't told you about the extremely interesting two days up to the Jostedalsbreen with the Thomases. I left here Monday morning early—picked them up at Balestrand and we went on together to the end of the Fjaerlandsfjord—where the scenery is according to our old way of estimating about 150%— above par that is. We got there about one o'clock had dinner and drove at once to my first glacier which Professor Thomas[5] called scornfully a "glaciere aux dames" it was so easy to get out. But I thought it was *superb*—beat anything I'd ever seen till we drove on to another area of it where we had to do some clambering. We stood and looked at the large river of ice, just quivering blue and white in the intense sunshine, and stretching far up above us to the top of the mountain where it was outlined against the sky in icy battlements and Professor T. expressed our feelings admirably by saying dryly "Well, that does very well, on the whole, doesn't it!"

We got back to the hotel at about ten o'clock me empty to my toes. We had— for a change—fish—salmon. It really was a change for me for we have a varied home-like diet here: but the Thomases collapsed in discouragement when they saw it. Paul[6] says they've had it for two meals a day right along.

The next morning we—Paul and I—rowed Professor and Mrs. Thomas about on the fjord, which is a milky pale green color from the glacier. At noon I left them and came back to Vik. They went on the next day to Laerdal and so overland to Christiania. I said good-bye to them for good. They have been so kind as you can't think and I have come to be extremely fond of all of them. "Cal" is one of the best men who ever lived and Mrs. Thomas is a rarely sweet and self-conquered soul. But do you know I was glad to leave them and come back to solitary Vik and my imaginings. Mrs. Thomas said so kindly as I said good-bye that I had been so "lively and jolly they'd enjoyed having me along. I was quite the life of the party." That's just it—I'm enjoying so beastly selfish a breathing spell now that I don't want to bother to be *anybody's* party's life—not even people I am as fond of as I am of them. I want to sit a whole morning long staring across the fjord at the glacier "ef I want ter!" I'd get tired of it, I suppose—indeed for all my intense enjoyment of it I am looking forward to my stay in Paris. That will do me quite as much good in another way. Oh, am I not the selfish pig to go loitering about the world doing such lovely things just to please myself. But don't you believe any Sunday-school stories about its not being any fun to be selfish!

"General-Consul-[Andword ?]" turns out to be the owner of the line of steamers I go on from Christianssand to Antwerp. He is to write to the captain for me, reserve a special cabin etc. Isn't that my usual luck?

Of course the foundation to my so care-free state of mind is the good news about Jim's[7] improvement. That is the sunshine that shines on all I do and think—that and the cheerful news about what a good time you are all having.

I've had a letter from Dorothy Gleed and one from Miss Patterson which I'll send on to you when I can find them. I fancy they are getting on as well as could be expected on the whole. But am I not a thankful girl I'm not there? *Am I not*—I ask. More selfishness! I'm on a regular spree of it!

Jim's letter *from Columbus* has just this minute reached me—dated June 30! But I don't care, its worth waiting for, goodness knows! You blessed *blessed* brother! Don't say you can't write "sweet" letters. That's like the most heartening call from you—as though I'd heard your dear old voice across all this water. Can you hear me call back?

A heart full of love to you all—
Dorothy

---

1. Probably Norwegian playwright Henrik Ibsen's *An Enemy of the People,* first performed in 1863.
2. *Gunhild* (1907).
3. A maternal relative of DCF's, who died in June 1924, just before DCF started writing *Her Son's Wife.* The novel is dedicated "To the memory of Aunt Phebe's spirit."
4. Ellery Sedgwick (1872–1960), American magazine editor. Sedgwick was editor of *Leslie's Monthly* (retitled *American Magazine* in 1906) and later the *Atlantic Monthly* (1909–1938).
5. Calvin Thomas (1854–1919), professor of Germanic languages and literature at Columbia University while DCF was a graduate student there.
6. Thomas's son.
7. DCF's brother.

7. To John O'Hara Cosgrave
[Late 1905 or 1906][1]
[New York, New York][2]

Dear Mr. Cosgrave:

I've been thinking with a seriousness quite surprising to me of your so very stimulating and helpful talk with me. Just now I'm grinding breathlessly away on a text-book contract[3] and haven't time for short stories, but as soon as this job is over, I mean to make a desperate effort to put into practice the many good resolutions I have made in meditating on what you said and to make some worthy use of the courage and inspiration I gathered from your wholesomely severe remarks.

In the meantime I am sending you something written some time ago and only now put into shape. I don't pretend that it is a short story so don't criticize it as such. It is a tract, I know, but there is a faint chance that it may interest you because of its subject. It's a subject about which I feel so bitterly, (having been placed where it has meant much to me) that I'm a little afraid I've fallen into the over-emphasis of the too single-hearted professional tract-writer. But at least it can do no harm to inflict it on you and I can tell more about its worth after I know the comments on it of "you-all" at *Everybody's*.

Very sincerely yours
Dorothy Canfield

---

1. Date: reference to "a text-book contract," probably *Elementary Composition* (1906).
2. Place: letterhead.
3. See note 1.

8. To Céline Sibut
May 11, 1906
New York, New York

My Dear:

I have let days and weeks go by, waiting for long leisure hours to come when I can write you volumes about things which I have to say to you, but this time never comes, so I am taking advantage of this present moment to tell you all the things which have happened since my last letter to you; I will say it all as it comes to mind. I went to the country, to my mountains, quite exhausted at the end of the long novel I finished the first of March,[1] hoping to spend two months in absolute solitude and complete repose. Well, never in my life have I spent two such exciting months as March and April. It seems like some sort of dream and I am in despair as I try to give you an idea about it all. I have talked to you in the past of several friends of mine—lovers perhaps, I said, but friends in any case. Well, I don't know why, perhaps because as we always say, "It never rains but it pours," and all the important events come at the same time, perhaps because people thought that I was so worried that I could not have any defense against any other emotion—I don't know why but all my friends (at least four) have turned, like magicians, into lovers, and I have lived in a sort of fever and excitement which is impossible to describe to you. I have never felt the demands of material things as I have during the last two months when each day—almost each hour—I thought of you, your counsel, your deep and comprehending sympathy with a surge of heart which was completely and sadly depressed by a realization of the immense distance between us. I can never be reconciled to the fate which has given me such love for you and which has placed me at the other end of the world—I cannot write to you all that I feel. I can only tell you, in so many words, that I am engaged—and that my happiness would be perfect if you were here! I really don't know too well how it all happened. I am accustomed to living in a world of letters, telegrams and unexpected visits. Yes, people have come all the way from New York to Vermont, and the village has been electrified several times by gentlemen from New York who asked the way to the Canfield house. I would step out from the children's room to be greeted by a man—serious, angry, composed or well disposed—as the case might be, until it all seemed quite comical, since my nerves were so tense. You know how I always have control over myself and how proud I am to be like that. Well, perhaps all this emotion was necessary to break the walls down and show me I am completely in love with the John Fisher I talked about last summer. I remember now that you said to me, with that keenness of character analysis which always fills me with admiration, "He is the one I like best and who would be the best for you." However, one would not say at first glance that we were made for each other. He is the football champion I talked to you about, the idol of the University's athletic field,[2] but he is much more than that—he is the most intelligent in matters of literature of all the men I know, the most sensitive in the area of art, and the best of men from the point of view of his character. He is as my brother is; so, there are two men of noble character in this world—at least two—and I feel optimistic these days that I have fewer doubts about the rest of humanity than I had in the past. I must be precise about John. He is very dark, with dark brown eyes and hair as dark as an Indian's. He is not tall, but built solidly, even a bit too much so to be handsome—with an air of strength and inexhaustible force. He has a very handsome head of a Roman type. His father was a very well-known physician in New York in the past, but he has now retired from active life because of his health and lives with his family in their country house in the mountains of Pennsylvania. His mother is a very cultivated and artistic woman who knows and has for friends a very literary and artistic circle in New York. John also has two charming sisters. He himself is poor, that is to say, almost completely without any private fortune and, according to the "independent" fashion of our young America, does not want to rely on his father in any way. But he has a good position in a kind of "literary office" which is well established, where he will probably have a good deal of opportunity for advancement; but all that will develop very slowly and it is more than likely that I shall be engaged for a very long time! That pleases me enormously for, even now, in the midst of so much happiness flowing about me each instant like a golden river—even now, I have a kind of fear when I think of marriage. John tells me gaily that he worked for two years to get me accustomed to the idea of being engaged, and that now he is going to change his tune and get me accustomed to the idea of being married. But all the same, even writing these words makes my heart beat faster. John says again and again, with his endless patience, "But see here, what is the trouble with you? You are not merely going to get married, which in itself would be moving, but you are going to marry me, which is the most natural thing in the world." I don't know—that feeling will come in due time, without doubt. I can't think of life going on without John—he has become indispensable, he is so gentle, so strong, with an affection so unbelievably good and necessary—but I am happy to have a lot of time to get accustomed to the idea of marriage.

Your
Dorothy

---

1. *Gunhild* (1907)
2. John Fisher was captain of the Columbia University football team.

9. To John O'Hara Cosgrave
September 17, 1906
Manchester, Vermont

Dear Mr. Cosgrave:

Your kind letter has just reached me and quite warmed my heart. I expect to be in the city toward the first week in October and shall be very glad indeed to go and see you and "talk things over."

I am very much pleased to hear that people liked the "Last of the Garrison."[1] I've heard a good deal about that and "Goblin Gold"[2] although my own immediate New England family cynically regard the endings of each as sentimental.

I've been having the most ultra-domestic and un-literary summer, keeping house, taking care of my brother's children, making hay and generally forgetting that pen can be put to paper: but it's been partly involuntary, because there was nobody else to do those things, and I'm beside myself with eagerness to get at my work again. I'm hoping for a long winter of steady and serious work, and the best beginning for such a winter I can think of, is just to take advantage of your more than welcome invitation to go and see you and get an inspiriting word of exhortation!

Cordially yours
Dorothy Canfield

---

1. "The Last of the Garrison," *Everybody's Magazine* 15 (July 1906): 61–67.
2. "Goblin Gold," *Everybody's Magazine* 14 (June 1906): 766–73.

10. To Céline Sibut
May 15, 1908
In the Clouds [Red Mountain, Arlington, Vermont][1]

My Dear:
Here we are in the forest to celebrate our anniversary, in a tent far from civilization. It is the anniversary of our marriage a year ago. We are really two savages who adore outdoor living. Our camp this year is far up (really in the clouds) on top of a mountain which belongs almost entirely to our family, and which is behind our little house. Our tent is about two thousand feet higher than the house, and the season here is almost two weeks later than it is in the valley. The lilacs are beginning to burst into flower in our garden, but here, until a day or two ago we were in snow. We have been here for ten days and I have become very sunburned and rash enough to start thinking seriously about a winter camp for hunting wildcats and foxes, of which there are many up here. There are also many deer but it is forbidden to hunt them except for one single week in October. The spring near our tent is a great favorite with all the animals on the mountain-side, and very early in the morning we can see a deer drinking, apparently without any fear of us at all.

Your
Dorothy

---

1. Place: stated.

— *Part 2* —

Letters, 1912–1919

11. *To Paul Reynolds*
November 3, 1912
Arlington, Vermont

Dear Mr. Reynolds:

Your letter of the first arrived yesterday evening, and my first impulse was to answer it in the form I have been using of late for all such letters, namely, that my output is very limited, because I have a great deal to do besides being an author, and that, so far, I have had no difficulty in disposing of what I do produce.

But when I sat down at my desk and looked in dismay at the pile of unanswered letters, and thought of the mountain of work which lies before me which I am very eager to begin, it occurred to me that perhaps I would be wise to hear what you have to say.

The situation is this; As I said above, I have never had much difficulty in selling what I write (if it is good enough to sell . . . I have four or five "queer" stories which I haven't been able to dispose of, but which nobody else could sell, because they are not magazineable) and without a word on my part, the prices paid by the different magazines have steadily risen. I have also had the most enjoyable personal relations with many editors, and have never had a disagreeable experience. This much against the advisability of employing an agent.

On the other hand, my correspondence is increasing enormously, I have a great many French and Italian letters to write, in addition to my usual mail, because of my connection with the Montessori movement.[1] My little daughter[2] is growing larger and needs more time and attention; and life in general, as it always does as one gets older, is getting more and more complicated, and needs more and more strenuous attempts to keep it simplified, if I am to have time for my work, and not become swamped in the flood of mere material details. If a literary agent would be a simplifying factor, and I could afford to employ him, wouldn't I perhaps, be wise to give up my personal touch with editors and the various details connected with sending out Mss. In other words, I am, for the first time in my life, open to conviction on this point. If you can convince me, go ahead!

It is, of course, the cost of employing an agent, which has seemed one of the most cogent reasons against that plan. Why pay a commission for something I can get for the price of a few stamps and a little time in addressing envelopes; for that part of my profession has never been in the least disagreeable to me, since I haven't at all the traditional sensitive artistic temperament and am not in the least cast down by the return of a manuscript . . . for one thing, I have now had a good many years' experience of that part of the business! If you can show me that, in the long run, it will be as profitable to have an agent as to do my own work, . . . why, I confess, I shall take considerable interest in what you have to say.

No, I'm sorry that I'm not going to be in New York during the next two weeks, nor, if I can help it, during the next winter! We were in Paris and Rome last winter and I've had enough big cities for a while. I am quite looking forward to a long, quiet, white winter of reading and work. So that you'll have to do your reasoning by letter, a process you must be pretty familiar with!

In conclusion let me thank you very much for your interest in my work, and your willingness to bother to try to have me for a client. If I have any agent, you certainly would be the one.

Faithfully yours,
Dorothy Canfield Fisher
(Mrs. J.R. Fisher)

---

1. DCF visited Dr. Maria Montessori's (1870–1952) Casa dei Bambini school in Rome in 1911. She endorsed the Montessori method of education in *A Montessori Mother* (1912), *A Montessori Manual* (1913), and *Mothers and Children* (1914). The Montessori emphasis on self-motivated learning and the development of self-discipline and self-confidence also forms the thematic underpinnings of *Understood Betsy* (1917).
2. DCF's daughter, Sarah (Sally) Fisher, was born on July 30, 1909.

12. To Paul Reynolds
June 21, 1913
Arlington, Vermont

Dear Mr. Reynolds:

Thank you for your last letter with the interesting and sympathetically sketched potential story in it.[1] I find the story very touching, indeed, and shall lay it away among my list of possibilities very near the head. If it doesn't "sprout" into a short story, I feel sure it will be an incident in a novel, where perhaps it belongs more than in a briefer treatment. Thank you very much for thinking of me in connection with it. I wish more than ever that I might have a *viva voce* talk with you. Perhaps I may, sooner than I think. Something may take me to New York . . . though I have just returned from a speech-making trip in Ohio (no, not on the suffrage!) and feel that it would take a good deal to tempt me again from the mountains.

I was very glad to see the check so promptly from *Harper's* . . . and my conversion to the advantages of having an agent is more wholesale than ever.

Will you, from your experience and good judgement give me a piece of advice. I have been asked several times to join this new Society of American Authors[2] . . . that isn't the exact title I believe, but you'll know what I mean. The annual dues are fifteen dollars, which means a good deal to people living on the small scale which is ours. I don't see that such a membership could do me a bit of good . . . I don't care a rap about "associating personally with people of my craft" liking plain folks as a rule a good deal better . . . and I feel that I am very well taken care of from a business point of view. But there are two things to be said. One is my incredulity as to the good an agent could do me, which has proved itself quite unfounded. The other is that my membership fee might do some good to authors not so well taken care of . . . what do you think? I'd really be very glad of your advice, which I'm sure will be sound. My publishers (Holt and Company) who are old friends as well as publishers, advise against it on the ground that it can't do any good to successful authors . . . but my conscience isn't quite clear about missing the chance to help the others . . . even if I am myself to [be] placed under the heading of a "successful" author. I have about the whole question of "success" a rather fatalistic doctrine that if one does good work one "succeeds" and if not, nothing can force success . . . but I daresay there is any amount of sharp practice among the lower grade of publishers against which unsophisticated authors need warning and protection. I never have had any such experience myself . . . but that proves nothing.

Forgive this long letter, and accept my thanks again for the story-germ.

Cordially yours,
Dorothy Canfield Fisher

[Handwritten] Do you hear anything about that rather unfortunately named story "In the Campo Santo?" I didn't know whether the Roman atmosphere would make it salable—on the contrary.

---

1. Reynolds told Fisher about a man who had been working on a manuscript for fifteen years before he died. The man's wife sought to have the multi-volume work published, but she was told that she could do so only at a cost of fifteen thousand dollars since the book did not make a valuable contribution to its subject and would likely have a very small sale. Reynolds advised the woman against publication, as did her friends. In his letter to Fisher, Reynolds proposed a happy ending to the story in which the book is published and proves to be useful to someone who desperately needs its information. I have not found such a story or episode among DCF's published or unpublished works.

2. Probably a reference to the Authors' League of America, founded in 1912. I have found no evidence that Fisher joined the league.

13. *To Paul Reynolds*
March 31 [1915]
Arlington, Vermont

Dear Mr. Reynolds:

I can't tell you with how much pleasure and interest I read your last letter about "Undine's Revenge." It does seem quite too good to be true to get somebody's judgment about a story (somebody that is, whose judgment I respect) before it's irrevocably published! The trouble with my husband's judgment, which is superexcellent, is that he knows so much about the genesis, thrashing-over, revisions and general history of a story that his judgment is almost as much from the inside as mine. And it's a judgment-from-the-outside of which I so very much feel the need.

All this as preface to saying that I don't see how I can possibly change the story as you suggest! I see your point of view perfectly and as I've said, I can't overstate the satisfaction I feel to know your opinion, nor the gratitude I feel for your bothering to give it to me . . . but in this particular story I just can't see my way to altering the end. The point is that such a simple-minded old countryman as my hero, *couldn't* know till it was all over, what was the real meaning of the sale.

But I do get from your letter a very valuable point, which is what I foresee I shall increasingly get from you, and that is a hint as to how to aim my shaft more directly at my audience . . . they get rather shadowy to an author, I fancy, and he needs to be reminded concretely that if he doesn't hit his readers, his shaft has gone wild. What I want the story to do for the "tired dressmaker and the worried clerk" is what it did for me in real life, to serve as a warning, and as a hint about the method to escape being "triumphed over by devils" ourselves. For you're quite right of course, that, and not the man's death, is the point of the story. And if you'll send the story back I will rearrange it a bit to bring out that idea, the idea that what happened to old Marshall Bigelow, happens more or less to everybody, the temptation to mistake an appearance for a reality, to give up something which is really satisfying and vital for what only seems to be a lot better. And I'll call the story (instead of that florid title which I disliked so much) "A Warning. . . ." And maybe one person in a thousand will see what I'm driving at?

And I'm ever so much obliged to you for your interest and the stimulating criticism . . . although it had an effect so quaintly different from what you meant!

The story will be better though . . . you see if it's not . . . and I've you to thank for it . . . which the same I do!

I've asked Holt and Co. to send you an author's copy of *Hillsboro People*. It's quite absurdly coals to Newcastle, if anything ever was! But I don't in the least mean you to read the stories! Only to accept them as a token of esteem!

Cordially yours,
Dorothy Canfield Fisher.

14. *To Henry Holt*
[September 14, 1915][1]
Arlington, Vermont

Dear Mr. Holt:

You *are* good to be reading that book! I didn't really believe you were going to be able to find the time for it. I can't in the least think how you do find time for all you do!

I'm greatly interested in your comments on the first fifth; but not so much alarmed by them as I would be if you'd read more. For I think by the time (if you're still miraculously continuing to find time) that you see how from my standpoint the "story" does begin at the very beginning. I mean, you see how there isn't any "story" except my Sylvia, and that what I'm trying to do is to tell what sort of clay she was made of, and into what sort of a vessel she was finally shaped by the moulding of circumstance.

Of course in that sort of a book, the "plot" in the Victorian sense, isn't the important thing: and the thread of the story does not run through a sequence of events but connects one phase of inner development with another.

How very nice of your brother to be interested in *Hillsboro People,* and to connect one of them with the contest in *Life.*[2] I flew to the volume at once, but a survey of the table of contents leaves me blank. My eye is evidently not so sharp as your brother's! Every one of those stories looks to me like everything I write (when I'm serious) a desperate attempt to get at and report what is inside of people's hearts. And I can't see myself doing that in fifteen hundred words. I wish to goodness I could! Maybe when I'm sixty, I'll have learned how.

I'm enclosing a picture of our darling Jimmy and his favorite mount. Do say he looks like my father. I hope so much he will!

Please thank your brother, and say I am turning again hopefully to a second consideration of *Hillsboro People.*

And thanks again to you for reading *The Bent Twig*!

Cordially yours
Dorothy Canfield Fisher

---

1. Date: appended, supported by publication date of *The Bent Twig* (1915).
2. In the fall of 1915, *Life* held a contest for the best short story of fifteen hundred words or less.

15. *To Alfred Harcourt*
[November or December (1915?)][1]
[Arlington, Vermont][2]

Dear Alfred:

Here is a letter I wish you'd read and help me to answer . . . you sicked him on to me, and so you're partly responsible.

The point I want to get at is this. Are there any more people who demand sugary optimism here than in England? Personally I don't believe a word of it. The majority of people everywhere, in every country at all times, have demanded and always will demand sugary optimism. That's my belief. What makes it seem acute now is that the majority of people are reading and writing, and are more important than they ever have been, that is, more obvious and out-standing than they have been.

What I'd like to know, is whether those English novels Miss Glasgow[3] thinks such a lot of have had any more *popular* success in England than similar, sound, sincere books have had here. If they sell by the hundred-thousand in England, I give up my point. But if they just have favorable reviews, why we can match that right here. No American reviewers take Gene Stratton-Porter[4] and Harold Bell Wright[5] seriously. And if they sell by the ten hundred-million, why so do Marie Corelli[6] and Hall Caine.[7]

You see my point. It's something the same as Syndor Harrison's in the *Atlantic*.[8] But what I want is a few facts, as to relative sales. Can you get me these without too everlastingly much trouble. It would be well worthwhile, I think to find out how Gilbert Cannan,[9] and the rest of them (personally I don't think they are such wonders as Ellen Glasgow does . . . but they're evidently what she has in mind) sell any better in England than Robert Herrick[10] and Ellen Glasgow (to be personal) and such writers do here. What she is objecting to is their popularity. If that doesn't exist, it would be interesting [to] bring out.

No news here . . . I'm pretty well worn to the breaking point with the suspense.

Lots of love to you all . . .

Dorothy

Say, can you tell me without too much bother, what is due us this month from you? We don't need it now, but it would make calculations easier if we knew what the size of the check would be.

Please send Mr. Gatlin's letter back. If I write that, I'd like to have it as a reference.

---

1. Date: based on the publication of an article by Henry Sydnor Harrison, "Poor America," *Atlantic Monthly* 116 (Dec. 1915): 751–63.
2. Place: implied.
3. Ellen Glasgow (1874–1945), American author.
4. Gene Stratton Porter (1863–1924), American author. Porter was known for her popular books for girls, including sentimental novels and nature studies illustrated by her own drawings.
5. Harold Bell Wright (1872–1944), American author. Wright's novels, often set in the American Southwest, were among the best-sellers of their time.
6. Marie Corelli (1855–1924), British novelist. Corelli was the world's best-selling writer during her lifetime.
7. Hall Caine (1853–1931), British novelist.
8. Harrison's article discusses whether "the gulf between orthodox good taste and the taste of the base American is quite so wide and awful as our conventional critics would have us believe."
9. Gilbert Cannan (1884–1955), British author.
10. Robert Herrick (1868–1938), American author.

16. To Robert Frost

January 14, 1916
Arlington, Vermont

Dear Mr. Frost:

That was by far the best part of my Boston trip—meeting you and hearing you voice my secret and up-to-the-present-time humble views about poetry![1]

I'm writing to tell you how much good it did me, and to correct an outrageous untruth I told you. You asked me if I'd ever written a play, and I said quite composedly no I never had. I don't know what I was thinking about! I have written one and it's been acted by a cast made up of our farmer neighbors, and with such success that we've had to repeat it, in near-by towns. We did it to make money for our district school house where Sally goes to school; and we did make a lot, that is over a hundred dollars which seems a big sum up here. I suppose I didn't really consider that a "play"—at any rate it was entirely absent from my mind when you asked me. It's absurd to be bothering you with this, when it can't possibly matter to you: but a fib (even an unconscious and trivial one) is better scotched than left squirming!

And anyhow I wanted to write you, to say thanks for your remarks on poetry. I've been talking them over and over with my much-interested husband ever since I came home!

With warm regards
Cordially yours
Dorothy Canfield Fisher

---

1. See Robert Frost entry in Notable Recipients.

17. *To Alfred Harcourt*
February 3, 1916
[Arlington, Vermont][1]

Dear Alfred:

You're right, we're glad to know that *The Bent Twig* hasn't given up the ghost. That's fine news . . . all your bulletins about that book have been fine. But there have been some gaps in them, naturally enough; and you've roused my curiosity so that I'd like to know just how many copies have been sold altogether. Yes, I noticed the page in the February *Atlantic*[2] . . . you're doin' grand by me! Did you see . . . I suppose there was some deal with you first . . . the page of Kerfoot's in the February *Everybody's*.[3] How much do those pages amount to? I should think quite something.

I heaved a long, satisfied sigh of pleasure to know that Mrs. Frost is as fine as her husband . . . though I'd known it ever since I saw him. He looks like a man whose wife is as fine as he . . . that's *one* of the ways he looks! I wish to goodness I'd have been with you, John and I. I do want John to meet Frost. And isn't that simply glorious about 6,000 *North of Boston*[4] and still going! I had a note from Ida Cerqua the other day. She says she's been ever so sick with the grippe, which is the reason she hasn't been to call on the Hartmans. But she is going as soon as ever she gets well.

Will you please send me up a copy of *Hillsboro People* as soon as may be. (Isn't it amazing how I can't keep a copy! I don't know *where* my last copy went!) John wants to read it over all in one piece, to see honest-for-sure how this "Real Motive" collection compares with it. Isn't he the conscientious, thoroughgoing comfort and mainstay!

My own impression of "The Real Motive" collection is that it is more uneven than *Hillsboro People.* It has quite a few stories which I think are better than anything in *H.P.;* but then again it has some others which maybe aren't so good. It's simply distracting to try to decide about the lighter ones . . . whether they're good enough to be permanently preserved! Just because they're lighter is no reason why they're not good, if they *are* good . . . but when you come on one after reading one of the very serious, deep-going ones, why, you feel it's pretty trifling . . . at least that's the way some of them strike *me* . . . but you said to leave them in to temper the tone of the whole volume . . . anyhow to leave them in till you and some other critic outside the Fisher family had seen them. So they go down to you . . . maybe John and I'll bring them down. I'm invited to address the Ethical Culture School,[5] and if I can fix the date so that it will co-incide with John's engagement of Feb. 18th, or anywhere near that . . . and if the children are as usual both well when that date comes, and if the thermometer doesn't take a notion to sink below zero about that time so it would need one of us here, and if I can get my cousin Hermie to stay here with Jimmy and Sally . . . If, I say, all these things be so . . . why, John and I are hoping to have the experience we so seldom have nowadays, a vacation trip TOGETHER! It's something to look forward to!

Anyhow, we're planning a trip to Swiftwater[6] the first part of May, going down by way of Pleasantville and stopping overnight with my brother, and coming back by way of Glen-Ridge and stopping overnight with you and Sue . . . and I assure you it seems quite natural to plan calmly (without consulting you) to stop overnight with you people as with Jim. It just now struck me, as I was writing our plan . . . the significance of that quiet assumption on our part. Pretty nice! So we'll be with you before so very long, anyhow . . . even if this February trip doesn't pan out for me.

Give my love to Sue as always . . . how she must have enjoyed the Frosts!

As ever yours
Dorothy

[Handwritten] Jim has just been up here for a few days and said casually he'd read somewhere that Roland Holt[7] was mixed up with a divorce-case. Is this so?

---

1. Place: implied.

2. A full-page advertisement for DCF's novels *The Squirrel-Cage, Hillsboro People,* and *The Bent Twig* appeared in the Feb. 1916 *Atlantic Monthly.*

3. J. P. Kerfoot's "A Row of Books" gave notice to *The Bent Twig* in the advertising section of the Feb. 1916 *Everybody's Magazine.*

4. Robert Frost, *North of Boston* (New York: Holt, 1915).

5. Ethical Culture (now Fieldston) High School, New York City. Felix Adler founded the Society for Ethical Culture in New York in 1876. The movement, based on the motto "Deed, not creed," holds that ethical endeavor should be the goal of human life, independent of religious belief.

6. Swiftwater, Pennsylvania: hometown of the Fisher family.

7. Roland Holt (1867–1931), American drama critic and vice president (1903–1924) of Henry Holt & Co., the publishing firm founded by his father.

18. *To Sarah Cleghorn*
March 4, 1916
Arlington, Vermont

Dear Sally:

Let me get over at once the telling of news which I suppose you will think is bad . . . everybody else seems to think so. I don't believe it will surprise you to know that John and I have been feeling more and more dissatisfied with what we were doing to help out in the war, and that we have about decided to do further. I don't know yet exactly in what form this will come. John has written to the American Ambulance Hospital Corps to see about the need for chauffeurs for ambulances,[1] and I have written to Céline Sibut[2] and Henry Baray about the need in their respective circles in France. The American Ambulance seems very glad of the application John put in (though of course this binds him to nothing, and he won't go with them if there seems more need somewhere else) but we can't hear from the French friends for a month yet. In the meantime everything is as indefinite as could well be . . . but I wanted you to know as soon as there was anything to know. Some of our vague plans are to this effect. If John goes to France this spring, I may go with him (leaving the children at Halcyon[3] with John's family) and see for myself what the conditions are over there, and if it would be possible to take the children over and settle somewhere near where John will be employed . . . you know of course that separation from John is about the desperate last resort in my mind, to be endured only if it cannot possibly be prevented. There are hundreds of thousands of French children who go on living in France of course, and Céline writes that life in Paris is about normal. But if I find the condition such that I think it would be dangerous for the children's health . . . why, of course I'll come back here and take care of them here until John can return. . . . This climate would be too severe to try to manage without him, and if we are here, next winter, and John in France, I think I'll probably go South somewhere; you could help with advice on that. But all this is too entirely vague to talk about. It may be that nothing will come of it at all . . . they may write from France that John can't be of help there . . . that they have plenty of help . . . but I doubt this. We'll see. In the meantime, though I face the future with unutterable apprehension, my heart is freed from that sombre desolation which filled it when I wrote you last. As you say, *now* is the time to stick to our principles . . . and it has made me sick to hear such crowds and crowds of Americans all writing vociferously to the papers that the Allies are fighting the cause of civilization for us, while we stand off in safety and profit by their blood and suffering . . . and yet nobody has done anything! Even John and I who have felt so keenly that France was standing between our world and all that threatened its permanence, have done nothing but send money, we haven't been willing to sacrifice our comfort and convenience . . . for that is practically all we are thinking of sacrificing now. There will be some danger of course, but not more than there always is in doing something worth doing . . . and it will be something always to remember, that John was able to help somewhat in healing some of the misery caused by the war. I too, if it turns out that I may take the children, may be able to help too.

Of course I needn't tell you . . . I couldn't, if I tried . . . what depths of prayerful and heart-sick meditation we have put on the question. Nor need I tell you, what the prospect of separation from the children (though I hope not for long . . . not more than five or six weeks I hope) nor perhaps, from John . . . means to me. I have spent many sleepless nights conquering the simple animal horror of the idea! But I didn't think I'd have been proud of my parents if they had given up what they thought right to do, because it might not have been exactly so good for the time being for Jim and me . . . and I hope when our children grow up, they'll feel that we did right. Anyhow, whether they do or not, I don't see anything to do but to go ahead and do it . . . or try to. I hope this won't seem just entirely insane to you . . . and yet I suppose it will. It seems to, to everybody else! Anyhow, I'm hoping for a word of comfort from you, and [handwritten] I love you very dearly and depend on you a great deal—your own

Dorothy

---

1. DCF's husband, John Fisher, left for France to work for the American Ambulance Corps in Apr. 1916.
2. See Céline Sibut entry in Notable Recipients.
3. "Halcyon" was the Fisher's home in Swiftwater, Pennsylvania.

19. To Louise Pound
[March 13, 1916][1]
Arlington, Vermont

Dear Louise:

I think that the picture the *Journal*[2] published is the funniest thing I ever saw! It was a snap-shot—I was leaning with one hand up against the white birch pillars of our porch, (which see above) but when the *Journal* printed it they blotted out all the back-ground (for no earthly reason I could see!) and left my upraised hand in the air, ridiculously like the hand of a bishop, bestowing the episcopal blessing. I'm fairly well hardened to the queer pictures that get into print, but I must admit I was aghast for a moment when I saw that! Why on earth did they do it do you suppose?

No, gracious no! I don't mind my pro-Ally sentiments being quoted. I wish I could print them in every newspaper in the country. It might well relieve my mind! There is now a chance that John and I may go to France to do relief work, children or no children—and take them along and settle down somewhere in a quiet place to the south of Paris (at least the children and I would) where we could see John once in a while, in the intervals of his work in a hospital. This never-ending inaction on our part is getting to be too much for us both. We *must* do something to help out.

I'm surprised by what you say of pro-German feeling in Nebraska. I have not yet met a single pro-German in this country—but it is generally thought, I believe, that the East is more solidly pro-Ally than the West, isn't it? Anyhow I've made addresses in a number of New England cities and towns, and, as I say, haven't chanced to encounter anybody but impassioned sympathizers with the Allies.

No, I hadn't heard that your learned brother had been made Dean,[3] but I knew he was regarded with great veneration by all Harvard people. They fairly [x] their [x] to the [ground ?] when he is mentioned!

Isn't this funny—and jolly and nice!—This sudden correspondence between us! It seems so good to me!

Cordially yours
Dorothy Canfield Fisher

[Keyed to photograph of DCF standing next to a donkey] Now if you know how big a donkey is, you can see how tall I am.

---

1. Date: postmark.
2. *Nebraska State Journal.*
3. Roscoe Pound (1870–1964) was dean of Harvard Law School (1916–1937).

20. To Henry Kitchell Webster
March 16, 1916
[Arlington, Vermont][1]

Dear Mr. Webster:
    Well, now I wish I'd plucked up my own courage and written you myself, instead of sending my message through somebody else, even somebody as very very nice as Miss Roderick![2] But I said to her, "I'd write to him myself . . . only do you suppose he ever heard of me?" And she said, considering the matter, "Oh, I wouldn't be surprised." So on the whole I thought I'd send the message through her . . . I hesitated to bother anybody as busy as you, with the congratulations of somebody you didn't know.
    Maybe, after that, you can imagine what a thrilling surprise and delight your letter is to me! I cried out to my husband, as I read and exclaimed, "Why for mercy's sake, he actually speaks of "The Great Refusal!"[3] I remember at the time, wondering about Mr. Sedgwick's enthusiasm about that story, for it

didn't seem at all his kind of a tale, and wondering vaguely if somebody else in the office had put him up to it, so to speak! To think of your having read Mss. on the *American* too! For that was, for a time, one of the innumerable jobs I have held. In fact I was still holding it, (I was sort of final reader,) when the magazine was sold, and we all lost our jobs together[4] . . . not that I hadn't at the minute five or six other ones, I was holding down. How New York does fairly claw at any young and energetic person! My life since my marriage has been (so outsiders think), fairly well diversified, with baby-bearing and tending, writing, housekeeping, gardening, lecturing etc. etc. . . . but it's a tranquil calm, compared with those hectic years in New York, when it seemed to me a new job rose up and grabbed me every time I went out of the house!

All this reminiscence stirred up by your reminiscence, and not a word yet about *The Real Adventure*[5] and I know Miss Roderick didn't begin to convey to you all that I think about it, because I didn't tell her half that I think—we were taking tea together in eight minutes before train-time at the Grand Central. And I assure you it would take me a great many times eight minutes to say all that I think about *The Real Adventure*!

Of course, you needn't be told how passionately the author of *The Squirrel Cage* (oh I am thankful to you for having read that!) was interested in your story as soon as I saw what you were driving at. It came as such a shock of delighted surprise too. I didn't notice the name of the author (I don't read much magazine fiction and don't know names very well anyhow) and I'd just been rendered almost physically ill by endeavoring to read Owen Johnson's *Making Money.*[6] I suppose that's libellous, isn't it, but I'll let it go! I was in such a mood of depression about American literature and magazines after I'd read an installment or two of that machine-made novel, that I started in on yours with as unfavorable a mental attitude as possible. And didn't I sit up and open my eyes and shout as soon as the situation began to develop. But I didn't trust you, I didn't trust an American magazine intended "for the family." I was *sure* that you would be betrayed somehow into sentimentalizing the situations, or prettifying those two splendid human beings, or smoothing over some of the difficulties of their situation. And I didn't relax my tension until the last installment! It seemed too good to be true, upon my word, it did! And I laid down the last installment with an almost solemn feeling of gratitude to you for existing! I kept saying to myself, "It's the *Squirrel-Cage* question, answered . . ." at least carried on much much further than I had had strength or insight enough to carry it . . . for the ending of *The Squirrel-Cage* was a palpable begging of the question the rest of the book had raised. Well, I'll have more courage to go on to the end of things, since this feat of yours.

I rejoice to say that I still preserve my reason enough, (in spite of my really preposterously indiscriminating admiration for your book) to see that you are absolutely wrong on one vital point . . . the treatment of the children. If I ever see you (and I hope I shall) I shall want to spend about one solid day in calling you all to naught on that point. That's no go! You and Mr. Wells (see *The Wife of Sir Isaac Harmon* and *The Passionate Friends*)[7] make me laugh with your casual waving away to a hypocritical perfect nurse with no nerves and perfect judgment about children, the fearful, tragic, distracting, and utterly fascinating problem for modern mothers of what to do with their own children. You might as well (honestly I'm not exaggerating) delegate being a wife to your husband, to some nice, easy-going girl with no nerves, who'll do all the comfortable things for him that a wife is supposed to do. If you do that, you're no wife. And if somebody else brings up your children, you're no mother . . . and anyhow, nobody else *can* bring up your children adequately but somebody quite as intelligent, well-educated, and *sensitive* as you are! The cow-like nurse would do finely for cow-like children of her own. She makes a million, vital and tragic mistakes every day, with children who have inherited their parents' nerves and intelligence and responsiveness!

And now comes a two-year-old baby, demanding his Mama, to save you from any more outpourings! This letter has been written, like all of mine, with children playing about, so you will please pardon lack of polish . . . also abominable typing! I don't pretend you can take care of your own without paying a price, you see!

[Handwritten] With many thanks for your letter, and more thanks for having written *The Real Adventure,* believe me.

Cordially yours,
Dorothy Canfield Fisher

———
1. Place: no reason to doubt Arlington.
2. Virginia Roderick, editorial staff member of *Everybody's Magazine.*
3. "The Great Refusal," *American Magazine* 58 (Dec. 1906): 202–10, reprinted in *The Real Motive* (1916).
4. DCF was a "final reader" for the *American Magazine.* Ellery Sedgwick (1872–1960) (see Letter 6, note 4), edited the magazine until its sale in 1906.
5. Henry Kitchell Webster, *The Real Adventure* (New York: Grosset & Dunlap, 1915).
6. Owen Johnson, *Making Money* (New York: Frederick A. Stokes, 1915).
7. H. G. Wells, *The Wife of Sir Isaac Harmon* (New York: MacMillan, 1916); *The Passionate Friends* (New York: Harper, 1913).

21. *To Henry Kitchell Webster*
March 26, 1916
[Arlington, Vermont][1]

Dear Mr. Webster:

If you doubt the ethics of answering an answer to a letter, what will you think of me, who take advantage of the excuse of answering an answer to an answer to a letter and inflict a whole book upon a helpless author-person, who has already too much of them in his life!

But it's not really a whole book which I am inflicting on you when I have my publishers send you a copy of my *Mothers and Children,* because all I want you to read is the last division (I *think* it's the last) called "Maternity no longer a profession for life." I'd send you just that, if I had it in separate form, but no magazine would touch it with a ten-foot pole, because they thought it too outspoken and grim, although goodness knows I thought I had kept it as mealymouthed and unfrightening as words could be! The other essays in the book came out, most of them, in magazines first; and then when Holt and Company published it in book-form, I took advantage of the chance to have my say out. You see that in theory I agree with you and Mr. Wells[2] and the rest (Mrs. Gilman[3] included) but that I insist the time isn't here yet, as a matter of hard fact. Honestly, you know, you did evade the question of what Rose is going to do about those twins when they get beyond the age when orange-juice at the right hour is the most essential thing . . . though I don't believe it's *ever* the most essential thing.

I'm delighted to know that you really know something about baby-tending, and can talk (when we have our discussion) on terms of equality of experience.

Do forgive me for sending you a book . . . I never did such a thing before, I assure you!

I hear that *The Real Adventure* is a best-seller, and I rejoice exceedingly. I'll warrant it's giving many a couple a thing or two to think about!

Cordially yours,
Dorothy Canfield Fisher

---

1. Place: no reason to doubt Arlington.
2. H[erbert] G[eorge] Wells (1866–1946), English author.
3. Charlotte Perkins (Stetson) Gilman (1860–1935), American author, lecturer on feminism and socialism.

22. *To Louise Pound*
April 2, 1916
Arlington, Vermont

Dear Louise:

I have another "interview" but I'm not going to send it because I am again referred to in terms of the minute and tiny, and I'm getting tired of that!

Thanks very much for wanting to print a picture and do a paragraph about me—but honestly do you think it worth while? What does all this "publicity stuff" amount to? Nothing of any value, does it. In my opinion the old adage of least said soonest mended ought to apply to writers. What difference does it make, *how* they look. And in my case, the less people know how I look, the more they'll think of me. Of course I'll send you anything you like, if you really want it—but I don't believe you really do. What's the use of being in the fashion, if it's a fool fashion?

John and I are tremendously stirred up over the possibility of going to France ourselves, to help out in relief work. John is thinking of going as ambulance driver for the American Hospital; and if our families aren't too *horribly* scared at the idea, I may take the children and settle down in France to somewhere near him: and to do what informal relief work I could. This is all very uncertain as yet. But we're simply *aching* to get out of this long inaction, and put our shoulders to a wheel ourselves. It's just sickening to feel so strongly as we do; and then not to be able to act.—cf. Freud and suppressed desires, I suppose.

What you say about open and active pro-Germanism astonishes me. My godfather from Topeka Kansas[1] has just been here and he reported an immense apathy and indifference—"What *does* it matter to a Kansas farmer who owns Belgium" etc. etc.—but *no* actual German sympathizers. I wonder if a fellow could do any good by writing on the subject? I've hesitated to say a word, because so many fools were rushing in. I'm no Kipling[2] maniac, and the talk about "exterminating Germany" makes me as sick as pro-German ravings. But I *can't* see that any sane person, (not of German blood) can possibly hesitate as to the rights of the case. Aren't *all* your pro-Germans of German descent? I bet they are!

Hastily—such apologies for this awful scrawl—
but always cordially
Dorothy Canfield Fisher

---

1. James Willis Gleed, lawyer mentioned in *Mothers and Children* (see Letter 26).
2. Rudyard Kipling (1865–1936), English author. Kipling's antagonism toward Germany intensified when his son John was killed by German forces in fall 1915.

23. To Paul Reynolds
April 26, 1916
Swiftwater, Monroe County, Pennsylvania

Dear Mr. Reynolds:

I haven't written you for some time, during which interval a lot of news has accumulated, some personal and other things professional. My husband sailed for France on the *Philadelphia* last Saturday, to take service in the ambulance corps of the American Ambulance Hospital at Neuilly. I intended to go with him, taking the children, up to the last moment; but was finally forced out of that plan by my alarmed family who thought in view of the submarine situation that it would be too reckless to take little children across the ocean. I do not feel that they were right, and bitterly regret that I couldn't go; but when one's parents and parents-in-law get beyond seventy, it is hard, not to say impossible, to refuse such anxiety as they felt.

You can imagine how very hectic and hurried the weeks have been with all this in the air. And of course that was the time when a lot of other business came up. Mr. Boyden wrote me asking (for the *American*) if I had anything like a serial to offer them. I wrote that I hadn't anything except the plan for a girl's book, which Holt and Co. have been wanting me to write for them.[1] I outlined this briefly to Mr. Boyden and asked him if he thought it might be anything to their purpose . . . it is a real juvenile, but one which perhaps might interest grown-ups, like Mrs. Burnett's *Secret Garden*[2] . . . in fact it is not unlike that in its general character although a very New England story. Mr. Boyden replied that naturally enough they couldn't tell anything about it without seeing a sample but that if I could have twenty-thousand words done inside six weeks from then (about the middle of April) they would be glad to consider it. He said there was nothing in the plan as outlined which would make it out of the question for them. In between our letters, they had written me from the *Woman's Home Companion,* asking for a serial, and I asked Mr. Boyden to turn over to them my letters to him (I literally hadn't an instant's time to write again). They read them and the synopsis of the story, and returned a decided negative. They must have a love-interest . . . the conventional grown-up story. So *they* are settled, which is at least something definite. Now comes the enclosed letter from some people of whom I never heard, and which I refer to you. Should I answer them personally, or is it something you can take care of for me? They sound to me just like another agent soliciting my stuff, only putting their request in a little different style from the usual formula in which that request comes to me. I am simply overwhelmed with work just now and would be grateful if you could say whatever needs to be said to them.

And will you also (if it's not asking too much) tell me what the *Ledger* means by the enclosed letter which sounds cryptic to me, and which I haven't answered yet. I don't see that there is anything in it which could interest me, do you? And I feel an instinctive distrust to anybody who writes "confidentially" he wants to tell me this or that, or that he wants something "not for publication." But those may be just ill-chosen phrases. Give me a hint, will you please, as to what I ought to answer them.

I think that is all for the time being . . . though it seems vaguely to me there was something else I wanted to report or to ask you.

My plans for the summer are indefinite. I'm afraid I couldn't stand Arlington without my husband, and think I will try to match my restless feeling of anxiety and care by wandering about. I am here for a month, with Mr. Fisher's family. Then I plan to be in Pleasantville, (Westchester) with my brother's family for another month, and then I shall hope to go in and out of the city and to see you once in a while. After that nothing is settled . . . perhaps a summer camp for Sally with her little brother and her mother boarding near by. I'm going to try to get that girls' story done if possible . . . though it is going to be cruelly hard to write at all.

I wish I had an extra copy of the synopsis of the girls' story, which I call "Understood Betsy," to send you. I'd like to leave that matter in your hands after this. Though it seems to me that I have talked it over with you, haven't I? Or was that with my Godfather? My mind is anything but clear these days. Pardon this disjointed letter.

Always cordially yours
Dorothy Canfield Fisher

---

1. The book, *Understood Betsy,* was serialized in the children's magazine *St. Nicholas,* November 1916–April 1917.

2. Frances [Eliza] Hodgson Burnett (1849–1924), English-born American author who wrote romantic stories and novels, many of them for children, of which the most famous is *Little Lord Fauntleroy* (1886). *The Secret Garden* was published in 1911.

24. *To Louise Pound*
May 16, 1916
Swiftwater, Monroe County, Pennsylvania

My dear Louise:
We planned to go to France, were all ready even to passports and tickets, but at the last moment the clamor of anxiety from the various relatives was too much for me—my mother who is over seventy-two, was fairly sick with apprehension—and we decided on a far far harder thing, to separate, John going on

to France without me. He is now driving an ambulance car near the Verdun front—and I am staying in this country to take care of the children! It is the first separation for more than a day, since our marriage nine years ago—and I can tell you, these days and nights are none too easy for me to live through. I'm here in the Pocono Mountains with my husband's family, and expect to spend the month of June with Jim and Stella in Pleasantville, the first long visit I've ever made there with the children.

I'm sending you with this a snap-shot said to be the best John and I ever had taken. It's never been published. You're welcome to make any use of it you please—or just to keep it for yourself, if you like. And I'm also sending the latest snap-shot of my Jimmy in his sand-pile, which is an excellent likeness of the fat little fellow. He is said to look like my father.

Write me again—do!

Cordially yours
Dorothy Canfield Fisher

25. *To William Lyon Phelps*
August 3, 1916
Waiting-Room, Grand Central Station, New York City

Dear Professor Phelps:
I've been trying desperately to find a moment in which I might write you, but packing and children, and getting our house ready to leave for the winter and saying good-byes have so more than filled every moment that it's only now, at five in the morning, as I arrive from Vermont on the early train, that I see a breathing-space, and feel I can write you the "report" I've been wanting so much to make to you. For, do you know, I feel that I owe you an accounting for what I do. That's one of the penalties you pay for your generous interest and sympathy! I really want you to know what I'm up to, for I'm counting on your help to make the most I can out of my life.

Sally Cleghorn—my very dear and close sister-friend—has written you that I am going to France, but she didn't tell you why, I believe. It's mainly for the very simple, elemental reason that my husband is there, and that we are the kind of husband—and—wife who find it almost intolerable to be separated. Life's too short to miss any of that perfect companionship! I'm not going into "relief work" (except what informal help I can give without interfering with my care for our children) I'm going to establish a quiet little French home in a suburb of Paris, near the American Ambulance in Neuilly where my husband will be, for the most part, in service, and just live there through the winter to come, instead of on our Vermont mountainside. I'm not going to write, because I've written a great deal this last year, and I want to give myself time to do a lot of thinking and living before undertaking anything new. And I hope our two children will enjoy their French winter as much as a Vermont one. You must remember there is nothing new in this for me. I was half brought up in France, you know, and have established French homes and lived there at intervals all my life. It all seems quite simple and natural to me, my husband giving up a year of his life to France, and I going to live near my dear French friends in this dark moment of their lives—like going to help out one's cousins in need. I think we'll both be happier all our lives to have done this. I hate war, I'm almost as much of a pacifist as Sally Cleghorn (though not quite!) but like nearly all of my generation I'm terribly, tragically bewildered by the complexity of the situation. And it will ease an aching heart to do the simple, obvious, human thing, even if it is not very deep or far-reaching, establish a home near my husband who is alleviating pain, and fill my house, small though it will be, with a succession of homeless Belgian and French children who can share in the mothering I give to my own. Perhaps I can think more clearly what it all means if I can stop the misery of feeling that I am doing nothing—not even the little I might do—to help out in the suffering.

I've written you all this as though you were my Godfather, to whom indeed I have recently written very much such a letter. He has disapproved very much of our leaving our comfortable Vermont home, but now, I hope and believe, feels more reconciled to it. I hope you will, too. It makes a good deal of difference to me—what you think.

With every good wish
Faithfully yours,
Dorothy Canfield Fisher

26. To Scudder Klyce
September 5, 1916
14 Avenue des Sycamores, Villa Montmorency, Paris, France

My dear Mr. Klyce:
Your unexpected, delightful, stimulating and wholly interesting letter has followed me here, and before I begin to answer it I want to give you a brief account of what I am up to, so that you can understand why I don't answer more at length . . . as I would very much enjoy doing!

My husband is in the service of the American Ambulance Corps (we neither of us could stand our inaction any longer, when there was such a tragic deal to be done here) and I've brought the children here to be as near him as possible and also to do what I can to help out. My help is taking the form of absorption in the needs of Men Blinded in Battle . . . perhaps you know something about the work of the Franco-American Committee which is working for them? I have undertaken the editing of a monthly magazine in Braille for the blind, and the creation of a good, sound modern library in French Braille now. Of course the men recently blinded have the habit of books, need them for a normal life, and desperately need them for a successful re-education.

This work together with the care of my children who of course always come first of all, as long as they are little, keeps me more than busy, as we are not rich people (to put it mildly!) and the cost of living in Paris is high, so that I must keep as close a watch as possible on household matters as well.

This explanation is given, partly because it may interest you, and partly as apology for a summary answer to your most interesting, almost exciting letter! In fact, I may say without exaggeration that it was exciting! To have such a bolt from the blue as that, makes a fellow sit up! To receive suddenly from a stranger such minute, discerning and accurate understanding of what I'm trying to say in my writing, takes my breath away. And to receive such commendation as you give me, makes me extraordinarily happy, and not a little incredulous! For I wasn't in the slightest degree overworking my intellectual honesty (in your own pungent phrase). I always feel very apologetic about writing anything dogmatic, and don't share your generous estimate about the relative percentage of sense and nonsense in such a book. I suffer so under the extreme amount of nonsense in such books written by other people that I don't in the least dare to hope that I have come off very much better in the enterprise, after all very chimerical, of telling people how to run their lives. You put your finger on the spot when you say that the only real way to do it, is by running one's own life as well as possible . . . and that is certainly job enough for anybody! Since I have begun to write (always I assure you with very shame-faced dislike of dogmatism) such "instructive" books, I have been invited to give lectures on the same subjects, and the questions put to me afterwards by my audiences have more than ever convinced me that one doesn't do much good by such would-be instruction. People always try to take you literally, to extract some minute rule-of-thumb out of you, and then apply it to all sorts of conditions! What do you honestly think about this? Don't you really believe that a lot of mothers, reading my *Montessori Mother* and *Mothers and Children* have gathered a confused idea that children must be allowed to do whatever comes into their heads? I'd really be glad of your opinion, which I know from your letter would be of great value to me. I've been on the point of saying that I would never write that sort of book again, but would stick to fiction, the flexibility of which gives one a better chance to be honest in one's portrayal and

interpretation of life. What would be your advice? It seems to me that in stepping up to a professor's chair (and you do, you know, in writing a dogmatic
book) you get out of focus. How about this?

The lawyer mentioned in *Mothers and Children* is my Godfather, Mr. James
Willis Gleed, who is a lawyer in Topeka Kansas and can be reached by addressing him care of Gleed, Hunt, Palmer and Gleed, Law-Firm. He is an extraordinarily intelligent man of about fifty-five, who has a passion for the Greek
authors and has been condemned to spend all his life making money . . . of
which he has, I believe, a goodly supply. He wasn't very well when I left America, and was taking a vacation, but by the time this reaches you, I'm sure he
will be back at work. If you write him, tell him you come from me and that I
have a very high opinion of your judgment!

I am filled with the greatest curiosity and interest in Mr. Eerwin's work and
in yours, and if this nightmare of a war ever ends, and my husband and I are
safe back on our Vermont mountain, I shall hope that Winchester isn't too far
away from us to hope for a visit from you. I am sure it would do a great deal of
good!

In the meantime please accept my warmest thanks for your generous and
heartening letter and believe me,

Cordially yours,
Dorothy Canfield Fisher
(Mrs. John R. Fisher)

27. *To Sarah Cleghorn*
December 28 [1916][1]
[Paris, France][2]

Dearest and Best:

Your first letter from Carl's[3] house arrives this morning, and I am going
about with uplifted heart thinking about what Mr. Howells says about *The
Spinster.*[4] Do you remember *now* the time when I sat on the stationery tub in
your Manchester kitchen and told you you were the real article, and I only an
imitation, who would be remembered solely as your friend? I am so proud of
myself for having known that the first of anybody.

John is back—brown, thin, bald and dead for sleep! He drops off anywhere,
any time! I think it is high time he was back from the front for a time, and he *is*
to be here for at least 3 months and maybe more!

I'm looking forward with extreme eagerness to your next letter with news of
how you get on teaching the children, and *how you are.*

What unspeakably horrible conditions for the negroes. One doesn't believe it until somebody like you writes it's so. The Belgian deportations[5]—that's unbelievable too—a real nightmare—inconceivable as refinement of torture. I *can't bear* to write you the details!

We're well here, though with occasional colds and *so* happy to have John with us! Write soon—write lots!

Your devoted
Dorothy

---

1. Date: 1917 appended, but reference to "what Mr. Howells says about *The Spinster*" makes 1916 more probable. Howells comments favorably on Cleghorn's novel *The Spinster* in "A Conjecture of Intensive Fiction," *North American Review* 204 (Dec. 1916): 871–72.
2. Place: biographical evidence that DCF was in Paris.
3. Cleghorn's brother in Macon, Georgia, whose actual name was Charles.
4. See note 1.
5. The Belgian deportations to German labor camps began in Oct. 1916.

28. To Louise Pound
February 14, 1917
6 Rue Pétrelle, Paris

Dear Louise:

I was so glad to get your letter, the first news I have had from you in so long. Yes indeed, I know where to apply the money. I am very much interested in two war children who, although not orphans, need help very much. Their father was badly wounded near Verdun and, although he has been cured of his wound in a hospital, he has been cured as, alas! so many of them are cured, only halfway. He is an iron worker by profession, and every time he has tried to go back to work to earn his living has fallen very ill again, his nervous system being very badly shattered. His wife is dead,—died since the beginning of the war. Now, his two little girls are not, of course, war orphans, since their father is still alive, and so they are not eligible for any of the State aid. I am trying to find someone to undertake to give regularly eight or ten dollars a month for their home in a little village, but who has not the where-withall to care for them. I have written to my sister-in-law, who, I think, will furnish the money, and in the meantime your cheque, together with what I will put with it, will enable them to hold out until the letter comes from Esther Fisher. So you see, it fell quite providentially.

Thank you very much for the long review by Miss Mann[1] about me. She keeps insisting on my being such a tiny wisp of a woman, in all she writes, because she is one of those big, upstanding creatures. I am really not so tiny as all that. Will you tell me, please, how Miss Mann, who is connected in my mind with the *Boston Transcript,* happens to be writing for the *Lincoln State Journals*? It sounds queer to me.

Don't you think it is rather fun to go around making speeches? You say you do not speak well, but I don't believe that, because you would not be asked to make them. You must get a view of bigger America, going from one of these remote spots to another, that is very enlightening. To think of your having seen May Lewis![2] I saw her for just one moment on the dock in New York the day I sailed for France, and carried away with me a vivid picture of her great black eyes.

I wonder if I have written you how much interested I am in work for the blind here? I am working in connection with Le Phare de France, which was organized by Miss Holt, of New York;[3] you know, the one who did so much for the Lighthouse work among the blind there. I have been organizing the printing press, which is to supply a magazine and as many books as possible to the war blind, many of whom were budding lawyers, mathematicians, political economists, and so forth, before the war. Of course they need books almost as much as they need bread. And I have been hustling hard to overcome the various obstacles which are in the way of any new enterprise attempted in a country in wartime. I am on the editorial side now, which is extremely interesting, and brings me into contact with some of the best minds in Paris. I do hope I will be able to get it in pretty good shape before the end of the war, because the end of the war means the return to America of the Fisher family.

Do you know, I wish you would write me another letter about what the state of public opinion is around you. I take so little stock in what the newspapers say. I would like to know what your opinion is how people feel about the diplomatic rupture,[4] and the curious pause that is following it. If you have only been skating three times, I have not been inside a theatre or a museum or a concert hall since I came to Paris. Busy times, these! It is not by principle, because it is my principle that you ought to go on amusing yourself as much as possible, even while working hard. But when night comes both John and I are too used up to do anything but tumble into bed. He is working very hard every day in the week, including Sundays, for the Paris Bureau of the Field Service of the American Ambulance.[5]

Do write me again, and let me know all Nebraska news. I've seen Adèle Lathrop's sister here, once or twice, she was head of the American Girls Club, rue de [Chereuse ?], before the war, and is still there, though there aren't any A.G. now, I believe! My handwriting isn't a bit more legible than yours. I've forgotten to say thanks for the D.L.M.[6] clipping. Of course I was glad to see it,—always pleased by kind remarks—though personally between you and me, I don't think I'm such great shakes as a writer! I do my honest best, but that anybody will read me fifty years from now, as Miss Mann prophecies—it'll take more than *her* say so to make me do anything but laugh at such an idea!

Bien à vous, toujours,
Dorothy

---

1. Dorothea Lawrance Mann, American author, literary critic, contributor to the *Boston Evening Transcript, New York Herald Tribune,* and various magazines.
2. May Lewis, American poet and contributor to magazines.
3. DCF worked for "The Lighthouse" organization (to which Winnifred Holt, Henry Holt's daughter, made major financial contributions) aiding the war blind of WWI in France. Her experience provides the basis for "Eyes for the Blind" published in *Home Fires in France* (1918).
4. On Feb. 3, 1917, President Wilson severed U.S. diplomatic relations with Germany over the issue of submarine warfare.
5. See Letter 18, note 1.
6. See note 1.

29. To Sarah Cleghorn
March 3, 1917
[6 Rue Pétrelle, Paris, France][1]

Dearest Sally:

Two letters from you, (February first and 9th) have just come in, in the wrong order . . . the American mail having tied itself into double-bow knots during the month of February. And those two letters rouse in me a great variety of emotions among which is quite prominent a considerable degree of exasperation . . . with you, with Jim-and-Stella, the Fishers and with Aunt Mattie.[2] It's on the subject of your not getting the round-robins. I don't see why under the sun some one of those people don't [line missing] There must of course be some reason why you don't take this step, or why they don't send them to you . . . but from across the ocean it looks like the greatest lack of enterprise and get-up-and-git on *somebody's* part!

Having thus relieved my feelings, which are you see, quite naively founded on the assumption that my round-robins are serious, important matters! . . . let me pass on to other matters in your letters. Yes I do take the progress of your colored student very remarkable. I have often heard it said that negro adults master the elements of reading and writing with remarkable rapidity. The first after-the-war northern teachers used to send back, I believe, the most astonishing stories of their application and quickness of intelligence. I have a vague idea that the accusation is made against them that they do not continue this quickness in more advanced studies, but that sounds to me just like one of those idiotic, lying, generalities which are so much indulged in against negroes. How absorbingly interesting intellectual development is, isn't it? In the midst of all my other occupations, I find myself constantly marvelling and rejoicing at the way Sally and Jimmy develop. Sally is speaking French very fluently now and is beginning to read it, and to write it a little. She has taken lately to writing a good deal . . . just dashing off compositions of various sorts for her own satisfaction. (Often she doesn't even show them to me . . . as for instance this "story" which I found in my waste-paper basket, "The little boy and the little girls." A boy found some girls. He did not know them and said "Will you play football with me?" "Why non!" they said, "What a funny idea!" The boy was ashamed and said to his maman, "Kill all girls! I hate them!" (I transcribe literally, mistakes and all.) How is that for quick action and savage denouement! And you will see in one of the last round-robins (for I take it after the above energetic exhortation, you *will* get hold of the back-files of those epistles) my account of a "play" which Sally wrote lately and which she and Jimmy and Mademoiselle Macquer acted with great effect thereafter.

As to politics, and the amazing things which happen . . . I feel despairingly there is little use to try to comment on them with you because by the time the letters go across the Atlantic and back there is a total transformation of the face of the world! The news this morning is of the German proposal to Mexico and Japan to form an alliance against the United States and conquer Texas, New Mexico, and Arizona. I find it almost inconceivable that the Germans should have done anything so calculated [as] to fire the last remaining element of the American people which was holding out for peace! John and I both think it sounds like a "fake." But so many things the Germans have done have sounded at first like clumsily wrought calumnies . . . the Belgian deportations for instance. I didn't believe those could be true, for a long time after we had conclusive proof of it! But what sounds particularly fake in this Mexican-German plot is that nobody says how that letter of Zimmermann's reached President Wilson's hands.[3] It's unthinkable that it shouldn't have been very closely-kept as a secret. It wouldn't surprise me a bit to hear that it *was* a fake.

Is Zephine's novel[4] out yet? I have seen it advertised in several places. It will be an important day for her when it begins to be reviewed. I've a notion that people will treat it very respectfully because of the excellence of the writing . . . if for nothing else. That makes me think of novels in general and of yours[5] . . . the negro woman servant! That's a subject so poignant and terrible that it makes me shiver to think of handling it. If *I* should try to, it would be wild and over-emphasized and almost hysteric, because the negro question always carries me out any sense of proportion . . . but I believe you (who did not come in contact with it in your childhood) will be able to give the subject the reserve-strength and restrained treatment which will make it effective. I think it a splendid, noble idea . . . and if there is anything under the sun I can do to help you in it, I'm even more than usually at your service!

I think it ought to be done! I don't see why somebody hasn't done it seriously before. Of course you know that novel of Howells[6] about the pretty girl who finds out she has some negro blood . . . but he begs the question in such a miserable manner at the end!

When does your book of verse[7] come out? I can hardly wait to see it . . . to see those dear and intimate denizens of my heart given to the delight and strengthening of others.

Don't you think *Fellow-Captains* has had very favorable reviews. Not a mocking note have I seen in anything you've sent me! And the other day I had an accounting from Holt in which they said over a thousand copies had been sold before January first . . . two months or thereabouts of sale . . . and I had sixty-nine dollars coming to me, which means you have the same amount and ought to have more . . . I have never been the least bit satisfied with that half-and-half arrangement, you know. Still seventy dollars apiece for two months sale seems good to me . . . but then Alfred Harcourt always laughs at my naive surprise that books bring in money. It always *really* seems to me that we authors ought to pay for the privilege of being allowed to express our thoughts as we choose, instead of being paid for doing what we enjoy more than anything else! My typewriter, as you see, is also somewhat on the blink, but workmen cost so like Sam-Hill nowadays in France, I'm getting along with it as best I can. The last time I had a few insignificant repairs made, it cost me twenty-five francs and I had to wait two weeks! I suppose workmen of that sort are as scarce as every other sort! My *o*'s are particularly recalcitrant, but if you once understand that peculiarity you can make out quite well what I am writing.

I have just finished in one day's intensive writing a series of thumb-nail portraits of different temperaments under the stress of active war-service which I called "Vignettes from Life at the Rear."[8] My tonsillitis yesterday mounted up into my ear and I had such an ear-ache I really feared an abscess there (my only good ear too, bad cess to this climate!) and I didn't dare go out, though there was a lot of work to do at the Phare. But being obliged to stay in, I took advantage of the enforced leisure and wrote furiously all day long . . . doing about five thousand words. It had all been ready to come out, you see and only needed to be poured out in a rush. I took the different soldiers whom I see, returning from the front on their furloughs, and set them down just as they are, the intelligent, educated one, furious with rebelliousness at the imbecility of the whole affair and frantic to think that the future settling of war or not-war will be at least partly determined by fat old politicians who have not gone to the front and seen the horrors which have left such a scar on his soul; then the good-natured, farm-laborer who doesn't (apparently) see anything at all out of the way in his new profession and takes it matter-of-factly as he would take anything else; the stupid one, "splendid first-line fighter" who hasn't any brains at all, but only capacity for bravery and obedience; then the refugee, man from the north of France whose wife and child are still there, held by the Germans, who is slowly going mad here alone in Paris; and finally for finish, my stepping into Notre Dame with the children in a mood of horrible depression . . . something of what the cathedral of Chartres did for me. I don't think it's of any special value, except as it may make people think. It was my purpose to try to make people at home REALIZE a little more of what war means. Not by the usual descriptions of battle-fields, but by showing how it affected men sitting by their own firesides and talking over their new life.

[Handwritten] I often wonder if I've at all given you an idea of how precious your letters are to me, and of how I've been rejoicing in your having the children to yourself and of what the winter has been to you.[9]

My best love to your Aunt Jessie—When do you go North?

Always your [x]
Dorothy

---

1. Place: letterhead.

2. "Jim-and-Stella" were DCF's brother and sister-in-law; "Aunt Mattie" was DCF's paternal aunt.

3. A Jan. 1917 letter from German official Arthur Zimmerman (1864–1940) directed the German ambassador to Mexico to offer that country alliance with Germany and support in reconquering lost territory in Texas, New Mexico, and Arizona. The telegram was intercepted and decoded by British naval intelligence and published in the U.S. It became a major factor in leading the U.S. into World War I.

4. Zephine Humphrey, *Grail Fire* (New York: Holt, 1917). See Humphrey entry in Notable Recipients.

5. Probably an unfinished sequel to *The Spinster.*

6. *An Imperative Duty* (New York: Harper, 1891).

7. *Portraits and Protests* (New York: Holt, 1916).

8. "Vignettes from Life at the Rear" was originally published in the *Delineator* (Jan. 1918) and is included in *Home Fires in France.*

9. Cleghorn was teaching her brother Carl's children in Macon, Georgia (see Letter 27, note 3).

30. To Scudder Klyce
April 3, 1917
[6 Rue Pétrelle, Paris, France][1]

Dear Mr. Klyce:

Your last letter which has just arrived has touched and moved me profoundly. The sympathetic and deeply divining clairvoyance which you bring to bear on my problems, ending with the information as to the facts of your personal life, and the unconscious revelation of which you have succeeded in making from those facts for your best self . . . it's not often in a life-time that one gets a letter so freighted with human significance. I have been meaning for some time to write you a more satisfactory letter than the very hasty notes which are all I have been able to compass with the children swarming about me and with my mind full of material details of the difficult life here.

It's curious, how the spiritual wind bloweth when and where it listeth! These letters from you form a strange and rather solemn episode in my life . . . (that a stranger, unseen, unknown should suddenly with so calm a confidence have thrown open doors I have always kept shut!) . . . and yet it comes in the midst of the noisiest, most confused and turbulent experience; as though, in the midst of work in a boiler-factory one should encounter one of the few understanding people in the world and as one toiled over clanging steel plates, should hear his voice proclaiming things one longs to meditate in peace and silence!

Well, there will be peace and silence enough on the side of our Vermont mountain when we get home. One of the lessons the years bring, is patience. I am putting your letters away carefully, to read again, under our great pine-trees: as dear to me as dear friends . . . I can say that to you without sounding sentimental, now that I know that you too love to contemplate things, so much less complex and unknowable than human beings.

There is an *ave-atque-vale* sound about this last letter which I acquiesce in if you think it best. I never have noticed that anything honest ever did any harm, but human beings are after all excessively complicated and unforeseen; it's quite possible that you're wise.

Thank you for the note about Fisher and Fiske *How to Live.*[2] I've a notion I may get some useful hints about the mechanics of the matter; although (as long as I don't get nervously tired) I have always had the most exceptionally good health. Twice in my life I have been nervously tired out and have been driven by an anxious family to consult those dangerous creatures "nerve specialists." They said, (one set in New York and one set later in Paris) that I was more than usually all right physically, but put together oddly nervously, so that nervous equilibrium is more necessary in my case than most. In the last analysis, it is (as it always is) up to the will residing in this body, to keep things straight. This

winter the trouble has been genuine physical fatigue, added to the mental fatigue of carrying too many unaccustomed details in my head. The children,
war-housekeeping, my husband's needs, and the very considerable complication of organizing an enterprise in war-time when workmen and raw materials
are practically unfindable, and industry all disorganized. However, my Braille
printing-press is now organized with a good force of competent work-people,
and really running well, turning out the best work of the kind done on the
continent, so somebody told me the other day to my immense surprise and
delight. I don't grudge the very painful effort I have had to put into it.

Since it has been possible to relax something of the eternal vigilance which
always accompanies the beginning of a new enterprise, I have been physically
resting. My best remedy is always a prodigious amount of sleep, and after
catching up on that, I find that, as I expected, I'm not so absurdly tense and
taut morally.

Yes, you're right, it's mostly a matter of being very much alone, and not
taking that condition too tragically. Only I think that everybody must be very
much alone; not at all that it is a peculiarity of mine. I feel sure that I am much
like everybody else. I couldn't feel so profound a kinship with all sorts and
conditions of folks if I weren't made just like them at bottom. They don't understand much, most of them, and don't care if they do or don't; and I make a
desperate effort to understand; but the stuff we're made of and the essential
conditions of our life is alike, I know.

I'm touched and amused at the idea of anybody looking up *Corneille and
Racine* . . . and then really reading it! I wouldn't do that for a good deal! I
don't remember much about doing it beyond that I suffered from much crude
youthful scorn of the futility of such kind of writing. I'm not so scornful now.
It's possible that any addition to the sum total of knowledge about anything, is
worth while.

My husband, like myself, is in a phase of tremendous material effort, working long hours, seven days a week with no let-up. As his mental processes are
slower than mine (and are far surer in the end!) I haven't tried to talk over
thoroughly with him the subjects raised in your last two letters. We just have
not the time! He didn't read the second one . . . I read parts of it to him . . .
and he won't read this one. He's *tired* and it's part of my job for the time being
to rest him and not to stimulate him to further activity which even though
intensely interesting to him as to me, is not as physically restful as somnolent
snoozing by the fire, pipe in mouth, and domestic chat of what the children
have been doing and how our limited store of money is withstanding war-
prices. I hope this doesn't sound too dull and prosy! It's not our usual life-in-
common which is very deep and full. This is a strange episode to us. But I am
thankful that we were able to come and do what we could.

I'm very much struck with the accuracy with which you analyze the phenomenon of your letters to me . . . from one of the very many points of view there are. You make me see very clearly a man who has lived so long with moral and physical ill-health that he had forgotten the feeling that comes with the knowledge that the rule of the world is as a whole good health. All the foolish, hampering conventions of society shut him away, as far as the circle close to him is concerned, although it probably contains a majority of healthful personalities, from a thorough-going enough, deep enough acquaintance with health in others to restore vividly his recollection of it. And then, a long way off, an ordinary, normal woman, very much like many normal women (happy wives, contented mothers and solitary souls none the less) instead of keeping her inner life to herself as the others do, happens to set it down in a more or less veiled form in fiction and essays. The man has an extraordinary gift for piercing veils and seeing the essence of things, and he is immensely relieved and comforted to see that the moral and physical ill-health which has been nearest him is not a bit universal, but is a painful exception. He knew it, of course, all the time; but he didn't *feel* it. And, saving your very intellectual presence, it doesn't do the human being a bit of good to know things if he doesn't feel them.

But, don't you see, that means that instead of having difficulty to find as you put it "one other example" that I have only to wave my hand around anywhere to find dozens, hundreds! You reason from me to other women and you're quite right because I'm just like them, only you've been able to see me more clearly than you do those you have actually seen, because you've looked at me through the magnifying glass of books. But the others are there . . . "one example" indeed! when you probably know five or six . . . the only difference is that they are not articulately and consciously aware of themselves. But anyone of your penetration can furnish enough articulateness for a dozen! All the same I feel very happy that I've chanced to be a sort of finger-post pointing you along a very familiar road which exceptional circumstances had happened to crowd from you. As for you, you've showed me the way along a road not at all familiar, and which it is quite possible I would not have seen if you hadn't been there.

Truly and sincerely yours
Dorothy Canfield Fisher

---

1. Place: letterhead.
2. Irving Fisher and Eugene Lyman Fisk, *How to Live: Rules for Healthful Living Based on Modern Science* (New York: Funk & Wagnalls, 1916).

31. To John S. Phillips
May 12, 1917
[6 Rue Pétrelle, Paris, France][1]

Dear Mr. Phillips:

Your more-than-welcome letter has just arrived (mail is a long time en route these submarinish days) and has given me a great deal of pleasure. You are connected with the very beginnings of my writings,[2] and I have always kept my great respect for your judgment, and my pride when you liked something I have done. So you can think with what delight I read that you think of me seriously, and would like to have your publishing-house handle my books. The fact that that is out of the question (except in the event of something entirely unforeseen) doesn't at all lessen my satisfaction that you remembered me in that connection.

I am under contract to Henry Holt and Company, who have been very kind to me always, and who consider me one of "their" authors. Mr. Henry Holt was a friend of my father's, and Mr. Alfred Harcourt is a classmate and close friend of my husband's so that the relationship has an element of personality in it as well as the satisfactory business-side. So that I must not think, as long as conditions are what they are, of considering another publishing-house. But as I say, that doesn't at all interfere with the glow of pleasure I had in hearing from you on that subject.

You can't think what a relief it is to know that America is putting her back into the war . . . at last. I discover that I have had an absurd and unbalanced feeling (sub-conscious) of personal responsibility for my country, and that that has added a strain of nervous tension to the very very hard work we are doing here. I never began to work so hard in all my life, and I've *never* been able to live a life at all at leisure. But here, now, one works the way you do when there is a case of desperate sickness in the family, and everybody stays up at night and works by day without a thought for anything but the bitter necessity that the work must be done. Only this lasts for so many weeks, so many months! You can think what a rest to one's mind it is to know that over there, there are hundreds of thousands of fresh and rested Americans who are putting their shoulders to the wheel! Bless America! No words of mine could ever remotely describe the effect of the declaration of war here. Such relief! Such pure and utter joy to find the principles of democracy not a myth, but acknowledged the most real of realities!

I'm hoping to go back to the States with my husband and children, next autumn, if the submarines aren't too outrageous. And I shall take the greatest pleasure in going to see you, if you will let me.

Cordially and faithfully yours,
Dorothy Canfield Fisher

1. Place: letterhead.

2. Phillips founded the *American Magazine* in 1906; many of Fisher's early stories were published in it. See Phillips entry in Notable Recipients.

32. *To Sarah Cleghorn*
September 5 [1917][1]
Crouy-sur-Ourcq

Dearest Sally:

Soldiers, hundreds of them are marching past my window as I write . . . a strange accompaniment to a letter to you! The regiment which has been quartered here at rest, is getting ready to be sent back to the trenches, and are going through preliminary exercises of marching etc. to get them into shape for active service again. They look . . . curiously just like anybody, just like the civilians-in-uniforms that they are. I am all the time struck by the contrast between our regular army of professional soldiers and these grocer's clerks and farm-hands and college-professors, with their worn blue-gray clothes. The strangest of all, though, to me, are the soldier-priests. A good many of them wear their black soutanes just as usual, only a good deal shorter, just about to the knee. With their chain and cross hanging over their hearts and their big spurred cavalry boots, and revolvers . . . don't they symbolize the world as it is! Almost without exception they are strong broadly built men, with serious, good faces and sad, earnest eyes. What *do* they make of it, I wonder. I wonder so much that I want to go up to them in the street and ask them! I can't tell you how eagerly I read your Journal letters[2] nor how deeply grateful I am to you for all the time you are taking to keep me close to what you are feeling and doing. I know that I'm not doing it for you . . . it's just from lack of time and strength! If I began I would never finish . . . and anyhow there is a wild incoherence about what I feel that I never could get on paper. It is mostly just pure suffering and horror. Here I come in contact with refugees, in close personal contact, and *feel* what the war means to them, as only personal contact can make you *feel* anything.

Don't children stump you! Jimmy said the other night as he was being dressed, "Me, I think that *le bon Dieu* is bad." "Oh why? Jimmy," "Because he made mosquitoes. If He isn't bad why did he make mosquitoes?"

And Sally, last evening, looking over some American newspapers, saw the cartoon in the *Post,* of the lynching of Little[3] and the ironic heading "Montana's short-cut to law and order." Of course she wanted an explanation. I explained as best I could which was pretty badly, and ended, "I think of course that the men who hanged him were as bad as could be. He had a right to express his opinion about anything. That's what America should be like." Sally pondered and asked, "If he thought people ought to steal, would he have a right to try to get them to do it?" So I had to fall back on the fact, which even a child's abrupt reasoning can't disconcert, that no matter what anybody did, he should be treated according to the law. And a minute later, she was screaming with laughter over the antics of the new puppy, and had forgotten apparently the whole dark and terrible question . . . which is quite as disconcerting as anything else children do.

This is started as an answer to your letter of August 12, with its dreadful news of the suppression of the socialist-press and the general running-riot of Censorship and "Public Opinion." I've just thrown into the waste-paper basket, and now think I'll fish out to send you, a letter from Horace, Henry, my father's old friend on the Pacific Coast. I suppose that is quite genuinely and sincerely how the matter looks to him and others of his generation. My God-father writes in the same strain, and says I ought to go home to "influence public opinion" to more active participation in the war and against the pro-Germans etc., etc. If I went, it would be to make the biggest kind of protest against gagging anybody with a tongue in his head. If that is to be the system employed, there's no use bothering ourselves to fight Germany. She's won the war already, and infected us with her methods . . . because it was just such hideous and unnatural unanimity which made possible the German invasion of Belgium. But I'm sure of my country, and I feel certain that this is only the usual fervent American reaction to any stimulant . . . this is the way they "took up" the blue glass craze,[4] and ping-pong and the Montessori system . . . to put together the most dissimilar examples I can think of. I mean not at all the serious earnest people on both sides, but this particular craze for unanimity I *know* it will give way to a more American way of thought. If I didn't think that . . . it would certainly be about the last blow necessary to convince me that the sooner this planet gets blown into star-dust, the better for everybody concerned.

The soldiers are coming back now, from where they have been drilling and look in on me wondering where I sit tapping on the typewriter . . . the only one Crouy has ever seen. They look a little tired, just agreeably so, and flushed and healthy with clear eyes and unconcerned expressions. As they pass one of the younger ones, while not losing step at all, manages to kick another one slyly in the leg. This makes the others laugh, and the young lieutenant look back at them sharply . . . and then that set passes out of sight and another files into view walking alertly, swinging their hands from one side to the other as French soldiers march, so vigorous, so *alive*. I send you this picture, taken as a snap-shot, to put in your war-Journal. They are so entirely human beings, like all others. Yesterday I saw a boche prisoner running a wheat-reaper, and noted with inexpressible interest, that he too looked just like anybody very calm and well-fed, much interested in running his machine right so the wheat would fall properly. I was on my way to send a package to a French prisoner in Germany to whom I have been sending food since the beginning of the war, and who is now working in the fields in Germany! I thought that very likely he is doing the work that his German-prisoner would be doing if he were at home . . . and found myself on the verge of that wild laughter which I imagine to fill mad-houses. Thank heavens I have Jimmy and Sally.

Do write often, my dear, dear sister. And don't mind if I don't, nor regularly. Really I cannot!

Your loving
Dorothy

---

1. Date: year appended, supported by biographical evidence that DCF was in Crouy in 1917.

2. Reference to Cleghorn's "War Journal of a Pacifist" (unpublished), written from Apr.–Sept. 1917.

3. Frank Little, an International Workers of the World union representative, was sent to organize a strike following the Speculator Mine fire, which claimed the lives of two hundred miners in Butte, Montana. His body was found hanging from a railroad trestle on July 31, 1917. There was no police investigation, and the strike failed some five months later.

4. The "blue-glass craze" refers to *chromotherapy,* the name given to the medical practice of healing by colored light. The methodic application of blue light was used to "cure" ills from eczema to cancer. DCF described its use by a quack doctor in *Her Son's Wife:* "On Tuesdays he brought with him a large, handsomely finished velvet-lined box, from which he extracted shining nickel and red rubber tubes and a strangely shaped hollow glass utensil. This last, after he had fastened the complicated apparatus together and connected it with the electric current, suddenly glowed intensely with a bodeful blue flame, and gave off a low roaring noise. . . . he pulled down the shades before he summoned this unearthly blue fire so that it was the only light in the room. . . . Then Lottie turned on her side and the doctor applied the diabolical glass tube (astonishingly enough, it was only comfortably warm) up and down her back in long sweeping strokes" (217–18).

33. To Scudder Klyce
October 27, 1917
6 rue Pétrelle, Paris, France

Dear Mr. Klyce:

Our little Sally is having typhoid fever—a pretty bad case—and I'm practically out of the world for six weeks more. I wanted to write you, but haven't now the time or strength to give to anything but our dear little girl. I know you'll understand. I've had a beautiful letter from Laura Kent[1]—it doesn't seem possible she's half around the world from me. I feel her not far away, at all, nearer than you, for instance. Which isn't logical.

I don't think I've ever written to thank you for such generous words about *Understood Betsy*. I thought afterward it had been presumptuous to send such a book to a philosopher. I wrote that little idyll, a year ago when I was sick with anxiety about my husband then at the front, and suffering acutely from the separation, the first since our marriage . . . isn't the human machine a curiously constituted one! I felt so bitterly the need of serenity and secure joy, that I had to create it—out of my head. I suppose *you* understand *how* that was done? I don't pretend to.

My very best greetings to the two of you
Dorothy Canfield Fisher

---

1. Klyce married Laura Tilden Kent, poet and children's book author, in 1917.

34. To "Folks"
March 23 [1918][1]
Guethary [France]

Dear Folks,

Just a line tonight to go with these films . . . nothing of any special interest, only I am trying to send you the films as I take them, so that you may select those you think worth preserving. I have to travel too lightly and have to be cluttered up too much with absolutely necessary things (like Jimmy's toy elephant and Sally's innumerable books) to carry an ounce of anything extra.

I feel very much up in the air these last two days . . . we are in a period of "no news" cut off by the Censor from everything . . . no newspapers, no letters . . . it is queer enough in the twentieth century not to get newspapers. Every once in a while this happens to this corner of France, I suppose because we are so near the Spanish frontier and everything in the world is seething inside that cauldron. But it may be that this present void period is because the great offensive is really "on" and is progressing so fast they don't want to let the provinces know . . . or it may mean nothing more than a wash-out in the railroad line somewhere . . . but your nerves get pretty wire-edged these days and when you don't *know* anything of what is going on, you certainly do get to imagining things! Of course for the same reason I don't know whether John is really going to have his long-deferred permission the first of April . . . in fact I don't know anything except that the children are very well indeed and very happy and Sally is getting on well with her studies, or so it seems to me. Goodnight to you all . . . this is a time for stout hearts isn't it?

Your
Dorothy

1. Date: appended, supported by biographical evidence that DCF spent the spring and summer of 1918 in Guethary while her daughter, Sally, recuperated from typhoid fever.

35. *To Sarah Cleghorn*
April 8 [1918][1]
Guethary, France

Dearest Sally:

I suppose you must be moving north by this time . . . or at least by the time this gets to America, but I don't dare address you anywhere but in Macon for fear of mistakes. I do hope that by this time you will be getting the round-robins again, but since that remarkable breakdown of that system for getting the news to you, I don't dare trust to it . . . and at the risk of repeating what you probably know, must tell you that we are still here in the south, and expect to be here until the end of April. John hasn't had his permission yet, and when he will, we don't know, but we hope sometime this month, and so are waiting on. In addition, everybody in Paris repeats the same thing, that we must not go back there with the children, to our fifth floor apartment. But I am so anxious to go on with that work for the poor children of Meudon,[2] that I can't bear to stay here any longer than is necessary. I think the suburbs of Paris safe enough to take children and almost certainly we shall go there and settle. I say "almost certainly" for of course it is out of the question to try to make any plans at all certainly which is of a certain difficulty when it comes to renting rooms! The children are well and very happy and jolly with lots of lively companions to raise Cain with, which they do! They play so heartily that I often think of Hazlitt's pet phrase and think that it would "put a soul under the ribs of death"[3] to hear their laughter and shouts. I suppose Fanny and Dalton[4] have done that for you this winter! Sally is quite recovered and doing very well with her somewhat irregular studies. Jimmy is well, but does not grow tall . . . it is possible that he is going to be little like his mother, which would be a pity.

You know the news from Zephine probably . . . that one doctor said she had a bad heart with a leaking valve which might go back on her any minute. She was alarmed, shocked . . . but before giving up everything went to another who after lengthy examination said "nothing of the sort," her heart was as sound as a bell, but that she had tuberculosis of the lungs! More alarm and shock to poor Zephine, who waited very apprehensive the result of laboratory tests of her lungs. HOW CAN DOCTORS do such things, say such things? I have known of so many such cases. I wish you'd just ask Carl for me, how it *can* happen. Wallace[5] waited around in Paris for all this time, not daring to leave

Zephine because of what the verdict might be. Now there is said to be nothing the matter with her beyond fatigue and general low condition, which last isn't surprising. She detests the air-raids and says she really suffers a great deal from fear . . . which is a very debilitating emotion. I have tried and *tried,* as I wrote you to get her to come down here, but in her last letter as in all the others she says she can't think of it. Here, I think I have her last letter here. I'll send it on to you. I can't write you, my dear, I *can't,* anything about the war. There are no words to begin to say what I feel!

I have just had a letter from Professor Phelps which has surprised me. He says, among other things, "I have renounced Pacifism and all its works ever since our country came into the war. I could not afford the intellectual and religious luxury of Peace when all my young friends were going into battle. I came to the conclusion that I *must* be wrong when nearly everybody I respected was for the war, this war." I own I was immensely surprised, having had no intimation of this change of feeling . . . it's a change of feeling that I had (it seems to me) the day the Germans marched into Belgium, but I have often thought that I never was a Pacifist, really; just as I often think that I never was nor can be a "literal" Christian. I am in the midst of a very Catholic circle here, as at Crouy, with priests and sisters of Charity and devout people of all sorts. I go a great deal to Mass, partly because it would hurt their feelings if I didn't and partly because I do like all churches, all religions . . . I wonder if this means I am really an irreligious person. I am given and loaned of course the usual number of books of piety, lives of saints etc. etc. . . . altogether a most devout Catholic surrounding . . . and I am even more startling convinced than ever how impossible the smallest degree of *real* religious conformity would be for me. If these dear people could see into my heart they would think me a "Monster of the Sin Pride of the Intellect" for it is literally inconceivable to me, resigning my judgment in any degree to any authority whatever. It seems to me that that would be the last sin, the worst crime against my better nature, the final abyss of cowardice and moral laziness . . . *to take somebody's else word for what is right.* I read their pious books with a sense of amazement which makes them interesting to me . . . and they are most of them fearfully dull! And yet I love to go to Mass and don't feel the least trace of the protestant horror which makes my irreligious mother bristle up at holy water and incense! And I feel perfectly at my ease with the most Catholic of all these people. On Ash Wednesday when Madeleine, our maid, brought back the ashes from church and marked the cross on all our foreheads, murmuring over Jimmy's rosy flesh, "Ashes thou art and to ashes thou shalt return" I thought it a most useful and profitable reminder.

It is curious your reading mysticism this winter, all the time protesting inwardly and citing "But thou meek lover of the good" and my being surrounded by Catholics . . . and thinking the same thing. I re-read "Brahma"[6] the other day and thought "Oh what's the use of writing 'works of piety' or books on mysticism . . . Emerson said it all, *all,* in those lines."

I haven't heard from you in some time . . . which isn't surprising with all mail irregular, but somehow, you have managed to keep me in touch with you so regularly (that's more than I've done with that miserable break in the round-robin circuit) that I feel very uneasy and a little apprehensive when I don't know pretty nearly what you are up to. And how your health is.

The last news from you was that it was really warm at last, that you were well, but that your aunt had strained her knee. I wrote a card at once . . . do things *ever* reach you! . . . and have been wondering how Miss Jessie was. I shall be glad to know you back in Vermont again for *my* sake, for your letters from there are breaths from the hills. I need them! I do!

We shall be here till May first in any case, and perhaps afterwards, but perhaps you'd better address letters to American Express. Do you know that maple sugar you sent Sally has never yet reached us. It has been in the customs in Paris for more than three months now, announced spasmodically by the Am Ex Co. who thereafter write that some new formalities have to be gone through with. Well, it will be mighty welcome when it comes and luckily maple sugar is something which keeps perfectly. It will last all the more in small sucking mouths, if it is very hard!

I have a new photograph to send you . . . although you may have seen it in the round-robin . . . IF you see those. I'm sending this for you to keep. It's really very good of the children, but fearfully retouched and smoothed-out, of me. Why will photographers do that! Haven't you a recent snap-shot to send . . . especially for the children to see. *I* don't need one.

Every once in a while, somebody, shivering and sick over the news of the terrible battle now going on, says that surely this means the end of the war. I don't dare to let myself think that . . . indeed to think of the end at all . . . and yet the idea is in my head! I wonder if we could survive the joy of knowing that all the butchery was stopped! I have been writing here, as I've told you, some sketches of people in France. Harcourt wants to publish them this June, but Reynolds wants (naturally enough) to have them published in magazines first. We shall see what they decide between them. I've had to leave it to Harcourt of course, I'm too far away to decide. Could you have time to read the proofs? I'd be so much easier in my mind if you could!

[Handwritten] A heart full of love and sympathy to you, dearest dear comrade-sister.

Your
Dorothy

1. Date: appended, supported by reference to "sketches of people in France" that Harcourt wanted to publish "this June," presumably *Home Fires in France* (1918).

2. DCF established a home for French children from invaded areas in addition to her relief work for blinded soldiers.

3. "And took in strains that might create a soul / Under the ribs of death" is from Milton's *Comus* (1.560).

4. Cleghorn's niece and nephew, children of her brother Carl.

5. Wallace Fahnestock, husband of Zephine Humphrey.

6. "Brahma" (1857), a poem by Ralph Waldo Emerson.

36. To Amelia Reynolds
July 31 [1918][1]
Guethary, Basses-Pyrénées [France]

Dear Mrs. Reynolds:

It was fine to get your letter of June 29th on my return from a horrible visit to the front, where I passed across the battle-fields of the Belleau woods, Bouresches and Château-Thierry just after the Germans retreated. I came home feeling that the dead men in the wheat-fields there were the only fortunate people in the world. . . .

But my own darling children are the cure for such moments of utter heart-sickness over the war . . . and next to them letters from home. Yours certainly counts as that! It did me such a lot of good to get your reassuring word about not hurrying to try to get work done, etc. That's what I feel myself, of course, but it stiffens my back to have you say it to me!

And I can't tell you how much pleasure it gave me to have you tell me that Mr. Reynolds has really liked what I sent to him of late. I have, you know, the liveliest regard for Mr. Reynolds' judgment on my work, and always feel that I have succeeded if he likes what I have done. He helped me write, you know, the best short story I have ever done (or it is my favorite, at least) "A Good Fight and the Faith Kept."[2] I took lunch with Mr. Reynolds while that story was still in the fluid state, and what he said induced me very considerably to alter it, greatly to its benefit!

Never mind about "Hats!"[3] I'm astonished at the speed and rate at which Mr. Reynolds has disposed of the other things. It is a fine percentage only to have "Hats!" left over. That is really rather too fantastic anyhow to suit the magazine public, I fancy.

Best regards to Mr. Reynolds and again thanks for your letter,

Cordially yours
Dorothy Canfield Fisher

1. See Letter 34, note 1.
2. Originally published as "Conqueror," *American Magazine* 81 (Mar. 1916): 11–14. Reprinted as "A Good Fight and the Faith Kept" in *The Real Motive* (1916).
3. "Hats!" was published in *Outlook* 119 (Aug. 28, 1918): 659–60. Reprinted in *Home Fires in France* (1918).

37. To James Hulme Canfield
November 23 [1918][1]
Versailles [France]

Dear Father:

Your letter with it's last entry of November 7th saying that the armistice terms had been accepted by Germany shows that you had the same false news that Melanie and Jeanne brought back from Paris to us here. But since I know that the Monday after you had the real news . . . I'd like to know just how you heard the great news, who brought it, and if you dared believe it at first!

Why about our coal, our cards give us a hundred and twenty pounds a month per family; but what you have on your cards and what you really get are different matters. A big poster up announced at the beginning of November that the military situation, splendid as it was meant that all the railway trains were used for troops and munition and that consequently the coal allowance would be cut down! That's all there is to say about it! What you do is go and get your little sack of coal, but you don't burn it . . . yet. You burn wood, or charcoal and you save month by month your allowance till maybe January or February when you have the real real cold snap of every winter, when casual means of heating won't do. Then you have enough for several weeks, don't you see. The gas has not given out here lately which is a comfort and makes cooking possible to everyone. And our sugar allowance of a pound a month per person was really given to us this month (the October allowance in full, not cut down to a half, or even a quarter as the last distribution in Guethary was). Perhaps the victory will bring a let-up in the restrictions. I do wonder what *is* the meaning of the completeness of the victory. The Germans have made such a terrible impression of duplicity on everybody's mind in the course of the war that nobody knows what to believe about them . . . it will take time to get that poise back like all the others. In the meantime the prisoners, horribly ill-treated, are drifting back in ragged, barefoot starving thousands . . . one of the worst nightmares of the war.

I must stop and go out with Jimmy to go to the bank and get some more money to pay for the wagon-load of wood which is now being deposited in our cellar, and am I not thankful that it is! By burning plenty of wood we can keep reasonably warm . . . and you can get plenty of wood here by paying the price. In Paris they are only delivering two hundred pounds at a time, and that lasts only a few days. Here I can get a whole wagon-load, two tons, at a time! It seems wonderful to think there is so much left of anything! Sally has come in for lunch and gone back to school, very rosy and bright-eyed and full of interest in her work. She is wearing the pretty blue broad-cloth dress with the green trimmings and she has a new green bow for her hair, and she looks very smart indeed. She had had an "examination" in history this morning and was full of interest in it. One of the questions was "who was regent during the youth of Louis Treize?" and Sally "almost" couldn't say it, but suddenly remembered Marie de Médicis just before it was time to hand in the paper. "And which was Turenne's greatest victory, should you say?" And "Of *course* they had to ask that silly question about who was Louis Treize's Minister after Luynes died, as if everybody wouldn't know that?" Of course this is all fresh in her mind from recent recitations, and I won't guarantee how much of it she really understands, but it is good that she is getting it now when memorizing is easy. Thanks for the letter from Fort Valley. I am glad they liked *Home Fires* . . . how far away from their life!

Such a lot of love,
Dorothy

---

1. Date: appended, supported by reference to "the armistice terms."

38. *To Paul Reynolds*
January 9, 1919
Arlington, Vermont

Dear Mr. Reynolds:

I ought to have written you long ago, and would have done so, if I had not been absorbed very sadly in a great family loss, the sudden and unexpected death of my old aunt here, the last of my father's family. This occurred almost immediately after I had received your last letter and I have ever since been occupied with those innumerable last things to be done, which are such a painful and inevitable part of the ending of a life which ends a whole period in a family's history.

I wanted to write that I have thought a great deal about what you say of trying to sell that novel[1] before it is written, and that, quite to my own surprise, I have come to agree entirely with you, and will try to make it possible for you to have something to offer. I can't get away to go to New York to see an editor personally, to tell him about the plan, and anyhow I doubt if that would be a good way for me. I don't believe I'm an impressive enough personality, to make an editor take me seriously. But I will try to write you out an outline, or summary of the story, which will be more in the nature of a description of the different people in it, than an outline of action. It has come to be more and more vivid in my mind, and I begin to have the excited feeling which comes when you are really on the point of starting in on a big piece of work, as you walk out towards the end of the spring-board and feel it begin to teeter under your feet, and know that the water is very deep . . . for the water I want to get into is deep all right. Can you give me any indications of how the summary would best be written, about how long a thing, and how detailed? I can make it just what you think best, in those regards.

I haven't much faith in the agreeable things editors say to you . . . they usually renege on them when it comes to the scratch, but when I was last in New York, both Miss Roderick[2] and the editor of *Everybody's*[3] (owner I believe) were extremely urgent in asking for the next novel. I didn't promise them anything of course, but I like Miss Roderick, and *if you think best* I would be pleased to let her have first try. But I want to leave the matter in your hands. The serialization of the novel would be to make money, and you know best how to do that. And such is my sceptical pessimistic view of editors, I own that I'll have the most agreeable surprise of my life, if you actually do get some editor to take it for a big price. It'll make a lot of difference to this family if you do . . . and I have come to feel the story so strong in my head that I don't believe the knowledge that it has been bought before-hand and that I've *got* to write it, will make a bit of difference to me, unsettle me in the least, once I get started on it.

Jimmy is having chicken-pox just now . . . there are bound to be a few interruptions like that, but I'm going to stop this foolish going-around and speaking, and being lunched and dined. It takes a lot of time and doesn't amount to a row of pins in one's work!

I don't think I have told you that I *think* the next novel is going to be good . . . but what *I* think is good and what editors think, aren't always the same. I *think* it is going to be very human. I think I'm going to like it . . . but I'm not sure, of course. I never did like *The Squirrel-Cage* very much, and there are parts of *The Bent Twig* that make me sick to look at!

Cordially yours
Dorothy Canfield Fisher

---

1. *The Brimming Cup* (1921), serialized in *McCall's*.

2. Virginia Roderick (see Letter 20, note 2).

3. Howard Duryce Wheeler (1880–1958) was editor of *Everybody's Magazine* from 1915 through 1919.

— *Part 3* —

Letters, 1920–1929

39. To Alfred Harcourt
January 28, 1920
Arlington, Vermont

Dear Alfred:

All right about that screed about how "Flint and Fire"[1] was written. I have decided forty times different ways, whether it would or wouldn't be a good thing to have it printed, and finally think I can manage so it won't sound like a "sure rule" for writing a story. My experience in didactic writing and speaking has made me all-fired wary about trying to tell folks how things are done, because the average run of folks are just crazy to get a rule of thumb and will grab one out of the most carefully constructed general considerations of any problem.

The stenographic report of what I said, was, as is usual with stenographic reports of what I say (I don't know about other people, maybe they talk less ramblingly than I) too utterly horribly formless to think of using. But I will turn to and write it out again very soon, honest injun.

We have been having a real siege here, with John in bed with a badly infected knee and a high temperature and us in quarantine with both children whooping it up with chicken-pox, and the thermometer at twenty below and me keeping fires night and day and tending to my sick-a-beds. Pretty strenuous materially, but not at all wearing morally as there was no anxiety about them, which is the only thing that ever bothers me in the care of the sick. John is up today pretty pale and peaked, Sally is up, pretty spotted and speckled, and I am back in my study to attack delayed work.

Thank Sue[2] for her good long letter, so full of all I longed to know about her and Hastings.[3] The Frosts decided finally after much hesitation to buy the place here, but waited too long, and somebody else got it. So they are going to stay on in Amherst.

More soon, when I send the screed.

Ever yours,
Dorothy

---

1. "How 'Flint and Fire' Started and Grew," an essay on the genesis of a DCF short story, was published in *Americans All,* ed. Benjamin Heydrick (New York: Harcourt, Brace, 1921).
2. Harcourt's first wife.
3. Harcourt's son.

40. *To Louise Pound*
January 28, 1920
Arlington, Vermont

Dear Louise:

Your long letter of the 24th is here, and tears me in several pieces! I have long wanted to revisit Lincoln and see the dear old friends there, and Mother's recent delightful visit there has freshened that desire.

But I do hate to be away from home and the children and my husband! I resolved solemnly when John came back from the front finally, in France, that nothing, *nothing* would take me away from home. Life is too short, the childhood of the children is so precious and so fleeting. And so I refused dozens of invitations when I first came home. But some few were especially pressing, or interesting, or would take me away only a short time (engagements in New England cities or New York) and I have spoken a little this winter, even as far west as Buffalo, where night trains run conveniently, so that I was only gone a short time, too.

If you will bury this in your bosom I will tell you how I happened to make the arrangement to go to Columbus, which I don't want to do at all. They wrote, asking me, very urgently, and to avoid just refusing outright, with no special reason, I thought I'd get out of it by asking double my usual rate, which is already so high I'm ashamed to mention it. I *knew* they couldn't pay that . . . but they wrote right back, sure, that was all right . . . and there I was, caught. (This is strictly for you, alone, you understand!)

So please can you give me a little time to think this over, this idea of going to Lincoln, which I *do* want to do, most awfully! But I might as well now give you a few details, in case it does seem possible. To begin with, I don't want to be *paid* for going to Lincoln! It's like going home! I couldn't afford to make the trip unless my expenses were paid, but I'd blush to take anything beyond that. But if you want to make money for something, especially money for France, the proceeds of the talk might go for that. If you advertised it this way, people might be interested in the purpose, too. I'd like it fine, naturally, if you were willing to give the proceeds whatever they were, to one of my war-enterprises in France, but that's not a bit important. So long as they go to something or somebody who needs them, it's all right.

The date in Columbus is April 17th or 16th, I forget just which. Would that be too late?

As for what I'd like to do, I'll do anything you think best . . . afternoon or evening, or both, read stories, make a talk . . . anything within my powers. I'm no professional speaker you know, and not having any idea that I am, it's no effort for me to speak or read. I just do it the way I would to the family, and let it go at that! I mention this, specially, so you won't be disappointed. I *can* make myself heard in almost any auditorium I ever tried, but beyond that, it's a plain and homely performance, let me tell you. And I almost hesitate to go back to Lincoln, for fear of shocking the old friends. Mother reports everybody so prosperous, and handsome and elegant, and leisurely, and good-looking, I almost hesitate to betake me very insignificant, indifferently clad, war-worn small person out there! But that's not serious. Between real friends, what are looks!

All this sounds as though I were really thinking of going, and I can't say I am. I can imagine the outcry to heaven of the children if the idea is proposed, for they grudge every minute of Mother which is not theirs. No don't say bring them along too. The journey is too terrifically long to undertake *en famille*.

But, if you *can* give me a little longer to meditate on this, I'll be glad, because if I had to decide today, I'd have to say no, and I would love dearly to go.

Cordially yours
Dorothy Canfield Fisher

41. To Paul Reynolds
February 6 [1920][1]
Arlington, Vermont

Dear Mr. Reynolds:

Poor Miss Beatty had a forlorn time getting here missing the morning train up, having to spend six mortal hours in the station at Troy, and arriving here on a train an hour late, about four in the afternoon, and leaving at eight.

She made a mixed impression on me. One of my older relatives said of her, "Nice girl, but only half-baked" which is what you mean by her "not having been through the mill."

She wanted to ask me if I disapproved of divorce under all circumstances, and when I said I did not, she said "Mr. Reynolds does." I said I doubted that, unless you were a Roman Catholic, which I also doubted. She also said that you had insisted that I meant this novel[2] as an attack on divorce, and I said I doubted *that,* too, and anyhow it was not so meant, but as an account of what happened to one woman, and I didn't believe in attacking things-in-general or defending them thus, because every individual case was so different from every other. She made the remark that Mrs. Reynolds quoted to me in her letter, (apparently it is a common one!) that "of course a divorce was a pity because it meant a failure and one hated to fail in anything, one's job, or one's marriage" and I opined that in my opinion it was a durn sight worse than any mere failure, being a deep moral wound. I didn't deny that a wound was sometimes better than some other things, just as I thought there were one or two things (*only* one or two) worse than war; but I thought it was always a dreadful tragedy and an irreparable loss. And so we went, apparently agreeing, she didn't say anything I *didn't* agree with, in actual words, but me with the typically arrogant "married woman's" feeling that she didn't know what she was talking about. (But I kept that to myself.)

I didn't mind any of that, nor did I object to her strictures on the fool-radical girl in the novel,[3] because I don't want to use her to make fun of radicalism, which I respect deeply when it is a sincere and honest attempt to improve the conditions of human life, but to make fun of the people who take up radicalism as they did ping-pong, or dancing, because it's the fashion.

But I *didn't* like, quite seriously it gave me a scare and put me off the notion of writing for her, her mentioning that she tried to have a "big crisis" for the end of each installment of a serial. I said earnestly that I wouldn't guarantee her that, nor even that I would in any degree try for that, and I wanted her to understand that fully, before she thought any more about the matter. In fact that I wouldn't guarantee her *any*thing in the way of style or "action" etc. And as that was towards the end of our talk I rather fancy that was the impression she went away with. But thanks to your letter, I didn't much care if she did!

I seem to have given the impression that I didn't like her. I did. I liked her candid, honest eye, and her certainty that she was right (She showed me a little diagram she has worked out which settles how we move up from the amoeba to God. Do get her to show it to you. Say I told you about it.) and I think her ideas on women's magazines are good, and I respect her trying to do something more than just increase the circulation, and I don't believe her ideas on marriage are really so radical as she lets on. I imagine she whoops 'em up a little with you because she suspects you (as vide that astonishing statement that you think there should never be a divorce in any circumstances!) of being very much in the other camp.

I'm much interested in knowing how it comes out, and simply delighted with that offer of Miss Lane's,[4] whom I've never met, but whose editorial work I greatly admire, from a distance.

Hastily, cordially yours
Dorothy Canfield Fisher

---

1. Date: reference to negotiations over the serialization of *The Brimming Cup* in *McCall's Magazine*.
2. *The Brimming Cup* (1921).
3. The character named Eugenia Mills.
4. Gertrude Battles Lane (1874–1941), an American magazine editor, became editor-in-

chief of the *Woman's Home Companion* in 1912. She built the publication into one of the most successful women's magazines of the 1920s and 1930s. The *Woman's Home Companion* was the third-largest magazine in the U.S. at the time of her death.

42. To Paul Reynolds
October 22 [1920][1]
Arlington, Vermont

Dear Mr. Reynolds:

Please, my best thanks to you and Mrs. Reynolds for taking the time to read through that bulky manuscript, and writing me so sympathetically about it, afterwards. I think I see how the habit of your mind doesn't make it easy for you to suggest changes, but I think if no startling criticisms occurred to you, no really glaring faults of construction or characterization, no "impossible" places, why that in itself is an indication to me. I'm glad Mrs. Reynolds liked the part where the children came in, because several people (who haven't had children themselves) have hinted that they found rather a good deal about children in the book!

I am writing now to try tentatively on you, an idea which has been slowly revolving in my head ever since I got the first draft of this novel[2] done. I won't try today to make a real outline of it, but only set hastily down about what it would be, to see what you think of the possibilities in it.

It would be the opposite-of-a-sequel to this story (I don't know any other name to call it) that is, it would be the story of Marise's life and Neale's in their youth before they met each other, then their meeting, and betrothal.[3] The end would be the same as the beginning of this, literally the same, the very same chapter.

The main idea would be a more "romantic" one than I usually treat, and it would be a sort of happy-ending story, in that you would see from the beginning two children growing up on opposite sides of the globe who needed each other to complete themselves, but who had not the slightest possible chance, in all probability, of ever laying eyes on each other's faces. I don't know that this has been done before, the tracing out of the tiny, incalculable causes which led, years and years before, to a decision which led to another, which led to another, all leading apparently to the meeting with the person who is the real mate. Marise's childhood is passed a good deal of it (you may happen to remember) in the old walled city of Bayonne in southern France, which I know very well, and which is picturesque and "different" with its part Basque color, to the last degree. Marise's father is an ordinary businessman translated to France as the agent of an American machine, a typewriter, or reaper. Her mother would be a very interesting type to me, the sort of last-generation American woman, like Mrs. Wharton,[4] who (so it seems to me) takes Europeans with a funny, prayerful certainty of their innate superiority. This American woman would consider that it was the opportunity of her life to become "cultured" and would do her pathetic, silly best to be like what she considers European women to be, even to the extent of trying to have a liaison with a young Frenchman, whom she drives to suicide, in the bay of Guethary. This is a real episode (this last) which I knew about, there, and it is the tragic story which I wrote you some months ago was continually haunting me. I think it is in its proper place now, as a part of a larger story.

The story of Neale is all in America of course, and I think could be extremely interesting, a young American of the very best sort, who doesn't know what path to take in the dark wood of this our life, and finds it with total unexpectedness in Rome, when he meets Marise and hears of the bequest of his old uncle to him of the small wood-working industry in Vermont.

Have I said enough to give you an idea? And will you please consider it, and let me know what you think. If you think the oddity of its being the opposite-of-a-sequel would not hurt it, I'll write out an outline, and let you try to dispose of it.

Sincerely yours
Dorothy Canfield Fisher

I think I could get this done inside the next year with considerable certainty. It ought to come out soon enough after the appearance of *The Brimming Cup* to profit by any interest the *B. C.* may arouse.

---

1. Date: stamped "received 26 October 1920."
2. *The Brimming Cup* (1921).
3. The "opposite-of-a-sequel" was *Rough-Hewn* (1922).
4. Edith Wharton (1862–1937), American author, who also spent time in Europe and set novels there.

43. To Alfred Harcourt
November 10 [1920][1]
Arlington, Vermont

Dear Alf:

There's such an accumulation of things to talk to you and Sue about, we'll never get caught up by letter. And so I've planned Christmas Vacation spent at Swiftwater with the older Fishers (Something I've wanted to do for years. I feel so guilty because John's parents see so little of the children) and then three or four days with the children still there, and John and me in the city, seeing you-all and hearing some music. How does that sound?

Then I'll tell you all about the election here,[2] in which John was defeated by an unholy coalition of stingy farmers, resentful of the new school and hard-drinking teamsters resentful of the prohibition laws. It was a spirited campaign, and I think did some good as startling all the better element of Arlington by showing what the other sort could do if they put their minds to it. It was intended and openly proclaimed as an attack on the project for the new school and now we are in for a lively defense of it at Town Meeting next March. It's all highly interesting to a novelist, and personally although we are very mad at the election as representative of a foul-mouthed, hard-drinking man who can hardly write his own name, we are personally relieved that we have tried to do our duty by the commonwealth without having the enormous bother of pulling up stakes in mid-winter to try to roost somewhere in Montpelier.

Then I'll also tell you what I think about Sinclair Lewis's *Main Street,*[3] which I read with the liveliest sympathy and interest and admiration, and certainty that Mr. Lewis takes a rather superficial view of human problems, but knows how to write a mighty good novel. The character of the husband, the country doctor, is I think by far the best thing in the book, absolutely "done," and finished and perfect, without a marring stroke on it, anywhere, an achievement that any writer in any age might be proud of, and mighty few could have done. But of course, knowing me, you can imagine how violently I protest from much of his thesis, and how naive I find his idea that a geographical change could achieve anything . . . *coelum non animam* for ever, say I! Horace knew what he was talking about, as did old Pestalozzi when he insisted that "help comes from the bosom alone."[4] I find a rather badly written editorial in the *Post,* that says a little of what I feel in the matter. It evidently refers to *Main Street* along with others like it, which shows what a success the book has had. I've noticed several very favorable reviews of it, and have rejoiced to see them both for your sake, and because it's fine to see that a book seriously, honestly, written in an attempt at accuracy and understanding of American life, gets attention and success although there is not a meretricious note in it, nor an insincere one. I don't believe the American public is such a blatant idiot as it is made out.

Everything here as usual. The Frosts are on their farm[5] now and the Lord he only knows whether they will make a go of it. John and I stand ready to do anything we can, from cookstoves to plumbing. If they only keep well.

I'm just about done with *The Brimming Cup,* and John is just about starting in to type it. The first bunch of it ought to be in your hands by the fifteenth. And say, while I think of it, will you please note down somewhere, to send one of the first advance copies to Professor Phelps of Yale. Whether it's bound or not, just what you're sending out to the trade.

What do you think? I've got the idea for the next novel . . . and it's simply the predecessor (instead of the sequel) of *The Brimming Cup* . . . all that leads up to that first chapter on the Rocca di Papa. How about it? [Handwritten] There's a lot of new material there on Marise's life in Europe.

Ever yours,
Dorothy

---

1. Date: references to "the election here" and the publication of Sinclair Lewis's *Main Street* (1920).

2. John R. Fisher ran for town representative of Arlington in the Vermont General Assembly in 1920 and lost. He was elected to the post in 1925 and 1937, was chair of the Republican County Committee of Bennington County in 1938, and was named to the Vermont State Board of Education in 1939, on which he served for ten years, eight as chair.

3. Lewis's *Main Street* (New York: Harcourt, Brace, 1920) and DCF's *The Brimming Cup* were first and second on the 1921 best-seller list.

4. Horace (65–8 B.C.), Roman poet. The colloquialism *coelum non animam* is from his *Epistles* (Book I, #27, line 27): "They change the heaven, but not the spirit, who travel across the sea."

Johann Henrich Pestalozzi (1746–1827), a Swiss educational reformer, is quoted in Emerson's "The American Scholar": "I learned that no man in God's wide earth is either willing or able to help any other man." In the "Introduction" to *Vermont Tradition* (10), DCF identifies Pestalozzi's and Emerson's self-reliance as a dominant strain of Vermont character.

5. DCF helped the Frosts locate the farm they eventually bought and named "The Gully" in South Shaftsbury, Vermont, about fifteen miles south of Arlington.

44. *To William Lyon Phelps*

November 10, 1920
Arlington, Vermont

Dear Professor Phelps:

What you've done for me and my writing means that when I am at work, you are always more in my mind than at other times. I've been hard at work now, for a good many months, ever since last winter, on a new novel, and as a consequence I've been feeling a slowly rising need to get in touch with you. So that it was almost like the answer to one of the many letters I've planned to write you but have not sent off, when I saw the envelope with the New Haven postmark on it, and your handwriting. And the generous mention of my name in the fine review of Mrs. Wharton's new novel[1] was exactly what I needed to brace me up in the inevitable ebb-tide of reaction that comes at the end of a long long pull at creative work. There's another mark of gratitude to chalk up alongside a great many others under your name!

I have wanted so much to talk over with you this novel I've been writing![2] It's unlike any book I ever wrote and indeed I don't remember ever reading one constructed like it. The technical idea of the method of construction came to me, one day last year, when a friend, a clever, modern, highly-instructed, well-read American woman, remarked to me, quite casually, as a matter of common experience, "But of course you always see more in characters in books than in people around you. You feel their human significance because the author tells you about it. People you know, always seem dull compared to those in books." I was immensely astonished by this, crying out to her that my own experience was quite the contrary, that the most casual grocer's-boy *living,* brought me a deeper sense of humanity than any character on the page of a book, that he was the rounded, complete, immeasurable, complicated and infinite whole of which even the best authors only succeeded in expressing a greatly simplified and mutilated part.

But on talking the matter over with all sorts of other people, I found that the experience of my friend is very common, that people quite habitually admit they find the actions of characters in books more interesting and significant than the actions of people around them.

Now I had in mind for several years (submerged by the material difficulties of our war-time stay in France) the idea of trying to write a novel which would deeply and truthfully analyze and depict a *successful* marriage. Why is not that a legitimate subject for portrayal in serious fiction as well as all the varieties of unsuccessful ones?

It occurred to me after that conversation with my friend, that I would try to tell my story of that marriage in a way which would lead the reader into some of the first-hand meditation on human character which authors habitually have. The method I worked out is this: with the exception of the introduction, each chapter presents happenings in the narrative told entirely from the point of view of one or another of the characters, never from the author's; and each chapter is meant to be a revelation of what lies under the surface of that particular character. I have tried to make a glass door through which the reader looks into the heart and mind of one and another of the men, or women, or children in the story, so that, once for all, he knows what sort of human being is there. From that time on, it has been my intention to leave the reader to interpret for himself the meaning of the actions of that character, without the traditional explanations and re-iterated indications from the author.

It seemed to me that the reader's reactions would be much more vivid and real if he could be stirred to understand for himself, without having the author in one form or another stepping in to tell him, what underlies the common surface of human actions. I have tried to set before him certain men and women and children, and make him realize what they *are.* Then I leave him to try to understand for himself the meaning of what they do.

Now of course to try any innovation in technique is a risky matter. I have gone to the heights of enthusiasm for this idea, and down to the depths with doubt of it. I cannot be sure until the novel is printed and read, whether I have succeeded in arousing the average reader to write his own interpretations of humanity. He may, even at the end, see nothing but what is on the page, instead of all the great, invisible, submerged meaning which all human actions have and which I hope he will read between the lines.

My husband, who has been the greatest possible help and encouragement in the writing of this book (he thinks it very much better than anything I ever wrote before) was speculating the other day on the possibility that readers won't understand what I expect from them. He cited one of the last chapters, which I meant to be a very touching and significant one, but which contains, in actual words, only a quiet description of the departure by train, from a country railway-station, of two guests, leaving behind them the family with which they have been living.[3] My husband said, laughing, "Anybody who picks up the book, turns over the pages casually and reads that scene as a sample will get one of the queerest sensations of flatness, he ever had! And it's always possible that the average reader may not take the trouble to do his own understanding of what lies back of these conventional gestures, and to realize the dramatic significance of the whole scene."

Well, we'll soon see. The book will be published next spring. I am just now toiling over the last revisions, and making a last attempt to find the "soft" places. I'll ask Mr. Harcourt to send you an advance copy as soon as it's in any shape to read, and I'll be grateful for any comments you can make that'll help me (as you've done so many times already) in this desperately difficult business of telling a little about human life as it looks to me.

I thought when we came home from France that I had done with it forever that I was too tired and dispirited from the dreadful ordeal ever to think of undertaking again the prodigious effort which writing a long serious novel entails. But in the blessed quiet and peace of our mountain life, much of the old, lost physical energy has come back, and with it the overmastering desire to pass on to others the wondering sense of the mighty miracle of human life, which comes to me with every day I live, with every contact with another human being.

The richness and endless variety of human relationships . . . that's what authors, even the finest and greatest, only succeed in hinting at. It's a hopeless business, like trying to dip up the ocean with a tea-spoon. Why do we keep on with it . . . especially anyone like myself but casually endowed with a very moderate capacity for it. Every novel I write falls so tragically short of my conception of it, I vow I will try another.

But, I know this sort of feeling comes from the reaction after a big effort!

And in any case I oughtn't to bother you with such a long rambling letter. I didn't mean, when I began, to do more than to thank you. The rest has come from an old habit of sharing my writing with you.

Thank you again, and with every good wish and cordial greeting

Faithfully yours
Dorothy Canfield Fisher

---

1. In his review of Wharton's *Age of Innocence* in the October 17, 1920, *New York Times Book Review,* Phelps wrote, "In the present year of emancipation it is pleasant to record that in the front rank of American living novelists we find four women. . . . The big four are Dorothy Canfield, Zona Gale, Anne Sedgwick, Edith Wharton."
2. *The Brimming Cup* (1921).
3. Chapter 28, "Two Good-Byes."

45. To W. E. B. Du Bois
January 3, 1921
Arlington, Vermont

Dear Dr. Du Bois:

I have returned from a ten-days absence from home, with no mail forwarded, and find your kind letter of the 22nd waiting for me. Thanks very much for the check sent to the Fort Valley School.[1] I appreciate entirely the difficulties of editing such a paper as the *Crisis,* and would not have thought of asking for any return for my story,[2] if I had not incautiously promised it to Mr. Hunt,[3] whose school needs help very much. Don't think of ever adding to it in the future. You have plenty of other responsibilities!

I have just finished a new novel, laid in Vermont, concerned with an intimate personal problem in the life of a Vermont woman and her husband. But I wish never to lose a chance to remind Americans of what their relations to the Negro race are, and might be, and so into this story of Northern life and white people, I have managed to weave a strand of remembrance of the dark question.[4] It is a sort of indirect, side-approach, a backing-up of your campaign from someone not vitally concerned in it personally, except as every American must be, which I hope may be of use exactly because it is not a straight-on attack, but one of a slightly different manner.

With best wishes, I am
Cordially and sincerely yours
Dorothy Canfield Fisher
(Mrs. John R. Fisher)

1. The Fort Valley [Georgia] Normal and Industrial School, founded in 1903 by Henry Alexander Hunt (1866–1938), prepared African-Americans for teaching positions, industrial work, and farming. The school is now Fort Valley State College.

2. DCF's "An American Citizen" appeared in the *Crisis* 19 (Apr. 1920): 302–8; 20 (May 1920): 23–29. *The Crisis: A Record of the Darker Races,* founded in 1910, is the official organ of the National Association for the Advancement of Colored People.

3. See note 1.

4. In a subplot in *The Brimming Cup,* Ormsby Welles, a retired business executive, leaves Vermont to aid in the struggle for African-American rights in the South. This was the first modern best-seller to present criticism of racial prejudice.

46. To Alfred Harcourt
April 6 [1921][1]
Arlington, Vermont

Alf:

Great Scott, didn't anybody answer that letter of yours about title and so on? I sort of thought John had, and he sort of thought I had . . . and the truth is we didn't realize that the time had gone on so since you wrote. but probably you didn't either, with Sue just getting off on her great adventure and all.

Anyhow you wrote you wanted a decision about the title, and serial publication, and all.[2] The title hangs fire something fierce. I think it is because John doesn't put his mind on it conscientiously. He says doggedly that "Converging Paths" sounds all right to him, what's the matter with "Converging Paths"?

And since that horridly corroding comment of Jack Knox's,[3] I am off the idea of "Two Halves." Anyhow, even without the football association of ideas, I'm afraid it sounds a little sentimental, like Two souls that beat as one, etc. What? And without John, who usually "does" the titles of the family I'm paralyzed. Yes, I know it's an important matter, and we ought to be less helpless about it. But I seem to have a deaf-and-dumb spot in my brain where that title ought to be. But as I figure it, you ought to have in your hands today a good big slice of Mss. (in its rough form anyhow) and maybe in looking it over you'll hit on the right phrase. I told Reynolds to get the Mss. to you as soon as the *Delineator* people had decided they didn't want it, and to tell them to come to that decision at once and not waste any time over it. We slammed it together into hasty typing, and sent it down to them three or four days after I saw you, just to quiet any questionings in ourselves about whether it wouldn't be foolish to turn down a very good offer for the serial. I know as well as I know anything, that no magazine editor in his senses is going to consider anything like that Mss, so it was only a question of giving them the sensation of having had the chance and a delay of a few days in getting the stuff for the dummy to you.

I put the first eleven thousand words (Neale's childhood) together at such a rate of speed that I haven't much idea how it does read. My idea about Neale's childhood and youth is this; (I might as well tell you now and get it off my chest) it is exactly the ordinary, normal, garden-variety of American boyhood and family life, with New England backgrounds, in a city near [New] York . . . nothing the least bit different from what everybody has seen around him or gone through himself, *but* it is "set" so to speak, in the complicated, double-and-twisted, European life Marise has, which will, I hope, bring out the colors in Neale's life, which Americans don't see because they don't know anything else! Neale is, for all practical purposes, not brought up at all by his parents, or anybody else. Marise is never for an instant free from somebody's bringing her up. Neale is never conscious of himself at all, lost in a perfectly natural freedom, where nothing is expected of him, except to be able to take care of himself and get his lessons. Marise is taught by precept, word, example, to be conscious of herself every minute, and perfection in anything she does is expected of her. Everybody around Marise lies to everybody else, as a matter of course, and so does she. And she hasn't the faintest idea whether what she is told is the truth or is something made up for her benefit. It never occurs to Neale to lie, or to suspect anybody else of doing it, for the good reason that nobody around him does. Music comes to be an integral part of Marise's life, and is her religion . . . all the religion that her life provides for her. Neale isn't provided with any religion, except success in athletic sports, which ceases automatically and abruptly when he gets out of college. Etc. Etc. Etc. The upshot is in Neale's case the production of a very strong, healthy, competent organism, that hasn't an idea in the world what to do with its competence. In Marise's a very subtle, keen, sharp-edged organism, busily engaged in cutting itself to pieces.

What I want to do is to make, by means of the European frame, the American scene visible to eyes that look right through it as a rule.

It's a complicated plan of construction . . . oceans of fun and *terribly* hard work to labor on it. But if there ever was anything not meant for a woman's magazine, this is it! It's going to take more hard work than anything I ever did, because of this Chinese puzzle question of equilibrium and balance and construction. I don't want Neale's life too closely, in detail to counterbalance Marise's . . . the counter-balance must be spiritual, and not material . . . and yet apparent to all but a stupid reader's mind. Oh, I warn you, I'm going to be dead to the world for about four months to come . . .

No more time . . . John waits with the car . . . and I've a lost feeling that there is something I've forgotten to say . . . having allowed myself to get telled off on this long discussion.

Ever yours,
Dorothy

1. Date: references to the first draft of *Rough-Hewn,* which DCF began in 1921.
2. See note 1.
3. A New York artist who was a friend and summer neighbor of DCF.

47. To Julia Collier Harris
April 13, 1921
Arlington, Vermont

Dear Mrs. Harris:

Thank you very much indeed for the good letter which has just come to me and which I have read with the utmost attention and interest. It would be a splendid thing for our country if more such reasonable, authoritative letters could be exchanged from one section to another. I am going to see that this one and the clippings you send are given a wide circulation among my friends, beginning with Sarah Cleghorn, the poet and novelist, a very old friend of mine, the god-mother of my little daughter, and from whom I got a good deal of the color which made up the small Mr. Welles episode in *The Brimming Cup.* [1] Miss Cleghorn's brother lives in Macon, and she has gone there to spend the winter for years, and given me yearly reports of what she found there. She evidently did *not* find such people as you, and if the South is like the North, there are alas! very few such people as you in any community. Would there were. So, having my report from a Northerner who had spent much time in the South, I put in the novel no more than that, the letters to old Mr. Welles from his cousin, who had lived in the South; that was all he had to go on, that and the certainty of the attempt to make the negro feel himself fundamentally inferior, which exists—I know it must exist—in the South among the meaner and ungenerous spirits, because it exists in the North, also. And you must have noted that I had everybody in the book feel that old Mr. Welles was going off half-cocked, (everybody except a little boy) with an exaggerated idea— but with an *intention* which being free from self-seeking and benevolent, had fine elements. I didn't make a single person in the book think he was justified. And I had him speak especially of the lack of external respect shown to educated colored people, because Sarah Cleghorn had given me innumerable cases of that which she had known, and because Mr. Welles, being a very humble-minded old man, wouldn't have ventured to attempt to untie any of the many complicated knots of that terribly complicated problem. He is only a character in a book, you know, whom I meant to depict as almost abnormally sensitive to what he might consider his duty; and I used the negro problem as the one which troubled him because I think that Americans can not too often be reminded of that tragic, serious, dangerous problem—here in the

North people forget all about it, and plan for the future as though it did not exist; and I want always to remind them that, until it is rightly and justly settled, or on its way to a settlement, the nation is on unstable foundations. I often tell my French friends, when they complain of the national problem, that they have *nothing* which can compare for a moment with the question of different *races* living together: and when I teach American history to my children, I always suppress an inward groan when I read of the first boat-load of negroes brought to Virginia. If only they had left them in Africa, where they belonged! But here they are, and there will be no rest for any of us till human ingenuity has found a fair and righteous way to let them live their lives, with as great chances for development as anyone else. I tell you, Americans ought to be (and here is one who is) profoundly grateful for Southern white people who keep their heads in the midst of the excitement, and labor towards the solution.

Your name is a household one in our family where my children are brought up on the classic and inimitable Uncle Remus stories,[2] I admire them immensely, and told my husband the other day that I thought them perfect classics, immortal. I was brought up with a number of little negro children for playmates, in the Kansas town where I lived as a child, and they went to our school, so that I heard the negro dialect a great deal. and as I read to my children (who have scarcely ever so much as seen a negro from a distance) I often laugh out loud at the turns of phrase so wonderfully rendered, that it takes me back to my childhood.

Forgive this lazy, hand-written and so badly written letter. I have writer's cramp badly and am scarcely legible, but my typewriter is out of commission and I don't want to delay in thanking you for your letter.

Won't you go on doing this once in a while if it is not too much trouble. Send us up a bunch of interesting clippings bearing on the points at issue, and let me give them a good circulation among my friends. You are quite right in thinking that we don't know enough of what the best white people are doing in the South, and hear too much of the bigoted uneducated, narrow class, which alas! is only too numerous in every community. For instance, I had not known that any Southern newspaper had taken a stand against the new Ku Klux. See here, why don't I subscribe to the *Enquirer-Sun* and have it regularly? I will, and read it regularly. Ask somebody in the office to let me know what the subscription is and I'll send it at once. With best regards to your husband (*can* he be the immortal "little boy" of the Uncle Remus stories) and thanks for your letter.

Cordially yours
Dorothy Canfield Fisher

---

1. See Letter 45, note 4.

2. Joel Chandler Harris (1848–1908), was the author of a number of comic sketches of African-American folklore featuring Uncle Remus, the first of which appeared in the *Atlanta Constitution* in 1879. Harris was Julia Collier Harris's father-in-law.

48. Scudder Klyce
November 16, 1922
Arlington, Vermont

Dear Mr. Klyce:

I wanted to rush to my machine and answer your letter the minute I'd read it; but I waited a couple of days to cool off and get my breath a little. You can't know how much good it did me. After such a long pull as is involved in writing such a full and complicated novel,[1] after living so hard into those other lives with the constant intense attention to the meaning of them . . . there is inevitably a period of reaction into a condition of flatness and fatigue and discouragement, when you wonder if anything you've ever done was worth doing! I know, I know this is mostly physical and I try not to take it too seriously; and for the most part try to defend myself against it by plain physical means . . . lots more outdoors than usual, and more exercise (I've taken to tennis since the proofs of "Rough-Hewn" were finished) and a change of occupation (I always clean house down to the ground after I've finished a novel) and when, in spite of that, the heaviness of heart gets hard to bear, I try to make myself think that it comes simply from having drained the pool pretty dry, and that the mere passage of time will slowly let it filter full again. But all such commonsense methods are palliatives, after all. There's a certain amount of real suffering, real disgust with yourself over your failings, that you have to live through, and stand the best you can!

It's into the middle of that state of rather grim endurance that your letter comes . . . blessings on it, and on you for the generous-hearted warmness of your encouragement. I keep it on my desk, like medicine to be taken at intervals! Thank you . . . more than you can imagine. I'm meaning to write a real letter to you two, soon. All about your article on Religion and Humor . . . which is mighty good medicine too!

Ever yours very gratefully,
Dorothy Canfield Fisher

---

1. *Rough-Hewn* (1922).

49. *To Julia Collier Harris*
December 8 [1922][1]
Arlington, Vermont

Dear Mrs. Harris:

Yes indeed, I am more than interested in your doings and those of Mr. Harris. I use you two people all the time as good examples of the right sort of Americans. Your work is an inspiration. I think it's so specifically fine that you are able to work together. Mr. Fisher and I do a great deal of work together, and I know how intimately satisfactory that is.

I'd thought my publishers had sent you a copy of *Rough-Hewn,* and I'll see that it is done at once. I hope you'll like the book. And I hope you won't be alarmed at the length of it! It is really two novels in one, I hasten to say in excuse. Yes, our summer abroad was a successful one. It was intended to have an opportunity to work uninterruptedly, and we really were able to put in two months of solid work such as I've almost never had before . . . for as a rule I work in the midst of a very stirring family and neighborhood life, with a thousand interruptions of all sorts. This is the first time I've been separated from the children for more than a day, since they were born, and the first time I've not kept house, the regular three-meals-a-day-routine, since I was a young girl. It seemed so strange to get up in the morning *with nothing to do except write*! I finished that very long and complicated novel, with less exhaustion than I've felt after any other book. Perhaps at forty-three, I ought to arrange my life with less demands? Perhaps the abounding energy of the twenties and thirties doesn't hold out inexhaustibly? The experience of the summer, and of the immense relief it was, make me think of such things. But how *can* one stop and take things more easily when there is such a cruel lot that needs to be done. This Board of Education business,[2] for instance . . . how I *wish* somebody else could take that. It is an unpaid position in Vermont, and quite a sacrifice for the five members of the Board, who have to give up other work, of course, to do it. But it is such necessary and such fine work, and it is really beginning to *go,* a little. The rural school situation is really improving. More and more are being brought up to standard, and the interest in them and public conscience about them is more and more awake. That's the sort of thing that can be done through *newspapers,* for every bit of the publicity which has aroused people has been done through the Vermont newspapers.

And that's the sort of thing, the slow change of public opinion which you and Mr. Harris are bringing about in your work. And it's the only kind that amounts to anything, I believe. I'm more and more of the opinion that the best kind of state laws, or rules of Boards of Health, or Boards of Education mean less than nothing, unless they are backed up by general public opinion, and that if public opinion is enlightened, almost any sort of laws will do! This is unorthodox I know.

I'm glad to know that you have a free hand now. You'll make something fine out of that paper for sure. Do send me occasional editorials when you think of it. Though I hate to ask you to add another item to your busy life and things on your mind. With my warmest regards and all good wishes

Cordially yours,
Dorothy Canfield Fisher

---

1. Date: 1926 appended, but DCF's references to her age being forty-three and the recent publication of *Rough-Hewn* make 1922 more likely.
2. In 1921 DCF became the first woman appointed to the Vermont State Board of Education.

50. To Elizabeth Jackson
February 25 [1923][1]
Arlington, Vermont

Dear Elizabeth:

Thanks so much for your welcome letter of the 21st. Yes indeed I'm "lotting" on coming to you if I do succeed in making that Boston visit, in April. I have to hear from Dartmouth first where I am to speak in April. If their dates can be made to fit, you'll see me *sure*. And thanks a thousand times for asking me. The book[2] is at a standstill just now because I've been awfully busy with other things for a while. I'm asked to be the William Vaughan Moody lecturer at the University of Chicago this year[3] and Robert Frost wants me to stop over in Ann Arbor[4] on the way and give them a reading. And what do you think. I've succeeded in persuading my Quaker-minded husband to go with me . . . of course *not* for the inevitable dinners and receptions and things, from which he is going to duck; but for the trip out and some quiet days together in Chicago which we have neither of us seen since we were children. I'm looking forward to the trip so much, for the sake of the honeymoon voyage it will be. And it will be interesting to see the west from a car-window too, after goodness knows how many years of not having a glimpse of it.

No. I haven't turned against the French, a bit. But I never did have the intense undiscriminating admiration of all of their traits which was in fashion during a short time during the war. I went to school a good deal of my youth in France you know, and I have I should say a good deal of the feeling I have for America . . . great affection, great admiration for noble and strong and lovely qualities, mixed with great exasperation and irritation over other qualities. I don't see how anybody could love America more passionately than I do, but there are times when I blush with shame to be an American . . . when I consider that the Ku Klux business is a real part of our American qualities, for instance. Well, that's the way I feel about the French a great deal. Just now I think circumstances are bringing out the very worst in the French national character, just as during a part of the war the very best came to the top. I didn't like the intense admiration of the Americans for France during the war for being based on a misconception as it undoubtedly was, it was sure to lead to a reaction. But I think the final outcome will be a sounder knowledge of both countries by each other, which before the war literally almost, knew each other not at all! At their narrowest and most selfish, the French bourgeois has more moral coherence in her life than the kind of American like my poor Flora Allen[5] because she has the selfish self-abnegation for her children. At her most foolish and futile, the kind of an American like Flora Allen has *aspiration* at least, for something finer and better than she has. At her most pretentious and shallow, the Eugenia Mills[6] of America are better than their ilk in France because they have an unquestioned physical purity, which is *something*. At their loosest and most unbridled carelessness of purity, the French actor like my old actor in *Rough-Hewn* has something better than the fine athletic American numskull because he has that passion for intellectual integrity and that respect for the things of the mind. That's what I was trying to say. Affectionate regards to you, always!

Ever yours
Dorothy C. Fisher

1. Date: reference to the William Vaughn Moody lecture at University of Chicago, which DCF delivered in spring 1923.
2. DCF was writing *The Home-Maker*.
3. See note 1.
4. In September 1922, Frost accepted his second one-year appointment in the English department of the University of Michigan, Ann Arbor.
5. Flora Allen is a character in *Rough-Hewn*.
6. Eugenia Mills is a character in both *The Brimming Cup* and *Rough-Hewn*.

51. To Julia Collier Harris
March 9 [1923?][1]
Arlington, Vermont

Dear Mrs. Harris:

Your letter and the column of colored news (so to speak) has gone the usual rounds, to everybody's great interest and approval. My father-in-law, who has done a good deal for industrial schools for Negroes in the south, and is much interested in the race, was especially appreciative and interested. Of course, the objection to calling them Mr. and Mrs. and Miss seems odd to us, so much so indeed, that many many northern readers of *The Brimming Cup* have written me about my mention of that fact, to say that they thought I must have made it up, because they never heard of such a thing, and don't believe it possible. But as you say, that is a detail of no special importance, compared to much greater elements of life. I only used it in my novel because it is a picturesque and colorful detail, completely unknown to most northern people. And the recognition of the social and educational life of the colored people by your column is a radical and generous departure, which cheers the heart to learn.

What you and Mr. Harris are doing is cheering anyhow, and has done us all more good than you can imagine. One of the people to whom I send the newspaper occasionally when there is an editorial which might interest her, is very rabid on the Negro question, and has the bitter blaming note in speaking of it which I deplore, always. Let me tell you what she said of this last detail of your work in Columbus, because it will interest you and may amuse you. "I never thought that *any*thing could convince me of the sincere good will of any southern white people towards the negro, in any capacity except that of workman or servant, but I must say that the Harrises have done it!"

Personally I feel about your problems as I do about the problems of the devoted souls who are struggling with the public schools in cities with an overwhelming foreign population; that the problem is so acute and puzzling, that I simply take off my hat to your devotion and courage. There is nothing in even the poor and rustic life of a little mountain state like Vermont, which can compare in difficulty with such problems, and I tell that many times to Vermont people who think we have much to contend with in inertia, and lack of money for necessary reforms, and general old-fashionedness and "softness" of mind.

I thought of you last night, and wished you could have been here to laugh at us. We were giving a little "concert" in our town-hall, a series of folk-songs Indian, Negro, Creole and Vermont, sung by our own local singers and the school-children. What made me laugh was the group of Negro songs, sung with the best will in the world, quite in tune and correct in time, but not remotely resembling the Negro rhythm, or gusto. I kept wondering to myself, "What makes them sound so queer and different?" and suddenly thought "Why these folks have never seen a real Negro in all their lives, much less ever heard one speak or sing!"

You see I was born and brought up, till I was ten years old, in Lawrence Kansas, where the Negro population is larger than the white, and where we all went to the public schools together, and played together, and the sound and lilt of the Negro rhythm has never left my ear. Our stiff, correct Vermont singers sounded no more like the rich luscious overflowing of Negro singers, than they sounded like opera singers. It had never occurred to me before that they had never seen a Negro . . . except a colored cook I had for a few years, when the children were little. He was a great curiosity, and considered a very fine talker . . . well, they have a gift *that* way, for sure!

This whole correspondence of ours has brought most vividly home to me the immense gaps that lie between different sections of our country . . . not between the travelled, educated people, but the plain ordinary folks. They really know as little about the South here in Vermont as they know about Europe, and I daresay the Georgia farmers have mighty queer notions about Vermonters . . . if indeed they ever reflected that there were any such people.

That's one of the jobs for our children and grandchildren to do . . . to bring the country together in a closer acquaintance, so that we'll be more of one family. A better understanding is sure to follow, don't you think?

With best regards,
Cordially yours
Dorothy Canfield Fisher

---

1. Date: 1927 appended, but contradicted by present-tense reference to DCF's father-in-law, Dr. William Fisher, who died in 1926. Reference to "the usual rounds" places the letter after that of December 8 [1922] (Letter 49) in which DCF asks Harris to begin sending clippings.

52. *To Paul D. Moody*
May 31, 1923
Arlington, Vermont

Dear President Moody:

I have just received, incidentally to an invitation to speak for a group of Middlebury graduates, a circular letter sent out by Miss Pauline Smith (or perhaps Mrs. Smith)[1] protesting against the "segregation" of women students at Middlebury. I didn't know that the proposition to separate the women students from the men students at Middlebury was a serious one, or that the authorities had really decided to do it.

I am of course familiar with all that can be said on both sides of the question, having been brought up on the discussion of it all my life. Equally of course I know that my opinion has no official weight (to put it mildly) at Middlebury. But I think it perhaps only fair to put my own opinion on record as being wholly against the proposed segregation of women (if it is seriously contemplated) as a very great and lamentable step backward. Of course you ought to know what people's opinions are, if you are to have data on which to make a wise decision, and so I'm sending you mine for what it is worth. There is no use in stating all the reasons on which I found this opinion. You too have been brought up on discussions of this question all your life and you know perfectly well what they are. All that is important (if that is) is to let you know that I consider those in favor of a full and free sharing of academic life infinitely more cogent, American, and forward-looking than anything that can be said against it. I wish I had known earlier that this movement to separate the sexes was a seriously meant one. It would, as you can see from the tone of the article which appeared in the *Tribune,* have made a difference with what I felt about Middlebury and said about it. It may be, however, that I am no better informed now than I was, and that I will find out that there is no such serious intention to reduce Middlebury just to the level of any other New England college, losing its particular quality which made it so distinctive nor to divide its financial resources which are none too complete as it is.

We will be sailing in a short time now, for our year in France, and I won't have time to think any more about the matter. I simply thought it more frank and open to let you know how one individual making up public opinion feels, although I know well enough that one opinion must, in the nature of things, count for only a little with the college authorities in making a decision.

With best regards,
Cordially yours
Dorothy Canfield Fisher

---

1. Pauline Smith (b. 1892), American educator.

53. *To Elizabeth Jackson*
June 14 [1923][1]
Arlington, Vermont

Dearest Elizabeth:

Yes I shall too thank you for reading the Mss.[2] so promptly and sending it back with all those invaluable comments! It was an immense help, and I'm so much relieved that you didn't find anything so very very wrong with my "store lingo" I carefully and religiously changed "stock closets" to "stock-cabinets" and "Advertisement writers" to "advertising office" etc. etc. blessing you the while! And I shall, as I have time reconstruct what is necessary to bring the story into line with the other more important changes you suggest. It is to appear in serial form in a woman's magazine next winter,[3] and this present version, with the changes you suggest (verbal etc.) will do well enough for the serial version which isn't very important. Evangeline will do as she is for them. I'm not a bit downcast by your not finding the store part interesting or life-like . . . indeed I smiled a little over that . . . you know so much more about it that it probably seems childish to you . . . but you just ought to see the absorbed breathless astonished interest with which several other readers devoured that part . . . "literary-minded" people who never had had the slightest idea of the background of that sort of work. I guess it'll do.

About the improbability of Jerome Willing's making such a success in such a small place, I took him almost literally, word for word, from Mr. Halle (Halley?) of Cleveland[4] whom I had such a scrumptious hour-long conversation in Mrs. Prince's office . . . a piece of good luck for which I can never be sufficiently thankful. Jerome's attitude towards his work, is photographically like Mr. Halle's, and I got statistics from Mr. Halle about the kind of store that could exist with a real live wire inspired proprietor, in a town of that size in the midst of a rich agricultural region. Mr. Halle told me of a man in Ohio who inherited a country store at a "cross-roads" with no settlement at all about it, who (with the aid of the ever-present automobile on every farm) had built up a real sure-enough department-store standing right there in the midst of the fields so to speak. And I know of another in Pennsylvania, in the Pocono Mountains near where John's family live. You see Jerome Willing is supposed to be the real thing, a second Mr. Halle . . . who by the way, made a deep impression on me. Blessings on Mrs. Prince for giving me that chance at him. I felt as a miner must feel when his pick-axe suddenly strikes into a vein of the purest ore that comes tumbling out in nuggets! Everything was so authentic, that came from him.

All the same I think your criticism is quite right that he is rather wooden in the story . . . the exigencies of space make it hard to do him justice . . . and get in any of the thousand-and-one touches which make characters live! He is needed only as the background. But I shall certainly work him and his wife over, during the winter, and see if I can't make them real persons, even though they are to be entirely in the background.

We're in mad haste . . . you can just see us packing wildly, trunks all around . . . having a good time over it as none of it is really important. All well, which is the only essential.

Ever so hastily, ever so gratefully, ever so affectionately yours
Dorothy Canfield Fisher

[Handwritten] I did tell you our French address is always American Express Co. 11 rue Scribe.
It's a *crime* your not getting paid better!

1. Date: references to the compositional state of *The Home-Maker*.

2. References to the department store setting establish the manuscript under discussion as *The Home-Maker*.

3. *The Home-Maker* was published serially in the *Woman's Home Companion* (Apr.–June 1924).

4. Samuel H. Halle (1868–1954), American department store operator, chairman of the board and director of Halle Brothers Co., Cleveland, Ohio.

54. To Elizabeth Sessums
August 16 [1923][1]
Arlington, Vermont

Dear Miss Sessums:

This is a very good letter of yours which just came in, and I'm glad you felt like writing it to me. You said something in it which interested me very much, and has given me something to say which is just what I have been looking for . . . when you say the Southern feeling about the negro is no worse than the northern (and everywhere) feeling about illegitimate children, unjust of course, but simply not to be reasoned out of existence. You're quite right, and I've always been trying to think of something to say to northern people which will bring home to them the injustice *all* modern civilization does to individuals when it blames them for something in their birth for which they are not responsible. There is often something so pharisaical and complacent in the attitude of northerners about their criticisms of southerners, I'm glad to have something to show them that they do exactly the same sort of thing . . . everybody does. If you'd spoken about the way the sensitive, cultivated, high-born Jews are often treated by the commonest, most ignorant people up here, you'd have had another good example, too, of that tragedy of being treated in a mass along with everybody else of your kind, whether you, yourself, individually are better than so-called inferiors.

If you'll notice in the "Fairfax Hunter" sketch,[2] I made but one comment on the facts . . . just presented them, in all their sadness. They *are* sad, you know, Miss Sessums, any sort of refusal to treat an individual on his merits, on his very own qualities, is sad. And you'll notice too that I did not at all lay any blame on the South . . . I said in the only comment I made, that I was ashamed "of our civilization" or of mine (I forget which) . . . taking my full share of belonging to an organization. I'm ashamed of the way the Jews are treated, too. I can't help hoping for better days, when there may be more sensitive and kinder relationships towards other peoples. And you may be interested to know that the story of Fairfax Hunter is literally true, the letter from his sister which came to me in France exactly as she wrote it. It needs no comments. My own share in it was not anything to be proud of . . . I ought to have tried harder to make some provision for that weak, sad, sensitive man. I placed him with a cousin of mine . . . kind enough, but not sensitive herself, incapable of even trying to put herself in the place of another human being, and of trying to bring into human relationships some acting on Christ's golden rule of doing unto others . . . Poor Fairfax is better dead. There was no place for him in the world we have all made between us. And isn't there something the matter with the world we have made when there is no place for a sensitive, intelligent, proud human being, whose only ambition would have been to improve himself and have the ordinary human recognition from his fellows of such improvement.

You see I've taken your good letter exactly in the spirit in which you sent it, and I've been glad to have a chance to talk this over a little with you.

With every good wish,
Dorothy Canfield Fisher

---

1. Date: based on the publication of "Fairfax Hunter."
2. This story of an African-American house servant living in Vermont was published in *Raw Material* (1923).

55. *William Lyon Phelps*
All Saints Day
November 1 [1923][1]
114 rue de Brancas
Sèvres, Seine et Oise, France

My dear Professor Phelps:
Your note about *Raw Material* was the first news I had of it, and it has stayed almost the only news! The book came out in August, I imagine, and I suppose some copies were sent me as usual, but customs, or slow mails or something has delayed them. I still haven't seen a copy. We were in Switzerland well on into September, and had no word that the book was published. I felt as though I had dropped it down a well. And then came your letter . . . can you imagine the effect? No you can't. I never had so vividly from any written communication the effect of a warm, actual handshake of encouragement. I woke up the next morning with the sensation of having really seen you in the flesh. And I certainly never had any comment on any book which gave me more pleasure. The process of struggling with one's weaknesses and faults of technic and taste, is such an endlessly long one it seems to me. I often wonder if I make any progress at all. And there is always the danger that too rigorous cutting into

faults may weaken the vigor of the creative impulse, the fire and life which after all, [is] what makes anything worth writing, or doing. You're never sure that you're on the right track! And a favorable comment from somebody who knows one's work from the ground up . . . it's the breath of life!

I watched some very carefully trained tennis-players this summer at Évian[2] (where we were playing this season) with a rather alarmed interest. They had had evidently the infinitely careful instruction which is given to leisure-class folks over here, their form was simply perfection, it was a delight to see them make one perfect stroke after another, like an artistic creation. But along came a middle-aged Englishman, who had evidently struggled along by himself, had any number of faulty habits, but who went right through their perfection like tissue-paper, simply because he had about forty times their motive-power. It made me think very hard about the art of writing (everything makes me think hard about that).

I'd give a lot . . . how many times have I said this! . . . for an afternoon's talk with you. When are you coming over? We are going to be right here, for the children's school. (They are in the Lycée connected with École Normal here.) We will be here till next July. Is there any hope that you'll arrive before that? I've just finished another novel (a short one this time . . . that I want to be like a knife-thrust at the heart of the reader) and feel the needed of lying fallow. I don't think I'll start on anything this winter, at all . . . just enjoy the children who are growing up with villainous rapidity, and do a lot of reading (re-reading rather) such as I've not had time for in the very busy American years of late.

Ever yours,
Dorothy Canfield Fisher

---

1. Date: appended, supported by reference to *Raw Material* (1923).
2. Évian-les-Bains, a resort on Lake Geneva, Haute-Savoie, France.

56. *To Paul Reynolds*
November 20, 1923
114 rue de Brancas, Sèvres, Seine et Oise, France

Dear Mr. Reynolds:

I've been outrageous about getting this article back to you, but it has not been wholly due to inertia. I've found it hard to put my mind with any calm on what Mr. Vance[1] writes, because of my impatience with what underlies it . . . I refer to all that "Nordic superiority, great white race" nonsense which is just making its belated way into our country. After seeing what idiots the Germans made of themselves for two long generations over that fantastic and so far, entirely unproved idea of Count Gobineau's,[2] and what a well-deserved punishment they got for it, it does seem as though Americans might leave it alone.

But I suppose it must be the fad of the hour, as America always does with ideas that are new to it. My only comfort is that American fads are usually short-lived as they are violent and we'll probably live through this and forget it, like the blue-glass cure[3] and ping-pong. The Ku Klux Klan (which of course has nothing but this Gobineau idea of inherent racial superiority at the bottom of its imbecilities) may make it odious enough to shorten its stay with us.

There is, however, another reason for my position in this article which seems to me valid. That is, it seems to me that the story of the success of the S.C.A.A. in the care of wretched children of poor parentage has no point whatever if we deny the immense importance of environment over heredity, cannot be made credible or intelligible unless that question is squarely faced. Here's a passage from Mr. Vance's letter, "You cannot take the son of a degenerate South European couple and make him into a good American citizen." (Why, by the way are South European parents always called degenerate in this kind of talk I wonder?) The whole story of the work of the S.C.A.A. is proof that if you can catch him early enough you can; just as is shown by the great change in any breed of cattle or horses when for a few generations they are given good care and good food. You can't keep Shetland ponies small, you know, if you give them shelter and enough to eat!

Well, this is just for your ear because I am sorry to have bothered you by my delay in this matter. If you think best, tell Mr. Vance the substance of this letter (couched in some decorous phrases of your own) or if you don't think that best, just pass the article along to him. But do make it plain that I have made every single change that I can and that I think it must appear in this form.

Best regards,
Cordially yours
Dorothy Canfield Fisher

This wasn't written about Mr. Vance and Mr. Wiggam,[4] but it might have been.[5]

---

1. Arthur T. Vance (1872–1930) was editor of the *Pictorial*.

2. Joseph Arthur, Compte de Gobineau (1816–1882), French diplomat, was best known for *Essai sur l'inégalitié des races humaines* (1854–1855) which advances the theory that the Aryan, or Teuton, is superior to all other human races.

3. See Letter 32, note 4.

4. Albert Edward Wiggam (1871–1957), American author and lecturer on heredity and eugenics, was a regular contributor to the *Pictorial* and other popular magazines.

5. Newspaper article enclosed: "If he were well-informed on the biographical facts about

which he prattles so decisively, he would be aware that the most competent authorities are inclining toward the view that far too much has been made of the supposed differences in the hereditary mental equipment of the races of mankind and that such obvious discrepancies as appear between the average Alabama Negro and the average inhabitant of Vermont are mainly due to environmental factors."

57. Alfred Harcourt
March 12, 1924
114 rue Brancas, Sèvres, Seine et Oise, France

Dear Alf:

Your letters of February 25th and 28th are here, and welcome as usual. The changes you made in the letter about arrangements with Mlle Salomon are all right, of course. She didn't know any more than I about what the proper thing was, and will, I know accept this. All right, I'll not sell any cinema rights (not that I'd ever have much chance to) but it will surprise me greatly, if anything of mine ever turns out to be *kinema-futter.* You remember what they wanted of *The Brimming Cup* was another book and a totally different one.[1]

I'm glad that you think the photographs are usable, though I have a little qualm about having them broadcast when John hates them so. But he hates practically all of my photographs except the ones that nobody else likes, so perhaps it's a deadlock in the nature of things.

You ask if there's another book on the stocks . . . nossir, I've been truly resting and lying fallow, feeling that I needed to do it. I'd been putting out a lot of stuff, you know since we went back from France after the war. It will do me good to be just a human being again. As a matter of fact I have not, of course, been able to keep my pen from paper entirely, but what I've set down has been something so different from anything I've ever done that I doubt if you could call it a "book on the stocks." It's this; for years now, ever since Jimmy could talk, we have "run" a series of what we call "Jimmy's made to order stories." He hates the banality of the usual book-story where he sees from afar the same old tricks about to be turned, and invented this way of getting stories that are bound to be unexpected. He gives his own recipe . . . "I want a story with a puppy and an ice-berg and a churn and a little boy and a dozen marbles." Thus avoiding the usual story of a puppy with a tin-can tied to its tail and a brave little boy-scout who rescues the poor thing which turns out to belong to the millionaire Lady Bountiful of the village or something of that sort. You can imagine that stories constructed with the ingredients which Jimmy gives out, are unexpected if nothing else. The whole point about them is that the unexpectedness must be in the incidents and not in the telling which is always matter-of-fact and serious. It has made a little narrative recipe which has amused

Jimmy and Sally for a long time. I must have told a thousand of them, more or less. They run off as fast as you can talk, you know, since you are bound by none of the usual rules of narrative. Well, in Switzerland, last Christmas time, I happened to tell one about an angry polar-bear which got the children to laughing so that they had the idea of setting it down for other children to laugh over. I didn't think myself that any of the real flavor of it could be decanted into cold print, and realized, what Jimmy and Sally don't, that most of their charm for us consists in the fact that they are a family tradition. But to please them I did put it down, and four others of the four days afterwards. I sent them along to Mildred Batchelder of the Horace Mann School,[2] as the best judge for that [sort] of thing I know . . . with many years of experience with children of about the age of those for whom these stories are told; and also a woman of ripe literary judgment. I told her that if she found, after trying them out on assorted children in the Horace Mann School, that they "went" to send them along to Reynolds, to see if he could perhaps place them with *St. Nicholas.*[3] In the same mail with your last, which came in yesterday, I had a letter from Mildred, saying the stories had had an immense success, and another note from Reynolds saying he had received them and would see what he could do with them (Reynolds' usual effusive epistolary style). If you think it's worth while, you might get them from Reynolds, if he still has them in his hands, and see if you think there's a volume in them for children's use. I could write any number needed, goodness knows. Perhaps Ellen[4] would look at them. Her judgment might be better than yours, in that matter. I remember she has a good flair for children's books. Personally I haven't the least idea whether they're not too trivial to consider. John thinks I've taken leave of my senses to have written them down at all.

All well here as usual . . . expect to be home about the middle of next summer, I think.

Ever yours
Dorothy

---

1. DCF refused to sell the cinema rights to *The Brimming Cup* soon after the book's publication in 1921.

2. Mildred Batchelder (b. 1901), American educator and librarian of the Horace Mann School in New York City.

3. *St. Nicholas,* an illustrated magazine for children published from 1873 to 1943 (see Letter 23, note 1).

4. Harcourt's second wife.

58. *To Alfred Harcourt*
June 7, 1924
114 rue de Brancas, Sèvres, Seine et Oise, France

Dear Alf:

Your two letters of May 21st and 22nd are here. I'm delighted that you find the "Made-to-Order Stories" entertaining but I continue to be astonished at the success of those funny little screeds. They are so entirely built for our own Sally-and-Jimmy fun that it has hardly seemed possible that other people could get (especially from the frozen black-and-white version) anything of their savor. However your liking for them confirms me in what I had begun to think from the report of Mildred Batchelder about the Horace Mann children from what the editor of *St. Nicholas* said about them, namely that it might be worth while to make a volume of them.

As to your terms, sure, ten percent is all right, as it is the usual juvenile arrangement. And I daresay I could have the book ready by fall, but I DO NOT WANT TO PROMISE THIS. I so mortally hate to have a promise hanging over my head (since I have the habit of keeping them) that if possible I never want again to agree before-hand to have anything ready by any certain date. I pretty surely could have ten stories ready by that time and that ought to be enough for the illustrator to start work on. But I'm apprehensive about the summer, and the crowds of folks which it will almost certainly bring upon me, and don't want to have anything actually promised as dark background to other vacation complications.

Everybody's fine here now, and we are enjoying tennis on the finest courts imaginable, in really fine weather. Just back from a trip in the Ford all through Brittany.

I haven't heard anything about *The Home-Maker,* except some heated matters pro and con which have already made their way here. One of them just raised the hair on my head . . . a woman in Massachusetts wrote me wildly that she would give her life if I had only written the book earlier, for her husband committed suicide last winter . . . an artist with no business ability, trying to make a living for her and her six children . . . she said "I understand now after reading *The Home-Maker* so many things I never dreamed of before etc. etc." Rather horrifying, I found it. Dorothea Mann[1] writes me that of course the book isn't the equal of my other novels, and that I mustn't forget the primitive element in people which is rightly alarmed at the idea of men becoming effeminate . . . ha! do you get this . . . from Dorothea? And an acquaintance writes me from Chicago that her neighbors are shocked by the utterly unexpected ending. These slight indications of interests are rather promising. if only people will find it interesting enough to disagree about violently, they may do some real thinking.

We're beginning to get ready to pack now . . . with mixed feelings very glad and rather regretful. France is a good home for me.

Best regards to you all as ever,
Dorothy

---

1. See Letter 28, note 1.

59. To Edith F. Wyatt
September 21, 1924
Arlington, Vermont

Dear Miss Wyatt:
    I've been quite absurdly putting off answering your letter, from day to day, because as long as it is unanswered, I have a valid excuse for keeping it open on my desk and re-reading it as often as I like. I can't possibly tell you how much good your generous words have done me, nor how immensely they have helped me. I suffer much from what I try to make it. It is enchanting to know that it is read with a sympathetic understanding eye which can divine my meaning so wholly as you have done. Praise from you means a good deal, I can tell you. I feel like shouting for joy that you noticed (apparently the only reader who did) the real vitality of poetry in Lester's life[1] . . . a conception over which I worked with all my heart on fire with what seemed to me the beauty of such an element in a man's life. And I feel a real deep gratitude to you for seeing that what I am always struggling so hard and so imperfectly to express is the poetry and tragedy and profound fundamental importance of the simple recurrent human relationships of daily life.
    Please thank all the members of your family for their share in a letter which has meant and will mean much to me. I'm more glad than I can say that you felt the impulse to write it.

Sincerely and gratefully yours
Dorothy Canfield Fisher

---

1. Lester Knapp, the husband-protagonist in *The Home-Maker,* is an avid reader of poetry.

60. To Paul Reynolds
September 29, 1924
Arlington, Vermont

Dear Mr. Reynolds:

Your letter of September 26th is here. It makes me very uneasy, as you know, to have any date definitely fixed when a story *must* be delivered. I'll do my best to get that story[1] done this winter, of course, but I don't want it to be absolutely promised for any date. I take it from your letter, however, that Miss Lane[2] doesn't insist on having it at any special date, but merely says that if she has it in the spring, it will be published in time for spring publication by Harcourt the year after. That's all right. And I fully expect to have it finished this winter. I read with attention your remarks on getting to work, and taking the dive into action, and agree with them. Everybody knows they are true, of course. The only difficulty is the human one of putting into practice what you know is an excellent maxim. But I do protest against being lumped in with the loafing authors who don't work unless they're hurried into it. No sir, by gracious, that is not me. Nobody *can* hurry me, unfortunately, and I really don't need it, if the work is on the right track. It usually ends by carrying me off my feet so that I can't think of anything else, and eat, sleep and breathe it twenty-four hours of the day, whether anybody even knows that I'm working on it or no. If it's not on the right track (whatever that mysterious process is) no amount of having promised it, can get it out of my skin.

All this of course just for you. Don't bother Miss Lane with it, for I really do expect to get the book done this winter.

Where does that little quatrain come from, in German? I'd almost forgotten it, and it's worth keeping up before one's eyes!

Faithfully yours
Dorothy Canfield Fisher

P.S. On second thoughts, perhaps you would better get in touch with Miss Lane on this matter of the date of delivery for that story, if you think there is any chance that she considers it essential to have it by a certain time. Suppose by some chance I can't get it done by spring? Then what? Would her contract be off? I think perhaps we'd better be quite definite in saying that we must be indefinite! She ought to understand that it is really impossible, in a matter of this sort, to promise by dates. And I suppose she does, after all her experience.

---

1. *Her Son's Wife* was published serially in the *Woman's Home Companion* (Feb.–July 1926).
2. Gertrude Battles Lane, American editor (see Letter 41, note 4).

61. To Alfred Harcourt
October 4, 1924
Arlington, Vermont

Dear Alf:

I've been waiting to write to you till we had a frost and the autumn coloring would make it just right for your trip up here to see the valley. But by gracious we *still* haven't had a frost. The memory of man etc. does not reach back to a fall when the first frost had not come by this time! Consequently the coloring, while autumnal and rich is not nearly so vivid as it usually is. But surely most any time now we must have the frost which brings out the flaming reds and yellows. I have doings on for a week from today the 11th, which will take me all the whole day and part of the day before, but nothing except that, as far as I can see, so suit your convenience, and look at the barometer readings to see which way it is going. The valley is plenty lovely enough to show Ellen,[1] even if it is not its usual wild splendor.

I have the "Made-to-Order Stories," practically all complete, only needing a little final revision and typing. There will be something over forty thousand words. Plenty. You don't want too much of that sort of highly flavored thing or people will get tired of it. I have tried out a few more on the meeting of the New York Library Association at Lake Placid, with considerable success. They all said that every library in the country would have to have several copies in their children's department, and old Mr. Hill of the Brooklyn Library said he would certainly put it in the adult department, also as it would please old boys as well as little ones. I counted the words in the Rootabaga stories[2] and found that there were not quite thirty thousand of actual printing, there. Most of it is pictures and blank pages and such-like. So I think you can easily make a full-size volume out of it. I'll be very glad if you can make a really good-looking thing of it, too, with good paper and illustrations. And on that subject, if you haven't anybody to illustrate it, I have a suggestion. Doris Webster (of the *Publisher's Weekly*) was here a while ago, and spoke of a friend of hers, who would be, she thought the right person for those stories (which by the way she liked very much). Her friend is Anne Moffett, at 130 East 57th Street, and I wish before you decide on the illustrator you'd see some of her work, and talk to her.[3] I think she'd take the liveliest interest in it, and her work has humor, and is not too fantastic. One of the details I'd thought of, is this . . . to have at the head of each story, a frieze, humorously conceived, of the different objects around which the story is constructed . . . pony-cart, fox-in-trap, house-fire, etc. Another thing, while I think of it. Now I'm in this country, I'd like to see the publicity, jacket etc. before they are decided on. I still think, you know, that the screed on the jacket of *The Home-Maker* did a good deal of harm, with its feminist color, and may have contributed really to the misunderstanding of that book. If I'd seen it before it was printed, I certainly would have asked to have it changed. And I think the "Made-to-Order Stories" are so very different from anything else of mine, and are so light and trifling, that the publicity ought to be carefully done, to avoid making people think they're something else than what they are. I don't want any serious-minded reader of my other stories to blunder into them, without having a pretty good idea before-hand of what he's going to find, or he'll get them from the wrong slant. And by the way, would it be out of the question to change the jacket of *The Home-Maker,* even now? I don't know about the material side of it, what it would cost in money and bother, but I think it would be a lot better to put something on the jacket about the way the book's been misunderstood and the way it should be taken, as a whoop not for "women's rights" but for "children's rights." Perhaps quote something from one of the understanding reviews, like the one in the *Evening Post* review, which called itself "The Cry of the Children"[4] and said, "the book will be misunderstood; indeed it has already been curiously misinterpreted as an outbreak of 'feminism' and 'emancipation,' whereas the real emphasis of the book falls upon neither husband nor wife, but upon children." Let me know if you think something might be done along these lines. I don't mind the book not selling so well as you thought, because its sold plenty well enough to satisfy me; but it does make me sore to have it so idiotically misunderstood, when the meaning is if anything too plainly inscribed all over it. Maybe when you come up we can talk this over.

We'll have to hear news of Hastings,[5] and you of Sally, too when we get together. I'll save the Sally-news till then, as it is various and full of ups and downs. She's getting lots of experience and learning lots of things about herself and other people she never could have learned with me by to keep things off her, too much, as is the way of mothers. I do hope Hastings is all right, and I believe he will be. He's old enough now, I should think, to be just about right for some life away from his folks. I'm eager to know how he takes to it. They are both having glorious weather for out-door life, these first few weeks.

All serene here . . . I've been putting in pretty hard the last few weeks as you can imagine, to get these stories done. I'm about ready now to start in on the novel,[6] which will certainly be the death of me! I dread it . . . and can't wait to begin it.

Ever yours,
Dorothy Canfield Fisher

---

1. See Letter 57, note 4.
2. Part of *Made-to-Order Stories.*

3. Dorothy Lathrop was the illustrator of DCF's *Made-to-Order Stories.*
4. H. L. Pangborn, "The Cry of the Children"
5. See Letter 39, note 3.
6. *Her Son's Wife* (1926).

62. *To Alfred Harcourt*
March 11, 1925
Arlington, Vermont

Dear Alf:

Thanks for your good letter of the 10th. Glad to know you are back all right. How much good Florida does you!

All serene here. John and the Legislature[1] on their last weeks of work, and going stronger all the time. He expects to be home towards the end of the month, *perhaps.* You'd better believe this stricken and deserted family will be glad to have him here again! Although Jimmy and I have had a beautiful winter, of a tranquility and peace too good to be true, with immense progress in school on Jimmy's part, and about ninety thousand words of first draught[2] on mine. I expect now it will be about a hundred and ten or twenty thousand. Hence it looks as though I might live through it. It has been deep, deep going . . . but it hasn't killed me yet, though I have been more ravaged by excitement and emotion over it, than over anything else I've ever written. I doubt if you or any man will be able to get into it, at all. But I bet you Ellen and a lot of other women will.

I don't want to stop to look at that dramatic version of *The Home-Maker*[3] now, because I'm not reading anything, except an occasional French book now. And anyhow as I haven't the least idea it will be played anywhere, coming in from an outsider like that, it's not very pressing. So I'll just leave it lay . . . where a million other things are laying, waiting for me to emerge into normal life again. But I did read *Arrowsmith,*[4] and found it what you know it to be, a very fine book indeed. When I see you, I want to talk it (along with many other things) over and over.

Mother's having the time of her life, hasn't missed a meal, the only woman in the 600 who hasn't been sea-sick yet.[5]

Ever yours
Dorothy

---

1. See Letter 43, note 2.

2. Date indicates that the work-in-progress was "Her Son's Wife."

3. The film of *The Home-Maker* was released by Universal Pictures in August 1925. It was directed by King Baggot and starred Alice Joyce and Clive Brook.

4. Sinclair Lewis, *Arrowsmith* (New York: Harcourt, Brace, 1925). See Letter 43, note 3.
5. DCF's mother was taking an around-the-world cruise.

63. To Paul Reynolds
March 28 [1925][1]
Arlington, Vermont

Dear Mr. Reynolds:

I'd forgotten all about those "Made-to-Order Stories" in your office. No don't bother to return them. I'm just correcting proofs on that book and won't read them. Just deposit them in the waste-paper basket and think no more of them.

I've been wrestling like Jacob with the new novel,[2] and have had a magnificently quiet winter in which to work . . . deep snows, the house empty all day (for Jimmy was at school, Mr. Fisher in the Legislature at Montpelier and Sally far away at boarding-school) and I have worked harder and with less nervous strain than ever before. It has turned out something which I have *felt*, terrifically, and still feel too deeply to have much idea how I have succeeded. I expect to finish the first draught in about a month from now (if all goes well) and will then read it over and begin revision. After I have been revising a week or so, I can let you know, I think, with some degree of accuracy, about when I can have it ready to send to Miss Lane.[3]

I think it will be a story which women will be interested in, (I hope which they will feel deeply) but I don't believe that it can interest any man. They have for too many generations had the possibility and the habit, of putting on their hats and melting away out of the house, when family relations got too uncomfortably tense. I rather imagine that they will put on their hats and melt away from the book at about the third chapter. But I hope that women who have had, for generations, to stick it out with no escape, may have a certain horrified interest in the story. At any rate, the fact that it is not at all a man's story won't hurt it for Miss Lane.

[Handwritten] Best regards to all of you,—and hopes to see Mary up our way for a week-end,

Ever yours,
Dorothy Canfield Fisher

---

1. Stamped "received 30 March 1925."
2. Date indicates that the work under discussion is "Her Son's Wife."
3. See Letter 41, note 4.

64. *To H. Robinson Shipherd*
July 10 [1925][1]
Arlington, Vermont

My dear Professor Shipherd:

Your letter of the 8th has just arrived and finds me most sympathetic to your purpose. I haven't any copy of *Americans All*[2] at hand (indeed I don't believe I ever saw that book except in proofs) and so haven't any idea what it is you wish to quote. But you're more than welcome to quote anything you can find on any page of mine, which will encourage young writers to revise and re-write. I don't know whether my case is typical or not, but it seems to me that the longer I write, the worse I write at first, . . . that is, the more I have to work over my draughts to make them nearer what I wished to say. This is probably simply because I know a little more all the time *how* to rewrite and revise. And this in turn would suggest that young writers are averse to rewriting because they really haven't any notion what to do. Rather than because they don't wish to make the effort. I can dimly remember a happy time when I could look at a page of mine and think "Well, I don't see what more I can do to that." Never any more! Any page of mine, taken at random, throws me into an acute fever of remorse for the mistakes in it, and an ardent desire to sit down and wrestle with it. This does not increase the joy of authorship, of course, but I hope it increases the quality of the product.

All this to show you how more than willing I am to be quoted as to the value of rewriting.[3]

Cordially yours
Dorothy Canfield Fisher
(Mrs. John R. Fisher)

---

1. Date: Shipherd's response is dated July 23, 1925.

2. *Americans All: Stories of American Life Today,* ed. Benjamin A. Heydrick (New York: Harcourt, Brace, 1921) contained DCF's story "Flint and Fire" and an essay on its composition, "How 'Flint and Fire' Started and Grew" (see Letter 39).

3. Shipherd quoted DCF's statement on the value of revision in this letter in *The Fine Art of Writing for Those Who Teach It* (New York: Macmillan, 1926).

65. To Alfred Harcourt
September 28 [1925][1]
Arlington, Vermont

Dear Alfred:

Thanks to all of you for the telegram about the movie-ized *Home-Maker.* Weren't you amazed? I was! They gave a special performance of it here, so that I could see it, and I watched with my mouth fairly dropping open with astonishment. They asked me to write them my opinion of it, and in so doing I laid special emphasis on my surprise, after all that has been said of what movie directors do to a story. It couldn't have been more faithfully followed, it seems to me, and even the moral atmosphere of the book was reproduced, as well as the facts. Now remains to be seen whether they lose money on it or not. I imagine from the talk of one of their representatives who came to see me here, that they undertook it in this spirit, as a sort of "call" to the outcry against bad movies by churches, women's clubs, parent-teachers associations etc. just to see whether there was anything in the demand which such righteous people make in the name of the public. They are trying to reach that sort of person, apparently, by their publicity, as an experiment, to see if there is anything in their ideas . . . that is, whether there is a living in it. Personally, I don't see anything in it which would at all interest (let alone entertain) a movie audience . . . to put it mildly. I should think it would fall absolutely flat, before people quite unable to see what it was all about. But I have thought that so many times of my work, and have been surprised that there seemed to be enough people interested in my sort of ideas. But whether there will be enough among the movie audiences . . . that's another matter!

Ever yours,
Dorothy

[Handwritten] Oh, say, send a copy of *Made-to-Order Stories* will you, please, with author's compliments to Annie Carroll Moore—New York Public Library. You know who she is, don't you? specialist in children's books.

---

1. Date: appended, supported by release of the film of *The Home-Maker* in August 1925 (see Letter 62, note 3).

66. To Alfred Harcourt
November 27 [1925][1]
Arlington, Vermont

Dear Alf:

Reynolds wrote me that Miss Lane[2] wanted to use the title "My Son's Wife" for that novel. I telegraphed that I had no objections to her using it for the serial version, but would prefer to wait before deciding the name for the book. Reynolds has just telephoned me that she wants to use the name for the book as the name for this serial, so it must be decided at once.

I've written her that I do not like "My Son's Wife," because of the first person; but that I will, somewhat reluctantly, consent to "Her Son's Wife" if you and she like that the best of the suggestions.

The relations of mother-in-law and daughter-in-law are not the subject of this novel, in any general sense; but the obligation laid upon a member of the older generation to sacrifice herself for a member of the younger, when she realizes that she is the only hope of the child. As far as Lottie interferes with Mrs. Bascomb's doing what's best for Dids, their relations are the subject of the book. But if there had been no child, they wouldn't have had any relations at all. So I'd like some title which would suggest what seems to be the vital point of the story, the relation on one hand of Mrs. Bascomb to her fine husband (the best influence in her life and one which determines her character) and her relation to his granddaughter. So here are my four suggested titles. I've asked Miss Lane to call you up on the telephone and talk it over with you.

John Bascomb's Widow

John Bascomb's Granddaughter

Her Son's Wife,

or, and this last would be my favorite, "Every Man to His Heritage." This phrase comes from a sentence in Proverbs, which runs,

"I will bring them again, every man to his heritage, and every man to his land."[3]

I'd print the whole text on the front page as explanation, as we did the quotation from Shakespeare, for *Rough-Hewn.*[4]

You can see without my explaining, in how many ways this would refer to what seems to me the real subject matter of the novel, the recurring of the heritage of John Bascomb from destruction or at least from deformity.

John likes the ring of "Every Man to His Heritage," and so do I. But you may have some good reason for preferring one of the others. Miss Lane must have it settled at once, so I send her to you.

Hastily, ever yours
Dorothy

1. Date: references to the serialization of *Her Son's Wife* in the *Woman's Home Companion* (Feb.–July 1926).

2. Gertrude Battles Lane, American editor (see Letter 41, note 4).

3. Jeremiah 12.15: "Then, having uprooted them, I will once more have compassion on them and restore them, each to his heritage and each to his land."

4. Quotation from *Hamlet* act 5, scene 2, line 10: "There's a divinity that shapes our ends, Rough-hew them how we will."

67. To Paul Reynolds

February 11, 1926
Arlington, Vermont

Dear Mr. Reynolds:

I have been thinking over your letter of February 6th, with the offer from the *Country Gentleman* about that Western trip. It interests me very much, just the kind of thing I'd like to do, and I think their pay is generous. But I don't believe I'd better consider it . . . at least not this year. I can't leave home very well for more than a fortnight; and I have such a lot of other work; and I don't believe I'd begin to see what I ought to, in such a short time. I'm not a journalist, you know, with the habit of writing of surface impressions of things. I have to live myself into my material before I feel sure enough to put pen to paper. I suppose I ought to have thought of all this before, and not bothered them to make a definite offer. But it has taken some meditation to discover what I really did feel about it. I think the job they offer should be done by a journalist, used to hitting the high places and to giving snap impressions . . . very interesting stuff it often is, too. But every man to his trade, and I've not been trained to that, and would hate to make the inevitable mistakes that are made in interpreting conditions seen so rapidly. Here's a little story of a journalist who came through our country here on a walking trip, and wrote an article about it for the *Freeman*. One of the things he said was that farming conditions were so poor here, and the rich people from the cities were [grinding ?] the faces of the poor farmers so (of course writing for the *Freeman* he had to say something of this sort) that the post-offices were plastered from ceiling to baseboard with notices of bankruptcy of farmers.

Our astonishment was immense, for of course farmers never "go into bankruptcy" as business people do, and anyhow nobody all up and down our valley has ever lost his farm to a wicked mortgage holder, or in any other way, except when the boys went of their own accord to the city. Well, we went out to look at the post-offices to see what it was they were plastered with, and found (so familiar a sight to us we'd forgotten it was there) many notices of executors of estates, the usual legal document, after somebody's death, to people to whom he owed money etc., to appear before the executors before such and such a date. Vermont-fashion nobody ever bothered to tear down those that were out of date, and sure enough there were lots of them yellowed with age, still clinging to the walls. The newspaper writer hadn't even bothered, apparently to read them, or else didn't know enough law to know what they were. Well, I tell all this story to show what it is I'm afraid of doing. You can pass on as little or as much to the *C. G.* people as you think best, but the upshot is that I don't believe it'd fit my equipment to do that work unless I could give a longer time to it (which I'd love to do some year) but I can't take a longer time till the children are older and both away at school.

I'm going to start in very soon on their "Farmer's Wife" article.[1]

Cordially yours
Dorothy Canfield Fisher

---

1. "Shall I Marry a Farmer?" *Country Gentleman* 91 (June 1926): 137–39.

68. To Julia Collier Harris
August 16, 1926
Arlington, Vermont

Dear Mrs. Harris:

Your letter was both a delight and a disappointment. I have been meaning to write you my enthusiastic delight over the Pulitzer award, which seemed almost too good to be true. Everybody I knew was enchanted with it, and I really think it has made a good many people think there is, after all, some merit in awards and medals and such methods of calling attention to merit.

But here you say it has really brought you a lot more trouble. Isn't that exasperating the way things go *dans ce monde*! When I didn't hear from you for some time, I worried often, for fear the strain you and your husband were under might really be too much for you; and it wouldn't have surprised me to hear of you as once more foreign correspondents for some fine American newspaper, enjoying American life. So the news of the Pulitzer award gave me news of you, and made me see you still there, on the outposts, holding out to do the work nobody else could begin to do as you two do!

Yes, of course I'll be much interested to see a book by a friend of yours,[1] specially any book about the success of a woman in business, which I think one of the most interesting new possibilities for women in this country. So large a majority of the fathers of our girls are heart-and-soul businessmen, it stands to reason that the girls themselves might do better if they were not automatically shoved off into being cultured teachers . . . although goodness knows our country needs cultured teachers enough sight more than business-people. Still, folks have to do what they are best fit for, and every opportunity for women means one less chance of a square peg living miserably in a round hole all its life.

I didn't know you had any Vermont blood. It makes you seem like a cousin. And from Craftsbury! Did you know that one of our cleverest young women in Vermont, is a Craftsbury girl.[2] She is (as few women do) devoting herself to political life . . . did you ever! . . . getting the best sort of education and experience she can to fit her to be a public servant of the state. She was in the State Legislature last term (as was my husband) and one of the most valuable members. She is now working in Washington, and adding to her splendid academic training the most first-hand experience of the realistic workings of political machinery. I expect great things from her, and am so proud that a Vermont woman has the initiative and imagination to strike out along that line. Also Craftsbury has done splendidly by its rural schools of late, and has very enlightened public opinion on that subject. No mean city, Craftsbury, although it has only just as many citizens as our little Arlington, about twelve hundred!

Do come on sometime to see it, and see us.

Cordially yours
Dorothy Canfield Fisher

P.S. Yes, I'll be glad to write something about that book that Harpers can use as publicity.

---

1. Helen (Rosen) Woodward, *Through Many Windows: The Autobiography of a Business Woman* (New York: Harper, 1926). Woodward is named in an Oct. 11, 1926 letter from DCF to Harris. She was in the advertising business in New York (1903–1923), and is said to have been the first woman account executive in the U.S.
2. Mary J. Simpson.

69. To James Weldon Johnson
[1927][1]
[Arlington, Vermont][2]

Dear Mr. Johnson:

Can you pardon the delay in my acknowledging the arrival of your beautiful book *God's Trombones*. I was away from home when it arrived and since then have been absorbed in the case of my little boy who has been suffering from a miserably complicated and long-drawn out attack of poison ivy.

I've not been too much absorbed to read the book, which I have done with an ever-increasing enthusiasm. I can scarcely tell you what a high joy the book has brought me. I find it heart-shakingly beautiful and original, with the peculiar piercing tenderness and intimacy which seems to me special gifts of the Negro. I have always been, as perhaps you know, a great admirer of certain beautiful traits which seem to me peculiar to Negroes; and it is a profound satisfaction to find those special qualities so exquisitely expressed.

Thank you very much for making my copy an autographed one. I shall always prize it greatly. Won't you tell your publishers please that I shall consider it an honor if they feel that they can use my name to bring your fine book to the attention of more readers.

Cordially yours
Dorothy Canfield Fisher

---

1. Date: publication date of James Weldon Johnson's *God's Trombones* (New York: Viking Press, 1927).
2. Place: implied.

70. To Julia Collier Harris
March 21 [1927?][1]
Arlington, Vermont

Dear Mrs. Harris:
Thank you a thousand times for sending me that delicious story of Harry Stillwell Edwards.[2] I was very tired last night, and sat down to look through the mail, after the children had gone to bed, feeling anything but hilarious. And I started in to read the little story only because I was too tired to get out of my chair. But in a very short time I was smiling, and before the end I was laughing till the tears ran down my cheeks. Isn't it too utterly racy and savory and delicious! I could hear every accent in it, and see every incident. And the rising number of rooms in that house and fountains on that lawn, is as funny as anything a Shakespeare clown ever said!

But you don't need to tell me who Harry Stillwell Edwards is (except that I'd no idea he was in politics, but thought of him as a professional writer like myself, because of the finish and professional quality of his work). I've admired his tales, as many as I could lay my hands on, for years. To think of there having been a chance of his being in the Senate! And oh heavens! to think that it was Tom Watson who defeated him![3] What a country we do live in to be sure!

I fell to thinking last night, wondering what there was about the Negro and the Irish element in our American life that gives us almost our only element of really uproarious fun. Mr. Dooley[4] has made me laugh like that, outloud, although alone in the room, laugh till I had to stop to wipe the tears away. And of course many of the immortal Uncle Remus' tales have that inimitable quality. But I don't know anything else in our American literature which has that hearty, whole-hearted amusement in it, do you? There is a great deal of humor and fun in New England life, but nothing of that Homeric quality. Is it because both the Irish and the Negroes are famous liars? (This is an indiscreet guess . . . keep it to yourself!) Or is it just because they have more vivid color of personality than Anglo-Saxons? At any rate, thanks again for giving me that delightful end to a tiring day.

And yet . . . isn't it queer . . . people who don't know Negroes miss the fun! I'm the only person in my very Yankee family who ever had anything to do with Negroes, as I had by chance because my father was professor in the Kansas State University.[5] And I find the others don't get the fun that I do out of good Negro tales, any more than French people see the fun in funny Irish stories. I tried to tell my husband something of this picturesque, colorful little tale, just howling with laughter over the characteristic Negro mixture of racing horses and betting on the races, with holding [a] revival meeting and preaching eloquently on the better life. And all he said was, "Well, it doesn't sound very probable to me!" So I had to have my laugh all by myself, knowing that it is more than probable . . . an exact picture.

Best wishes always
Dorothy Canfield Fisher

---

1. Date: 1927 appended.

2. *AEneas Africanus* (1919) by Harry Stillwell Edwards (1855–1938), American author.

3. Thomas E. Watson (1856–1922) was elected to the U.S. Senate over Edwards in 1920 by a vote of 124,630 to 6,700. The League of Nations was a key issue in the campaign; Watson was an anti-League, anti-Wilson, anti–war measures Democrat, while Edwards was a pro-League Independent.

4. "Mr. Dooley" was a comic character in a series of popular stories by Finley Peter Dunne. *Mr. Dooley in Peace and in War* (1898) was the first of the series featuring the Irish saloonkeeper, which concluded with *Mr. Dooley on Making a Will* (1919).

5. DCF's father, James Hulme Canfield (1847–1909), was a professor of political economy and sociology at the University of Kansas in Lawrence (1871–1891). DCF lived in Lawrence until the age of ten.

71. *To Alfred Knopf*
August 15 [1927][1]
Arlington, Vermont

My dear Mr. Knopf:

The time must be approaching for the appearance of "Death Comes to the Archbishop," and I'm writing to offer my services if you think there is anything I can do to help the distribution of that exquisitely beautiful book.

It was a great disappointment to me that it was not chosen by the Book-of-the-Month Committee for the book to be sent out in September.[2] The other members of the committee, although appreciating its loveliness, said they felt it was too contemplative and had too little "action" (whatever that means!) to appeal to a very large and very miscellaneous audience.

As soon [as] I'd read the book I wrote to Miss Cather to express my really unbounded pleasure in it, but I don't know where she is this summer,[3] and had no address but the Bank Street one, so I'm not sure that the letter ever reached her.

I'm so far out of the current of what's going on in literary talk that I've no idea whether my name as an admirer of a fine book would be considered an assct or a liability. You will probably know whether I can be useful in any way to Miss Cather's beautiful book. Please call on me if you think there is anything I can do.

Sincerely yours
Dorothy Canfield Fisher

---

1. Date: reference to the impending publication of Willa Cather's *Death Comes for the Archbishop* (New York: Knopf, 1927).

2. The book-of-the-month for September 1927 was Rosamond Lehmann's novel *Dusty Answer* (New York: Holt, 1927).

3. Cather moved out of her 5 Bank Street apartment in New York's Greenwich Village at the start of the summer in 1927. She spent the summer visiting relatives in Wyoming and Nebraska.

72. *To Robert Frost*
[1928][1]
[Middlebury, Vermont][2]

Dear Robert:

I was all but torn limb from limb by my tennis-playing men-folk when we straggled home from the Equinox expedition at nine Tuesday evening, and found you'd been there at last to play doubles. Of course I wasn't in the least to blame for their missing you—that mountain climb had been their idea entirely—but I caught it all the same. Is there any chance at all of your giving them another chance before you sail?[3]

But that's not what I'm writing about. I've just made one of my wild breaks up here and want to warn you off. Perhaps you knew already that Grant Overton[4] is a Catholic convert of recent date? If you did and let me come up here without a warning—! I waltzed right in to the subject in my headlong incautious way and found in the midst of my remarks that he had turned R.C. last year. Since you're coming and will meet him I thought you'd like to know.

Love to Elinor always
Dorothy

---

1. Date: appended, supported by reference to Frost's impending trip.
2. Place: letterhead, Bread Loaf Inn, Middlebury, Vermont. DCF was teaching at the Bread Loaf School of English in Middlebury, Vermont.
3. He sailed for France on August 4, 1928.
4. Grant Overton (1887–1930) American novelist and literary critic.

73. *To Scudder Klyce*
January 6, 1929
Kingwood Park, Poughkeepsie, New York

Dear Mr. Klyce:

It's fine to have a letter from you again (although I wish you'd put more "family" news in it! I have a great interest in and sympathy for your wife, you know, and in the little Dorothy) and it's fine to know there's a new book of yours[1] available. Thank you very much for thinking of sending it to me. I shall be mighty glad to have it. On account of the health of my very old and frail mother, who is now in my care, we have come down from our rough little mountain cabin home in Vermont, for the winter months, and are at Kingwood Park, Poughkeepsie, N.Y.

I agree to your comment on *The Brimming Cup* if you are not meaning to say that all women are idealists and all men are realists. I have put on the other side of this page a clipping[2] that says something of what I feel in the matter.

The ideal mating is of an idealist and a realist, to complete each other; so of course being a man and realistic you think you like all women to be idealists. But if you were a man *and idealistic,* I bet you a nickel you would gravitate towards the realistic type of woman, and think (as many men do) that women are the really practical members of the race, incapable of idealism but very useful for keeping things going smoothly.

I once wrote a book (*The Home-Maker*) intended to show the tragic (and quite unnecessary) sorrow and suffering caused by the blind pressure of public opinion which insists that all men are realists and all women idealists, and if they are not, at least they must make a life-long pretense that they are. The book horrified a good many people, but I had (among shocked letters) a good many which were written by people very grateful for a statement of and some sympathy with their predicament.

Send along your book. I'm eager to see it.

With warmest regards to you both,
Dorothy Canfield Fisher

---

1. *Dewey's Suppressed Psychology* (Winchester, Mass.: S. Klyce, 1928).
2. The article, "Each of Us Is Manly and Womanly" (author and source unknown), discusses feminine and masculine characteristics with reference to the opinion of Dr. William White. DCF highlighted the following sentence: "Much of the confusion on the question of masculine and feminine characteristics arises, Dr. White believes, from the tendency to regard the 'introverted' or inward-looking type of mind as essentially feminine, while the 'extroverted' type is essentially masculine."

74. *To Robert Frost*
[October 7, 1929]
[appended to October 7, 1929, CCTL to Arthur W. Peach: 3 pp.]
Arlington, Vermont

Dear Professor Peach:[1]

I'm not going to be able to go to Burlington for the 9th, and so am sending you by writing what I'd say about the proposed "Authors' League" or "Writers' Association." Since the meeting in Springfield I have been thinking seriously on the subject and have talked the situation over with several of the writers from this part of the State. It would be, I believe, an honest Vermont thing to let you and the committee which is deliberating on the advisability of an organization of writers know how I feel about it. I'm sure you won't make me feel unduly responsible by giving any more weight to what I say than it is worth—just a personal opinion.

I know I am not alone in thinking that one of the great, seriously great drawbacks to American life is over-organization. We have done wonderfully well as a nation by our competent organization of enterprises which can be organized and have improved American life in many ways by regulating our material life in an orderly systematic manner. But there is a well-known danger in too much reliance on organization, for there are many fine human activities—creative authorship for instance—which cannot be regulated in a systematic manner. It is hard for such intimately personal individual efforts as writing and painting and music to find a breathing-space and elbow-room in the typical American scene where everything else is done more or less in unison. Creative work cannot be done in unison to any degree whatever. One of the joys of Vermont life for me has always been that in this respect it is not the typical American scene. I have always thought there could be no more bracing and wholesome background for the inner struggle with his own limitations which is a writer's life, than the Vermont tradition of personal independence.

Attempts outside of Vermont to form literary associations have resulted as far as I have known them either in the United States or elsewhere, in the formation of social organizations, with the pleasant and unpleasant features of all social groups—never literary. How could they be literary, when writing is the most solitary business possible? It has seemed to me in keeping with Vermont honesty and fact-facing, not to have an organization which seems to offer its members something it cannot possibly give; which even runs the risk of wasting purely social contacts and in hopes for results from social contacts, their strength and resolution which is all needed, every fibre, for the hard business of mastering their art.

There is also, I feel, another danger in a formal Vermont organization of this kind, the danger that the sane and loyal localism which we all hope will always continue in Vermont might easily through it harden into self-conscious narrow sectionalism. It is hard at best to hold that balance true. It seems to me there is more chance that we Vermont writers may avoid the two extremes of colorless cosmopolitanism and self-admiring provinciality if we keep our relations to Vermont casual, spontaneous, personal and unorganized. [Handwritten in margin, keyed to paragraph above: "Oh there, Cady!"]

If I were on a committee considering the desirability of forming a Vermont literary association I should welcome the expression of opinion from all concerned, and I take for granted that your committee does, also. I have talked with Zephine Humphrey Fahnestock, Bertha Oppenheim,[2] Margaret and Walter Hard[3] and with Robert Frost, not only the greatest writer Vermont has ever had the privilege of claiming but a man of wisdom and much experience of conditions outside the state. I find that they all feel about as I do that it would be wonderful good fortune if Vermont writers instead of following those of other States along the well-trodden conventional road of organization could continue to do their own gait. It is a delight for Vermont writers to be treated as Vermont has always treated its authors, not as differentiated from other people but just as human beings and fellow-Vermonters.

But of course it is not for us to decide. If your committee thinks best to form a literary league, association or organization of some sort, we shall all acquiesce, will try to do our share, and will come to meetings as often as circumstances permit.

With warm personal greetings,
Sincerely yours

Dear Robert:

This is the letter I copied off (slightly better typing than this) and gave to Zephine Humphrey Fahnestock to take up to Professor Peach. I hope it's somewhere near what you'd like to have said and that I haven't expressed myself too strongly. I think Zephine thought I had, a little. I ought to have taken a little more time to writing it, instead of putting it off till the last.

Tell Elinor I have Saturday next at four written down on my calendar and also in my cheerful expectations. I'm so glad you two are near at hand.

Yours ever
Dorothy

---

1. Arthur W. Peach (b. 1886), American poet and educator, was Professor of English at Norwich Academy (Northfield, Vermont).

2. Bertha Oppenhcim, American poet.

3. Margaret Hard (1888?–1974), American bookseller and author, was best known for *A Memory of Vermont* (New York: Harcourt, 1967), an account of her experiences as owner of the Johnny Appleseed Bookshop in Manchester, Vermont.

Walter Hard (1882–1966), American poet, husband of Margaret Hard. DCF wrote the "Introduction" to Hard's *A Mountain Township* (1933). His *Salt of Vermont* (1931) is dedicated: "To Dorothy Canfield, who has seen to it that the salt has not lost its savor."

75. To Alfred Harcourt
December 12 [1929][1]
Arlington, Vermont

Dear Alf:

I'm sending back the biographical sketch with a few alterations. Those personal remarks in the first paragraph were very kind, and thanks to the person who thought of them, but I believe I'd rather have the thing less personal because I often have this leaflet sent out from here in answer to questions sent me. And so it may seem to the people who get it from me, that I'm talking about myself. It's bad enough to quote what other people say, as we do at the end.

The next paragraph I rewrote entirely, because of some mistakes as to dates, and the one after to take out another slightly too personal remark. I was ten years old when the family left Kansas for good, so of course didn't do any of my undergraduate work there. And Father was professor there, and president of Nebraska and Ohio.[2] The two poplar trees are dead, killed by the cold, and we are going to plant some new little ones next spring, but they may not live, so it's safer not to mention them.

On the last page, I wish you'd put in a little more mention of *Why Stop Learning?*. I'd like not to have people forget that book. I've said some things in it I'm glad to have said. Can't you find something brief that somebody— maybe John Cotton Dana,[3] who liked it very much—has said about it. I send along a single review I happen to have—no, I have two.

I've added a comment from a Danish magazine which somebody has just sent me. I like to be liked by the Scandinavians because I like them.

Which picture are you going to use? This is important because I get so deadly sick of looking at one I don't specially like.

My thanks to whoever wrote the little screed about *The Deepening Stream*. It's excellent.

Oh say, what do you think—the idiocy of modern methods of editors and magazines. Miss Lane has for some time contracted to take for the *W.H.C.* the next novel I write, and now has just signed a contract for the next after that![4] How dare they take such risks? Suppose I don't write anything more (ill health or cussedness or something) for fifteen or twenty years, and am then all out of date and favor and left behind by changes in taste? They'd still have to take whatever I wrote and pay for it. If I were an editor I'd never do it in the world!

It was fourteen below zero last night, and this morning ten below, in such a sparkling world of silver and blue that I can hardly bear to sit here at my machine writing to you. Mother doesn't even know it's cold—we have put double windows on every window, glassed in her porch, banked and weather-stripped and tar-papered all sorts of things, and her house (which has always been a Cave of the Winds in winter) is as tight and warm as can be. Not so ours. John hasn't gotten around to all those winter precautions yet. But I do hate high temperatures in a house, you know. And I'm certainly suited, right now!

I wish you could look out as I do and see the smoke from our kitchen chimney rising straight as an arrow into this crystal air.

Here's to you all—I hope Hastings[5] is out on skis somewhere this minute!

Yours ever
Dorothy

1. Date: appended, supported by references to "the screed" (advertising copy) for *The Deepening Stream* (1930).

2. DCF's father was chancellor of the University of Nebraska at Lincoln (1891–1895) and president of Ohio State University (1895–1899).

3. John Cotton Dana's review of *Why Stop Learning?* appeared in *Libraries* 33 (Feb. 28, 1928): 104–5. The review begins, "That is just the right title for a book on adult education; and the book itself is just the book to be read right now by every library worker. It is wise, witty and convincing. It is not an exhortation to librarians to busy themselves over adult education; for it shows that from the first days of public libraries, librarians have been helping adults to keep on learning."

4. *The Deepening Stream* and *Bonfire* were published serially in the *Woman's Home Companion*, June–Nov. 1930 and June–Nov. 1933, respectively. DCF received thirty thousand dollars for the rights to *Bonfire*. Gertrude Battles Lane, American editor (see Letter 41, note 4).

5. Letter 39, note 3.

1. Fisher in 1885, age 6.

2. *Fisher with father, James Hulme Canfield, at Columbia University, c. 1902.*

3. Fisher with mother, Flavia Camp Canfield, c. 1897.

4. Fisher with husband, John Redwood Fisher.

5. Fisher near the front in France, 1917.

6. Fisher with son, Jimmy, and daughter, Sally, 1915.

7. Fisher, 1917.

8. Fisher with husband, John Redwood Fisher, September 1942.

9. Fisher at home, date unknown.

10. Fisher's residence in Arlington, Vermont, 1936.

11. View from front porch of Arlington home, 1943.

— *Part 4* —

Letters, 1930–1939

76. *To Elinor Frost*
September 15 [1930][1]
[Andermatt, Switzerland][2]

Dear Elinor:

You can't know how much good your long letter of August 8th from Baltimore, did me! It came to me in the period just after I had received my brother's telegram, saying that Mother had died in her sleep,[3] when I was—although it would be wrong to grieve over Mother's release from her worn-out body—full of bewildered pain and *incredulity.* It doesn't yet seem possible to me that my mother, life-long intimate element of every plan I have ever made, is no longer there! I don't suppose I can really take it in till we are home again. It seems to me now that I will find her, lying quiet in her bed, as she has been for the last two years. Such news has of course been expected for years, but it was quite unexpected, too, for Mother's condition—except mentally—had not changed for a long time, and the doctor saw no reason for thinking that her end was near. Mentally she had failed greatly in the last year—but of the times when she was herself, she was quieter, more serene, more contented than I had ever known her—such a sweet quiet loving smile, as came on her face at such times— a new expression on her always-animated, restless face. In some ways, strange as it seems, this last year of extreme bodily feebleness and mental failing, was one of the best of her life. I am thankful she lived to have it.

It is hard, indeed as yet impossible, for us to readjust ourselves to this new phase of life, and I daresay it will take a long time to get used to Mother's absence. We are coming home as soon as Sally is installed in her Oxford college,[4] which is October 14. As soon as possible after that we'll get passage to New York. I do hope you and Robert will still be in the Gully. I do want to see you both, so much! It pleased me more than I [can] say that you like *The Deepening Stream*—gave me a big lift up! I am so overwhelmed by the manifold faults of my work, that I'm grateful beyond anything for opinions of people whose judgment I value, that it is a little better. If I could only stick to things, small things, like the *Made-to-Order Stories,* that are quite within my grasp! But no, I must go on tackling big themes! Its splendid that you like this last one!

We've left Jimmy in his pleasant, friendly outdoor German school,[5] but will return for a last glimpse of him before we go with Sally to Oxford—sounds like your trip to visit Marjorie and Lesley,[6] doesn't it. I am so deeply interested in Marjorie's success in her training, so enthusiastic about it and so proud of her courage and perseverance! I think she's wonderful. I wish I could see her! Think of her working in the children's ward, with responsibility for lots of babies at once![7] Give her my love when you write, won't you! And how I do hope we'll see you when we get back towards the end of October. My first trip will be to see you. My best to Robert as always,

Affectionately your friend
Dorothy

---

1. Date: reference to death of DCF's mother, Flavia Camp Canfield, who died on August 15, 1930, at age 86.
2. Letterhead.
3. See note 1.
4. Sally Fisher received the A.B. degree from Somerville College, Oxford University, in 1932 and the M.A. in 1934.
5. Odenwald-Schule, near Heidelberg, where Jimmy Fisher studied German.
6. Robert and Elinor Frost's daughters.
7. Marjorie Frost was admitted to the Johns Hopkins Nurse Training School in February 1929.

77. To Paul Reynolds
November 3 [1930][1]
Arlington, Vermont

Dear Mr. Reynolds:

I wouldn't need to hunt around for an idea for an article—gracious, no! I have several that are tormenting me to get written.

One came repeatedly into my mind all during this last summer of European travel, and during the reading of several very unfair French books about America. It is a meditation on one of the most frequent causes of international bad feeling, I think.[2] It is borne in on me, especially last summer as we wended our way through not only my second-home country of France, but Germany the Scandinavian countries and England, that every country, including our own, is (being human) made up of two strongly contrasted types of people. There are the civilized, decent ones that make you glad to belong to the same race with them, to be found in all classes, in every country I ever set foot in. And there are the odious unendurable cads and dumb-heads, also to be found in all countries and all classes.

I'd like nothing better than a chance to make a few thumb-nail portraits of both kinds, balancing up and pairing off the awfulness of certain European and American types and the delightfulness of others. I think something amusing and *true* could be done here.

Now it is my guess that most of the harsh judgments passed on all nations come from comparing one class in one country not with its corresponding class in another, but with another one altogether. From Sinclair Lewis's *Main Street,*[3] where no American civilization is conceived of as existing, to the opposite, the blatant American tourist who sees nothing decent in Europe provincials but with a small highly cultivated elite somewhere else; or else comparing European professional life with that led by small-town merchants in America etc. etc. It is positively laughable, how exactly they duplicate each other's mistakes. Americans are apt, you know, to think of French women as light-minded and pleasure-loving and travelling French people are sure that American women are utterly conscienceless about their home-making—always comparing one kind of French woman with another kind of American.

I have a life-time of accumulation of material on this subject and if you think an editor would be interested in it, I'll be glad to go to it.

Sincerely yours
Dorothy Canfield Fisher

---

1. Date: reference to "Motes, Beams, and Foreigners," *Harper's Magazine* 162 (Mar. 1931): 436–46, an article on international relations.
2. See note 1.
3. See Letter 43, note 3.

78. To Pearl Buck
November 7 [1930][1]
[Arlington, Vermont][2]

Dear Mrs. Buck:

Your letter and Mr. Buck's book[3] are safely here, giving me a very great pleasure. I know something about agriculture (living in a state where it is by far the greatest industry) and think I shall be able to make out a good deal of that learned book's priceless information. Not the graphs, probably! My generation is not at home with graphs, not having been brought up with them as my children are.

I am writing for a volume of Vermont information which I mean to send to Mr. Buck in the hope that he may find something of interest in it. You too perhaps, though you haven't your husband's professional personal interest in this poor and dearly loved old mountain state.

I can't tell you how happy it makes me to know that you too felt something of the impression so vivid to me, on meeting you, that we can speak together without misunderstanding, *at once.* It so seldom happens! A rare and lovely and heartening experience. It gives me more confidence in myself! We will be looking forward to your visit—don't talk about "a call." Can't you spend part of the Thanksgiving holiday with us? We haven't much to offer except the warmest welcome! But our small mountain home has several extra beds in it in the winter-time when the children are away at school and college, and it might interest Mr. Buck to have a glimpse of the way in which Vermont farmers "manage." Do come for as long as you can spare the time. It would be a joy to have you both. My husband joins me in the warmest hopes that we may have this pleasure. Christmas vacation would be quite as convenient for us, if it suited you better.

With every good greeting
Cordially and faithfully yours
Dorothy Canfield Fisher

---

1. Date: references to a book by John Lossing Buck, *Chinese Farm Economy* (Chicago: University of Chicago Press, 1930).
2. Place: implied.
3. John Lossing Buck (1890–1975), American missionary to China, educator, and government advisor on agri-economics. Married Pearl Buck, 1917; divorced, 1934.

79. *To Elinor Frost*
November 10 [1930][1]
Arlington, Vermont

Dear Elinor:

No, you've got another guess coming. Those men who wrote to ask me, as a R.F. specialist, some points about Robert's poetry, were not at all editors, or anything professionally connected with writing. One of them was a real-estate man (from his letter-head) in Philadelphia, and the other was a Chicago lawyer. Just sure-enough Readers, they were, authentic readers, people who buy a book to own it and read it—sometimes a fellow gets to thinking when New York has been yelling especially loud in his ear, that there aren't any such left, only professional readers, exhausted by their job, whose reading is their *gagne-pain* and whose fun and pleasure are golf and bridge. The last time I saw old Professor Phelps he showed me with a martyr's pride his study. You never saw such a sight! It was in autumn, just after the flood of fall books. There wasn't a place to sit down, hardly to set your foot. Books in their bright paper jackets piled shoulder high on a sofa and chairs and his desk. Thank God, say I, for the real-estate man in Philadelphia and the Chicago lawyer. I hope I have a few such who read my books!

I'll be delighted, if anybody will give me the chance to write a review of Robert's collection; certainly I can grab it away from H. Canby[2] for the *Bulletin of the Recommended Books,* for the book-of-the-month organization, and I understand that lots of books (relatively speaking) are sold by listing them there. Yes, I'll write tonight to them, asking for the job. Canby wouldn't let me, I know, do it for the *Saturday Review,* and I suppose he's right. He'd want a poetry shark to do it there. If anybody else from anywhere asks me to review it I'll jump at the chance. I hate to have Robert spend one of his author's copies on us, when I ought to be able to graft one off'n his publishers. Tell him not to send it, till I see if they won't send me one as a reviewer! There are so *many* people to whom he'll be having to send it.

I feel for you about that dress to be altered, for I'm far from gifted, myself, in that line. And Sally who's a wizard at it, is far away. We travelled with no baggage to speak of, this summer, I had only one tiny suit-case, so I couldn't buy anything in Paris where things fit me better than anywhere else. (The "small-woman" styles in ready-mades in New York are made for the small Jewess apparently, with opulent bust and hips, and they hang on me almost as badly as the big sizes). I got only a travelling suit,—and that's all I've got now, except a corduroy skirt and some shirt-waists, and that embroidered black silk dress which is now starting on its third year. It's perfectly preposterous! But I don't have to appear, as you do there in Amherst, once in a while. Maybe I can get an afternoon dress the next time I'm in New York. But I ache all over at the thought of the struggle that involves. Must be Skinner-Farmism[3] coming out in me, don't you think. I'll be wearing a felt hat with a hole in it, yet, as Nat Canfield does.[4] That reminds me, have you had the announcement card from Ruth, about her new son? Another James Canfield in the family.

I'm almost settled—that is, have almost disposed of the things that were waiting to be decided till I got here. The huge pile of periodicals I just carried out to the barn, still in their wrappers, to wait till I could look at them. And I find that such a restful way to dispose of such things that I'm going right on doing it. It's wonderful. It always did depress me to look at "literary" magazines, for instance. Their unopened brown wrappers are simply joys to me eye!

I'll see what I can do with the "neighbor" article.[5] I think the way we neighbor is true-Vermont, anyhow, once in six months. And that with no decrease of esteem or affection. But I do wish we *might* manage it a little oftener, and rejoice in your prospect of being here next winter. For we surely shall be.

What did you-all say to the Nobel prize in Literature? It made one happy man, if no more—Alfred Harcourt.[6]

My fingers fly madly along over the keys, probably turning out awful typing—to hear from you and to write you is next best to seeing you. I am sorry we missed you. But I don't believe I could pry John loose from Arlington for a while, There is so much here he *must* do before winter—you know how it is— and he was also wildly impatient to get back home. Oh well, I can just wait till you come back for something—or till spring—or maybe we'll be in New York at the same time.

With love to you all, as always
Dorothy

[Handwritten] I thought of course you had a copy of *The Deepening Stream* or I'd have sent it myself. When you wrote this summer that you'd read it, you know. I can easily graft one to send, and will at once. I'm so proud you want it.

---

1. Date: appended, supported by reference to Alfred Harcourt's pleasure over Sinclair Lewis's winning of the 1930 Nobel Prize for Literature. Harcourt was Lewis's publisher.
2. Henry Seidel Canby (1878–1961), American author, editor, and educator, was editor of the *Saturday Review of Literature* (1924–1936) and served on the BOMC Selection Committee from 1926 through 1955.
3. "Skinner-Farmism" is derived from the surname of John S. Skinner (1788–1851), the founder of the first agricultural journal in the U.S., *The American Farmer* (1819).
4. DCF's cousin.
5. DCF's essay "Robert Frost: A Neighbor of Mine" was published in *Literary By-Paths,* ed. Mabel A. Bessey and Monica D. Ryan (Chicago: Lyons & Carnahan, 1928).
6. See note 1.

80. To Fred Lewis Pattee
November 24, 1930
Arlington, Vermont

My dear Professor Pattee:
    Yes, I did get the *Creative Reading* booklet and read every word of your analysis with the keenest interest and appreciation of your friendliness and of the close attention you had given *The Deepening Stream.*[1] I don't think it's as autobiographic as you indicate—its handy, you know, to use as *backgrounds* scenes familiar to the author, but the people acting their parts before the background are often not at all the real ones who belong there. I do wish I had been there this summer to have a talk, or to write you a long letter about that question of yours. It would have been interesting to analyze the part which familiar backgrounds play. But in the long run, most novels are a sort of autobiography I suppose—even in my case such a novel as *Her Son's Wife,* which had in it not one single character or incident or background I had ever personally encountered. But that too, was a sort of imaginary autobiography, that is, I lived through in the character of Mrs. Bascomb what would have happened to me if I had been there.
    Is this pretty metaphysical? I think I mean something by it. And certainly *The Deepening Stream* is much more close than that. In a deep way you are right,

of course, since it treats of the growth of personality in a normal woman under such and such circumstances, there must be, beneath the surface, perhaps more than I realize of autobiography.

At any rate you've done a beautiful job of analysis and a generous work of appreciation, and I feel grateful to have such a sympathetic and understanding reader.

You didn't mention,—or did you?—no I don't think so—one element which I meant to be fundamental—the encounter in Matey's youth with evil in the shape of disharmony between her parents, which was a real preparation for her for the later encounter with cosmic disharmony. Conquering one, coming to understand it as a part of bigger whole, really strengthened her for the later part of a bigger whole, really strengthened her for the later test. Perhaps you thought that too obvious to need to call to anyone's attention? That was, to me, the base of the story.

One more thing, a small detail. I never felt, as a child that our family life was uprooted, although we moved from one town to another in the West when I was a little girl. The point was that I never felt that was our home at all, but that this particular piece of the globe where I now live, and where all the Canfields have kept a footing since they settled here in 1764, was our home, which never changed at all. Our travels here and there, were like travels to me, always. Arlington—no, not even Arlington but this very side of Red Mountain, was the stable thing in life. The description I gave of Matey's feeling uprooted is done from divination not from experience, and I take it as a compliment that it sounded so real to you as to make you think it something I'd lived through.

Well, the next time you're in Vermont, do come to Arlington and drive up our hill to our little shack and make us a call. I'd love to talk over a thousand things with you.

Cordially yours
Dorothy Canfield Fisher

---

1. "Dorothy Canfield's *The Deepening Stream,*" *Creative Reading* 3 (Oct. 1930): 578–91.

81. To Merle Haas

December 14 [1930][1]
Arlington, Vermont

Dearest Merle:

The photograph of your handsome Bob is here, and much gazed at by both of us, as we try to see whether it does him justice or not. We don't think it does,

although it is a fine thing. But something about the expression—life, perhaps—
is missed, don't you think? But we're delighted to have it, and have put it up on
the mantel-piece in our little living-room, to watch as we come and go and read
there. Why is it a secret? Christmas? Don't the children know it's taken? Anyhow I'll not tell them, or anybody, till you say it's "released" as the newspaper
people say. And thanks so much for letting us have one. Do you know what it
makes me want to do—to make a portrait of him, myself, in my own way, some
time, as I made a portrait of my father-in-law in "Adrian's father" in *The Deepening Stream,* or a portrait of you-know-who in Matey's father, Morris.[2] And by the
way, you are still the only people who know who, apparently, though I get a scare
once in a while. Willa Cather in writing me of the book was especially interested
in that character, said that the professor was simply absorbing to her, she found
him "absolute reality" etc., till it made me sort of nervous.[3] You two haven't
been talking in your sleep have you? Gracious! Will I ever be so taken aback as
when you asked me was it a portrait? I try hard never never to put people into
books so that they can be recognized—only meditate endlessly on their characters till I think I see what is the basis of it, and then put that alone, and no merely
outward circumstantial resemblance. Never till you two asked me so straight
out about that character, has anybody, so far as I know, guessed at one. It certainly did give me a turn! Did you see my jaw drop? Well, my father-in-law
wasn't exactly in detail like Adrian's father, but I think I put into the book what
was the basis of his character—at least what he meant to me. And someday,
years from now probably, when it's had time to mature in mind, I'll try my hand
at a portrait of your Bob, drawing a character that grows up into all sorts of
manifestations of the absolute essence of honor which is its root.

And speaking of writing things, do you remember an evening we had together last year, when you two told me something about the race-prejudice
which so absurdly complicates your lives and that of the children of the future.
I'd never happened to come in contact with it at all before—that particular
kind—and was as astonished as shocked at some of the things you told me.
Well, its been lying in my mind ever since, moving me to want to deliver a
blow at the vestige of barbarism that it is. I've circled around all sorts of ways
of doing it, and finally hit on the indirect way as the best one. Grown-ups are
like children, if you get their prejudices aroused, first off, they won't listen to
you—*can't!* So I started in from another aspect of the matter—international
bad feeling—and developed (or hope I did) a line of reasoning which insensi-
bly slides the reader along to a position in which racial bad feeling seems as
absurd. There's little or nothing in it about anti-Semitism—one reference by
name, to pin it fast—but an attempt to show how ridiculous it is to think that a
national or racial label on somebody really shows anything about *any one individual living human being in question.*

I've been working on it lately and finished it last week.[4] It goes to *Harper's,* but of course must go through Mr. Reynolds' office. I had it sealed up in the envelope to go to him, when I suddenly thought I'd sort of like to have you and Bob read it first and make any comments you thought helpful. So I pasted another label over Reynolds' name and its going to you. If you think it's all right, just send it along yourself, will you, to Mr. Paul Reynolds, 599 Fifth Avenue, marking it as coming from me. If you'd like anything changed, send it back here.

Much love as always
Dorothy Canfield Fisher

---

1. Date: appended, supported by references to *The Deepening Stream* (1930).
2. Probably DCF's father, James Hulme Canfield. Fred Lewis Pattee draws the connection in "Dorothy Canfield's *The Deepening Stream,*" which DCF responded to in Letter 80.
3. Cather to DCF, December 1 [1930].
4. "Motes, Beams, and Foreigners." See Letter 77, note 1.

82. *To Merle Haas*

[1931?][1]
[Arlington, Vermont][2]

Dearest Merle:

Just a line before starting in to autograph a lot of books that have been waiting for several days—what a funny idea getting authors whom you don't know personally to write in your books! What satisfaction *can* it be! To have Robert Frost put his name and a line down in a book he himself has given me—yes, that's something I'm proud to pass on to the next generation. (only alas! I don't value so darn highly most of the books autographed for my father, now I think of it.)

I've been glancing through another one of the eccentric French periodicals that come to me, and just on the chance that you may like to see what sort of thing they are doing, send it along. *Rassurez-vous,* I'll never send another! I subscribe to it because it is struggling for an existence, sponsored by some doctors I know, who are trying to use this means of spreading abroad some ordinary information they want to get to the public. Every year they think they'll have to give it up, on account of finances and then grit their teeth and stick it out another year. But it is so unattractively printed and published! Who would want to read it! Perhaps Bob might like to peruse the review of somebody's thesis on *les entorses du genou chez les sportifs.* It's a topic of burning importance to tennis players. They may be good doctors and public-spirited men but aren't they the unskillful editors and publishers!

I think of you every day and many times a day—with pride. I hope Betty will some day fully appreciate what kind of a mother she had. And I bet she will.

I'm having hard going with my writing just now—*priez pour moi* when you have a spare minute—approaching a crisis and trying to bring up four or five characters to jump the hurdle at the same time. They get out of hand, I find one slipped from my control, and rush to catch it before it gets loose altogether and by the time I have brought it back—are the others waiting patiently there for me? Not so you'd notice it, any. Some mornings as I start over to my writing-lair in the outdoor study (not the one in the pines, but the other one nearer the house) I feel a real panic, as though it were some great danger I were approaching—only ever so much more scared than *that*! So—to put it [in] yet another language, *sancta carissima, ora pro me,* in the intervals of your own big creative job. I bet you too feel moments of panic—let's swap prayers!

With so much love
Dorothy

---

1. Date: appended.
2. Place: implied.

83. To Margaret Sanger
October 4, 1931
Arlington, Vermont

My dear Mrs. Sanger:

Thanks for your invitation to be a member of the reception which your Committee is giving to Mr. Wells[1] on October 23rd. I feel myself in regard to this invitation as in the whole matter of birth control, in a position that takes a little explanation to be intelligible. It is, of course, of no consequence to people in general whether my position is intelligible or not; but since your invitation brings the matter up between us, it seems perhaps suitable—at the risk of boring you—to try to explain it.

I have just been considering a very tempting invitation to be one of an American Commission which is to travel in the Orient during this coming year, make certain observations about conditions there, and on returning to the United States, publish a report of their opinion on those conditions. I have just, very reluctantly, refused this chance at a most interesting piece of work, because, although deeply interested in the Orient and quite aware that our own welfare in the future is far more closely tied up with the welfare of Asia than was dreamed of in my youth, I am so ignorant of most of the innumerable elements of the complex Oriental situation, that I felt no confidence that my opinion would be sound, and so refused to assume the responsibility of giving a public opinion. And I feel that to refuse in the same way and for the same reasons to give a public opinion for or against birth control is the only wise and honest—though not at all dramatic attitude for me to take.

To have a valid opinion on any subject one needs not only to have sufficient first-hand information about the facts, but to have put a good deal of careful thought on those facts. In regard to the Orient and our relations with Asia (though I know the subject is of highest importance) and in regard to birth control (certainly one of the most important questions of our time) I have not the first-hand information about the facts, nor have I put on the few facts in my possession the thought that would enable me to guess at their importance in relation to the whole of two situations as complex as any that have ever confronted the human race.

It would have been perfectly truthful to write you simply that I have not the time or strength to give to public dinners and never attend them. But I have so great an admiration for your courage and whole-hearted devotion to a cause you consider vital to human happiness that I owe you, personally, an honest explanation of why I do not accept this invitation, rather than the easy evasive "regret because of previous engagements" with which one puts off a casual person.

Sincerely yours,

---

1. H. G. Wells (see Letter 21, note 2).

84. To Ruth Suckow
October 8 [1931][1]
[Arlington, Vermont][2]

Dear Ruth:

I can't remember just what I said about Mr. Knopf and the Book-of-the-Month Club, but whatever it was, it's yours to read to John Farrar[3] if it will help clear up your somewhat complicated business situation. And if you want any more like that sample (whatever it was) say the word and I'll cut another length off that piece and send it to you with all my heart. Yes, I did notice that a bunch of you were being sold around like baseball players, and I was rather pleased with the news, preferring very much to have you with Farrar than the *Cosmopolitan*. You know of course that Farrar is a Burlington Vermont boy.

I'm *glad* you are going to that State University conference, of which I have heard and which I am interested and where I'd be too, if there were only a few more of me than there are. Give Mr. Foerster[4] my best greetings, please, and all my good wishes. I do hope for a considerable success for his plan which sounds like a good one to me.

You'll get quite a surprise I think when you read the new Sigrid Undset book.[5] I did anyhow. She's a convert who is a genius, but the first-fruits of conversion all the same. I found it baffling and disconcerting.

I was writing Willa Cather the other day (we've been exchanging letters at a great rate this summer over an odd little matter of publishing a foolish young thing we did together a million years ago)[6] and happened to mention your last book[7] with the admiration I feel for it. She has just written in answer and says she is going to get it as soon as she comes out of the woods where she has been resting and meditating. All my men-folks found *Shadows on the Rock*[8] too dim even to see. It was really funny to see my brother, who is a class-mate of Willa's[9] and has always been one of her most loyal admirers, struggling to make anything out of it—"sounds to me like something to be read at a Catholic Sunday School picnic"—. But I didn't find it so. I think Willa was trying to write something in pastels instead of oils—and why can't she be allowed a change in medium once in a while, I asked my brother and husband? It was written during the three years that have been so hard for her because of her mother's slow dying. I think that ought to be remembered, too.

And—one last item in this madly hasty rattle—I shouted and threw up my hat when you spoke those wise words about "Comrade Jesus."[10] I think it is simply thrilling!

P.S.—that Massachusetts farmhouse where Neale spent his vacations in *Rough-Hewn,* was just down over the line between here and Williamstown—practically Vermont, really Vermont, you were right. Lots of sympathy about Ferner's[11] hay fever. Robert Frost has it frightfully too, and has to go up into New Hampshire or somewhere high at the hay-fever date, or almost perish!

John and I had dinner with Elinor and Robert the other evening, and had a grand time—except that about eleven when we simply could not stay another minute, being already far later than we ever go to bed—Robert was as usual just getting limbered up!

So much love
Dorothy

---

1. Date: references to *Shadows on the Rock* (New York: Knopf, 1931) and Norwegian novelist Sigrid Undset's (1882–1949) "new book," probably *The Wild Orchid* (New York: Knopf, 1931).
2. Place: no reason to doubt Arlington.
3. John Farrar (1896–1974), American publisher and author, with Farrar & Rinehart

(1929–1944), chairman of the board of Farrar, Straus & Giroux (1946–1974). Suckow's last book published with Knopf was *Children and Other People* (1931). Farrar & Rinehart published her next book, *The Folks,* in 1934.

4. Norman Foerster (1887–1972), American educator and literary critic, received an honorary Ph.D. from Rockford College (Rockford, Illinois) with Robert Frost and DCF in 1934.

5. See note 1.

6. DCF and Willa Cather published a short story, "The Fear That Walks by Noonday," in the 1894 University of Nebraska yearbook. A limited edition of thirty numbered copies, with a "Foreword" by Ralph Allan, was later published. *The Fear That Walks by Noonday* (New York: Phoenix Book Shop, 1931).

7. *Children and Other People* (New York: Knopf, 1931).

8. Willa Cather, *Shadows on the Rock* (New York: Knopf, 1931), book-of-the-month, August 1931.

9. DCF's brother Jim was a classmate of Willa Cather's at the University of Nebraska from 1891 to 1895.

10. "Comrade Jesus" is the title of a poem by Sarah Cleghorn originally published in the *Masses* (April 1914): 116; I have been unable to identify Suckow's "wise words."

11. Ferner Nuhn (b. 1903), American author, Ruth Suckow's husband.

85. To Paul Reynolds

January 29, 1932
Arlington, Vermont

Dear Mr. Reynolds:

Your prophetic soul gave a groan of misgiving, when I first outlined the plot of this new story of mine,[1] first told you it would be "ironic" in character. I remember well that you looked unhappy at that word. And my prophetic soul, as I told you at lunch last month, has been groaning ever since the depression over a premonition that that price was too high to be possible. The enclosed letter from Miss Lane[2] shows that we are not bad prophets. I insist that I am as good a one as you, for I feel in my bones that the price of the story is one element in Miss Lane's dissatisfaction with it, and naturally enough.

Honestly, she's wrong about its being any more for serial publication than any others of mine (they were all rather queer serials, *I* thought). It's just like all my work: *The Deepening Stream* had much less suspense element than this (in fact it hadn't any) must have been much harder for readers to hold in mind from one month to the next, hadn't any outward events. It did have a love-story—after a long long time of slow sledding, but every bit of the courting took place off stage and was left to the readers' imaginations. *The Home-Maker* hadn't any love-story and no suspense. And *Her Son's Wife* was solidly made up of thoroughly tiresome and disagreeable people, till towards the very end when Mrs. Bascomb became slightly more likeable and the little granddaughter emerged.

Of course it would be a waste of time to bring this up in an argument with

Miss Lane. It can't be argued about. And it would be equally futile to lay much weight on the testimony of a good many people who have read this Mss. so far and who have all found the quality of the writing the best I've done, and who moreover have all (except you) commented on its having much more of the suspense element creating much more eagerness to know what happens next than any of my other books.

That's not the point. I take it that Miss Lane is justifiably nervous about the whole magazine situation and naturally wants more certainty about the success of her serials than ever before. I think every point she makes in this letter could have been made equally well about any other book of mine, so that this one shouldn't have surprised her in the least. It must be her own attitude that has changed. But we'd get nowhere by saying that. I'm writing to ask you what shall we say? What is the best thing to do? I'm sending her today a non-committal letter, a copy of which I enclose so that you can be *au courant.* But before I see her, I'd like to hear from you. It's quite a serious matter for us both. What would you say to going to her with the enclosed letter? Mr. Fisher is not very enthusiastic about this, but is willing to if you think it right and wise—and expedient.

Cordially yours
Dorothy Canfield Fisher

---

1. The work under discussion is *Bonfire* (1933), serialized in the *Woman's Home Companion.*
2. See Letter 41, note 4 and Letter 75, note 4.

86. To Merle Haas
[February or March 1932][1]
Arlington, Vermont

Dearest Merle:
I did some shopping in the extra time in Troy, and with parcels in my arms like a commuter approached the train north at a little after one. I wasn't going to try to get into the chair-coach for that short trip—didn't know whether they'd have kept it all the time for a passenger who didn't appear at Harmon, but as I walked down the platform, the porter sprang forward with such a relieved, welcoming look, seized on my absurdly tiny bag as if it had been a Gladstone, and said, smiling all over his face, "Well, Mis' Fisher, I surely am glad to see you. I began to think you was *lost,* for fair." To my look (you can imagine how astonished I looked) he said, grinning, "I hear you got on the Empire State at Harmon this mo'nin'. Just would do it!" I cried out, "For goodness sakes, *how*

did you hear that?" And he said proudly, "Oh they passed the word along up the line. I was lookin' out fo' you here. They said you said you'd take the train at Troy."

Can you beat that? That's what it is to live in a State so small that it only has one express-train south and one north everyday. I didn't know they counted the passengers, one by one like that! And could you have *imagined* that on the New York Central, up and down the Hudson, they'd gossip like that! I was fairly abashed at having my idiotic mistake trumpeted around all over the place, and said peevishly, as he escorted me to my place in Car 18 Seat 21, "What do you suppose possessed me to make such a mistake! Of course I usually take the Flier down and hardly ever up, except sometimes in summer," and he even had a charitable excuse ready for me, a theory, based on some other people who had showed a confusion of mind inconceivable to me if I hadn't just shown a like one, and who, thoroughly mixed and confused by the shifting of day-light-saving time (never recognized you know by the N.Y.C. trains) had come an hour ahead of time to that train. But personally I think that was just Ethiopian courtesy and imaginativeness. I think he made them up for my special need. I still remain an imbecile in my own estimation.

I haven't read a magazine in I don't know how long, but seeing a *Harper's* on the newsstand at Troy, I remembered what Mr. Haas had said about that Alice Beal article,[2] and bought the copy. I like the article fine, and being the proud mother of two Odd Children and the wife of an Odd Husband, every one of whose differences from the common mould is cherished by me, I echoed loudly her defense of the Odd Child against the teachers of the new schools who certainly have the group-conduct idea so fixed in their heads that they can't ever remember there is any other kind possible for human beings. And then while I was about it, I read the whole magazine, saying to myself that a man as completely a man and a brother as that Fred Allen ought to make a good sheet.[3] And I liked it all, and thought maybe I'd even subscribe (although I don't take periodicals out of the wrappings much any more, except a violent Communistic sheet from Paris which gives me news of a corner of life I never would know otherwise) and when I got home, there was a letter from the energetic Mr. Reynolds, who had taken an idea of mine for an article on international criticisms, and sold it to *Harper's*. So I'm not only a convinced reader, all at once, but one of their writers, and if Billy Sunday[4] can beat that for a sudden conversion, let me hear of it.

One of the letters in the mail is the enclosed from Sally, and I'm sending it to you on the chance you may like to share a little in my children as I *love* to step into the world where yours live. You won't be able to understand all the allusions (Miss Darbyshire, for instance is her very Oxfordian Tutor. Frankie Folsom is a Rhodes Scholar at Merton, Frank Meyer is a Balliol man (British) and Eleanor is Eleanor Flexner, the daughter of Dr. Abraham Flexner—(the other American student at Somerville).[5] I repeat, you won't be able to follow all the allusions, and its not especially interesting, but it gives a picture of young life in Oxford, of a certain kind—and its Sally! So I just take for granted you will be interested in it. Send it back when you've glanced at it please, and *please* send me word at the same time, that your so-very-nice and so-very im-portant husband has, exasperated by feminine fussiness, been driven to go to a doctor who has given him a clean bill of health, so that he can laugh at my aunt-like intrusive anxiety!

Ever so much love, always,
Dorothy Canfield Fisher

---

1. Date: "midwinter 1931" is appended, but February or March 1932 is more likely, based on the March 1932 publication date of the *Harper's Magazine* under discussion.

2. Alice Beal Parsons, "Shall We Make Our Children Commonplace?" *Harper's Magazine* 164 (Mar. 1932): 489–500.

3. Frederick Lewis Allen, "Radio City: Cultural Center?" *Harper's Magazine* 164 (Mar. 1932): 534–45.

4. William Ashley Sunday (1862–1935), professional baseball player who became one of the most popular revivalists in American history.

5. Eleanor Flexner (b. 1908), American author. Flexner's works include a biography of Mary Wollstonecraft (1972).

Abraham Flexner (1866–1959), American educator who founded the Institute for Advanced Study at Princeton and signed Albert Einstein as its first staff member (1930).

87. To Paul Reynolds
February 25 [1932][1]
[Arlington, Vermont][2]

Dear Mr. Reynolds:

Yes I believe I could do an entertaining article with considerable sense in it on the subject of "Lo, the Poor Introvert!"[3] or words to that effect. I have long, now, been saying when I am asked to speak on education and child-life that the world has been helplessly in the grip of extroverts for the last century, and that there is a great danger in trying to force naturally introvert children into being chatty and sociable and gregarious and all the other extrovert virtues, forget-ting that there are greater and deeper ones of which they are capable. The loss from the modern world of religion has much to do with this, too, of course, religion being the natural stamping ground of the introvert. But could you sell such an article?

About Miss Lane[4]—it's by no means so cheery as you take for granted. She was sweet and cordial and nice as only she can be; but she was from Maine, every inch of her. She listened attentively to the story as I told it to you, and said at the end "But that is a very cynical disagreeable story!" It's just the same one I told her a year ago. And "The central figure is this intensely disagreeable girl in whose place nobody would want to put herself." I said something about the great success both as a serial and as a book of *The Red-Headed Woman*[5] which gave her a little pause, maybe. But only a pause. I agreed to rewrite the first chapter—perhaps the first few, and to give at once to the reader the information about why the young doctor is so grumpy, and to change the time of day when he and Lixlee are shot from the compromising two o'clock in the morning in her bed-room, to nine o'clock in the evening and in the kitchen. But I do NOT think Miss Lane is reassured. And neither am I, not really. But I am an author, and the moment I got back and set to work on the story I forgot all about her and the chance she may think it impossible, and have been ploughing away in my own perverse fashion, doing it as I want to do it, with in the back of my mind, the notion that I'll do a whole other version, more or less, for her, making the action more direct and taking out all the local color etc.[6] That's where we stand. I write you as I always do, just as it seems to me, pouring it all out, and hoping you'll get it straight. There's nothing to do but to go ahead and see what happens. I'll write you again about how I get on, in about a month—time enough to let Miss Lane know if I can't deliver it in June.

I enjoyed that lunch with you, very much, though it did give me too confident a feeling about Miss Lane—for she did not react, seemed to me, at all in as much relieved a fashion as you did, on hearing that action and goings on.

Well here's hoping—no bones will be broken, no matter what happens.

Always cordially yours
Dorothy Canfield Fisher

[Handwritten] Oh, say, I *hate* to bother you, and I wouldn't only I've been bothered—a friend of my husband's sent me the enclosed story for me to send to a magazine. *Could* you or Revere[7] glance at it, and address the envelope to whichever magazine you think would be most likely to be interested and drop it in the mail-chute? It won't compromise you, at all. I don't know the author, nor anything about her—she's only a friend of that friend of my husband's. An imposition all around.

---

1. Date: stamped "received 27 February 1932."
2. Place: no reason to doubt Arlington.
3. "Lo, the Poor Introvert." *Harper's Magazine* 166 (Dec. 1932): 77–85.
4. See Letter 41, note 4.
5. Katharine Brush, *The Red-Headed Woman* (New York: Grosset & Dunlap, 1931).
6. In the book version of *Bonfire* (1933), Anson Craft and Lixlee are shot at 2 A.M. in a

bedroom; the time and location are unspecified in the serial version published in the *Woman's Home Companion* (June–Nov. 1933). See Letter 75, note 4.
    7. Paul Revere Reynolds, Jr., American literary agent.

88. To Alfred Harcourt
March 1 [1932?][1]
[Arlington, Vermont][2]

Dear Alf:
    Why, I answered that Doremus letter direct to him—I thought it would be nice to do this. And I'm afraid I didn't keep his letter after my answer had gone out. That was funny—that old business coming up after so long. The point was that at the time (years and years ago) I was writing so many stories and *Munsey's* were accepting so many, they hardly knew what to do with them all. Magazine etiquette is strongly against using two pieces by the same author in the same issue (why?) and so for a time when they used two of my stories they attributed one to a made-up Stanley Crenshawe. I didn't see any harm in it, but after a few times I asked them to stop because I got tired of explaining to fan-letters writing to Stanley Crenshawe, who I was. I remember I had a letter from Reynolds (who was already my agent) saying he had been struck with some story or other appearing under that name and would like to be Stanley Crenshawe's agent. So I called them off and haven't thought of it since. For an instant as I read Mr. Doremus' letter I was stumped—only something very vague stirred in my memory and then it all came back. What *does* anybody do who has something really to hide??? Everything seems to come out—that awful old story of Willa's and mine,[3] and now this absurd little quirk.
    Yes, that's grand news about the sales of those two books.
    I hope you all four are well, especially Hasting's wife. My best to Ellen.

Yours always
Dorothy

---

    1. Date: appended.
    2. Place: no reason to doubt Arlington.
    3. "The Fear That Walks by Noonday" (see Letter 84, note 6).

89. To George Palmer Putnam
March 22 [1932][1]
[Arlington, Vermont][2]

Dear Mr. Putnam:

I have had, as usual, a number of manuscripts and proofs on my desk wait-ing to be read, and knowing from your letter that Miss Yezierska's novel[3] was not to be published till next autumn, I felt there was no hurry about it, and have only today opened the package of galleys of her so finely-named book.

I have just now laid them down, and turn to my typewriter to write to you that I think the book much improved since I saw it, although still, it seems to me, much too close to exact portraiture of individuals. You know that was what I told Miss Yezierska when she showed it to me a year ago, that I thought she brought over into her book from life too many details of personality that are literally like the originals in her mind. I know that she has been making a real effort to make a change in this respect, or at least she has talked to me a good deal about understanding more about the desirability of making her char-acters less easily identifiable.

However, this is of course no responsibility of mine, and is something for her to decide. I mention it to you since you ask for my word on her work.

But I do feel very strongly that in the last part, the last chapter really, which is a description of her life in Arlington and some of the people she has met here, she has left in some touches which, if published as they now are, would really pain some of the village people who have done what they could to be kind to her. She is so kind and warm-hearted herself, I am sure she would not wish to do this, especially since the changes are rather minor.

Nobody of course has any right to offer unasked for advice to an author so I shall, in writing her now, only say that I have some ideas about minor changes in the last chapter, and ask if she would be interested in having me write her in detail about them.

I'm telling you this to let you know I hope, if it does not conflict with your convenience too much, you will feel like postponing making the page proofs till I have had a chance to hear from her.

With best wishes
Sincerely yours

---

1. Date: based on the publication date of the novel under discussion, Anzia Yezierska's *All I Could Never Be* (New York: Putnam, 1932).
2. Place: implied.
3. See note 1.

90. *To Paul Reynolds*
March 28 [1932][1]
[Arlington, Vermont][2]

Dear Mr. Reynolds:

I have a letter from Miss Lane,[3] a very nice one as always, saying that times get worse and worse, and that "this last week the bottom apparently has dropped out of business all of a sudden" etc. She says they have all had a substantial salary cut and have been asked to cut prices and size of books to the limit. "This does not of course apply to prices that have been contracted for such as the serial you at present are working on for us. It may be an absolute necessity however, for me to ask you for a reduction in the serial to follow this if in the future you do one. If by any chance you should decide to postpone book publication of your serial it would be a godsend as the problem of cutting on the new book sizes is going to be terrific. If however, you are able to finish it we shall keep to our bargain."

This probably won't surprise you, close to the field of combat as you are. Nor does it surprise me. I will write her (after I have heard from you) that I will postpone getting the serial in her hands till six months after the date promised—this will bring it in January of next year.[4]

Now I would also like to write her, as I have wanted for some time, that I would like to make a reduction in the price of this serial. But I want your opinion on this of course. My feeling is this: "It was contracted for at the peak of prosperity and since everything else has shrunk since then why should that stay the same?" Mr. Fisher retorts, "If prosperity had gone on swelling, and prices had risen, there would have been no talk of raising a price contracted for. Why should there be now?" I feel that this depression is the sort of thing that breaks all precedents, and logic too, and really would like to do this if you don't feel too strongly against it.

If you do agree to it, how much do you think would be enough to make a real difference to Miss Lane?

In any case I'll write her that I'll postpone delivery for six months. And I'll try to rewrite it, having the extra time for it, so that she won't have such a tough job of cutting. I don't mean to cut it myself, but really prepare a version for serialization different in technic from the more leisurely presentation I usually employ.

Let me know, will you what you think of this, and any odds and ends of information you have that bears on the matter.

Always cordially yours
Dorothy Canfield Fisher

1. Date: stamped "received 29 March 1932."
2. Place: no reason to doubt Arlington.
3. See Letter 41, note 4.
4. The work under discussion is *Bonfire,* serialized in the *Woman's Home Companion* (June–Nov. 1933). See Letter 75, note 4 and Letter 87, note 6.

91. *To Anzia Yezierska*
March 31, 1932
Arlington, Vermont

Dear Miss Yezierska:

Your letter is just in, saying you would like to know in detail what came into my mind about the last part of your novel,[1] and I hasten to set down my ideas and forward them to you by air-mail as you suggest.

First I will say what I thought you intended this novel to be—the story of the struggle towards understanding and spiritual peace of an ardent impulsive girl capable of thought but not at all naturally given to it. She is obsessed by the miseries due to race prejudice and can't see anything else wherever she turns. After many experiences, all beginning in ardent emotion on her side and ending in disillusion and sadness for her, though with faint glimmers of a meaning in her experiences not wholly grasped by her, she finds in a little old-American country village the same sort of feeling that some are inferior and some are superior which she had thought came from race feeling alone. She sees the problem then as one of the major ones of humanity, all humanity, to be solved by everybody's learning to see and understand the other person's point of view, and coming to know that other people even of very different temperament and gifts have contributions of value to make to the human whole.

I hadn't seen the ending you wrote but supposed from what you told me of it that you meant to use the wanderer to bring into her life someone who, by firmer grasp on this conception of life and by a more complete and impersonal hold of it would strengthen and confirm her own groping notions of it. I had supposed you meant to show, when the villagers wouldn't let him in, and when Fanya fell instantly back into her old fixed habit of scorning and hating and looking down on people who didn't do as she thought they ought, that the wanderer, a riper and stronger soul than she, would recall her to her dimly glimpsed ideal of understanding, would, for instance, just reasonably put to her the many perfectly good reasons why country people with an age-old habit of seeing only familiar faces, should, in a world so filled with violence as the modern world, hesitate to take an unknown man living the traditionally irresponsible life of the roamer, into their homes. I expected this so confidently from what you said about it that I even thought I recognized the place where the great dramatic turn away from her old habits of thoughts would be made, when she says the villagers have thimble minds etc. I thought the wandering philosopher would say "But see here, they are human and so they have minds like yours. Aren't you showing a thimble mind in passing such hasty judgment on them? Put yourself in their place, think what you would be with a century and a half of static life back of you in which the ebb and flow of the gypsy-element of change has played no part etc. etc. Just see how it looks to them etc. etc." Instead of which he seems with his "But why let thimble minds hurt you?" to agree with her that those complex human beings can be safely condemned because of one action, to fall in with her own superiority-complex which has caused her so much pain in the past, her feeling that what she wants is righteous and if other people don't want it it can only be because they are small and mean and not generous and warm-hearted as she is. The wanderer might even—something the reader thinks at once,—point out that the fact that he is presented by Fanya (by that time the villagers would have learned that many of her standards were not familiar to her and hence would have felt that they could not tell beforehand what she might do in any circumstance) that his presentation by Fanya might have made them less willing to take him in than if he had presented himself alone, or better yet, following the local folkways always the wise thing to do, had gone to a local official, told his story, given the official in this way a chance to gather an impression of his personality, and to decide which family would be most likely to take him in. At this point I had thought—this from what you had told me of the ending—Fanya would be struck by the strength of soul he shows in being able thus to see the other person's point of view when *he himself is uncomfortably involved*—something the poor girl is so little capable of, herself—would for the first time really if only for a moment see and respect another point of view than her own, would recognize in the wanderer a soul farther along the road than she, would feel the possibility that he might mean much to her in the future, and would look forward with an intuition of happiness to come, to the possibility of creating with him a beautiful human relationship, would feel that at last her tempestuous soul has found someone to help her develop without bitterness and scorn her own natural gifts for free and spontaneous feeling and action, and to help her make a contribution to life of real value.

I can't but feel that the present ending, their becoming almost at sight, actual physical lovers, will make your readers think that they have been mistaken in thinking that Fanya is a rare personality, will make them feel that she is only that common phenomenon a woman looking for a lover to satisfy her heart and body, rather than that rare human being looking for some meaning in the wretchedness of life that will satisfy her mind and soul, as well as her heart and body. Won't she seem to the reader to be doing with this wanderer just what has brought such misery to her right along—ignoring the element of growth and time in human relationships, trying to snatch a blossom from a relationship of which she has only just planted the seed. Experienced people will say "She is just going around and around the same vicious circle. This too will end as badly as all her other attempts to love and be loved." I should think an intimation—a delicate faint one—in Fanya's mind at the end, that some-time—and that now she can wait on growth with trust instead of grabbing what needs time to develop—I should think that would be a more artistic end-ing and would much more accurately produce the effect you wish. Unless in-deed you *want* to indicate that poor Fanya is really and truly doomed by the limitations of her personality, and never will do anything all her life but make too-snatching beginnings which all end in the same disheartening way? But no, I am sure you meant the book to show a movement forward.

Then, I think that Harmon West is still pictured so exactly and literally in all details—save the one that he is a man and your dairy farmer is a woman (and by the way she simply couldn't have been a woman in New England. No New England woman would ever attempt with her own hands to carry on a dairy-farm with no help etc.) that he and everyone else in Arlington will see that he is described as a filthy outcast—and I am sure that would deal him a deadly blow of pain, and he is so harmless and humble and gentle an eccentric that I can't bear to have that happen. I am sure he has no idea—who of us has—that he looks from the outside as you describe him. To have the dirt and disorder of his poor home and person so photographed and displayed to the big world—it would cause him the most painful humiliation. I know, I know you show that you as an author think the villagers mean and narrow and unimag-inative not to overlook his eccentricities, but that would seem to him only your personal notion, which might or might not mean much to him. Whereas the picture of those eccentricities present the facts of his life—suddenly presented to him as other people see them. It would, I am sure, seem to him and to everyone else that it would have been infinitely kinder not to take those facts out of their familiar setting and obscurity and hold them up for all around the world to see. A more complete transposition would of course do away with this difficulty and would not, I should think, be at all hard to do.

You asked me to "tell anything and everything that occurred to me" and I have hurried to my typewriter to do that, and to catch the first mail out, though if the book is not coming out till autumn I should think there would be no extreme haste.

I don't want to waste your time in apologizing for making such suggestions about what is no concern of mine. I take you at your word as I know you want to be taken, and put this quickly tapped-off epistle into the envelope without re-reading. I do hope your sister's difficulties are lessened.

Hastily, faithfully yours
Dorothy Canfield Fisher

---

1. The work under discussion is *All I Could Never Be* (see Letter 89).

92. To André Maurois
April 7, 1932
Arlington, Vermont

My dear M. Maurois:

I am rich indeed in these days, with two books of yours in the house—*Le Cercle de Famille,*[1] so precious to me with its gracious autograph on the fly-leaf, and the translation *A Private Universe.*[2] I read the first in one long fascinated seance, coming back from New York after the last meeting of the Book-of-the-Month Committee; and have been keeping the second on my desk, reading it slowly, and keenly savoring its rich mellow wisdom and the astonishing under-standing of varying racial mentalities which marks your attitude beyond that of any writer I read. *Le Cercle de Famille* has been passing around my own *cercle de famille,* from one enthusiastic reader to another, to the tune of enchanted comments on this or that particular phase of the book. My sister-in-law, a most intelligent French woman who knows French life at first hand, was struck by the art with which you created the whole of a French town and its inhabitants, so that one walked around its streets and heard its clocks strike as if in real life. My husband found the conversations on politics and the European situation in the latter part of the book, the only real intelligent talk he had ever found in a novel—and exactly like the talk of really intelligent men of differing points of view. And I had no choice between one part or another—except perhaps that I found the very beginning, the scenes at the seashore full of poignant beauty that was poetry as well as the most expert delineation of character. Thanks so much for sending me this copy. I am honored to have one with your autograph.

I have been meaning to write you ever since your last visit to the United States—first to thank you for the pleasant picture you give of some of the pleas-ant sides of American life—like the delightful little vignettes from Princeton which to my delight I find again in *A Private Universe.* And then to tell you of a story about you which is going the rounds in America, which may please you, and which you may not know—at least not from the point of view from which it is told. An intelligent middle-aged American, a successful professor of chemistry by profession, but with a cultivated interest in literature, wanted to hear you speak—I think it was on Balzac—and noting that you were announced as lecturing somewhere in New York, looked up the place where it was to be, and taking with him a professor of English Literature, also a man of taste and cultivation, went there at the appointed hour. I don't know where it was— perhaps at the French Institute?—but evidently some mistake had been made about publicity and people did not realize you were to lecture there. The audience consisted of a mere handful of plainly dressed women—school-teachers by their looks. The two experienced men were at once deeply interested in seeing what your reaction would be to this, telling themselves that if the lecturer had been an Englishman of your distinction, he would have felt no compunction in showing brutally by a rough scornful slighting manner, his resentment of such a lack of appreciation, punishing those who were there because of the absence of those who were not as is the frequent practice of public speakers. I don't know that the two Anglo-Saxons went so far as to make a sporting event of the episode, and in the Anglo-Saxon manner make bets with each other as to what you would do, but they awaited your arrival on the platform with as lively an interest as ever they felt in any drama. When you appeared on the platform, they said, you gave not the faintest sign that you so much as noticed that the audience was not large and distinguished, but as animated and alert, and attentive to the matter in hand as if the finest critics in the world were before you, you proceeded to give of your richest and most sparkling best for an hour—lavishing on those shabby humble and now dazzled teachers as much care and thought and attention and personality as if you had been addressing Carnegie Hall. Certainly you can never in all the course of your public speaking have had before you more utterly admiring listeners than the man of science and the man of letters who came away proclaiming, "There is civilization! There is the fine flower of a fine root! There is delicacy and conscience and an imaginative good-breeding that justifies the claims of France to being the home of civilization," etc., etc.—The pretty story has spread like the circles around a stone thrown into a pool of water, and has gladdened everyone who has heard it. Having been in America and having heard stories of the way in which some English (and German) lecturers have treated their American audiences, you can perhaps imagine the impact which this graceful act of yours has made—an act, I daresay, which seemed to you the simplest of common decency. I thought you might be interested in this incident, and have meant, as I said, to write you before about it. But the multiplying of letters is one of the fatigues of modern life, and I hesitated to add to the size of the bundle which must arrive every morning on your desk. Feeling justified in writing you because of *Le Cercle de Famille* I add this account of an evening of yours which you have probably forgotten, but which will not be forgotten by many admiring Americans.

With every good wish and hopes that you may soon be returning to these shores,

Sincerely yours,

---

1. *Le Cercle de Famille* (Paris: B. Grasset, 1932).
2. *A Private Universe,* trans. Hamish Hiles (New York: Appleton, 1932).

93. To Thomas Dinesen
August 12, 1932
Arlington, Vermont

Dear Mr. Dinesen:

Yes indeed I remember every detail of my short visit to Copenhagen a couple of years ago, and can still see you as you came down the long wharf to meet our aeroplane when it came in from Lubeck. Any connection of my dear Mary Westenholz[1] would never be forgotten by me, you can be sure of that.

I have read your sister's stories[2] with extreme pleasure and interest. I had not thought that anyone could possibly use a language not his own with the sureness, richness, ease and subtlety shown by your sister. They are quite strikingly fine in quality—although I feel, perhaps rather obscure and complicated as to the construction. But that obscurity is a charm for many people, (I am among them,) and I don't think it will be a drawback for those capable of delighting in the unusually fine quality of the writing and of the reflections contained in these extraordinary tales.

A friend of mine, who is one of the best New York publishers,[3] was visiting us when the stories arrived, and hearing my exclamations about the quality of the writing, he began to read them, and has taken them back to New York with him to show them to his partner. He agrees with me that there is little possibility that any magazine could use them serially, (they are too long, and with too little of what is called "narrative interest" for that, we both think) but the book publication by an American publishing house is apt to be rather more profitable to an author than the British publication. Although of course in this miserable year of depression and failure everywhere, it is impossible to predict anything at all. At any rate, if he is interested I will have him write you direct about any proposition he feels able to make.

There are, as you suggest, some grammatical mistakes in the English; but some of them positively add to the exotic charm of the style, and the few others could easily be corrected, by anyone whose native tongue is English.

When I have heard definitely from the publisher who is now reading the stories, I will write you again about the matter. In the meantime let me thank you for letting me see this most original and unusual work.

Dorothy Canfield Fisher

---

1. Aunt of Karen Blixen and Thomas Dinesen. *Fables for Parents* is dedicated to her.
2. Under discussion is an early manuscript of *Seven Gothic Tales,* which was later published by Random House (1934). See Karen Blixen and Thomas Dinesen entries in Notable Recipients.
3. Robert Haas of Random House.

94. *To Paul Reynolds*

December 5, 1932
[Arlington, Vermont][1]

Dear Mr. Reynolds:

I'm sending down to you under separate cover some stories written by a Danish connection of mine. They seem to me most original, strange, interesting and rich in texture. Whether any publisher could be found for them is another matter. Would it be asking you too much to look at them and see what you think? If you agree with me that they are worth doing something with—trying, at least—will you see what some publishers think about them, and greatly oblige me? The author, the Baroness Blixen, would like to have them published in magazine form. If not that, in a volume. Will you see what you can find, and many many thanks as always from

Dorothy Canfield Fisher

---

1. Place: implied.

95. *To Paul Reynolds*

[Mid-December 1932][1]
[Arlington, Vermont][2]

Dear Mr. Reynolds:

No I don't think you were at all too drastic in your remarks about [the] short stories. I understand you. And I feel for you. But I go right ahead bothering you relentlessly. I too don't think really that the Blixen stories could possibly be taken even by the most "literary" of our magazines. And I don't know whether any publisher would be interested in them. Don't put yourself to much trouble about them. The opinion of two or three readers should be sufficient indication, I think. Just pass these on to me when you get them, and we'll call it a day and many thanks. I think it would be well to try the most literary-minded of the publishers—for instance, Knopf—don't you.

Hastily and gratefully yours
Dorothy Canfield Fisher

---

1. Date: DCF is responding to Reynolds's letter of December 8, 1932.
2. Place: no reason to doubt Arlington.

96. To Paul Reynolds
[January (19?) 1933]¹
[Arlington, Vermont]²

Dear Mr. Reynolds:
Just send back those Baroness Blixen stories to me. We've definitely established the fact that everybody thinks them charming—and not publishable at the present time.

I like to have you give advice, and once in a while I take it, you must have observed. This is one of the times. I shall say nothing to nobody about being through with serials—I did *not* say through with long stories! I shall want to write other novels I'm sure. I meant through with the business of trying to please a magazine editor with a novel—the serial game. But I won't say anything rash about that. As you say, who knows what's before one—especially in these days.

As soon as I'm in shape to work my head again, I'll start in on the last revision of the book version of "The Bonfire," and after that write two or three short stories for the *Delineator* and the *American* or so I now think.

Cordial greetings always
Dorothy Canfield Fisher

---

1. Date: stamped "received 21 January 1933."
2. Place: implied.

97. To Merle Haas
[April (1933?)][1]
[Arlington, Vermont][2]

Dearest Merle:

Here's a letter that should have gone back to you and Bob long before. I don't know how it got marooned in my files.

The umbrella, and rubbers, which certainly did save my life that outrageously bad Monday, are also going back, lashed to a board, very soon. My satchel just came in, with the mail tag tied to it. I didn't know you could send baggage that way by mail! There are some things the poor old gov't is good for, anyhow!

Vermont is in its most heavenly mood this week—the spring flowers are here with a rush—hepaticas, blood-root, colt's-foot, arbutus—and my garden is like a lovely chamber-music piece, with the blue scillas for violins (exquisitely played by God) and the white crocuses for second-violins (bowed, say, by the Arch-angel Gabriel) and the golden crocuses—millions of them the violas, and the big dark pansies the 'cellos, played by all the hosts of heaven—those pansies went through the winter in my cold-frame and grew roots and roots and roots—four times the size of roots of ordinary pansies. And now they are let out into the spring sun, they leap into bloom big big velvety flowers, such as I've never had in my garden.

And when you look across the valley at the mountains, throbbing with color, with that mauve bloom of April thick on them, you think it is all foolishness to grow flowers because the mountains are more flower-like in color than any garden.

In short, spring is in Vermont. Words can say no more!

The Mears[3] waylaid me for news of you-all, and wanted to know how Bobby looks. I said he couldn't look better. Also that he had not forgotten them, which pleased them. Baseball is in the air. I see all the boys out pitching and catching till it's too dark to see the ball. Our four kittens are quite big now, with open eyes—and little Pinky their mother, showed that blood will tell,—the other night she transferred them all to our bed, just the way her grandmother used to cart her kittens around. I had thought her perfectly satisfied with the box in the woodshed.

(Love to Betty.)
And love to dear all of you, always, from your
Dorothy

[Handwritten] *Make* Bob tell me when he has a book that I wouldn't like to miss!

<hr>

1. Date: year appended. April is stated.
2. Place: stated.
3. Clif and Nettie Mears were Arlington neighbors of DCF.

98. *To Karen Blixen*
April 30, 1933
Arlington, Vermont

My Dear Baroness Blixen:

I can't tell you how remorseful I feel for the delay in answering your letter of January 22nd. It was caused by my great desire to write you fully about my impression of your work, which I greatly admire. But I have been really swamped by my work and correspondence this winter, physically unable to cope with it all, and now see I would have done better to write at once, as I am writing now, a brief note to say that I will be delighted to be of any service to you, will be honored to write a review of your collected stories when they are published and to see that they get as wide attention from reviewers as possible.

I do hope you will have found by this time an English publisher who will show more appreciation of those enchanting and curious stories of yours than our American publishers did. Not that they didn't enjoy the tales, and really appreciate the rare flavor of your style. But they couldn't get up their courage in the face of the depression to publish them. The trouble is, I think, that American publishing, like too much else in this country, is organized for operation on a large scale only. Our publishers say that they simply cannot, without losing much money, publish anything which can't be printed in large editions and sell many thousands of copies. English and continental publishers manage somehow to be able without ruining themselves to print smaller editions and find the smaller and more select audience—or so it looks from this distance!

Do let me know—if this is not adding a burden to the others you are carrying—what happens to these remarkable stories, and don't forget that I shall count it a privilege to review them, or do anything else I can to bring them to the attention of the many readers who would find the keenest enjoyment in them.

Yes, I agree with Mr. Haas and with several other people who read the stories, that a novel from your pen would be an event. But since I am by way of being a sort of novelist myself, I know something more than those gentlemen do about the vast expenditure of time and vitality needed to write a novel. If you are not in good health, and have just been through trying and troubling experiences, it would be madness for you to start in on the tremendous undertaking of writing a novel. But it would be hard for me to think of any literary event that would interest me more than a novel by you about the Natives of East Africa. The very thought of what such a book would be—with your extraordinary knowledge of that region, all warmed by your love for the people and the country—is exciting indeed.

I note that you speak of the possibility of your putting up a security to the publishers to assure them against any financial loss in publishing the stories, and that because of the rate of exchange it would be easier to do this in England than in the United States. At the rate our dollar is falling on the world's exchange, that will soon no longer be true. I would be so glad to see the book published in America! If it is published by an English firm, won't you let me know by which one, because very often American publishers take over a book already printed in England and give it American publication under their own imprint. I would like so much to help along such an arrangement.

And please be sure that since reading your stories I am more than ever at your service for any help that I can give. I know some English publishers too, if that matter is not already settled. With every good wish for your health and strength, and every hope that I may have the great pleasure of reading more of your work soon, and finally with renewed apologies for my unforgivable delay in answering your welcome letter,
I am

Cordially and heartily yours
Dorothy Canfield Fisher (signed)

99. To Alfred Harcourt
May 3 [1933][1]
[Arlington, Vermont][2]

Dear Alfred:

I'm ever so much pleased and encouraged that you like "The Bonfire"! That's the best of news! And I think your suggestion about cutting the first part is good. I'll do something with that, when I once more start at the beginning for the last reading and last touches.

I think too your idea about having the end papers drawn by somebody more than just a draughtsman is good, and that something very nice could be done by the right person. But I think Wallace Fahnestock[3] would be better to ask than Jack Knox.[4] I don't know whether Jack can draw at all. He paints agreeably but neither John or I could remember ever having seen a line of his drawing. And anyhow I see him so seldom it would mean any amount of writing back and forth. But Wallace does draw very very well—I like his line drawings much better than his paintings. He is right here close to us, so that I could see him often and easily, and he knows the Vermont mountains like the back of his hand. Do tell me how much the job would be worth, and price in hand, I'll drive up to Dorset and ask him. Till then, don't approach anybody else. I believe something quite good can be made out of that, and am so glad you thought of it.

I can't tell you how glad I am that you see that Lixlee is not just a wild-cat, but a human being with a heart and with pride of her own, totally misunderstood. A short chapter near the end will perhaps make the reader more aware of her side of it. Though I do not want ever (this just technical) to have anything shown from her side. She is the only character, you'll have noticed, whom you don't see from the inside. I wanted the reader to make up his own understanding of her from what he sees of her, just as he would in real life.

And *how* nice that you thought the Northern Lights scene[5] successful! It is the climax and turning point of the book, and it shows the old hand you are that you picked it out as such, even without having the last part to read.

So now I unmake the date with the draughtsman on the 18th—hoping that it will be Wallace Fahnestock up here. Just let me know, will you, as soon as may be.

Hastily, ever yours
Dorothy

---

1. Date: appended, supported by impending publication of *Bonfire* (1933).
2. Place: implied.
3. See Letter 35, note 5.
4. See Letter 46, note 3.
5. The "Northern Lights scene" occurs in part 4, chapter 5.

100. To Alfred Harcourt
October 5, 1933
Arlington, Vermont

Dear Alfred:
Thanks for your letter of the 3rd with its promise of the Rockwell Kent book and frontispiece.[1] (I feel for you, having to find a tube to send that, having stuck fast in many such a sending, myself, for lack of tubes!) I know I shall like both of them very much, and be glad to have them.

Thanks too for the invitation to stay overnight at Riverside and see Ellen's[2] school. You know that's something than which I wouldn't like anything better.

I'll see if I can't manage it some time when I'm in the city. But not this time as this is to be one of our semi-annual visits to Swiftwater and John's mother and sisters, and also Swarthmore, where I am to speak for their Forum. So my stay in the city will be something like the twenty-minute sojourn of September. But there are lots of other times.

Yes, I like that announcement, and I think Harry Scherman's review *very* kind, and well-put. But I'd *like* not to have the book spoken of as though Lixlee were the only character in it. And oh *how* I would like somebody to mention the fact that here is a siren who did not spring full-fledged from the head of Venus, so to speak, but started a human being with human feelings, and grad-ually by the force of circumstances and her own (at first hardly recognized by herself) gift for being alluring, was pushed into the role of siren. Nobody is ever willing to allow a siren any real human feelings, such as sorrow, or disap-pointment. John says if I wanted people to realize that about Lixlee—that she really *was* an ignorant girl at first, that she really was terribly in love with Anson, and that her life broke right in two (just as much as if she were a "vir-tuous" woman) when she found that he was incapable of loving her as she loved him—that I should have told them so in the character of the author. But I hate that sort of telling. When you show characters acting—oughtn't your readers to draw their own conclusions from their actions as you present them? Well, maybe some of them will. You certainly did, when you first read it—I remem-ber your speaking about the tragedy that her marriage was for *her,* as well as Anson.

Not that—for goodness gracious sakes—I think any of this should be put into a sales-announcement! It just came into my head as I rattled the keys here.

I thought you looked in super-excellent condition, the other evening—never saw you looking any better or more vital. Which the same, at our time of life, is worth commenting on!

Yours ever,
Dorothy

---

1. Probably an advance copy of Rockwell Kent's *Salamina* (New York: Harcourt, 1935). The frontispiece depicts the book's title character. In 1919, DCF loaned Kent money to buy a house near Arlington. She wrote the "Introduction" to his *Wilderness* the following year.

2. See Letter 57, note 4.

101. *To Harry and Bernardine K. Scherman*
[1934][1]
[Poughkeepsie, New York][2]

Dear Bernardine and Harry:

Jimmy and I are here for a few hours (we found a good dentist here in those three winters we spent here,[3] and still keep him.) and I am moved to write you a word about that story of mine "The Moran Scandal."[4] I'm afraid I sounded as though I were claiming to have "made it up out of my head" entirely and I didn't. I took it from life, as anything that's true must be taken of course; all that I did was to put a narrative of material facts (that I *did* make up out of my head) around something that everybody has seen and felt—the way in which, in thinking about men and women in love, everybody carries to an even greater than its ordinary intensity, the human unwillingness to consider the individual case on its own merits, and applies with a real passion some general rule, without the slightest examination of its general truth, or its particular application to the people involved. We all have felt this, suddenly hot in the air in the course of a chattily gossiping talk about acquaintances a bitter insistence (not in words, of course, but in voice, expression, flash of eye, tone of phrase) that nothing must be permitted to question the dictum that in love between man and woman, exclusiveness and possessiveness are all there is to it, all that makes it alive, all that makes it love in each and every case, and for *always,* without any possibility for growth and change.

What lies back of that quick savagery is, I suppose, something very vital to the race,—and to love. It is a quick instinctive defense of love from laxness, and looseness and general softness of fibre, because it must be tense enough to be turned up to a clear note, or it's not love. But that instinct to defend is all mixed and confused (human nature being what it is) with one of our worst, laziest and most cruel instincts—which shows itself in race prejudice, the instinct to make a rule and then apply it (without examination of it) to individuals, without examining *them*! One of my passions—which has led me into a good deal of championing children who are peculiarly helpless under this process, is for the honest look at any individual situation, act or personality, without applying, slam-bang, some rule of thumb that may not have any connection with *this* reality, and which once clapped down, precludes any sensitive or honest taking of thought about it. The law, "The Law", is bad enough, seems to me, with its enforced generalization and it is necessarily very bad indeed,—without having all the rest of us, ignorant and prejudiced and full of ourselves as we are, setting up little Supreme Courts where we hand down decrees based on precedent (of our imagination often) and rule, not on human consideration of the facts before us.

That's an abstract idea, of course (*but taken straight from observation of life*) and to anybody it, really, in a story takes every device one can lay one's hands on to keep the abstract quality out of it; hence the choice of the first-person narrator which always helps concreteness, and of the other elements of back-ground that might suggest that it was taken from actual material experience. And hence my enchanted delight when Sally Cleghorn asked if it weren't real—in the sense of being a literal transcription of an actual story. Well, I've worn you out with this scrawling—I who so seldom talk about my work with anybody am always pulled out of my shell by you two, I notice.

Jimmy continues very enthusiastic about the Russian possibility[5]—I never saw him jump at anything like that. I do hope John won't think we are crazy!

Thanks for considering him—thanks for liking that story. I hope I haven't spoiled it for you by all this, or bored you too much. I daresay I still haven't said a thing of what I feel about it—words are so tough.

Hastily—though you'd hardly believe it!—and devotedly yours
Dorothy

P.S. I hate to be secretive, but it might save me trouble with people I should have seen in New York and didn't if you didn't mention that I stayed over to Friday!

---

1. Date: publication date of DCF's "The Moran Scandal," *Story* 5 (Aug. 1934): 41–54. Reprinted in *Four-Square*.
2. Place: letterhead.
3. The Fishers stayed in an apartment in Poughkeepsie in the winters 1925 through 1927, partly to be near their son, Jimmy, who was attending a nearby boarding school, and partly to spare DCF's elderly mother the rigors of winter in Vermont.
4. See note 1.
5. DCF's son, Jimmy, traveled to the Soviet Union with author Maurice Hindus in 1934 (see Letter 102, note 6).

102. *To Ruth Suckow*
October 7 [1934][1]
Arlington, Vermont

Dear Ruth:

I was terribly put out when I saw that *The Folks*[2] was published, without my having seen it—for I coveted it as choice for the Book-of-the-Month Club. When I wrote John Farrar asking with some heat why in the world I hadn't seen it, I was told that "it came in late, too late for the B. of M. and was given to the Guild"[3] (I took this with the usual grain of salt one uses for publisher's statements, and thought probably there was something else I didn't know about) but that a copy would be sent me. And yesterday's afternoon mail brought me two copies, two—one from the publishers and one from the Book-of-the-Month Club for of course it is to be on their list, and you'd better believe I shall grab the chance to write the review of it.

Well, I had been (literally) dozing over a life of Oliver Cromwell,[4] which is one of the books-to-be-read this month.[5] I'm interested in Cromwell all right, but I am congenitally unable to read accounts of battles—you know, "the left front formed on the slope of Byrne Hill, facing the cavalry drawn up in something-or-other order—." John had come in to the study and seen my head drooping over the book, and had taken me to task—for he adores reading about battles. And then the mail was brought in with two copies, two, of the book I had been longing to see. And I started in—and behaved from then till a very late bed-time like a cat long deprived of catnip when a large branch is offered her! I rolled and purred and leaped around and revelled and wallowed in satisfaction. And I read and I read—snatched dinner—went back to reading. My eyes began to hurt (for I was gulping down the pages at top speed) and I remembered the oculist had threatened me with dire things if I didn't stop when a grain of sand came into my right eye. A grain of sand did come into my right eye—and I just read on and on. It got as big as a boulder—and I read on. My feet got cold (we haven't started the furnace fire yet) and I thought "This is mad! I might just as well finish it tomorrow!" But I kept on reading. I said to myself "Oh here is a section that can't be as good as the rest!" But it was as good. And finally I finished it at I'd be ashamed to tell you what hour of the morning.

Then I crawled stiffly to bed, but insisted on waking John up to exclaim. "It's great! It's simply wonderful! It's perfect! Oh gosh! what a pity the Book-of-the-Month couldn't have sent it out as a choice, they reach so many people." John said sleepily, "Don't forget that some people—some men specially—feel about that kind of work just as you do about accounts of battles." (He's always saying something dashing one's unreasonable spirits like that.) And I said, "Yes, of course, it has its limitations as every art-form has its limitations. But granted those, Ruth has filled her form with pure gold, heaped up, pressed down, running over. And oh the use of detail—combined with luminous light—*Vermeer*—a sort of anguish of pleasure in the exactitude and yet the transfigured quality—."

And this morning, with my right eye blood-shot and swollen, I'm sitting down to say there's no use my trying to tell you how much I like the book, all of it—the New York Village section is *just as good* as the rest—better than anybody else has ever done that, seems to me. You must be feeling proud and happy and *serene*. Don't try to tell me you are dissatisfied with it—you can't be!

I must be off to bathe that miserable eye in hot water—congratulations, *thanks*—I do hope you and Ferner are sometime coming our way again. We would so much like to have you—and we have any amount of room now that both children are away most of the time. A spare-room apiece if you wanted! Have I told you that I am a grandmother? Sally has the sweetest little baby girl, with a smile that would melt icicles, and the best of health. Jimmy went to Russia last summer, with Maurice Hindus,[6] and saw an eyeful. Do come to see us!

Congratulations and thanks some more.

Affectionately
Dorothy

---

1. Date: publication date of Suckow's novel *The Folks* (New York: Farrar & Rinehart, 1934).
2. See note 1.
3. The Literary Guild book club.
4. Probably Hillaire Belloc's *Cromwell* (Boston: Lippincott, 1934).
5. DCF would typically read fifteen books per month in her role as a member of the BOMC Board of Selection.
6. Maurice Hindus (1891–1969), Russian-born American expert on the Soviet Union and author of *The Great Offensive* (1933), book-of-the-month, Nov. 1933 (see Letter 101, note 5).

103. To Bernard De Voto
September 29, 1935
[Arlington, Vermont][1]

Dear Mr. De Voto:

I've just been trying to clear out my letter-files, and came across this note from you, which ought to interest you. Do you remember my having with me, the summer of 1932, some of the manuscript of what was later published as *The Seven Gothic Tales*. They'd been sent me by the brother of Baroness Blixen, who wanted my advice and help in getting them published. I asked several people whose judgment I respect to help me decide whether I'd have a good chance of getting them published, and to tell me what their impression was of the strange and unusual style. You were the only person who, at that time, liked them at all! I was interested just now to see with what unhesitating certainty you rate the quality very high indeed. I wish I could send some of the other comments! You'd be amused. But that would be too malicious. But take it from me, you stood entirely alone at that time, more honor to you. I think, as a matter of fact that this book was rather wildly overpraised when it did appear—it wasn't as supergood as all that. But it had certainly the most extraordinary *quality*— which you recognized even from that one short sketch.

I hope you're well, all of you; I wish your travels had brought you up our hill again this summer. Mine may take me in your direction,[2] or at least to

Boston, more often now than before, as my dear and only son is just entered for the long grind at the Harvard Medical School, God help him!

With best greetings,
Faithfully yours
Dorothy Canfield Fisher

Don't think of bothering to acknowledge this! You must be submerged in work.

––––––––

1. Place: implied.
2. De Voto was teaching at Harvard University in Cambridge, Massachusetts.

104. *To Robert Haas*

February 22 [1936?][1]
[Arlington, Vermont][2]

Dear Bob:

I've read the Blixen story,[3] and think I'll tuck it into Priscilla's[4] suit-case (how could it get lost that way? It couldn't.) to send it back to you the quickest and safest way.

I found it extremely beautiful. For me it had all the inexplicable glamour of her other stories, but with a straight-fibred sincerity very different from the somewhat perverse and twisted self-consciousness of the *Gothic Tales*. I can't imagine what anybody would do with one such story. You'd have to have enough to make a volume, but if you had—you'd have *something*! Her attitude towards the Negro—or aren't they Negroes? Anyhow the natives—around her, seems to me extraordinarily fine, penetrating, sympathetic, and with a complete lack of the usual pretense of "understanding" them wholly, which is balm to my heart. I am so much offended by most of the ways in which white people "take" peoples of darker skin, that I've been told there's no pleasing me—I *hate* people to look down on them, and I think people who look up to them in a muddled way as D.H. Lawrence looked up to the Mexican-Indians are being silly, I'm always bristling up with resentment because there's condescension in the white attitude towards them, and I think it is just as bad to overestimate them. In fact I don't know any other instance of finding a white person's attitude towards "natives" quite to *my* taste, as in this study, But not all of it. There is so much pure beauty in the writing that it fairly makes a lump come to your throat. The study of LuLu[5] is perfection! There too, I LIKE the author's attitude towards animals and their world. From the business point of view I dunno. There's no narrative of course, no movement. If you can afford the risk, it seems to me the great distinction of the work would make it a credit to any house to publish. As far as anyone can see from this one sample.

I have one small objection—just a notion—I'm sort of tired about hearing that [the] Prince of Wales ate dinner at her house. The last mention in the story seemed the work of a supererogation, in a manner of speaking. But this is personal.

Your little daughter is being—I'd hardly like to say the perfect guest, for she doesn't seem like a guest at all, just like a little girl who belongs to us, and to the house and mountains. I'm not being in the least motherish towards her, thinking she might like to be treated like an independent entity—I mean I have no suggestions as to things to be done—like goings to bed, or gettings up, or taking baths or anything. She does it all, all right—as well as anybody, and with manners which I call perfection because they are so natural and unconscious. In short we are enjoying her stay! The whole gang is off on Bromley mountain this perfect sunny winter day—the eight of them—two Mears, two Wymans (Harold and Edith) three Conroys[6] and one Haas—all on skis and crazy about the sport. Roger has no skis, and whatever my charms may be, I am *sure* that Priscilla would enjoy Roger's company on a picnic more than mine, and my skis, boots, heavy stockings, poles are just right for him, so off he goes with the others, with a radiant face that simply warms my heart to the bottom. They are to go up the Long Trail to one of the Green Mountain Club's open lodges, get fires started, cook their lunch (sausages, hot chocolate, sandwiches, doughnuts, marshmallows, bananas—what one might call a calorific meal, for folks who will have been ski-ing on a mountain) and ski around—perhaps go farther up the Trail, and back to the road by four. This brings them out while the sun is still high and before the cold drops like a panther into those woods, as the sun disappears. We are still having five or six below zero every single night. But now that the sun is higher, the middle of the day feels quite warm to me, not exactly thawing, but cosy and comfortable in the sun. This evening, if they are not all too exhausted by ski-running, we are going up to the ice rink at Manchester back of the Equinox Hotel, to a skating carnival (probably of very modest country proportions, with some fancy skaters down from Rutland). This will probably not interest Priscilla with all her skating experience as much as the country children. But she may have a chance to show off some of her new figures to their bedazzlement and delight. You and Merle were good to let the dear child come.

I'll look at the Silone[7] as soon as may be—I'm sort of swamped just now with fighting off demands on me to "lead" something or other—the fight of the strikers against the Marble Company, the fight against the new Parkway, goodness knows what—oh Joseph Conrad, how truly hast thou said "But I am not a wise man, only a writer of fiction."

I *wish* Merle could have come, but she wouldn't have seen much of her child if she had unless she could have followed along on skis, for Priscilla has spent almost every daylight hour since her arrival, on skis. She has on my ski-boots, by the same token now (an extra pair) and I beg to report Merle (who, it seems priced some ski-boots which were SIXTEEN DOLLARS) that Bass and Company of Maine make some perfectly good and properly cut ski-boots for four dollars and fifty cents. The prices of those Fifth Avenue stores on sporting goods is really beyond scandal! I saw some skis at Saks for $35! When at Hambro's in Boston, where they have the best that's made anywhere in the world, their highest price is $15 or $16, and you can get good skis for $12.50. Do remember anyhow, that for winter things, a Vermont general store, or a Bennington department store is the place to go, rather than New York—in the nature of things.

Love to Merle, always, she says not to send you condolences on the death of your aunt, as it was the ending of one of those terribly long illnesses—but all the same I do. Each death leaves a gap in the circle—you can reach the hands of those you love across it, but the gap is there.

Ever and always yours
Dorothy

---

1. Date: year appended.
2. Place: implied.
3. The work under discussion is *Out of Africa* (New York: Random House, 1938), established by reference to "the study of LuLu." Dinesen writes of her pet antelope in part 1 of the novel, "Kamante and Lulu," book-of-the-month, Mar. 1938.
4. Haas's daughter.
5. See note 3.
6. The Mears (see Letter 97), Wymans, and Conroys were Arlington neighbors of DCF.
7. Ignazio Silone, *Bread and Wine,* trans. Gwenda David and Eric Mosbacher (New York: Harper, 1937), book-of-the-month, Apr. 1937.

105. *To Paul Reynolds*
[October (8?) 1936][1]
[Arlington, Vermont][2]

Dear Mr. Reynolds:

Our letters about Miss Lane's decision must have crossed, both of us writing promptly.

Yes, I thought that probably putting in so living a controversial subject as race prejudice[3] would not be to her editorial taste. She is probably quite right—the readers of her magazine wouldn't like to have such a red-hot poker picked up in their presence.

Yes, that part of the story is an essential part of it. T.C., a highly intelligent man feels all through the first part of the story that he has been out of the real battle-field of human life, has been off in a safe corner, where there are no red-hot pokers lying around. His love for Susan is partly a fumbling reach for something to fill that void. Then when the ugly modern octopus flings a tentacle so far afield that it reaches his quiet little corner, his chance comes to strike a real blow—at a real risk to himself—for the cause of decency and human dignity. And that sends him on into the next phase of his life, very much more satisfied—feeling that he has after all made his life count for a good cause.

So you see, the story would lose its point if that strong element were left out. But I think it quite possible that most editors would react as Miss Lane did, that it is really too disagreeable a subject to think about—(of course one of my purposes is to make people, comfortable in their own remoteness from the problem, think about it!)—and to be mentioned in an audible voice.

Why don't you—just to show good will, show it to the *Ladies' Home Journal,* if you think they would like to have seen it, and then we could feel that we had not shut them out, because of the *W.H.C.* commitment.[4] And then, if they don't want it, as I'm pretty sure they won't, you might try *one* more serious magazine, I don't know which one, you'd know better than I. And if they don't want it, just send it back to me to work on at my leisure and in peace. How's that for a plan?

I hope I've made myself clear on the Jewish question. I think race prejudice is creeping in insidiously to American life (for instance I bet you a nickel that the Country Club of your own town of Scarsdale is closed to Jews—without regard to their individual refinement or desirability). I'm ashamed of it, and I think most decent Americans would be ashamed of it, if they stopped to think about it. T.C. is a decent American. Q.E.D.

Cordially yours
D.C.F.

---

1. Date: stamped "received 10 October 1936."

2. Place: no reason to doubt Arlington.

3. The work in question is *Seasoned Timber* (1939). The subject of racial prejudice is raised when the officials of Clifford Academy must decide whether to accept a million-dollar gift bequeathed to the high school by a wealthy trustee on the condition that they not enroll Jews. Timothy Coulton Hulme ("T.C."), the principal, leads the successful fight to reject the gift, book-of-the-month dividend, 1939; alternate, Jan. 1954.

4. *Seasoned Timber* was not serialized in the *Woman's Home Companion.* Excerpts from it were published in *Scribner's Monthly* 105 (Feb. 1939): 22–24; *Scholastic* 34 (May 13, 1939): 11–14, and (May 20, 1939): 27–29.

106. To Mrs. Haven
April 5, 1937
Montpelier, Vermont

Dear Mrs. Haven:

I read your letter over attentively, laid it down and thought hard about a person who is much in my mind of late, even more than usual, because she is going through a hard period of anxiety and care. Whatever comes to me I turn around to see if there is something in it for my dear Sally Cleghorn.

What occurs to me is this:—would it be possible for your program committee (without of course telling Miss Cleghorn that the idea was mine) to invite both Miss Cleghorn and me, for the same evening, I to read a story or make some remarks, Sally Cleghorn to read some of her lovely poetry—ballads or lyrics. And the twenty five dollars to go to her, who really needs it. (I wouldn't have accepted a fee anyhow, I never do from my Vermont or New Hampshire neighbors).

This would give Miss Cleghorn a pleasant change from the restrictions of a life mostly spent in caring for a very old aunt, and a little extra money. I'd drive her over and back. We'd both immensely enjoy a chance for a visit together.

What do you say?

Cordially yours,
Dorothy Canfield Fisher

107. To Bernardine K. Scherman
[1938][1]
[Arlington, Vermont][2]

Dear Bernardine:

If thoughts were airplanes, I'd have risen like a rocket and flown through the air to you and Harry yesterday, when your letter came in. There are ten thousand times ten thousand things I want to talk over with you about this novel.[3] It's been a wonderful experience to have you both read it in this still-plastic condition. Although I do mourn over your having seen it with many moulding touches still left out, and actually with several chunks of it unwritten. I never showed such an unfinished piece of work to anybody before.

But my mourning isn't very deep because it is quite evident that you and Harry "get it" in spite of the lack of modelling in many places. Yes, of course, the story is of the growth—as growth takes place in middle age—of a fine specimen of the human race, and the struggle over the bequest is (for me) not the story of the book, but another occasion when the real stuff of which he is made comes out into visibility. So the entirely unorthodox (from the novel-writing-rules point of view) strategy of having the girl vanish from the reader's sight about the middle of the book, is from my point of view all right. There is no (inner) break in the story—only a rising from one plane to another. I just won't try at this distance and with my fatigued old fingers typing, try to go into detail with you about the points you bring up, and the many many others I want to ask you and Harry about. We'll talk those over when I see you—glory be, that I'm going to!

But I will tell you what'll interest you I know, that I have gone over with and shown to two Principals of Vermont Academies near me here, the main story of the bequest and what is done about it at election. And they agree with me that *it is true to Vermont life*—mixed up and human as it is. And that reminds me to tell you the real reason why I made the Principal of Clifford Academy look like Jack Knox[4]—as he does very plainly. It is a very delicate matter for me to write about Vermont people as I do, living right here with them, and the only way I can manage it is by pretty careful transposing and camouflage. This particular novel was especially difficult because there is a real danger that the near-by Academies or Seminaries will think it is meant for a photograph of them. The Principal of the Seminar in Manchester is short and swarthy and musical. So I first, when I first began thinking about it, made my Principal tall and blonde and sort of a rough-neck (but kept Mr. Howe's [keyed in margin: "of Manchester"] music which I really wanted). But then the Principal of Townsend Academy came to see me about some details of the financial part of the story, and wasn't *he* tall and blonde and a rough-neck! So I finally asked Jack if he would mind if I took his looks quite recognizably, just to head off other identifications. He looked rather startled and dubious, naturally, but I assured him that nothing more than his physical appearance would be necessary, as the personality of the Principal of Clifford Academy is almost amusingly different from Jack's. And now, having done it with his permission, I feel rather apologetic to him, because as I went on, I sort of forgot it was his looks I was using, and in the latter part had a good many rudely realistic things to say about scraggy necks and deeply lined faces, which can't be very pleasant reading for Jack. But never mind, the camouflage is working finely—Merle said she quite recognized the "original."

Yes, you are of course quite right, there must be a scene with Susan, after the bequest is announced—the notes for it are all down, but not yet in shape. But it is at Miss Peck's of course, with other people around, so all Susan's fervor of approval strikes Timothy as quite impersonal.

And yes of course there must be a description of the effect on the town of the election, as well as the description of people going to vote and Mr. Dewey's talking to them and the painful wait of Timothy and Mr. Dewey for the result.

And the missing chapter will make (I hope) a GREAT difference in the ending. For in it I mean to try to show that Timothy's crust was broken by the upheavals he has been living through and he is released into a much deeper satisfaction with his profession—the satisfaction middle-aged people feel with their work, when they are finally forcibly pushed out of hoping to get anything more for themselves. That gives Timothy a rich full content for the years before him—not just intellectual as he has been about his teaching, but emotional too—with Eli Kemp as the particular case showing him what he means to some of the students around him. This puts the very ending—Susan and the baby—into a much better proportion. It is not all he has, by any means, and although it is still sad and I think rather bitter (for it *is* bitter, the utter unconscious selfishness of the younger generation having pushed him into the situation of older generation (to them) whose business it is to help them live). It is only part of the whole of his life which is very much bigger, surer, more massive and more rich than when the story starts.

Well, I have written you something although I was only going to say thank you thank thank you for help now and to come. For I do hope you and Harry won't have forgotten the details when I see you for I want to ask you a great many questions—for instance *is* the statement of one of the biggest themes of the book, when Canby goes out to the car when Timothy leaves them after his first visit to them after their marriage, and Timothy tells him that as you grow older you find to your surprise (what no book ever admits) that there are many ways to love—is that too baldly outspoken???? You'll remember that at the beginning he is thrown into a panic by the intimation that he is getting too old to love? I mean part of his growth to be into the realization of the wide horizon of love, open before those who will step out into it. But is that too plainly said? It is one of the main things the book is about. More anon—some more thanks. Apologies for the HORRID version you read.

Love
Dorothy

---

1. Date: based on the composition history of *Seasoned Timber,* which DCF began in 1936 and continued to work on through 1938.
2. Place: implied.
3. See note 1.
4. See Letter 46, note 3.

108. To Mary C. Jane
February 7, 1938
Arlington, Vermont

Well, my dear Mary, when I scribbled that hasty note while the Christmas vacation crowd of young people were still with us I had no idea it would be so long before I wrote you a proper letter. The obstacle had been physical—a wretched arthritis or neuritis or writer's cramp or whatever, which has gripped my writing arm and right shoulder and made writing so painful that I've done as little as possible of it.

But though I've not written I've thought of you a great many times. Your letter I've kept on my desk where I could dip into it. You can't imagine what it means to an author to know that books written from one's very heart have gone to another's heart. Your actually knowing some of the scenes from them—it takes my breath away with pleasure. I do wish you and your husband had stopped the day you passed through our pine woods out by my Octoberish garden, and told me who you were. I would have laid aside everything to take you up the mountain path to look-out rock, on which Sylvia and Austin came out.[1] The next time you come this way you must give me the chance to do this—and to talk over with you some of the points raised in your letter.

The matter of successful marriages as the solvent of doubts and distrusts of life, for instance. I told my dear Sarah Cleghorn (Do you know her *Threescore*?[2] If not do get it from your library. I know you'll like it.) what you said about marriage and she said, "There! I've told you you must write a novel about a spinster. Marriage *does* take up too great a place in your work."

Well, the novel[3] I'm now working on has a hero, a wifeless, middle-aged, school teacher, the head master of one of our old Vermont academies, who finds his way up from the personal and impermanent to the impregnable fortress of security which integrity is, without marrying. You shall have a first copy of that (if it ever gets itself written in spite of the demands on me from the outside.)

You see, all the time I've been writing, there has been a strangely marked "literary fashion" to decry marriage, to decry and disbelieve in any form or growth towards strength and wholeness. The careful study of disintegrating forces has alone seemed worth while to most serious and conscientious writers of fiction. Perhaps the great admiration my generation felt in its youth for the Russian novelists (of the old regime) had something to do with this. They were mostly occupied with the study of human weakness yielding to the overwhelming odds of Fate. I'm sending you today a book of short stories of mine published last autumn[4] in which the story called "The Forgotten Mother" was written under something of the same impulse to correct an exaggeration which has made me write so much about happy marriage; since the new lore about child-psychology and Freud's study of sub-conscious impressions I've been struck with the same tendency on this part of writers; that is, to describe only the disintegrating effects of bad and confidence-destroying impressions in early childhood, never those other impressions (which after all, must be in the majority or we would all be in the insane asylum) which build up personality and put firm ground under our feet.

But I don't at all mean to imply—this goes without saying—that happy marriage is the only solvent of the great knotty problem of living and growing, nor that mothers do not often plant the seeds of doubt and despair in their children's lives—any more than I meant to imply that the Beethoven Fifth is the summit of musical experience. As a matter of fact the Tchaikovsky's *Pathetic*[5] moves me as deeply as it moved you. I chose the Fifth because it is noble and fine, and because I thought it perhaps better known to American readers than most other symphonies.

That you did get the very essence of what I'm trying to say in my novels— and how happy you made me with that comment in your letter—you show when you say you knew at a moment of doubt in your life, that I wouldn't want to "tell" anybody what was best to do in his own life, that what I most hope for in anybody is that he may slowly (for it comes slowly) learn to use his inner strength to make his own decisions. That is what I wish passionately to say to young people . . . "You have strength within—look for it, find it, cherish it, help it to grow and you will savor life—and catch glimpses (for we cannot hope for more) of its deepest meanings."

As for your thinking that you are an "ordinary" person, less gifted, less cultivated than Sylvia or Marise, your letter makes that idea a laughable one! If either of them could ever have written a letter so full of thoughtfulness, of maturity, of fine quality—I'd have been proud of them! And they were not extraordinary young women anyhow. Poor Matey took forever to learn anything. Just a school teacher.

You speak of not liking *Bonfire*. Was that I wonder perhaps because poor Lixlee was too savagely primitive for your tastes? I wanted to show there a primitive not at all intelligent nature which in sound, "natural" primitive conditions would have been straight-fibred and strong, really crushed into crookedness by lack of understanding, proper care, room to grow *in her way*. She was strong and vital and so did not succumb entirely, but was forced into devious ways by social demands on her far beyond the capacity of her limited intelligence to grasp or meet. You see there I *did* make a study of disintegrating influences on a personality—my interest in it being this:—that what happens to one happens to all of us, that it is not safe ever for us to stand off and let a personality go to anarchy and disorder, because as it goes down it takes down with it all it touches even the smug, righteous people who seem to themselves to stand afar off in safety, and who do not feel the need to sharpen the antennae of their sympathetic understanding, in order to help along a human being on a very different plane from theirs. But I evidently was not skillful enough or subtle enough in my portrait of Lixlee to get this over to you. And if not to you, evidently as understanding a reader as any author can hope for, not, I'm afraid to anybody.

You ask me one of the most disturbing questions in the world now, and one to which I would give I'm afraid a different answer from the one my dear Sarah Cleghorn, confirmed pacifist that she is, would give. No, I don't believe if really pushed to the extreme that I believe ANY peace is better than ANY war. Do you? Does your husband? I am trying to use my influence just as far as it will go, against Fascism and for democracy. I'm for the legal government in Spain and against the Rebels. I'm passionately against Hitler and Mussolini. Would I advocate fighting, if it came to that, to resist Fascism's spread? I'm terribly afraid I would—well as I know the hideousness of war. The hideousness of the "peaceful" life now being lived under the Fascist regimes seems actually more hopeless—dead.

I've never written so to anyone before—perhaps no one ever before asked me so point-blank that deadly question.

Well from the length of your letter to me and mine to you, it looks as though we had too much to say to each other to get in to letters, doesn't it? You must try to come back again, and let's take a walk together on our mountain. In the meantime thanks again with all heart for your deeply satisfying letter. I don't say, "May you be happy. You deserve to be," but, "You will be happy because you deserve to be." That's my credo.

Faithfully yours,
Dorothy Canfield Fisher

---

1. The scene featuring Sylvia Marshall and Austin Page, the protagonists of *The Bent Twig,* occurs in chapter 27, "Between Windward and Hemlock Mountains."

2. Sarah N. Cleghorn, *Threescore* (New York: Smith & Haas, 1936).

3. *Seasoned Timber* (1939).

4. *Fables for Parents* (1937).

5. Peter Ilyich Tchaikovsky (1840–1893), Russian composer. *Pathétique,* Symphony No. 6 in B Minor, 1893.

109. To Franklin Folsom
June 23, 1938
[Arlington, Vermont][1]

Dear Mr. Folsom:

I've been away from home for some days and on returning find your letter, accompanying the protest by Mr. MacLeish of the suppressing by the Detroit Public Prosecutor of Ernest Hemingway's *To Have and To Have Not* in the library and in the book stores of that city. Also the telegram saying that Mr. Brooks agrees to sign the letter of protest.[2]

I don't feel like signing it myself. To take issue with the Roman Catholic Church is a major operation and to be effective needs a basis less open to question than the "we are further informed that the real reason is" etc. of the first paragraph of Mr. MacLeish's letter.

The accusation of political animus in the suppression of a book ostensibly because of its too great outspokenness, would also have far greater force in the case of a book not so outspoken as Mr. Hemingway's. It is really an exaggeration to say that "only a prurient mind could possibly find the book offensive." I know several able, mature, intelligent, experienced American men of letters, not in the least prurient who found certain pages of it decidedly offensive.

So I don't think the case made out in Mr. MacLeish's letter is sound enough to stand what it's sure to get, skillful analysis and both violent and subtle opposition.

Sincerely yours
Dorothy Canfield Fisher

---

1. Place: implied.
2. Based on complaints by the Detroit Council of Catholic Organizations, Hemingway's *To Have and Have Not* was deemed obscene by local authorities in 1938. The League of American Writers (of which Franklin Folsom was national executive secretary) protested the ensuing citywide ban against the sale and library circulation of the novel. In a letter published in the *Nation,* Van Wyck Brooks, Archibald MacLeish, and Thornton Wilder claimed, "The real reason for the suppression is Mr. Hemingway's known sympathy for the Spanish government in the civil war in Spain and his activity in securing ambulances for the service of the Spanish army and the bombed population."

110. To Robert Haas
August 10 [1938][1]
[Arlington, Vermont][2]

Dear Bob:

How will this do for the Blixen book?

"It is almost incredible (N.B. or if that sounds too heated, astonishing) that

the author whose style in *Seven Gothic Tales* was wreathed with sculptured gro-
tesqueries and stained through and through with strange glowing colours unlike the light of day, should be able to give us in "From an Immigrant's Note-
Book"[3] (N.B. Is that the title? I can't remember exactly.) a book of classic, im-
perturbable simplicity. Classic is the adjective which comes again and again
to the mind of the reader:—the feeling for beauty, for pain, for effort, for night
and day, and animal-life wild and tame, for humanity white and black, is poignant and searching. But it is always expressed with a reticence and restraint
that gives this story of life on an African farm a singularly aristocratic quality.
The last section is heart-rending in sadness, but composed, measured, with
the stern quiet dignity of tragedy."

Was that something like what you wanted—to give an idea of the book's
quality? If not, you know without my saying so, I'll do it over.

I forgot to tell you that I've heard from Joslyn[4] who has begun to look into
the accumulated research material of the Youth Commission,[5] to apply his
slide rule to their statistics, to get his well-trained teeth into it. He reports there
is plenty of material for a good book, but he doesn't think (from this first
glimpse) that he is by any means always going to draw the same conclusions
from it as the staff of the Youth Commission. I think he means that they are
much dominated by Mr. Owen D. Young and Newton Baker[6] (or maybe have
that kind of mind themselves) and just naturally sheer away from economic
conclusions, turning to the safe non-controversial old-American idea of education as the cure for all ills. I've written him that his own judgment is what you
and I want, and that he is free to make up his own mind without reference to
the official opinion (only there isn't any, yet) of the Youth Commission. But
they may, it is quite possible, be driven to conclusions outside their usual dog-
mas by the material itself. I've seen Mr. Young succumb entirely to the evidence about the need for Federal Aid to schools. He was utterly opposed to it,
hotly, at first, as Federal interference etc. But when the statistics from the south
and other underprivileged places came in, together with the fact that all cities
over one hundred thousand fail by thirty percent in replacing their own popu-
lations, he was perfectly capable of putting the two figures together and bowing his head to the inevitable.

Merle was here yesterday for a minute—she and Bobby rounding the corner of our drive, looking like brother and sister. Bobby had been fishing with
Merle for company and had caught a BIG trout in our mill brook—biggest
I've ever seen taken out of that little stream. He certainly is getting the hang
of it.

Angie's not so well—curses!

There was something else I wanted to ask you about, but I'll save that till I
see you.

Did you make out all right about *The Deepening Stream*?[7] If not, I'll let out a holler. I'm so pleased about that.

Ever yours
Dorothy

---

1. Date: year appended, supported by the publication date of the book under discussion, *Out of Africa* (1938).
2. Place: implied.
3. "From an Immigrant's Notebook" is the title of part 4 of *Out of Africa*.
4. Carl Smith Joslyn, American sociologist and a "first reader" for the Book-of-the-Month Club.
5. DCF served on the American Youth Commission of the American Council on Education from 1936 through 1940. She helped prepare the Commission's report *Youth and the Future* (1942) and amplified her own views on the state of American youth and education in *Our Young Folks* (1943).
6. Newton D. Baker (1871–1937), American lawyer and public official, U.S. secretary of war (1916–1921). Owen D. Young (1874–1962), American corporate executive, chairperson of the German Reparations Conference (1929).
7. Refers to the publication of *The Deepening Stream* in a Modern Library edition (1938).

111. To Arthur H. Quinn
September 5, 1938
Arlington, Vermont

Dear Professor Quinn:

Why, you've broken my heart! I don't know when I've had such a shock as you gave me by the casual phrase in your letter, "I felt that the hero should have done something more essential and important at the end than the leading of an athletic parade!" I could lay my head down on my desk and weep that you should think that poor broken Anson Craft was the *hero* of *Bonfire,* he whom I intended as the *ne plus ultra* of a failure, the blackness of his defeat the night against which the soaring triumph of the *heroine* of the book, his sister Anna, rises on a parabola of glorious happiness into the only heaven her generous soul could know, fulfillment and hope for some of life's disinheriteds!

I intended the pattern of the book to show the decline into defeat and failure of Anson, for I can't imagine any failure more abject than a grown man of brilliant intelligence who can get joy *only* in the adolescent triumph of an athletic team of boys; and the rise from disheartenment and apparent hopelessness (as far as personal happiness goes) of a great-hearted woman whose passion was to open prison doors and let out those unjustly shut up inside.

At the beginning of the book the line of Anson's life starts high in promise: vital, intelligent, established in the finest profession known to humanity, with a beautiful young girl in love with him; Anna's position in life seems a poor thing far below the boldly up-soaring curve of his, for she is no longer in her first youth, not beautiful, she is convinced that she has inherited melancholia, she has found no joy in her attempt to "do as she pleased" when she left her laborious position in Clifford to go to Paris, to easy well-paid work. But because Anson's attitude towards life is materialistic, cynical, non-generous, everything he touches turns to ashes, and it is the very violence of his failure [Keyed to "failure" in right margin: "I refer here to the scene where Anson has the attack of angina, and startles Anna into an emotional crisis in which she realizes her love for Fred Kirby."] which breaks Anna's reflex-habit of not taking the personal happiness then at her hand, and sets her free for personal joy. This, in my visualization of the pattern is the point where Anson's descending and Anna's ascending lines cross.

Anson loves and marries in a materialistic reaction from all that makes love and marriage more than bodily love; and is betrayed to misery by just that, when poor dumb Lixlee takes him at his word and honestly tries to live as though bodily love were the supreme good. But no, the spoiled boy must have his cake and eat it too. He must have physical love as the supreme emotion, but it must *not* be supreme at the moment when his professional training makes him will to put something else first. Poor trapped bewildered Lixlee would have been better off with the wild man from Searles Shelf who *did* set his passion for her above everything else, and who meant what he said, as he showed when he killed himself at the end when she went away forever from Clifford.

When in your analysis of *Bonfire,* you said the "ending is weak," it gave me a literal start, for the last chapter of that book is—for me—by all odds the most powerful and satisfactory I've ever written, almost too symmetrical and yet, I thought, true. You see Anna's life soaring in blessedness—she is not only happy herself with an adored and adoring husband, a lovely child (why did you suppose I wrote the little vignette of her child asleep upstairs and the closed bud of the adolescent country girl getting her first intimation of the beatitude of maternity from looking at her?) with a second child on the way, but—equally important for her great soul, her darling project of rescuing those ignorant, poverty-stricken young people from the back-roads farms *is a success,* as you can see from the way those Merrill young people react to it.

I was church-thankful as I wrote, because I had for heroine a woman of so large a nature as to be incapable of that complacent satisfaction with her own personal satisfaction and happiness (or sorrow over her own personal unhappiness) which is all that most heroines of novels can (apparently) feel. She is in a kind of heaven on earth, Anna Craft is, there in Dewey House which is giving those needy adolescents what she had risen from the nether hell of personal unhappiness to fight for at the Town Meeting. And from the lighted windows of that heaven of fulfillment she looks out on poor Anson in the dark capering foolishly like David before the ark (why did you think I had him actually prancing with all sense of dignity gone, with a woman scorning him as she looked down on him from a window above, except to make my readers think of the gambling King David and another woman looking down in silent scorn on him[1] and then across her heaven falls the shadow of perplexity and wonder (which is the beginning of a wider wisdom) at the unguessable complexity and confusion of human existence, where everything turns out so differently from what you expect, where you yourself who never tried for happiness, nor hoped for it yourself, are drowned in bliss and your cherished brother who had it all in his grasp, is broken and defeated.

I *meant* her confession of bewilderment at the very end, to suggest to the reader (if he were subtle enough) that she was on the brink of realizing that she herself was a prime factor in Anson's defeat because she gave so immoderately to him all her devotion—and so that she is on the brink of a new kind of wisdom, a new painfully acquired love of living which will enable her hereafter to "be devoted" more wisely and to realize that even in devotion the necessity of keeping things in right proportion still exists.

Well, I never before, I think, tried to defend a book of mine from criticism. I see their faults so clearly I always take for granted that criticism is justified. But when I defend I rather go into it with all my might, don't I? I really didn't know what you meant by saying the end was "weak," and wanted to ask you. Your letter speaking of being disappointed in the end to which "the hero" had come, was a revelation to me of how totally you had (so it seems to me) mistaken my meaning. Was it all my fault that you did, do you think? Where was it that I failed to make that meaning clear?

Was I mistaken in thinking that I was strong enough to take on as "heroine" the kind of woman in real life goes almost invisible, quite unrecognized? Did I risk too much in defying the unwritten literary convention that the person in the book who has the most vivid sex-experience is necessarily the central figure? Do let me know, won't you, if you have the answers to these questions?

Cordially yours,

---

1. In the Old Testament (1 Chronicles 15), Michal, the daughter of Saul, looks down upon David with scorn as he dances before the arrival of the ark of God.

112. To Ruth Suckow
January 7, 1939
Arlington, Vermont

Dear Ruth:

The two beautiful white cats (I'd have known them for yours and Ferner's clear across the room without the welcome line in your hand writing) came in while the house was full of children and grandchildren, for this old Vermont friend of yours now has two married children and two grandchildren, making six in the younger generation to come home for the Christmas holidays. And while they were all here, racketing around, the January Harpers came in and I pounced on your story in it,[1] so I've two fresh links with you—though I don't know your street address. I've been so eager for news of you. "Hollywood Gods and Goddesses"[2] I think I wrote you about. I meant to anyhow, liking it greatly. But I am greatly taken by "What Have I?" every word of which I read twice, once in the great first gulp, again to get out the marrow. It's better than ever! Winifred is absolutely alive on the page, a person—and the American woman (her kind) too. I could smell the perfume Nancy made her try, I could touch that slightly-wilted, innocent, childlike, touchingly soft cheek, I could see her troubled (but not deeply troubled) pleasant eyes. I fairly ached with the "pleasure of recognition." It's wonderful news to have from the notes at the back of the magazine that you are writing a novel. Keep your health. We need that novel![3]

Dorset is grown enormously chic and cock-tailish, so that plain folks don't go up there much any more. Manchester languishes on the leavings of the Dorset summer folks. Arlington is as always, with a few more old houses sold to artists and writers, but not enough to change the immemorial Arlington social inertia, which we all so greatly enjoy. John and I are well, but lots older, both of us struggling with sea-sick horror and disgust over the international situation, and the creeping in of anti-Semitism to the U.S.A. (Dorset is entirely given over to it, alas! alas! and just now is making an impassioned effort to exclude Jewish skiers *from their fields and hills*—which fortunately geography being what it is is hardly possible.) I've just finished a novel, maybe a little better than most of mine, on which I've been working for the last three years— one episode of which deals with anti-semitism in a Vermont village. It's to be called "Seasoned Timber"—from one of George Herbert's poems.[4] Rather a nice name, don't you think?

Now come on with a bulletin of news from you and Ferner. We haven't heard a thing in a long long time—too long! I do hope you're well, and Ferner too. That the beautiful cats are, I can see for myself.

With affectionate greetings to you both,
Dorothy

---

1. "What Have I?" *Harper's Magazine* 178 (Jan. 1939): 126–37.
2. "Hollywood Gods and Goddesses." *Harper's Magazine* 173 (July 1936): 189–200.
3. *New Hope* (New York: Farrar & Rinehart, 1942).
4. Quotation is from George Herbert's "Vertue":
"Onely a sweet and vertuous soul, / Like season'd timber never gives; / But though the whole world turn to coal, / Then chiefly lives" (ll. 13–16).

113. To Bernardine K. Scherman
[December 1939][1]
[Arlington, Vermont][2]

Dear Bernardine:
Somehow you've become the Bach-specialist—well, you were the first to speak of that brief passage in *Seasoned Timber*.[3] So I send along another letter from another professional musician,[4] a man this time, and—of all things!—teacher in a boys' military school! *Don't* bother to send it back. We won't be here anyhow, since we are bursting all bonds of routine, and going off unexpectedly to spend Christmas with Sally and Paul and the grandchildren in Indiana, and won't be back till next week. It'll do me good to be a grandmother and nothing else for a while. I've been working with machine-gun speed for rather too long. But oh! I had five hours of such joy lately—I must tell you as a fellow-writer about it, it'll amuse you. I had gone on that tiresome dirty long trip to Grand Rapids to speak for the Children's Crusade,[5] and had left home twelve hours earlier than I needed, hoping to see and argue with the National President of the Parent-Teachers Association,[6] who is being canny and prudent about committing herself about the Children's Crusade. She lives in Detroit. I stopped over there, telephoned the house (I'd already telegraphed trying to make an appointment) and her husband said he was sorry, she was in Chicago. The next train—to Grand Rapids—didn't leave for six hours. Six uninterrupted hours! My heart leaped up. I've had a sketch about a sixteen-year-old girl in my head for *months*, all ready to set down, but not a minute did I have free from the incessant letter-writing etc. for the Children's Crusade, except when I was too tired to sit up any longer.
But this was in the morning—I'd slept pretty well on the sleeper! I rushed to buy a bottle of ink from the news-stand girl and borrow a pen (none on sale) from the Express-office man. And there in the abominably dirty smoky "women's room" of the station I had five hours of forgetfulness—I was up Mount Mansfield seeing a sunset, I was sixteen, half greedy child, half sensual young woman,

I was climbing up a beautiful cliff, I was—well, you know the blissful idiocy of the story-writer! Aren't we the loons!

Do you know I'd like very much to have a talk with *you*. It begins to seem too long a time.

Affectionately
Dorothy

---

1. Date: December 8, 1939, letter from Charles L. Reid ("another professional musician") and reference to "going off unexpectedly to spend Christmas with Sally and Paul."

2. Place: implied.

3. The passage, in which the protagonist T. C. is moved by a recording of Bach's *St. John Passion,* occurs in chapter 30 of *Seasoned Timber.*

4. See note 1.

5. In October 1939 DCF spoke to the State Commissioners of Education Convention in Grand Rapids, Michigan, to promote the Children's Crusade for Children, a charity to aid European children who were war victims. The crusade, begun in September 1939, asked American youths to contribute pennies to help their European peers. Over $130,000 had been raised by the end of the crusade in April 1940.

6. J. K. Pettengill.

Part 5

Letters, 1940–1949

114. To Willa Cather
October 9, 1940
[Arlington, Vermont]¹

Dear dear Willa:

What I felt on finishing *Sapphira and the Slave-Maid*² (what a perfect title!) was not like shouting out the "hurrah!" of congratulations on a beautiful piece of work, just heart-felt thanks. The lovely little book is a priceless gift to our gloomy anxious times. I know beforehand that its readers are going to be filled with the same sort of personal gratitude to you that I feel.

When I came to the happy ending, that sunlit, actual, not-to-be-doubted happy ending, I took out your letter to me about *Seasoned Timber*³ (I hadn't far to reach! Prizing it too highly to have it far from my hand, I've kept it on my desk ever since it came) and read again what you said in it about more and more shrinking from sadness and frustration. Well, my darling Willa, you've helped everybody to turn away from frustration, in this exquisite tale.

With devoted love
Your
Dorothy

---

1. Place: no reason to doubt Arlington.
2. Willa Cather, *Sapphira and the Slave Girl* (New York: Knopf, 1940), book-of-the-month, Jan. 1941.
3. Cather's letter praising *Seasoned Timber* is dated November 8 [1939].

115. To Eva Robin
March 15, 1941
[Arlington, Vermont]¹

Dear Mrs. Robin:

The Book-of-the-Month Club has just forwarded to me your letter of the 12th. I am rather surprised and somewhat daunted by the influence you attribute to the book-of-the-month choice, and to what Dr. Canby² and I say and write. It's a great compliment of course and I take it as such, very appreciatively. But I can't but think you over-estimate the influence we have. We of the Book-of-the-Month Club do our very best, as seriously and conscientiously as we can, to select books which will be (a) read by the subscribers to the Book-of-the-Month Club, for, of course, no matter how fine a book is, if its subject matter is in some specialized field in which only a few people are interested, it's no use to send it out. People won't read it. Then (b) we try energetically to have only authentic books—not books written by people with whose opinions we agree, for that would sadly limit the range of choices, and diversity of taste is the very savor of life, but books by authors who, as far as we can find out are sincere, mean honestly what they say, and who are telling the truth as they have seen it. We put off voting on whether to send out *Out of the Night*[3] for a month, during which, as far as possible, the details of the story were verified by responsible people in a position to have the necessary information. Only after this had been done, did we vote for sending out the book. As to the opinion of the author about Soviet Russia, you must remember that we have sent out other books about Russia, notably *The Russian Primer,*[4] so favorable to the Soviet Union as to bring down on us a great deal of embittered criticism from people who don't like modern Russia, and who felt—only the other way around—as you do about *Out of the Night.*

(c) Another consideration we try to bear in mind in making our choice, is that it is advisable to have a variety in the books we send out as choices—a variety in genre (some fiction, some history, some biography, some in politics, etc., etc.). A strange, "different" kind of a book like that by Valtin makes a great break and change in the series of books sent out and, other things being equal, this is considered. You see this is only one of twelve choices in a year. It is not an expression of the convictions of any of the judges, but a powerful statement of one aspect of the opinion of our times.

Have I, I wonder, made any clearer to you the reasons for the choice?

With sincere good greetings,
Dorothy Canfield Fisher

---

1. Place: implied.
2. See Letter 79, note 2.
3. Jan Valtin, *Out of the Night* (New York: Alliance Book Co., 1941), book-of-the-month, Feb. 1941.
4. M. Ilin, (pseud. Ilyia Iakolevich Marshak) *The Russian Primer* (Boston: Houghton Mifflin, 1931), book-of-the-month, May 1931 (with *The Square Circle* by Denis Mackail).

116. To Mary C. Jane
July 16, 1941
[Arlington, Vermont][1]

Dear Mrs. Jane:

I am going through an experience quite new to me, a very serious illness which culminated in an operation last December and a long convalescence ever since.[2] It interferes with all kinds of things which I used to carry on without thinking about them. But I'm not going to let it interfere with sending you some kind of answer for your letter of June 26th which gave me, as all your letters do, an immense amount of pleasure.

I have kept it on the corner of my desk since it came in, reading it from time to time, and meaning to show it to my dear and only daughter when she comes on for a visit this summer with her husband and children. But I find I haven't even told you that it has arrived safely. And that I am going to do without waiting another day.

There are so many things in it which I'd like to talk over with you, that it's a sort of exasperation just to send an acknowledgment without plunging into the long discussion of anything you bring up which I'd like so much to do.

What you say about *Seasoned Timber* interests me enormously. I'm touched that you were able to read it so carefully as you evidently have, for I had expected that younger women could no more read this study of a middle-aged intellectual man than middle-aged intellectual men have ever been able to read my stories of the vital young home-making women so dear to my heart. Most of the letters I have had about *Seasoned Timber* have been from men and this has seemed quite natural to me. I agree with you that there is something exasperating about Timothy's not reaching out his hand to take what he could get. And it's much more than half a loaf, you know, which one gets by accept-ing ordinary life. You may remember that the young Canby thought it would be very natural for his Uncle Timothy to marry the home economics teacher. And how enraged that made Timothy! I think probably Timothy's rigorous training and experience in music (his aunt's fiercely "professional" attitude, that it must be "just right," or it was nothing) may have had something to do with his attitude towards life. There may have been a confused mental "carry-over" into the complex field of human relations of that tyrannical demand for perfection which alone gives distinction to artistic creativeness. Such standards ignore the obvious fact that human life is vast and diverse and rich, immea-surably beyond any art-material, and cannot be restricted and pruned off and cut down as the artist restricts and cuts down on his material to get even a little selected piece of it into the frame-work of his art. But of course one great factor in Timothy's situation was that he was just leaving physical youth behind him!

But here I go, so stirred and interested and stimulated by your letter that I'm starting off as though you were sitting here in my study, with a long eve-ning of talk before us. It's a deep and fascinating aspect of Timothy's life—of everybody's life—which you bring up, as a result of such thoughtful reading of *Seasoned Timber* as any author couldn't but be grateful for.

It is as hard for me to resist plunging into a long talk with you about the war, as about what was the matter with Timothy Hulme's way of taking life (especial thanks for bringing that grand Browning quotation to my mind!).

But I'm headed off from that too, by this new necessity to use what strength I have sparingly and cautiously because there's not enough of it to go around. It would of course take a long book to set down what comes leaping to my mind as I read your questions and observations on our world's tragic situation. But I can't let a letter to you go off without one outcry of real horror over your English rector's attitude, which seems to me as dreadful as anything ever said by Hitler. It would be poison to me, to be in the same room with a man capable of such words. And yet I don't feel that Lindbergh has any grasp at all on what the problem really is.[3] I'm afraid he is carried away by a feeling so many of us have (don't mention this to your English rector!) of intense personal distaste for English people, and intense long-standing disapproval of British imperialism.

But I feel that, just as we must, when a great personal sorrow comes to us, make an epic effort not to let our lives be bounded and limited by that grief, but enlarge our hearts till they can harbor both faithful old sorrow and also the new joy which life is willing to bring with every dawn—so, in this terrible crisis, we must enlarge our natures till they have room in them for such personal distastes and dislikes, and *also* for acceptance of all men as (potential) partners and sharers of life. Until we accept them, there can be no partnership. We have shut the Germans out. We must not shut out even your English rector.

It seems to me that this dreadful convulsion is (or may be) part of the struggle to bring to birth a new conception of the oneness of mankind. (This was the idea Timothy was so wildly struggling to try to grasp and pass on to his young people, and by the way, this was what he *really* cared about much more than about Susan Barney!)

Now many an effort to bring new life into being, results in death. Perhaps this *may* be such an effort—just too great for the human race to achieve. We may not be able to rise above our dreadful human faults like a horse, fumbling with his nose at the latch of a gate, not able to perform the simple operation of lifting the latch and going forward. But there's a chance that, this time, we *may* learn how to lift that latch. The very violence of the convulsion may drive us to transcend what we have thought were our powers. A chance to succeed is a challenge!

With such gratitude for your letter,
Your ancient and appreciative friend
Dorothy Canfield Fisher

---

1. Place: implied.
2. DCF had surgery on an enlarged thyroid in fall 1940.
3. The American aviator Charles Lindbergh (1902–1974) was a noninterventionist.

117. To Carlton F. Wells
March 30, 1942
[Arlington, Vermont][1]

Dear Mr. Wells:

I am returning herewith the very interesting and moving and alarming material which you sent together with your letter of March 26th. Mr. Best of the Viking Press had given me some idea that this sort of protest is being made against the John Steinbeck book, and has suggested that I write an answer. But I'm not at all inclined to do so, because I think there is a good deal to be said on that side. It had not occurred to me at all when I read the book, and when I wrote the review,[2] that it might be taken as minimizing the horror of Nazi rule. I had become alarmed by what seems to me a tendency among Americans not to realize that the war, the Germans, are factually real. The great American audience has had so much experience with movie horrors of one kind and another that I feared they were almost incapable of recreating any form of reality for themselves out of the journalistic account of Nazi doings. It seemed to me that from that point of view that Steinbeck's book might have a real propaganda value.

But I can see, now that you and others have called my attention to it, that there may be a danger of its presenting too soft a picture—ironic as that is. However, I think all these protests will help minimize the danger if it exists. I am glad they are being made therefore and have no intention of trying to refute them.

With thanks for your thoughtful letter, I am
Sincerely yours,
Dorothy Canfield Fisher

---

1. Place: no reason to doubt Arlington.

2. Steinbeck's novel *The Moon Is Down* (New York: Viking Press, 1942) was the subject of controversy for being too soft in its depiction of the Nazi occupation of Scandinavia. DCF endorsed it in the *Book-of-the-Month Club News* (March 1942). Among the materials Wells enclosed was a letter from a Polish refugee who called Steinbeck a Fascist and said that his book grossly misrepresented the reality of a German occupation, book-of-the-month, Apr. 1942 (with *Cross Creek* by Marjorie Kinnan Rawlings).

118. To Pearl Buck
July 20, 1942
Arlington, Vermont

Dear Pearl:

My great-grandmother kept the bell in the tower of our old church tolling solemnly from dawn to dark on the day eighty-three years ago of John Brown's execution. Eighty years ago my grandfather was with Henry Ward Beecher in England,[1] on the American mission to influence British public opinion in favor of the Union and the abolition of slavery. My father, when he was President of Ohio State University,[2] set all half southern States by the ears, forty-four years ago, by inviting Booker Washington[3] (as the President of another institution of learning and hence a colleague) to lunch with us in our home. You know something of my life-long attitude—let me tell you that all those four generations of Canfields rise up to shout "Hallelujah!" over your new book.[4] We were, all of us, too provincial Americans to realize (until Kipling appeared to shock us awake in horrified protest) what was going on in Asia. But, it is so entirely a part of what we did know, all too well, that when you point your strong sure finger at it, we recognize it as another aspect of the dark shadow which we have all felt, all striven vainly to enlighten.

As I read the speeches and essays in this volume of yours, I kept thinking wonderingly, "Wonderful how Pearl can make her voice heard against the sodden blanketing of moral inertia, when we never have been able to." And just now, it occurred to me that maybe we—I don't mean just the minute-to-invisibility cluster of Vermont Canfields, I mean all the many Americans who have not—not ever—accepted the iniquity, who have steadily kept the fight against it a part of their lives, though overwhelmingly busy with all kinds of other work—maybe *one* of the reasons why your voice is being heard is that some of us stood faithfully (although smothered by opposition to the point of apparent ineffectiveness) by the principles which, as you state them, emerge into total visibility, even for the great public.

It's wonderful to have this book, with your generous warm-hearted words on the fly leaf.

Your old—I really am now one of the oldest, am I not?—and devoted friend,
Dorothy Canfield Fisher

---

1. Henry Ward Beecher (1813–1887), American clergyman, editor, and abolitionist.
2. DCF's father, James Hulme Canfield, was president of Ohio State University from 1895 to 1899.
3. Booker T. Washington (1856–1915), African-American author and educator, was the

first president of Tuskegee Institute (from 1881), an influential Alabama trade school for African-Americans.

4. Pearl S. Buck, *American Unity and Asia* (Freeport, N. Y.: Books for Libraries Press, 1940).

119. To Robert Frost

September 12, 1942

[Arlington, Vermont][1]

Dear Robert:

Every once in so often—and more often of late, it seems to me—I'm approached by somebody or other who wants me to tell him something about you, which hasn't been published, so he can write about you. You know the kind of thing they want—intimate reminiscences of how you looked or what you said or did on some occasion—or some unpublished and hitherto unknown items about your family life, or relations with other writers and critics. They seem to be ready to snap at almost any bone.

Now I don't know just what to do about this. It's not so simple to dodge them as it seems. Detesting as I do, people who snoop around in my past, my impulse is to cut them off pretty short, with some phrase which means, "none of your business." But, human nature being what it regrettably is, their reaction to this is a certain horrid expression of the eye which means that they think I am suppressing some shameful (and hence juicily desirable) tidbits. The very fact of my not being willing to say anything is regarded as a proof of—oh, something or other objectionable. You can just see them more determined than ever to look through the keyhole of the locked door.

As we all get older, this prying gets pushinger. In my own case, I have hopes, pretty well founded, that it will first lessen and then stop altogether, as folks just forget that I exist. But there's no doubt about it, they are not going to forget that you exist—not for a cent! Nobody with any sense can possibly think that the interest in you is going to be noticeably less in our lifetime—and thereafter, into the bargain.

Now you're the person most concerned. Have you invented any formulæ in which you'd like to have these questioners answered? If so, send your suggestions along, and I'll apply them faithfully. I really need some general instructions from you on this point. Maybe some innocuous afternoon-tea anecdotes, delivered impressively as if I thought I were saying something, might be a better defense against this meddlesome curiosity. What do you think?

I liked *The Witness Tree*[2] so much, I made a bid to write the review of the book for the *Book-of-the-Month Club News*. But Benét wanted to do it too, and it was evidently thought that I'd written enough praise of your work to last for a while, so his review went in. But those were my sentiments too—I don't need to tell you that.

On the train when I went down to New York, the last trip I made, were a lot of Bread Loaf[3] students going back from the summer session. What they said about you (and they didn't know I knew you) simply enchanted me—and couldn't have but pleased you.

How well Lesley looked, when she stopped here with her girls, on her way to see you. She says that Irma[4] is in fine shape too.

Ever yours,
Dorothy

---

1. Place: implied.
2. Frost's *A Witness Tree* (New York: Holt, 1942) won the Pulitzer Prize for poetry.
3. The Bread Loaf School of English in Middlebury, Vermont, where DCF lectured (see Letter 72, note 2).
4. Lesley and Irma Frost, Robert and Elinor Frost's daughters.

120. *To Robert Haas*
October 6, 1942
Arlington, Vermont

Dear Bob:
It came to me in the night last night that I had written you since I had received your letter with those marvelous little masterpieces of description of the Dinesen stories,[1] and had not mentioned them! I don't keep much track of my correspondence when it's of the fluent and spontaneous kind like my letters to you, so I'm not sure I had written you since then, or that if I did write you, I didn't mention them. But on the chance that I didn't, I want to go on record as saying I think they're really quite wonderful. What an amount of effort goes into such compressed statements only another author knows! I still haven't read the new ones in the complete collection which has come in, partly because I've been saving them for just the right time. But I regret to report that Jack Knox[2] has been here for his usual autumn foliage visit, and since I was very busy I turned over the collection to him to occupy his time. He was as dazzled as anyone by the way in which they were written, but he said mournfully (and I hadn't told him that the Book-of-the-Month people had said the same thing) that he really did not know what they were all about. I'll have to see what John says. But I am going to take my stand firmly on the superlative fine quality of the writing. It is simply too good to pass over.

Love to you all always,
Dorothy

1. The Dinesen book under discussion is *Winter's Tales* (New York: Random House, 1942), book-of-the-month, June 1943 (with *Combined Operations* by Hilary A. St. George Saunders).
2. See Letter 46, note 3.

121. To Paul Reynolds

[October (7?) 1942][1]
[Arlington, Vermont][2]

Dear Mr. Reynolds:

I've been trying for days to find time to write to you something about my story, "The Knot-Hole."[3] I think it is as good work as I have ever done, from a literary point of view. And I was slightly dismayed to have *Good Housekeeping* see in it only something "interesting but too depressing." But it is of course something cheerful they are looking for.

I meant to suggest to you that it will not be worth while, probably to try it on women's magazines, even though they do pay so well. And—unless you have already sent it both the *Atlantic* and *Harper's,*—when you send it to one of the more serious magazines, I believe I'd like, by a great exception to my usual rule, to write a little note to the editor to go with it. If you have already sent it to those two magazines, and have it back—here's hoping not!—how about the *Yale Review?* If you try it there, I'll write a brief note to the editor too.

Unless, you think this would really not be a good thing to do. It occurred to me that maybe, just this once, a sort of push to the editorial elbow might be useful.

What do you think?

I'm working now on one of the two articles Mr. Markel[4] wants for the *Times,* and hope to send it to you to send to him, in a few days.

Always faithfully yours
Dorothy Canfield Fisher

1. Date: stamped "received 9 October 1942."
2. Place: no reason to doubt Arlington.
3. "The Knot-Hole," *Yale Review* 32 (Mar. 1943): 493–517. The story won second prize in the O. Henry Prize competition for 1943.
4. Lester Markel (1894–1977), Sunday editor of the *New York Times* from 1923 to 1964.

122. To Christopher Morley
[1943][1]
[New York, New York][2]

Dear Chris:

I find I can't go to sleep in this hotel room (even after an absurdly busy day) without making a protest about a remark you dropped today—when *you* were making a protest against my feeling about Santayana.[3] You said "But the man of the Renaissance was heartless." The rush of talk was going at such a clip I didn't want to try to hold it back while I explained that when I used the word "heartless" about Santayana, I wasn't using it in the sense of "unkind." I meant unfeeling—that Santayana certainly is, and that the man of the Renaissance certainly was not, almost by definition. He cared passionately about something or other—art, or learning or getting rid of an enemy. I think Santayana's attitude is more like the late seventeenth and early eighteenth century—in France at least. As I read that marvelous self-revelation, I kept thinking of Chamfort (not the Revolutionary one) who lived to be almost, or maybe it was more than, a hundred years old. He survived all the court intrigues for all that time, all the campaigns, all the changes of opinion and ups and downs— by a pattern of life rather like Santayana's, a quick appraising eye for people from whom he could get something he wanted, a masterly technic in not observing the existence of people who might call on him to give them something they needed, were it only sympathy or compassion. And when he was—still in the best of health and spirits and witty and animated—nearly a hundred, a young courtier asked him marvellingly, "How *do* you do it? How *is* it that you have outlived every one of your contemporaries?" Chamfort smiled, tapped himself on the heart and said proudly, "Nothing there! Absolutely nothing there."

It's not the hot-blooded Renaissance that Santayana belongs to with his detached tourist's attitude, but Chamfort's period. Or at least that's the way it looks to a now awfully sleepy

Dorothy

Thanks again for the *Illustrated London News.* I'm so touched by it, and by your getting it for us.

---

1. Date: selection of Santayana's *Persons and Places: The Background of My Life* (New York: Scribner's, 1944) as a book-of-the-month, Jan. 1944 (with *The Signpost* by E. Arnot Robertson).
2. Place: letterhead, Commodore Hotel, New York, N.Y.
3. See note 1.

123. *To Albert Einstein*
February 20, 1943
Arlington, Vermont

Dear Dr. Einstein:

The enclosed carbon copy of a letter to Mrs. Katherine Salter explains itself, I think.[1]

I never have met Mrs. Salter, and I imagine that you have not. I think probably our interest in her has the same basis, that we thought her an energetic and vital descendant of the anti-Fascist cause in this country. I said about a year ago that I would be willing to write an introduction to a collection of her letters to newspapers, if she could find a publisher for them.[2] But I note in the article which she wrote for the *Churchman* she speaks quite definitely on the fact that I *will* write the introduction for a book of hers and that you will recommend it to any publisher.

But I have the uneasy feeling that she has changed her ground somewhat since you and I knew about her work. Her forceful and, I thought, sound protest against the fascist propaganda, seems to center now entirely on the Catholic church. As I say in my letter to her, I think here she is on ground where she must make more distinction than in combating such an enemy of democracy as in Father Coughlin.[3] There were many Catholics who did not at all approve of Father Coughlin and I think she does not take that into account.

I feel a little uneasy about the carte-blanche which she seems to assume you and I give whatever collection of letters she may wish to publish.

May I venture to ask whether you agree with me that there may possibly be some trouble ahead for us here?

Since this is the first time I write to you, perhaps it will be as well to say that if you will speak to Dr. Aydelotte[4] about me, he can reassure you as to my own reliability.

With admiring greetings,
Sincerely yours,

---

1. I have been unable to locate the carbon copy of Salter's letter.

2. Salter's book was not published.

3. Charles Edward Coughlin (1891–1979), American clergyman, was famous for radio broadcasts in the 1930s and for supporting the pro-Fascist Christian Front.

4. Frank Aydelotte (1880–1956), American educator, director (1939–1947) of the Institute for Advanced Study at Princeton, was associated with DCF as a fellow member of the Honorary Committee of the Women's International League for Peace and Freedom (1935). Aydelotte, as president of Swarthmore College, presented DCF with an honorary Ph.D. in 1935.

124. To Pearl Buck
June 22, 1943
Arlington, Vermont

Dear Pearl:

I saw that nice sister of yours the last time I was in the city, and after a delightful, although all too brief, interview with her, I find myself moved to write you something about her undertaking, an undertaking, by the way, which I endorse with all my heart. I think a really truthful, penetrating biography of you for our younger American generation is one of the most useful books that could be published.[1]

I had the impression in talking with her that it was going to be hard for her, as it always is for anybody who writes a biography of someone still living, to get any shadow into it. There is something very flat about any story which doesn't set down some real difficulties overcome. When I spoke about this to your sister she said that you and she had thought that to put in the story of your daughter and her difficulty, and the shadow and effort that that brought into your life would provide the relief which I was so sure would be necessary. But I don't think that's enough. That is a shadow which comes from circumstance. It was a kind of accident and will seem so in the story of your life.

What I think is needed is some inner shadow, because of course all young people have inner shadows. Adolescents are, nearly all of them, in a state of inner conflict—with themselves, with circumstances! Since each one knows only himself, he can't help thinking that his difficulties are different from and harder than those felt by other people. I don't think anything is more helpful to young people than to hear about adolescent difficulties in adjustment which were felt by people who afterwards overcame them, and grew into well-poised and powerful personalities.

Now I don't know anything about your adolescence, of course, and I don't know whether you had any inner difficulties. But you certainly were a rare bird if you didn't have! In my own case the particular shadow which darkened my adolescent years was a complete lack of harmony between my father and mother. I've never spoken about this to anyone but you, this minute. But I remember very well how it seemed to me a burden greater than I could bear all during the time when I was growing up. Yet there was no open quarreling or dissension— just a complete lack of ability to make each other happy. Now from your two books about your own father and mother,[2] I should guess that you too must have struggled hard to make some synthesis of the spirit out of that element of discord in your life. I don't know whether you would be willing to have your sister speak of this, or of anything else which may have given you passing difficulty when you were the age of the young people who will read this book.

And another thing, I think the book will be incomplete unless the young people have the feeling as they finish it, that you did not slide smoothly into life like a canoe launched with the bow on but splashed sideways into it as most of us do. Nothing is so encouraging in learning about a creative enterprise such as a successful life is, as to know something about the failures which accompanied the earlier phases of it. Because nearly everybody does have failures, and if he reads about somebody else's efforts which apparently got along without any, he thinks he's so poor at the business of living that he'd never succeed.

You're used to sudden appearances of mine at your elbow when something brings you especially to mind, so I hope you won't mind this one, and will pay no attention to it if it doesn't seem to you to have anything in it to your purpose or to the purpose of the book.

With affectionate greetings always,

---

1. *The Exile's Daughter: A Biography of Pearl S. Buck* was written by Grace Sydenstricker Yaukey under the pseudonym Cornelia Spencer (New York: Coward-McCann, 1944).
2. *The Exile* (New York: Reynal & Hitchcock, 1936), a biography of Buck's mother; *The Fighting Angel* (New York: Reynal & Hitchcock, 1936), a biography of Buck's father.

125. To E. B. White
August 25, 1943
Arlington, Vermont

Dear Mr. White:

Ever since my return from the last meeting of the Committee of Selection of the Book-of-the-Month Club, I've been turning over in my mind your letter to Mr. Scherman, which he showed us. I don't think that I now venture to write to you about it solely because of our disappointment that you don't feel it possible to be one of that Committee.[1] That disappointment is very great. All four of us were warmly agreed that you would be just the right addition to our work. We had the most cordial welcome waiting for you. Perhaps I especially was hoping with real intensity that I could look forward to working with you, and having the benefit of contact with your mind and taste. No, not I, more especially than we all were. Everybody was stricken with disappointment on reading your letter.

Nothing is more tiresome and objectionable than to beg somebody to reconsider a decision. I wouldn't be writing now (as I'm doing on an impulse) if I didn't think that perhaps you made that decision without knowing some of the facts you'd need, to see what is really involved. I hope I'm not speaking out of order in passing on to you some of the items in my own experience with the

Book-of-the-Month Club organization. I don't see that such a personal letter can do any harm, (except that it may be sort of a chore to read) and maybe you'd be interested in hearing something about the seventeen years—can it possibly be that long?—of my connection with the organization.

To begin with, I shied off at the first mention of such a connection just as you do. We live in the country for exactly the same reasons as you and Mrs. White do, and all through the thirty-six years we have been here, in my old Vermont hometown, we've been suspicious of any proposition that would threaten what we get out of country life. Whenever somebody has emerged from the New York barn with a measure of corn in one hand and a halter held behind his back in the other, we've always flung up our head and cantered off at top speed to the far reaches of the upper pasture. So when the matter was first proposed we agreed to it only in the most tentative way.

What appealed to us in it were these things: the certainty that it would not involve living in the city, the fact that it was work we could do together more or less—and that would be true of you and Mrs. White, of course, and the fact that, no set office hours being involved, we could shove it to one side, for days at a time, when some pressure from country work made that more desirable— if a frost threatened and we had to hurry to cut the corn and cover the tomatoes for instance. On the other hand, we didn't like the general sound of it any too well, and had never heard of the two men at the head of it. So, like cautious farmers who won't sign their names to any document for fear it may turn out to be a mortgage on the home place, we accepted the offer very tentatively, making the most explicit, written-down agreements which left the door to escape wide open behind us. Well, we've never even thought of that door, because so far as we can see, we have come and gone as freely as though it had been taken off its hinges.

And I too had ever so many writing projects in my mind. Most of them have been carried out, really better as far as I can see, since my connection with the reading for the Book-of-the-Month Club. I hadn't thought about that until your letter, with its fear that you'd have to give up certain writing plans of yours long held if you took on this work. Then I looked back over the years we on the Committee have been working there, and saw that all of us have done our best work in that period of our lives. We're no world-beaters as authors, any of us, to put it mildly; but such as we are, we have produced our best in the last seventeen years. This is no proof, of course, that—as I think has happened in my case—the absence of the recurrent thought as to how to pay the grocery bills usual with free-lance writers has given me such greater peace of mind, that we could, with no economic pressure, plan for endlessly long writing work, with no feeling that it had to be pressed in order to get royalty income. It has seemed to work that way in my case—to make a frame-work of security inside which long-time plans could be made in all quiet. But that isn't positive proof of anything. It is certainly negative proof that the professional reading done for the Book-of-the-Month Club has not interfered with the authorship of four people of such entirely differing temperaments as Morley, Canby, White and me.

Your phrase about the danger of having "money and power" also set me to doing some fresh analytical thinking about the job. Why *don't* we all sink beneath the consciousness of the responsibility of such "power" as the Book-of-the-Month Club certainly has come to wield? One reason is certainly because in the first years so little "power" was involved that not even the most over-conscientious person need worry about it. But largely I think because of the basis on which our choices are made, and this bears too on your feeling that you'd be driven sort of distracted by the need to make up your mind about the merits of a book.

From the first day on, what we on the Committee of Selection have been asked to do, and the only thing we have been asked to do, is to say what books we ourselves have really *enjoyed* reading. From time to time, since all of us, like most experienced literary folks are, more or less, in a manner of speaking, literary critics too, we have started in our monthly discussions, to wander off into the paths of literary or sociological (sort of) relative values. Mr. Scherman always brings us back to first principles by reminding us that our part is not to decide whether a book is likely to please American readers in general and the subscribers to the Book-of-the-Month Club in particular (the Archangel Gabriel isn't smart enough to make a guess at the answer to that wrapped-in-mystery question) nor whether it would be good for Americans to read such a book, (which would be offensive presumption on the part of ordinary people as we are). All that we are asked to do is to report on which books we ourselves personally enjoyed reading, or actually, ourselves, found especially interesting. The idea—I should think by now the idea has been proved a sound one— is that members of the Committee of Selection are, take them by and large, with their different temperaments, backgrounds, traditions and interests, quite representative of a large number of other Americans. If we on the Committee have all thoroughly enjoyed reading a book, the chances (long-range chances) are that a whole lot of our fellow-Americans will enjoy it too. And sure enough, that's the way it has, in general, turned out to be.

We are especially warned against any attempt to gauge the mental ability of those who get books from the Book-of-the-Month Club service, and scale down the books chosen to meet any hypothetical lack of literary judgment on their part. Mr. Scherman sits in on all discussions at meetings but scrupulously refrains from throwing his own weight around, even a pound of it, when it comes to making decisions. What brings him out of his observer's corner with a rush is one question, which is still once in a while incautiously made,—the question as to whether a certain book which we have very much liked may not be "over the heads" of other readers. We are—almost—innocent in reverting to that question, for such an endless lot has been written by people specializing in looking down their noses at others, about the low-browism among Americans. It sticks, some of it, just because it is so often repeated, even though our own experience in the Book-of-the-Month Club reading contradicts it. Well, if any of us ever wonder whether a book we ourselves have enjoyed is maybe too high-brow, Mr. Scherman recalls us to the basic principle on which the organization is based—that we are representatives of American readers, quite a large number of them to keep such an organization going. "If you've enjoyed it—if a majority of you have really enjoyed it more than any other book you've seen this month, that's all you have to think about."

We ourselves supply mentally the rather shamefaced challenge implicit in this, "What makes you think you're so much better and smarter than your fellow-Americans?" What indeed, we ask ourselves silently, and turn our back to the single-minded search as to which book or books we ourselves really found most enjoyable, or most worth-while, or most interesting, or most freshly informative.

Don't you think that those long deliberations and uncertainties of judgment of which you speak so feelingly in your letter are concerned with the question of how a book should be, fairly and accurately, "rated" on the literary scale, in comparison with other books? I always fall into a centipede-like inability to know which foot goes before which, the minute I try to hold up some sort of literary or historical yard-stick to "measure" a book. But I always know whether I myself—not as a literary person just as an American woman—have really enjoyed reading a book.

You can see that the considerations of "power" are pushed far to the background of our thoughts. And of course another thing which keeps it pushed back is the system which makes it so easy for the "subscriber" not to take the book we have selected, but some one of the twenty or so other books offered to them every month on the same terms in the *Book-of-the-Month Club News.* I rest my very soul on the knowledge that a large portion of the subscribers don't pay any attention to the book we choose, but pass it over to order some other one— among those which we have also liked, and which are listed in the *Book-of-the-Month Club News.* That calm ignoring of our choice by such a lot of subscribers takes a lot of the cuss out of the "power" we are supposed to wield.

When I said that Mr. Scherman does not try to influence the opinions of his Committee of Selection, I don't mean to imply that there is any sultry, genteel suppression of anybody's opinions in suffering silence. We all talk at the tops of our voices in the freest most untrammelled interchange of opinion it's ever been my experience to encounter, in the course of a long and pretty active life. To give a concrete instance:—not long ago we chose as book-of-the-month a book by a man we all personally dislike very much. Mr. Scherman too, more than any of us. We all said we had taken the book up violently prejudiced against it, but we had been forced, as we read, to find it absorbingly interesting, fresh and important. Mr. Scherman writing me a few days later about something else, said with the most honest violence of phrase that he thought it had been a poor choice, and was surer even than ever that such a fellow was simply incapable of writing a true or honest book. I took his remarks as he intended them, as an open blowing-off-steam expression of his opinion, differing from ours, not at all as any attempt to "influence" the choice—if he'd wanted to do that, he'd have blown off steam at the meeting when the choice was made. I cite this to give an impression of the honestly free atmosphere of Book-of-the-Month Club talk.

It's rather rare, I think, to have such wide open discussions without anybody's trying to put anything over through influence or pressure, and I'm not without other experiences of group effort as measures of comparison. I worked for years as a member of the Vermont State Board of Education[2] and enjoyed that very much, finding the men I worked with honest and true Yankees. And I worked for six years on the Youth Commission (a General Education Board activity)[3] with such widely differing people as Newton D. Baker, Owen D. Young, President Hutchins of Chicago, Matthew Woll of the American Federation of Labor, Monsignor Johnson of the Catholic University, Ralph Budd of the Burlington Railroad system, and old Chester Rowell of the San Francisco *Chronicle*.[4] The discussions (such endless ones!) around that table were as honest as those at Book-of-the-Month Club meetings. Nobody tried to put over anything, not a trace of steam-rollering from any direction. But—perhaps exactly because the members of the Commission were so extraordinarily different by tradition and background—there was, or at least I sometimes felt there was—a rather troubling anxiety not to step on anybody's toes, not to shock anybody's convictions, not to rub anybody's susceptibilities the wrong way. Living as I do, in Vermont, with lots of elbow-room, moral as well as geographical, and with little ceremony, I sometimes felt a little oppressed by such careful restraint. I'm more at home in the occasionally vehement, always absolutely spontaneous and unstudied equal-to-equal discussions around the Book-of-the-Month Club table, when you can sing out heartily an unfettered "Oh you're crazy!" to a fellow-debater, without breaking any windows.

Well, you'll have to take an evening off to read this epistle! I'm using the Ediphone of late for my correspondence. (I can't write a word in a story or essay except in long hand). Everybody warned me that the ease of talking into that speaking-tube would lead to garrulously long letters. This one seems to prove their point. It goes to you with very friendly good wishes for you and Mrs. White from

---

1. Heywood Broun died in 1939, but the four remaining original members of the Selection Committee (DCF, Henry Seidel Canby, Christopher Morley, William Allen White) did not seek a replacement until 1943. E. B. White was their choice, but he declined. When William Allen White died the following year, Clifton Fadiman and John Marquand joined the group.
2. In 1921, Fisher became the first woman elected to the Vermont State Board of Education.
3. See Letter 110, note 5.
4. Newton D. Baker (see Letter 110, note 6); Owen D. Young (see Letter 110, note 6); Robert Maynard Hutchins (1899–1977), American educator, president (1929–1945) and chancellor (1945–1951) of the University of Chicago; Matthew Woll (1880–1956), American labor leader, vice-president of the American Federation of Labor (1919–1956); Monsignor George Johnson (1889–1944), American religious leader, educator, Associate Professor of Education at Catholic University in Washington, D.C. (1921–1944); Ralph Budd (1879–1962), American railroad executive; Chester Rowell (1867–1948), American newspaper editor, Republican political leader of the 1920s and 1930s.

126. To Pearl Buck
August 26, 1943
Arlington, Vermont

Dear, dear Pearl:

How you and I always feel the impulse to put our heads together, to clasp hands closely, to share what is in our hearts, in grave moments of crisis! Your letter comes in just as I was about to write you—partly because Dick[1] startled me by saying you had a kidney infection which was keeping you in bed for a while; partly because my constant thoughts about you were focussing again into an impulse to write you; and partly because I wanted to break over the rules governing group-effort of all kinds and (confidentially) tell you what no single member of a committee is supposed to say about a decision by the committee as a whole, that I felt as you did about the Walter Lippman book.[2] Like everything else in our mixed complicated human life, the advantages of group-action are not to be had without paying the penalty of some disadvantages. The moment you do not act as an absolutely independent single individual (as you so valiantly do) you are put into situations which do not truly represent your own personal convictions—this happens often in our New England Town Meetings, when, after prolonged debate, the minority must accept *and act upon* a decision made against its will by the majority. In the long run, in general, it can be said that such group-action has more advantages than disadvantages. What one has to do, of course, is to balance the times when one is made to seem to be part of an action not in keeping with one's convictions, against other times when concerted action (with all that it involves of giving up individual expression) makes possible much greater power to forward one's personal feelings and opinions. The disadvantages must not occur so frequently as to outweigh the advantages. But, (at least in our Anglo-Saxon discipline) it is unrealistic and willful to give up the great advantages because of a single, or a very few instances of the opposite.

But before my pen—not nearly so quick as it was even ten years ago—touches paper to write you, in comes your letter showing you are thinking of me as I of you.

Yet there is so much to say, dear Pearl, that I should never put it all down, in the rich complication of detail as it is brought to me sweepingly from one of our terrifically complicated, nervously tense, angry, frightened modern world. So I'll set a little of it down with short-hand brevity. I used always, when I heard you criticized, to spring quickly to contradict, to defend you. Now I don't always, because I want to hear exactly *what* it is felt by the people who resent your attitude (so very few, *never forget that,* in comparison to the astoundingly large number whose hearts are reached by your every word.)

They seem to feel (I think I've written you this before) that your protests against racial prejudice, against the idiotic assumption of the superiority of the white race, oversimplify a situation, by leaving out of it the myriad complexities of the economic and political aspects of the matter.

They feel that you do this because you are primarily a splendid writer of fiction, who really does not understand the economic elements in the international situation. Suspect in fact, so little about them, that you are not even aware of their prime importance, and so are quite sincere and single-hearted (but none the less over-simplifyingly mistaken) in putting into the foreground in an exaggeratedly important position, the matter of racial relations. Remember I am only reporting as accurately as I can what I gather your critics—the honest ones—feel. These are no opinions of mine.

They feel—here the historic difference of opinion between "the gradualists" and the "revolutionaries" of ideas comes acridly to the fore, as so many times in the last two centuries—that your approach to the question is dangerous, because (whether you say or only imply this) your readers get from your expression of opinions a terrific impact of "immediacy" (if there is such a word!). They gather that what you think should be done is instantly to sever ties and connections which, having lasted a century or so, have grown into organic connections and hence, should be (will have to be they think) untangled slowly; like a good surgeon performing an operation who patiently lifts one nerve after another, separating one muscle from another, compared to the hasty one who slashes straight through, causing mortal danger of "shock" to his patient. Here again *I* think that the urgency of the hour should be taken into account. There may not be time for the gradual untangling of fibres. In the fact that there is *not* time, (perhaps) we are paying the deadly price for not having begun earlier to do the untangling. It takes perhaps just such clear compelling voices as yours to make people *begin* to untangle.

The people of the United States were profoundly shocked, in the real medical meaning of the word, by the horror of the Civil War, and the awful price that was paid for the settling by the sword of a matter that should have been (as in England in 1833 by the Emancipation Act) settled without bloodshed. The hundred million dollars (wasn't it something like that?) which was the price to the British of a non-violent, non-bloody political and sociological solution of a matter settled in our country by violence, was infinitesimal compared to the dreadful moral wounds and scars left in the U.S.A. by an abrupt ending of a wrong, known to be evil by all decently civilized men and women. I think (I've never heard anybody else say this, it comes just from the long, passionately intent meditation on our national history by an old American woman) that deep in the American sub-conscious mind, there is now a dread of such quick endings to ancient wrongs.

All this is only such an explanation as my observation brings to me, of the reasons underlying the resistance to your anti-imperialist thesis (to which in theory every decently civilized man and woman assents) on the part of some of the better-grade responsible, fairly well-informed Americans. Of the others, the Jew-hating, Negro-baiting ignorant mob, I say nothing, because they are primitive "nativism" unqualified by any intelligent thought at all—such members of the mob were supporters of Hitler, exist alas! in all nations and are only kept from power by the concerted efforts of more civilized people.

I think that outspoken anti-imperialists are needed just as the Abolitionists were indispensable in the first half of the nineteenth century to the awakening of the conscience of our nation, although those crusaders knew nothing and cared nothing about the huge economic elements involved in the question of Negro slavery. We inch along so painfully—if indeed we do advance even slowly— our poor human race, it takes all kinds of workers to push against evils, the ones who advocate quick action, the quicker and more sweepingly complete the better; and the ones who want to take the time patiently to untangle the interwoven muscles and nerves, rather than to cut them. In the battle-field hospital, the operating surgeon cuts, desperately, knowing the danger of shock is less than the certain death if the gangrened tissues are not removed. Perhaps we are now actually on the battlefield, when gradualism is no longer a possibility, when it is a choice between dangerous "shock" and certain death—to (as you say and as my heart forebodingly tells me) our sons and our grandsons, who, in the years to come, will pay the price of our lack of courage and decisiveness now.

I was asked not long ago by the *New Masses* to write a statement about racial prejudice for their columns. I never lose an opportunity offered me to speak out on that dreadful wrong and fatal error. But I did not, as their invitation suggested, write about "Measures legal, political and social which might be taken to combat this deadly evil"—because I felt as an ordinary woman might feel if asked to advocate one or another way of producing synthetic rubber, a daunted ignorance of the facts involved.

So I wrote the article which I enclose with this.[3] I don't think it adequate. I wish I might have felt informed enough to speak with positive conviction on some of the political and social and legal aspects involved. All that I can claim for my approach and the limitations of my statement is that *if every decent citizen* made as outspoken a statement from all varied occupational standpoints and experience they have, a complete and adequate statement of this complex problem would be the result. Of course they won't.

Hence the inadequacy of my approach, I admit this with sorrow. I don't say it is the right one. With the limitations of my experience and my life-long mental habits, it is the only one I myself can, in honest sincerity, employ.

As to unthinking, generalizing criticisms of your attitude, lumping your firm anti-imperialism as one with anti-British convictions they, I'm afraid, will have to be taken as part of the clatter and roar and clash of arms of our troubled times. Some of them come from an honest feeling that since unity of the Allies is vital to the immediate success of the war-effort, any anti-imperialism expression is a risk to military success.

In any case, St. Peter opening wide the pearly gates to let you in as a stalwart defender of the brotherhood of man, will never have heard of them. You'll have a much larger and more golden harp (as is right for your more powerful hands) to play, than the little plain one which may—if things turn out better than I often fear—fall to the lot of your devoted, now venerable friend,

---

1. Richard Walsh (1886–1960), American publisher, Pearl Buck's husband (m. 1932), and president of John Day Publishers.

2. *U.S. Foreign Policy: Shield of the Republic* (Boston: Little, Brown, 1943), book-of-the-month, July 1943 (with *Western Star* by Stephen Vincent Benét).

3. "How to Combat Racism," *New Masses* (July 27, 1943):20.

127. To Otelia C. C. Connor

May 16, 1944
Arlington, Vermont

Dear Mrs. Connor:

Your note of May 10th is here, bringing me a great deal of pleasure. I think such writing as you are doing for the local newspapers on serious topics is as useful a work as anybody can do with a pen. I so often hear from young people scattered here and there over the big nation, who say they would like to "become writers." They all have one idea which is to go to New York, and be in close touch with the publishing business. I always write them the same thing, that nobody can learn any art or even a trade, without a period of apprenticeship. And if they would write on topics which really interest them, *for their local newspapers,* they would gain an invaluable experience and lay a foundation for the practice of writing, far beyond anything that they could get in a big city strange to them.

Of course it's very pleasing to me that you find *Our Young Folks* has material enough in it for such articles. It is what I hoped when I wrote *Our Young Folks:*— that intelligent and thoughtful Americans might use it as the starting-point for developments of their own, working out ideas as, in practice, they would be appropriate to different parts of our great Federation. So you see your work is my ideal realized.

As for the statement about English teachers, I think you will agree with what I meant, which evidently I didn't put as clearly as I might. You see in *Our Young Folks* I was writing about adolescents. I think the difficulty with many English teachers is that they give their students when they are still too young to appreciate unusual literary qualities, some classics from the past which just seem dull and uninteresting to them. The eighteenth century in particular has a quality so different from that of our own times, that I think it requires the perspective of some added years for modern readers to appreciate it. My feeling is that in literature as in food, one should be careful not to offer nourishment which is not suited to the age one is trying to serve. No matter how much one likes sauerkraut for instance, no matter how much one realizes that there are valuable vitamins in that food, it would be neither appetizing nor digestible for a child of two. I have the same feeling about some of the classics from the past. One runs the risk of making young people turn away from the good-quality writing altogether, if good-quality writing of a period the style of which seems strange to them, is presented to them at too young an age. It's just a question of waiting a few years when they'd be more likely to appreciate it.

Does this clear the point? I hope so.

With many thanks for your letter and every good wish, I am
Faithfully yours,
Dorothy Canfield Fisher

128. To Richard Wright
July 1, 1944
Arlington, Vermont

Dear Mr. Wright:

Mr. Meredith Wood of the Book-of-the-Month Club, has just sent me a copy of Mr. Aswell's letter, and your proposed new ending for your latest book.[1]

I admire, as I did when you accepted with what seemed to me such an intelligent reasonableness, some changes in *Native Son,*[2] your freedom from the traditional author's prickly touchiness.

And I greatly admire the three pages you have written to end your fine narrative of your childhood and youth. I think they will help to make the book intelligible and hence more fully moving and convincing to the many readers it is going to have. You have put into this material, as I hoped you might, poetry and spiritual beauty, which make a noble ending.

I have read these pages several times over, with the closest attention for they are vital to the impression made by the book. And the last time I went over them, it was with pencil in hand, to see if perhaps I might have a helpful suggestion or two to make, as from an older writer to a younger comrade in authorship.

You write with such finished skill—how could you have acquired it so young, and against such odds!—that very few possible changes occurred to me, as you will see from the copy I enclose with this. I've drawn a pencil mark around only two or three words or phrases I think might be improved, like the phrase marked on page 3 which seemed a little awkward and involved. Perhaps the idea could be put through the process of distillation (you, as a writer, will know just what I mean) and clarified into a verbally simple statement which will more surely and directly give its essence.

I have questioned the last part of the last sentence, because I am not sure that I know accurately what you mean by it. After the magnificent vision of "men being able to confront other men without fear or shame," that last phrase might mean that part of your vision (or as you put it soberly and realistically your "hazy notion") was that any man, all men might hope to catch a brief glimpse of glory beneath the stars. But as the idea is now set down, I fear that some readers may construe it to mean that you yourself hoped for the "luck" of having some personal glory, some individual success. I may be wrong about the possibility that some readers might construe your use of "one" as referring to yourself. But I set down this question because it would be a pity to have anybody tarnish by such a misconception the gold of the phrases "that life could be lived with dignity, that the personalities of others should not be violated, that men should be able to confront other men without fear or shame."

With considerable hesitation, I add to these verbal suggestions one idea which came into my mind as I read. I hesitate because I dread to seem to put any pressure on you to say more than you feel you sincerely can. Sincerity is always for everyone, complex and confusing as human life is, one of the most difficult moral achievements. Especially so for people placed in the position of the American Negro. Your own sincerity is extraordinary in its integrity. I would feel guilty if I thought I had made it harder for you to keep it intact.

And yet, perhaps an elderly woman writing to a young man may hope to speak objectively enough about a troublingly delicate matter, to be of service.

My idea is this:—you ask (a question all of your many readers have asked themselves about you, with an eagerness full of anxious hope) "What was it that always made me feel that way? What was it that made me conscious of possibilities? From where had I caught a sense of freedom?"

We too ask ourselves that question, we, meaning those Americans who, following the example of their parents and grandparents, have done what they could to lighten the dark stain of racial discrimination in our nation. What we have hoped—faintly hoped—was that those efforts of men of good-will have somewhat availed—a little—enough so that those suffering from racial injustice might catch a passing glimpse of the fact that such efforts are rooted in those "American principles" so mocked and degraded by the practices of racial discrimination. In what else could they be rooted? That they exist is a proof that American ideals are not the tawdry pretense they are so often accused of being.

In the South, it is frankly violent brutality which bars the way to free Negro development. In the North it is hypocrisy—the failure to do what is admitted to be right to do. But when La Rochefoucauld[3] said that "hypocrisy is the tribute paid by vice to virtue," he was saying by implication that hypocrisy is a proof that the conception of virtue really does exist, valid enough to make men ashamed of not living up to it. To keep that conception in regard to decent race-relations alive and growing has been the aspiration of generation after generation in many an American family, judging by my own, and by those I know.

To receive, in the closing pages of your book, one word of recognition for this aspiration, if it were possible for you to give such recognition honestly, would hearten all who believe in American ideals. We would never dream of asking it—we were told by our parents and have told our children never to ask for it, or wish for it, but to do what we could out of simple respect for human dignity and veneration for the basic principles of our nation. We have understood that the American Negro needs all the vitality he can summon to carry on his part of the long struggle for human rights, that for him to keep his well-justified resentment intact is natural, to be expected, is indeed probably a source of vitality.

Yet when Paul Robeson[4] —who never in any other way known to me, has publicly shown that he is even aware of the heaped-up honors given him by his admiring fellow-Americans—went so far as to make his magnificent voice the medium for singing the ballad "I Am an American," a good many anxious and heavy hearts were lightened among those doing their best to lessen the wrongs of which all decent Americans are ashamed.

What I'm trying to put in such a tentative way as not to make it a suggestion, much less a request, is the question whether it might be possible for you, somehow, somewhere in this fine epilogue, to answer your own question "What was it that made me conscious of possibilities? From where had I caught a sense of freedom?" Perhaps you might answer it by another question such as I put to myself, only I put it into old-fashioned phrases, "From what other source than from the basic tradition of our country could the soul of an American have been filled with that "hazy notion" that life could be lived with dignity? Could it be that even from inside the prison of injustice, through the barred windows of that Bastille of racial oppression, Richard Wright had caught a glimpse of the American flag?"

The briefest recognition of the existence in our nation of this long-held aspiration, reaching you, valid enough to help keep alive in your heart that "consciousness of possibilities" which has continually led you up into wider and finer development—what a benediction that would be! In your third paragraph when you refer to what books were to you in the South, it might be possible to say (if this is what happened) that in books you heard of the existence of Americans who believed enough in the American principle of fair play to the individual as to be at least ashamed and sorrowful over each failure to put that principle into practice.

But, of course, (this goes without saying) if you don't honestly believe this is true, if I am mistaken, even a single word would be a dreadful travesty

With friendly greetings,
Faithfully yours,
Dorothy Canfield Fisher

---

1. This begins a series of letters between DCF and Wright in 1944 concerning the publication of his autobiography, *Black Boy,* and its selection as a book-of-the-month. At the request of the Selection Committee, Wright cut a longer autobiography (*American Hunger,* published by Harper & Row in its entirety in 1977) and wrote a conclusion for the newly shortened version, which he titled *Black Boy.* DCF recommended changes not only in word choice, but also in the tone and content of the final pages. *Black Boy* (New York: Harper & Brothers, 1945), book-of-the-month, Mar. 1945 (with *Apartment in Athens* by Glenway Wescott). See Janice Thaddeus's "The Metamorphosis of Richard Wright's *Black Boy*" and Arnold Rampersad's edition of Wright's *Early Works* for a full discussion of the Wright-BOMC connection. Meredith Wood (1896–1974), Book-of-the-Month Club vice-president. Edward C. Aswell (1900–1958), Wright's

editor at Harper & Brothers. His letter informing Meredith Wood of Wright's decision to cut *Black Boy* at the BOMC's request is dated June 26, 1944.

    2. *Native Son* (New York: Harper & Brothers, 1940), book-of-the-month, Mar. 1940 (with *The Trees* by Conrad Richter).

    3. François de La Rochefoucauld (1613–1680), French moralist, author. The quotation is from his *Réflexions, ou sentences et maximes morales.*

    4. Paul Robeson (1898–1976), American singer, actor, All-American football player, and son of a former slave. "(Shout! Wherever You May Be) I Am an American." Words and music by Paul Cunningham, Ira Schuster, and Leonard Whitcup (1940).

129. To Richard Wright

July 12, 1944
Arlington, Vermont

Dear Mr. Wright:

Thanks so much for your letter of July 6th. It makes me wish more than ever for a chance to meet you. Don't you suppose that some time when I'm in New York for my once-a-month trip to the city for the Book-of-the-Month Club Committee of Selection, you and I might have a chance for half an hour's talk together? It would give me great pleasure.

The changes you have made in response to my suggestions seem excellent—especially the change in the very last paragraph. The beauty and nobility of your thoughts there, now shine clear to every eye.

As to my more general suggestions, you are—it goes without saying—the person to make the decision about that. I won't question whatever you decide to do. Your book is a first-rater, and with this epilogue has a fine finish. Anything I say is just a personal notion of mine, and you must not take it too seriously. But if I may permit myself to make a verbal suggestion, I'd like to say that the expression "novelistic narratives" doesn't seem a very good one. Perhaps a simpler form like "stories and novels that I have read" would cover the ground. And as one novelist writing to another I protest against the phrase "unreal lives." I have always felt that the lives in good novels (I don't mean only great novels but just good, sound, honest ones) are in many ways for the reader more "real" and true than the lives of their flesh-and-blood neighbors, because the author has put his whole heart into the effort to know more, understand more, and tell more of the essential meaning of human lives than most people can possibly know about their neighbors. Hegel said, you know, that there is more reality in a work of art than in factual reality.[1] Do change that phrase, which really does not do justice to our craft, yours and mine.

I gather that you cannot bring yourself to use, even once, the word "American" in speaking of "the tinge of warmth which came from an unseen light"— such a beautiful, sensitive phrase! Some of the novels and stories you read were—it is probable—laid in your own country of America. Hence some of the characters in books through whom you had "glimpsed life's possibilities" were fellow-Americans of yours. These "unseen lights" which shone through them upon your faith were reflections of American efforts to live up to an idea. Those characters could have been no other than products of an American tradition. However dimly that light came through to you, suffering so acutely from the rough denial of the very existence of American ideals, part of it must have come through American delineation of American characters.

Or am I mistaken about this? Was it only in Russian, and British or French fiction that you found anything to give you tidings from afar that there were human brothers of yours on the globe, who had ideals, who tried, however fitfully, to live up to them, who never dreamed of denying their validity, as for instance the Nazis have denied the validity of the ideal of human brotherhood. Did you not, in any book character, encounter a white fellow-citizen of yours who tried to live up to that ideal? It seems to me that, factually, whether you were at the time fully conscious of this, part of what it meant to you to be an American Negro, must have been a distant echo, however blurred and dim, from fellow-Americans of yours who, generation after generation, have loved that ideal and have sorrowed because its realization seemed so long in coming.

I'm dictating this letter in rather a hurry, trying to catch the one mail out from our tiny village and may not be saying exactly what I mean. But I'm sure that with your sensitive ear you can catch the over-tone. I do hope you also catch the over-tone of my unwillingness to say too much about this. *You certainly are the best judge.* Whatever you decide to do, I'll accept without question.

Certainly the new ending, the last paragraph of your book, is a beautiful thing.

With warm congratulations,
Sincerely yours,
Dorothy Canfield Fisher

----

1. German philosopher Georg Friedrich Wilhelm Hegel (1770–1831) develops this idea in his *Aesthetics* (1835).

130. To Richard Wright
July 21 [1944][1]
[Arlington, Vermont][2]

Dear Mr. Wright:

Wanting to quote that beautiful last paragraph of yours in my review of your book for the *Book-of-the-Month Club News,*[3] I telegraphed Mr. Aswell[4] to send me a copy of those pages. His answer "Wright is finishing revision in line with your suggestions, copies will be sent you tomorrow," makes me very uneasy for fear you are going beyond what you really feel is honest. I'd never forgive myself if (in my own attempt to be honest) I had stepped beyond the line of permissible influence on a younger writer! Don't you put in a single word which is not from your heart, like all the rest of your fine books! You have a grand ending as it is. I feel I shouldn't have written as I did, that second time!

I'm sending you herewith the review (minus the quotation of your last paragraph.) I'll hold it till I hear from you whether you'd like a change of tone or pace (or substance) somewhere. It does not need to go in to the Book-of-the-Month Club office at once. I've been working on it, to get it in shape (sort of in shape) in time to have your judgment on it before I send it in for publication.

Hastily—forgive this scribbled note in my tired elderly handwriting, and the badly typed script. My secretary is taking a vacation.

With friendly greetings
Dorothy Canfield Fisher

---

1. Date: internal evidence places this letter in the *Black Boy* series.
2. Place: implied.
3. DCF's review of *Black Boy* was published in the *Book-of-the-Month Club News* (Feb. 1945): 2–3. She prefaces the quotation from the book's final paragraph as follows: "Richard Wright strings your nerves taut. He communicates his anguish to you as by a piercing cry of pain in your physical ears. Yet he finishes his book with disciplined self-control—and power to spare, so that in the last pages he sweeps his readers out from the concrete and definite, with their crushing weight of literal fact, into a spacious realm of thought, poetry, beauty and understanding. Like a musician composing a brief, deep-hearted largo after passionate and agitating pages, the American Negro looks calmly at himself, at his country, at mankind, 'in the aspect of eternity.' He quiets his deeply troubled spirit—ours with his—by drawing a long breath under the open sky of the universal."
4. See Letter 128, note 1.

131. *To Richard Wright*

July 23 [1944][1]
Arlington, Vermont

Dear Mr. Wright:

Your letter and the final version of your ending comes in, to give me the greatest satisfaction. You have *not* said a word beyond what you really felt and feel—I might have known you'd be incapable of that—the ending is a beautiful piece of writing and deeply full of meaning. How proud you will make the authors you mention—Mencken, Dreiser, etc. and what an interesting discussion (in your letter) of the value of the revolting spirit in literature. For me, a girl, brought up to the innumerable intangible, smothering restrictiveness of the late Victorian period, it was Thoreau, with his total doubt of the roles of our conventional society of capitalism, it was Emerson, looking out from his mountain-top, who gave me courage to try to be myself, not what the conventions of my time would have a girl. But I had so many more helpers than you—a father who detested and despised the then-unquestioned idea that only in being inferior to men (except in physical attractiveness) could women be of value to society. And a mother, an artist, who laughed at conventions of all kinds. And the most generous-natured husband, brought up in the Quaker tradition that women are needed as whole human beings and must be allowed, encouraged and stimulated to grow to their full human stature. Thoreau and Emerson helped—but not as vitally as Dreiser and Lewis helped you.

I'm venturing to send you my last book (not a very picturesque or interesting one, although written with all my heart) because of a few pages in it, comparing the general attitude towards women to that towards Negroes. It's only an analogy, partial, but may be worth your looking at it.

With hearty congratulations,
Dorothy Canfield Fisher

---

1. Date: internal evidence places this letter in the series about *Black Boy.*

132. *To Harry Scherman*
July 27, 1944
Arlington, Vermont

Dear Harry:

Miss Stoller (or somebody from the office who wrote me about the reviews due) said that the review of the Richard Wright book need not be written for a while.

But I thought the comment on that particular book, under the circumstances, so important to get right, that I've been working away on it for some days. I sent it to Wright himself (minus the page which I have marked marginally after the script had gone to him) to make sure that he found nothing to object to, in it. The color situation is so outrageously tense with emotion in our times and our country, that I feel every word should be well considered.

His answer I send with this. He approves as you'll see.

But the comparison of the pressure kept up by Southern white people on Negroes to the pressure kept up through the Gestapo on the population of

European countries occupied by Germans—it's a pretty strong one. Several people up here, to whom I have shown the review have said that they think it a dangerous one. I asked what "danger" they saw in it. They had a precise answer—danger to me in arousing hate towards me in the South (but I certainly can't be much cherished there, as it is!) and danger to the Book-of-the-Month Club in losing all their Southern subscribers. You ought to take that into account, of course.

I think the passage I have added, which shows that their attitude is no monopoly of theirs (of Southern whites) but is another aspect of an instinct which has operated in other times and other countries, should take off some of the cuss of the review—make its position more universal, and less uniquely directed at Southern whites in 1944.

My secretary (in Poughkeepsie) is taking her annual vacation, and my right arm is having a spell of writers cramp, hence the pretty bad typing. But legible I hope.

Do you think that, since Wright saw the review without that passage, showing that the Southern white attitude is pretty universally present in all unregenerate human hearts, he should see the review with that passage added? I wouldn't think so—but I have the feeling of an infantry-man making a cautious way forward over a strip of territory thoroughly strewn with hidden mines. And I'm so used to walking around as I feel to, that I'm never sure when I have been cautious enough.

Since there is no need of the review at once, there is time for you to consider these points.

Ever yours
Dorothy

133. To Richard Wright
August 23 [1944][1]
Arlington, Vermont

Dear Mr. Wright:

The tables are being turned on me. When I sent my review of your book (by the way all of us on the Book-of-the-Month Club Committee like "Black Boy" very much as a title) down to Mr. Scherman and Henry Canby etc., they all said to me just what I said to you, that I was not being fair to those Southern white people who do not constitute a Gestapo. That is, I was ignoring the fact that there are such Southern white people. They point out that the Gestapo in Germany is official and governmental, a policy upheld by force and enforced on every citizen. And that the "Gestapo" of the South to which I refer, which watches with so anxious and disapproving an eye any signs of character-superiority in colored people, is made up, not of all but of part of the white population. A large part, the great majority, but still not all.

After I had taken time to cool off, I realized that they are correct and accurate, and that it is up to me to take a lesson in patience, and reasonableness and ingenuity from a man young enough (I assume) to be my grandson! So now I am sitting down to revise that review, trying to do as you managed to do when you revised those passages in your last chapter which you and I discussed—that is, to keep the honest heat of my feeling fully expressed, without weakening my point by overstating it.

I'm so glad you are having a real change and vacation[2] —for so Revere Reynolds told me over the telephone. What a loss to those of us who have had old Mr. Reynolds take care of our business affairs, to lose him.[3] But he was over eighty, and even a sturdy, nervously energetic Massachusetts man can't expect to work much longer than that. He had been my literary agent for—I think—almost forty years. I'll hardly know how to manage without him. Such integrity, such sound good judgment, such resourcefulness, we needn't expect again to find, I suppose.

With friendly greetings,
Sincerely yours
Dorothy Canfield Fisher

---

1. Date: references to *Black Boy.*
2. Wright spent part of August 1944 in Montreal and then traveled to Ottawa, where he stayed until early September of that year.
3. Paul Reynolds, Sr., died August 19, 1944.

134. To Anna P. Broomell
September 8, 1944
Arlington, Vermont

Dear Anna:
Your every letter makes me long to *see* you, to have at least one, good, creative hour's talk with you. This letter-writing business—it is a good deal as though you stood in the woods, half-way to the cabin and I stood on our front porch for a "conversation." Lots better than nothing, I admit.

Now this return-to-fiction idea—there is so much to be said on that point! Since the invasion of France,[1] I have not—until the other day—written anything in the way of fiction except "The Knot-Hole"[2] and that was more like a groan of anguish than a story. I have written incessantly, articles and state-ments, in which I have tried to uphold the civilized decent attitude towards life. Articles and statements can be produced by the single effort of will, pur-pose, concentration.

But fiction—that's more like falling in love, which can't be done by will-power or purpose, but concerns the *whole* personality, which includes the vast areas of the unconscious and sub-conscious, as well as those processes within the control of purposefulness. This element of the unknown puts into the writ-ing of fiction an element of the uncontrollable. And fiction written *without* the whole personality is not fiction (that is, re-created human life, interpreted) but only articles or statements in narrative *form.*

Now that the war has progressed to the point where we can be *sure* that the Nazis will not actually, literally invade and hold our country, now that we are *sure* that none of us will ever be tortured to make us betray our friends, not to speak of the lessening of the unbearable burden on the heart of horrified sym-pathy for Europeans who *were* still under that threat, that grim reality, I feel an immense lessening of emotional tension. And the other day, sitting down at my desk to write yet another stream of articles, I felt the old impulse, buried so long beneath the great deposit of anxious moral concerns, to write something because I *wanted* to, because I felt like making one of those comments on hu-man life by *implication,* which, if successful, turn out to be creative fiction.

So pushing the duty things to one side, the endless Kaufman biographies,[3] the work on the text-book series,[4] the *Christian Herald* articles,[5] etc., etc., I wrote the enclosed—an intimate thumb-nail study of a baby!—unexpected, almost disconcerting result of the stirring to life of the "whole personality" freed to be more nearly "whole" than for long, by the lessening of the pressure of urgent, material, immediate dreads and shames and sympathies.

I send it to show you how that inner spirit which creates, bloweth where it listeth, not where one tells it to blow. Only when you have (as I have) behind you the long years of experience, you don't try to tell it where to blow. You wait with humbleness what is sent. With hope as well as humility. For so I wait.

Alas! Sally Cleghorn is having a severe and exhausting experience. Aurelia (the old Negro woman, now "on the town") has been in the hospital in Albany for her very serious asthma. She was pronounced well enough to leave the hospital, and Sally, feeling that she should have friendly and sympathetic care (not just poor-house care) invited her to "make a visit." Aurelia almost at once had a terrible recurrence of the asthma, has had to have bed-care (doctor com-ing for adrenalin treatments three times a day). Sally has carried trays up and down stairs, sat up all night, tried to order food, prepare it, keep the house, give Aurelia nursing care—she looked eighty years old, yesterday when I saw her briefly, her eyes sunk deep into her head, deathly pale, emaciated, on the point of collapse. Aurelia is to be taken back to the hospital today—I hope not too late for Sally. She has simply gone far beyond her very limited strength. Mrs. Porter was there, "reading the riot-act" as she said, to Sally anxiously. I feel anxious, myself, but hope that possibly, if she survives (!) this may be an experience proving to Sally some of the material limitations to which (no matter what our good will) we are all subject.

With so much comradely affection to you, my fellow-pilgrim in life,

---

1. Germany invaded France on June 5, 1940.
2. See Letter 121, note 3.
3. DCF wrote biographical sketches to accompany the portraits of famous Americans by Enit Kaufman, *American Portraits* (New York: Holt, 1946). Kaufman, a Viennese World War II refugee, lived for a time in the log cabin on the Fisher property.
4. DCF worked on a series of public school readers with LuVerne Crabtree Walker and Eunice Crabtree, *Crabtree-Canfield Basic Readers* (Lincoln, Neb.: University Publishing Co., 1940).
5. DCF contributed articles on a variety of topics to the *Christian Herald* throughout the 1940s.

135. *To Zephine Humphrey*
January 10, 1945
Arlington, Vermont

Dearest Zephine:

I'm very happy over your letter of January 3rd, because it shows that we are in almost complete agreement in the matter of religious ritual. Of course you know our attitude puts us among the heretics for any but Quakers and Unitarians I suppose. For any symbolical interpretation of ritual is particular anathema to the orthodox.

I don't know if you know Eric Gill the Roman Catholic sculptor and artist.[1] He's one of the famous English converts. I remember reading in his autobiography[2] last year his account of how he got himself converted. He felt just as you and I do, but was extremely anxious to become a Roman Catholic. The priest who was in charge of his preparation, sent him across the channel to a Belgian monastery where he said there was a monk especially gifted in the preparation of Protestants to Roman Catholicism. When Eric Gill got to the monastery he found that the monk spoke no English. He himself spoke no French. And yet he was told to stay there for a week or so and engage in conversation with this monk. The only English words which the monk had learned were these "Not symbolical. Literal. Actual." These he repeated over and over day after day as Eric Gill tried to get over to him something of his feeling about ritual.

Finally Eric Gill says "I got tired of this and said to myself, I've always wanted to be a Roman Catholic and I'm going to be one. Then I just won't think about all this." So he went ahead and joined the church on those grounds—if you can make out what they are!

Alas, the history of all religion seems to be about the same, that a founder with a beautiful and mystic grasp on reality, tries to tell his followers something of its essence by means of symbolism. And after his death, and sometimes before, they turn it into literal, rigid, dogmatism. It's repeated over and over. Just at present in the Episcopal church (at least in the Vermont diocese) the literal and materialistic interpretation of ritual is absolutely triumphant. And indeed in the Roman Catholic Church the reaction against this attempt to consider their ritual as symbolical and not actual reality and in matter, is growing more intense. I don't think you or I would be welcome, saying our own kind of prayers, in either High Church or Roman Catholic Church, nowadays, because our heresy has been labelled with increasing definiteness, as absolutely untenable.

I'm awaiting more news of your sister with anxious concern—for you—for her!

Devotedly yours,

_____

1. [Arthur] Eric [Rowton] Gill (1882–1940), English sculptor, engraver, and typographical designer.
2. *Autobiography* (New York: Devin-Adair, 1941).

136. To Christopher Morley
April 18, 1945
Arlington, Vermont

Dear Chris:

After all, more than any splendid poetry, it's a piece of unplaned oak from an ancient ballad, in words of one syllable, which has stood by me in these very bad hours and days.[1] Do you know it?

> "Fight on, my men," Sir Andrews said,
> "I'm sorely hurt, but not yet slain;
> I'll just lie down and bleed awhile,
> And then I'll rise and fight, again."[2]

Affectionately yours
Dorothy

1. DCF's son, James, graduated from Harvard Medical School, completed his internship, and volunteered for the medical corps in support of the war effort in 1942. His battalion was converted into a ranger commando unit in 1944; he was killed while attempting to liberate American prisoners of war in the Philippines on January 30, 1945.

2. The ballad is commonly known as "Johnie Armstrong."

137. To Robert Frost
June 8, 1945
Arlington, Vermont

Dear Robert:

Whit Burnett,[1] indefatigable anthologist, is getting up a new collection of pieces, this time for college (or perhaps high school) readers. He wants to use a brief sketch which I wrote about your talk here one day—when one of the Wilcoxes, our neighbors, came over to ask if we had seen a lost cow, etc., etc. And he wanted me to write two or three paragraphs about the sketch to give his young readers the reason why he chose it.

I've done the enclosed script (if that's what moderns call it) and send it to you—not expecting that you'll read it, for I highly approve of your ruthless not reading or answering of miscellaneous mail. How else would you ever get anything done? But just to take the cuss off writing about you in public without giving you a chance to have something different done, if you'd like.

We're looking forward to seeing Lillian[2] up here soon—not so very well, she writes, with some heart trouble she didn't know she had. Does she have the bad luck as to health, poor girl! But she says Prescott[3] is quite strong and well, and is to work in New York this summer. I can hardly realize that that boy will be twenty-one his next birthday!

I think your Job poem[4] is just as good as I expected it would be, after what you told Margaret Hard[5] and me about it, last June—and believe me, that is a superlative of praise. What a bonfire of delight in it has been lighted in its reviews—all the ones that I've seen.

Ever yours,

1. Whit Burnett (1899–1973), American author and anthologist.
2. Lillian LaBatt, Robert Frost's daughter-in-law (Mrs. Carol Frost).
3. Prescott Frost, Robert Frost's grandson (son of Carol and Lillian Frost).
4. *A Masque of Reason* (New York: Holt, 1945).
5. See Letter 74, note 3.

138. To Frederick A. Pottle
August 22, 1945
Arlington, Vermont

My dear Professor Pottle:

Now at last I'm back from my travels and can really sit down to dictate an answer to your most interesting letter of August 6th: I regret that I am dictating it because I don't dictate very well, having begun to use that method of writing very much too late in life to have mastered it. I never dictate anything except letters. So you'll have to consider this a letter and not an addition to my lecture.[1]

As I have written you, there are two points I'd like to have changed—in fact I think you really will have to change them to be accurate, but all the rest of your essay is extremely interesting to me, and shows a quickness and flexibility of apprehension of the writing process which is a delight to the writer. Every such teacher of English, raises the level of reader appreciation, and that always raises the level of writing skill.

My first point is in comment on a statement of yours on page four in which you say that I was "near the edge of a nervous collapse." That really is an inaccurate memory of what I said. Because I remember that I especially stressed the fact that this kind of heightened awareness is *not* a condition which goes with ill-health in any way, nor is it—as artists and creative workers like to think—peculiar to them. I especially underlined the fact that everybody, without exception, has days when he is more aware of what goes on around him than on other days. I went to look up my notes on that lecture, I had only one note page of the briefest kind of memoranda, but I found enough to make me sure that I did say that on those days a person not a writer or an artist of any kind is aware of this condition of unusual sensitivity by noticing more the things which happen around him—as that he really sees that a sunset is beautiful, or is indignant over a newspaper account of some injustice which often would leave him untouched, or is frantically irritated by the squeaking of a door or somebody rocking in a chair, small sounds which usually he wouldn't observe.

I pointed out that the ordinary person simply suffers and feels more deeply at such times when his awareness is more acute than usual, but does not make use of it in any way. The artist, writer, or any other form of creative worker, knows that his material and the impulse to creative work comes through that particular state of sensitivity. Robert Frost used to say that when he felt that state of unusual consciousness of everything around him, both for happiness and unhappiness, he "went up into the attic where the clothes were hanging to see which set of clothes would fit that."

I make this point especially because I notice you say I was near a nervous collapse. That's inaccurate in fact, for I have never been near a nervous collapse in my life, have always been indestructibly healthy, like the descendant of New England country people that I am. I was tired on that day in Norway and somewhat strained from a great effort to absorb a new language more quickly than was really possible. But my quickened sensitivity was no more than everybody has had, from the filling-station man to the professor conducting research in a laboratory. It is a common human experience—this change of rhythm in awareness.

The other point I wish to comment on is on your page five. In which you say, underlining it "Mrs. Fisher had *only made a story* out of the facts. But she stopped being hurt by the recollection as soon as her mind had evolved a plot." There's a very important element in writing involved here which I think you overlook. The very end of your essay makes me think that it has just escaped your observation, close as that has been. I think the pain had gone out of the recollection because a new understanding of what has happened to you in the past comes into everybody's mind as he gets older. It is one of the benedictions of increasing years. For the inability to understand is the real unbearable tragedy of human existence as you point out in your quotation from William James in his comment on the tragedy of Job.[2]

Our position, I mean the position of the human race, in regard to understanding its own behavior and the forces of its behavior, is in ignorance, I think, very much like the ignorance of the cave man in regard to the physical phenomena of the world. He knew nothing whatever about the sources of the physical phenomena—nothing about the law of gravity, the succession of the seasons, had only the dimmest ideas of what sunlight did for the world. My impression is that, as far as knowledge of human nature is concerned, we are still wandering in that kind of foggy and dim guessing. So that any moment of vision which brings even a little crumb of understanding of any human phenomenon is a priceless event.

The non-writing person, accepts that new understanding and incorporates it with his own personal life. The impulse of the writing person is to share this new understanding with the rest of humanity. He feels its importance as a help to understanding what takes place around us, and can hardly wait until he has put it into some form in which, he hopes, others may see the significance of events in human life which they have been taking perhaps callously, perhaps just with dull or slow lack of understanding.

What had come to me, there in the Norwegian garden, was a vision of the universality of sensitiveness among all human beings. The slow-witted and dull and unattractive, they who are usually left to one side because they don't seem as alive to ordinary people as those with more gift for articulate expression, I had suddenly perceived that not only my old kinswoman, but all like her, can if placed in favorable situations or circumstances, enjoy life much more deeply than they do. Never again, I subconsciously felt, would I be able to overlook and disregard such a human being in any circle of which I was a part. And my feeling about writing the story was, subconsciously or not, that I was eager to pass on this deeper understanding to others, so that they too would have their eyes opened to the spiritual significance of unassuming people around them, those who do not claim aggressively their share of the goods of life.

So I don't think it was simply that I had "thought of a story that could be made" out of that experience which gave me relief from the pain. It was the feeling that the pain had brought me more understanding of human life which I might, by incorporating it into a fable, pass on to others.

I'll be very much interested to know what you think of this statement of mine, and I hope very much that you will incorporate something (phrasing it very much more carefully than I have in this dictated message) in your essay. For I think it is of vital importance in the understanding of the art of fiction writing. Especially in making the distinction between the two kinds of fiction writing—the kind of story writing which offers the reader an escape from human life, and the kind which is an invitation to him to reflect more deeply than he has upon the significance of human life.

Now one last thing, I wonder if you would be willing not to use the name "Aunt Helen" for that was her real name. I had forgotten I used her real name. I'm afraid some of the cousins in our family would feel hurt. Can't you make it Cousin Margaret. I think nobody would recognize that.

With cordial greetings, and many thanks to you for letting me see this text of your essay before publishing it, I am

Faithfully yours,

---

1. Pottle was preparing an essay based on DCF's lecture at Yale in 1928 on the composition of "The Bedquilt." The essay, "Catharsis," was published in the *Yale Review* 40 (Jan. 1951): 621–41.

2. In "Catharsis," Pottle writes: "William James somewhere has a fine remark to the effect that Job did not complain because God had allowed him to be afflicted, but because he was unable to see God's purpose. If he could only be assured that God had a purpose, he would be content to suffer" (629–30).

139. To J. W. Lane
November 3, 1945
Arlington, Vermont

My dear Dr. Lane:

Your letter of October 15th has just now been forwarded to me from the Book-of-the-Month Club.[1] You see I am a country dweller, living far from the city up in the hills of Vermont.

I found your letter singularly unenvenomed for one on the subject about which you write. Most people always get so excited and unreasonable when that subject is brought up. I read your letter all through with much interest, laid it on one side on the pile of mail which had been read and went on going through the letters which had come in. In one of them was enclosed the proof of an advertisement which is soon to appear in Boston. I don't believe I can answer your letter in any better way than by sending you this advertisement which is to be signed by a number of literary people.

The whole question at issue is really a complex one, the adjustment of literary standards to other standards. In your case one of your standards is of exact medical accuracy. My husband's father was a doctor and my only son was a doctor so I know something about the feeling of doctors for this and can appreciate it. But for writers of creative literature the question of exact accurate nomenclature is not so important as the human accuracy of the picture as a whole. And the opinion of the tremendous majority of competent writers and critics who have read Richard Wright's book is that the human picture as a whole which they present is intensely real.

All those who have spent their life-time working in the literary field, whom I know, have expressed themselves in the greatest admiration of Richard Wright's gift as a writer. The Committee of Selection of the Book-of-the-Month Club, composed as you know of five people who have spent their whole lives in perfecting their skill in the field of literature, both as writers and as critics, were without exception unanimously enthusiastic about the fine literary quality of the book as a whole. If we sincerely felt that it was a fine book, true to human experience as it came to this stepson of our American civilization, we felt we were justified in sending it out to American readers.

Yes, of course we think a great deal, deeply, with anxiety and much earnestness, about the question of sending out books which may not be beneficial to certain kinds of readers. We do the very best we can, on that difficult question. You may be sure that the five of us, elderly, sincere, earnest, American citizens think over the whole situation before we come to a decision.

With thanks for your thoughtful letter on a subject of vital importance I am

Sincerely yours,
Dorothy Canfield Fisher

---

1. J. W. Lane, a physician from West Chicago, Illinois, wrote to DCF on Oct. 15, 1945 to express his disapproval of *Black Boy* on the grounds that it was medically inaccurate in detail and contained obscene language.

140. To Zephine Humphrey
December 18, 1945
Arlington, Vermont

Dearest Zephine:

Yours of the 14th is in today, just as I send off to you something I found among other proof sheets on my shelves. It is the messy set of proofs of that anthology on which Sally Cleghorn worked. I'm not sure that all the pages are there but there are plenty of them to show you that it was a very big undertaking.

I think it would be quite an interesting undertaking—doing this work with Mr. Soskin.[1] My principle has always been as you can perhaps guess, to take on all the work I could possibly swing, no matter from which direction it came. And I think that from a practical point of view that's not a bad way of keeping connection with the publishing world, when one lives far away from it as we do here. And in almost every case I've found something well worth doing possible in the job. I rather imagine you will too.

I simply can't imagine why Mr. Ober[2] does not answer your letter. Is it possible that they can have moved from Scarsdale? The last I heard of them they were right here as they had been for many years. I'll make inquiries and see.

Oh yes, of course I understood about Sally Cleghorn and her cat. Such a minor clash of relative values makes up plenty of the amusing elements in everyday events. When it's just a question of the cat, and somebody's teeth at break-fast time, it's just amusing. When it's a question of doing the best thing for a good cause, and alienating people by an excess emphasis on the details— then sometimes it's rather agonizing. In the back of my mind I always take such episodes as a large question-mark to me myself, as to whether I'm keeping my own relative values in proportion and perspective. Nobody does, I suppose. But it's a good idea to question once in a while about that point. It's not exactly a moral point, and so I think the real moralists hardly ever think of it. It's a question as to the composition of each day's activity, like the question an author asks himself about the composition of a novel—is he getting the various details in the right proportion. Oh a novelist I say? I mean a painter too of course. For I always have conceived of everyday life as needing very much the sort of constant effort at composition—that is shapeliness, elimination of unnecessary details, choice of details—as any other work of art.

Drop me a post card won't you when you make up your mind about doing the book for Mr. Soskin? I'd be really very much interested to know what you decide, and I think I hope you will take it on.

With ever so much love always,

---

1. The "undertaking" was a history of New England social life and customs: *A Book of New England* (New York: Howell, Soskin, 1947).

William Soskin (1900–1952), American editor and publisher. Member of the Book-of-the-Month Club editorial staff.

2. Harold Ober (1881–1959), American literary agent. Head of Harold Ober Associates, which represented Pearl Buck, William Faulkner, F. Scott Fitzgerald, and J. D. Salinger among others.

141. To Mrs. M_____

[1946][1]
[Arlington, Vermont][2]

Dear Mrs. M_____:

Your letter of June 20th has just come through to me in my Vermont home, and I have such a fellow-feeling for you (I'm not only a mother like you, but a grandmother) that I am moved to sit down at once and answer as clearly as I can the various points brought up in your letter.

What is in question, of course, is the basis of selection for the Book-of-the-Month Club books. Three of the five members of the Editorial Board, Dr. Canby, Mr. Christopher Morley and I are of Quaker background. That is, I think you will agree, a guarantee of our sober, careful upbringing in our youth, and of our recognition of moral values during our adult life. We have children and grandchildren, so that the whole gamut of the younger generation is very close to us. Mr. Marquand has young children, and so, I think, has Mr. Fadiman. I really think nobody could be more anxious to do the best thing for the young people of our nation than we five responsible, experienced Americans.

But if all the books written by Americans were arranged and restricted so that they could be read by inexperienced young people without shock or harm to them, we would have a very superficial literature indeed—suitable for the immature, but not for those facing the dark complexities of adult life. There are deep and black and grim parts of human life, about which every grown person has needed to meditate and reflect deeply. It might be said that novels could be divided into two classes, those intended solely to entertain or amuse or please, and those intended as invitations to the reader to deepen his understanding of the meaning of human life.

Fiction which is intended to inspirit, encourage and entertain young people is of a very different quality. There must be plenty of that, of course. But to restrict fiction to subjects and considerations suitable only for people under twenty would be very unfair to older people struggling with the deeper problems of life, who need help in interpreting what they actually find around them in twentieth-century life. It is unfair to people entering upon mature life, or in the midst of it, to make them think that human existence is other than what they find it to be. Reality—in fact—comes as a dangerous shock to those who have been led by the books they read to expect from human life something quite different from what any of us are likely to encounter.

I am an elderly (nearer seventy than sixty) rural Vermonter, and I am repelled as you are by what seems to me the overemphasis laid in modern novels on sex-relations. But I feel that if there is in our American twentieth-century life as it is lived by large numbers of people, in actual reality, such an overemphasis, with its resultant misery and dreariness, it would be ostrich-like for our serious novel writers to ignore it. No good is ever done, I think, by pretending that anything is different from what it really is, either in our explicit statement, or by implication. The prettifying of human relations in conventional old-fashioned, mid-nineteenth-century fiction, was responsible for some ghastly shocks when the readers of those pleasant books came up, in real life, against something which the novels they had read had led them to assume did not exist.

I wholly agree with you that inexperienced people should not be exposed, too young, to ugly aspects of adult life, even though such aspects are part of our nation's life, alas! How to protect them from such contacts, and at the same time not force our American writers to work on the juvenile plane, is a great problem to all those responsible for the welfare of the younger generation, and for the protection of literary standards.

But to ask that every novel written by an experienced, reflective author should provide, for young people, a guide to what is "accepted conduct" as you express it—that would result in very superficial and unreal fiction, not at all worthy of the great traditions of literature, which, we all hope, our great country will carry on.

The theme of *The Hucksters*[3] is this, don't you think: the really horrible power over human beings of the greed for money and the really revolting results when men value money more than self-respect. Those men in *The Hucksters* who trembled so when the rich old tyrant came into the room—they were free, able-bodied Americans. Nothing in the world (save their own eagerness to make a lot of money) held them there to be insulted and humiliated by the rich man, as completely as the people around Hitler were insulted and humiliated. Any one of them could, at any minute, have put on his hat like a self-respecting man (as the hero finally did), could have left that horrible set-up, to earn his living like a decent man. The only reason they did not was because they couldn't resist the temptation to get more money from the disgusting old man than they would in some other work.

All in their personal lives that disgusts you and me and any other sane person, resulted from the nervous tension, panic, fear, and bitter self-contempt which filled their wretched lives. They were driven half crazy by their ignoble relation to that old man. Yet his only power over them was that he had money they wanted.

If there ever was a book which said at the top of the author's voice, "Stand up, straight! Keep your dignity! Don't value money more than self-respect!" it is *The Hucksters*. What might be called its "message" is one which would be a salutary warning to any young person about to begin earning his living. The horrible coarse details are a part of telling truthfully this story of one corner of American commercial life.

We read in the Epistle to the Romans that "The wages of sin is death." But "moral death" is an abstraction that doesn't mean much to people without wide experience of human life. What the author of *The Hucksters* has done is to show what "moral death" really is, in terrible, frightening detail. We who live ordinary, respectable, self-disciplined lives, devoted to our families, surrounded by quiet, pleasant people, we are far away from such dreadful danger as that which ruins the lives of the employees of that coarse old millionaire. Yet an adored son of ours might inadvertently stumble across some analogous danger as he works for his living. We can hardly imagine them, and so could never warn our children against them. But I can hardly imagine a person reading *The Hucksters* who would not recognize, in real life, even in some quite different outer form, the terrible danger of valuing a high salary more than his self-respect. The great question, of course, is at what age young people may safely begin to encounter, in soundly written books, some of the various aspects of that actual reality which faces them in their adult life. That question has to be answered differently for every young person, of course. And it is a question for parents and teachers. Fortunate are they whose parents put the best and most courageous thinking they are capable of, into getting the right answer to this vital question—as you are evidently doing.

If you really feel that the Book-of-the-Month Club should send out only books suitable for the reading of young people in their teens, or books which always ignore the dangerous moral failures so often made by men and women in real life, wouldn't it be better to cancel your subscription? For a few years, anyhow, it might be safer, till your own cherished younger generation have grown up to an age where they could profit, begin to encounter, occasionally, in a book, some of the things from which no parent can wholly protect them in real life. Don't you think that perhaps just to keep out of the house any books you think unsuitable for young people might be the best solution of the problem you describe with so much sincere anxiety in your letter?

With every good greeting,

Faithfully yours,
Dorothy Canfield

_____

1. Date: publication date of Frederic Wakeman's *The Hucksters* (New York: Rinehart, 1946), book-of-the-month, June 1946.
   2. Place: stated.
   3. See note 1.

142. To Margaret Mead
January 3, 1946
Arlington, Vermont

Dear Dr. Mead:

I was asked to give a talk at Boston to the annual convention of the Teachers of Social Sciences the day after Thanksgiving. And I took the opportunity to speak for the thousandth time, it seems to me, about the social pressures, invisible and tyrannical, which the United States puts upon its women and girls.

I had no sooner reached home from Boston than the people who heard me there began to write me that you had an article in *Fortune* which I should read since you and I were evidently in entire accord on this subject, and I don't know how many of them have sent me the article.[1]

It goes without saying that I like it enormously and that I am very thankful that you have written it. I'm so glad of my one glimpse of you when we spoke together on the same platform once some years ago, to see that you looked very young, robust and vigorous. For you have a great deal of work to do and are very much needed in the American future. It does me a lot of good to know that you are on the ground ready to lead where there is so much need for leadership.

And because I think everybody on the same side ought to have some idea about his fellow-workers, I am giving myself the pleasure of sending you a recent book of mine called *Our Young Folks*. Don't bother to read it all—you have far too much to do. And you know it all anyhow probably.

But take a look at the section called "Something About Girls." It represents my struggle to get something said in the sake of the universal ignoring (so it has seemed to me for many years) the real problems of American women.

And I'm also sending you—what I hate to have anybody send me—a carbon copy of a typescript. It is the memorandum for my talk before the Social Sciences Convention. It seems to be the only copy I have of that talk so I'm going to ask you to return it to me, and I've put in a long envelope, stamped and self-addressed so you won't have to make an extra motion to get it back to me. It is, as of course your experienced eye will recognize, just a hasty note for a talk, not at all a finished production. But I think all we who are on the same side ought to stand together and use each other's arguments if they can be of any use. I'd be honored to have you make any quotation from me, with or without quotation marks—just to have you use it for the good cause would delight me.

I've been struggling with this problem since before you were born I think, and have felt as though I were talking down a well, as the old saying goes. I never seem to get anybody to listen to me at all—or at least to take any action on what I've said. It delights me to have your voice apparently so much more audible than mine.

With friendly and admiring greetings,
Faithfully yours,

---

1. "What Women Want," *Fortune* 33 (Dec. 1946): 172.

143. To Christopher Morley
January 11, 1946
Arlington, Vermont

Dear Chris:

One of the many things I have been set to learn since the news came of my son's death,[1] is not to weep, even when the heart is deeply, deeply shaken. I didn't know at all that tears—too many tears—could literally threaten the vision of one's physical eyes, until, with the sight of one eye very much impaired, I went to see my oculist, who told me that he could do nothing to help me, that I must just stop crying or I would lose my vision.

I was horrified at the thought of my uselessness were I to lose my eyes, and at the idea that I might bring on that uselessness, my only way of living up to my golden-hearted son's example, by lack of courage in bearing what was given me to bear—lagging far behind Jimmy's example who stood up to what was given him to do,—up to death and beyond. So I have been learning how to live in wild turmoil of unspoken pain, of pride, and sorrow,—without crying. Or mostly without tears. Every once in a while some shaft suddenly thrusts too deep, too suddenly. The Christmas season has been a hard one to live through on these terms, for Jimmy was born—in the room where I still sleep—almost on Christmas day, and the old house which was his home rings constantly, and especially at this season which was so especially his, with echoes of his light elastic young step, and a thousand visual memories of his comings and goings.

I am moved beyond myself to tell you all this, because your note has, almost astonishingly, been a very great help. I did not weep over it—because I have learned how to keep back the tears, even when I am stirred to the depths, as I was by your kind, kind friend's divination of the sorrow I am trying to transmute to something I can carry forward with me into what's left of life for me. It's almost surprising, human life being what it is, and we all what we are, that you *could* have the spiritual intuition in the midst of your own life so rich in affections and satisfying work, thus to divine the silent inner struggle going on in another's heart. It impressed me greatly. And it was comforting.

I used to say—before I had known overwhelming sorrow—that nobody could understand another's pain or really share it, or really bring any comfort to it. I know better now. Such an unexpected message of sympathy and understanding as yours—it steadies the faltering step which is trying to find its way forward. I'm very grateful for it.

It's sweet to have you include "those of my house" when you send your compassionate thought toward John and me. Please thank your wife for sharing your impulse to stretch out a kind and loving hand to those in distress.

Your

---

1. See Letter 136, note 1.

144. *To Robert Haas*
April 16, 1946
Arlington, Vermont

Dear Merle and Bob:

Do you know I believe, in my focused and concentrated interest on the last Blixen book[1] that I never told you the overwhelming news that her Aunt Mary, my beloved Mary Westenholz, is not dead at all. She is very old, eighty-five years old, but in excellent health. The Norwegian-American clergyman who gave me this news, apparently from absolutely first-hand information from people escaping from Denmark, was just mistaken. He has died since he told me, so I can't find out where the mistake lay—he got it from people escaping to England and from thence to Canada, for military training. It's quite possible that they mixed up her sister who was the mother of Baroness Blixen with Mary Westenholz. They were about the same age and of course very close to each other. Anyhow my dear Mary is still alive and I have had a letter from her. Do you remember that beautiful passage in the Beethoven *Missa Solemnis*[2] where the chorus suddenly bursts into almost hysterical joy on the phrase *Et ressurexit*. Well, something like that was in my mind when I read this news. What I'm writing to you now is one last confidential speculation about Isak Dinesen the writer. You know I consider it somewhat intrusive thus to peer openly into the depths of another person's personality and speculate on what is there. I do it all the time of course but I usually keep it to myself. As long as you do that I think you're reasonably decent about it. But now I want to give you one other guess of mine which may be to Bob's purpose as her publisher.

One of the things which Mary writes me is about her niece of whom she says "She has passed a serious operation and cannot recover health or strength."[3] This from a serious responsible member of the older generation means a great deal. It probably means that Tania will be more or less an invalid from now on. For anyone of her tastes and aspirations this will be an extremely serious blow and alteration of her life.

You may remember that I was struck by a certain likeness in her character to that of Oscar Wilde who was also extremely brilliant when I wrote you that hastily scribbled-off letter. Well, you know that the one really serious knock-down blow which Oscar Wilde had was his term in prison,[4] and that he wrote while there "The Ballad of Redding Gaol" which has become one of the English classics, there's no doubt about that.

Now it seems to me quite possible that this complete alteration in Tania's life may break up forever her work as a writer, or it may on the other hand deepen it to a new spiritual significance which it has never had before. She may become a really great writer not only through skill and subtlety, but through death.

Maybe not. Illness and weakness can destroy the creative impulse, but they haven't in a great many invalid authors with something seriously the matter with their health.

I thought you might be interested and that Bob really should know about this sentence from Mary Westenholz's letter which presages apparently continued invalidism. Bob treats his authors so entirely like human beings that I know he will want to know this item in the human existence of a brilliant writer.

Affectionately always,

---

1. *The Angelic Avengers* (New York: Random House, 1946), book-of-the-month, Jan. 1947 (with *Mr. Blandings Builds His Dream House* by Eric Hodgins).

2. Beethoven's *Mass in D* (1822), known as the *Missa Solemnis*.

3. In Feb. 1946 Dinesen underwent stomach surgery for duodenal ulcers.

4. In 1895, Wilde was sentenced to two years' hard labor for his romantic affair with Lord Alfred Douglas.

145. *To Raymond Holden*
November 16, 1946
Arlington, Vermont

Dear Mr. Holden:

I have been writing you, vastly enjoying the process, a leisurely letter-in-my-mind, as I have read your poems,[1] slowly, as I love to read poetry and as your beautifully thoughtful poems should be read. A thought-comment on each one, as I read it, has been tucked away in my mind.

But before I could get pen to paper to set down these "meditations on first-rate poetry," and to thank you, more than I can say, for the inscription in the book which made and makes me so proud, which was and is so reassuring to my sense of not amounting to much in spite of honest efforts,—in comes Miss Stoller with your note to me about someone who'd like to talk to me about Robert Frost.

And that brings up a question which is, to me, so poignant, that I sit down as soon as I reach home, to write you about it.

I just never do, for anybody, what this biographer of Robert Frost would like to have me do—that is, talk about an old friend, to someone who is going to pass on what I say to the reading public. We Fishers shared life, as friends and neighbors, with Robert Frost and his wife and his children up to the time of Elinor's death.[2] What one comes to know about one's friends by this sharing of life during a period of years has its intimate aspects. And I am deeply colored by the Vermont and Quaker tradition of keeping intimate details for those who have an intimate knowledge of the framework around the details. In passing them on to people who don't know the context, there is, inevitably, a risk of inaccurate presentation, of having them seen in a perspective which makes them appear other than they were—are. I wouldn't like to have an old friend of mine interviewed and questioned about what he had come to know about my family and me in the course of years shared together. I don't see that anybody could take out of his whole acquaintance with our life a part for somebody to use for publicity, without distortion. I'd be obliged to a friend who would protect me from that risk.

I have written several pieces about Robert Frost,[3] some of them with facts about his personality, which give expression to my great, almost extravagant, admiration for his poetry in a way that's carefully planned to be suitable for reading by people who don't know him personally. Why not use those, as "sources" and call them enough? They must be listed, I imagine, in *Poole's Index*. I have also written a slight, short sketch about him in a book just about to appear (early in ,December) published by H. Holt & Co., entitled "American Portraits."[4] Holt & Co. would give you, I am sure, a set of the proofs of this book, and probably permission to use any part of this—although it is not to be "informative" as to details, and might not be to the purpose of a biographer.

I seem to have mislaid your note, in the flurry of getting home from a Book-of-the-Month Club meeting with all the sorting over of papers involved in that process. So I'll have to ask you to pass on the gist of this letter to the biographer. You'll be able, I am sure, to think of some way to put it to him, less Vermont-brusque than what I have written you impulsively, without trying to find conventional phrases.

With every heartfelt good greeting to you, and so many renewed thanks for the gift of your deep and noble poems,

Faithfully yours,
Dorothy Canfield Fisher

---

1. Probably Holden's *Selected Poems* (New York: Holt, 1946).
2. Elinor Frost died Mar. 20, 1938.
3. For example, "Robert Frost: A Neighbor of Mine" (see Letter 79, note 5), and "Robert Frost's Hilltop," *Bookman* 64 (Dec. 1926): 403–5.
4. See Letter 134, note 3.

146. *To Meredith Wood*
November 16, 1946
Arlington, Vermont

Dear Meredith:

My head was swimming when I turned away from that long telephone-talk with you about the whirlpool centering on the Steinbeck book.[1] How you got through that complicated re-arrangement beats me! You must have been a wreck.

Now that I've had a little time to settle my thoughts, I find two items to bring to your attention. One is this:—the Steinbeck book is not gross, like *The Hucksters*[2] because of the peculiar environment set around a group of people, which acted upon and influenced all in the same way. In Steinbeck's book the group shown came together from a variety of backgrounds and experiences, and *yet* they all have one obsession—sex. This fundamental conception of the story seems to me false to human probability, and makes the constant under-lining of sex seem a contrivance of the author's (either for financial profit or because he himself has a peculiar personal taste for such underlining)—it is no longer an attempt to portray human life.

I hope some of the most offensive passages will be taken out but I haven't much hope that the changes can alter the basically (it seems to me) phoney and artificial nature of the story. The brilliant quality of the actual writing will have to be the explanation of its choice. There is certainly no brilliance in the creation of character and no power of real understanding in the portrayal of personality. But many readers seem satisfied with a bright surface of adept and vivid style, such as Steinbeck certainly has.

(2) Among the many protests which I've been reading about *The Hucksters,* it seems to me the only really justified ones come from subscribers who said that the long review of *The Hucksters* in the *Book-of-the-Month Club News* had *not* given them any idea of the coarse outspokenness about sex which to them had made it intolerable. Such readers said that they didn't attempt to decide what kind of books the Committee of Selection decides to send out; but they do think (and I think so too) they have an inalienable right to know before they agree to accept a book whether it is likely to shock and offend them and their families. They admitted that the right to select given to subscribers by the Book-of-the-Month Club opens to them a perfectly possible way to escape books they are ashamed to have their families see, but only, of course, if in the description of the book, sent out a month beforehand, they are given a clear and unmistakable indication about the character of the book being described in this respect.

I feel this position is logical and reasonable and I think the person who writes the long review of *The Wayward Bus* should make this point clear. Really clear. Not to be missed.

Once, years ago, when in talk with Harry,[3] I made this point he said that alas! such an indication by a reviewer of something sexually shocking in a book simply brought more readers to it. Any book so described was sure to have a sale from people looking for something pornographic.

This is likely, human nature being what it is; but such people take the responsibility for their choice of their reading on themselves. It is no longer our responsibility.

I haven't much real hope that the book can be made decent because the conception of the story seems to me based on a deliberate falsifying of human probabilities, limiting the interests of all those diverse people to one of the many possible tastes and interests of men and women; but I don't see any reason why the review can't set up a sign-post that will give a warning perfectly visible to every reader.

Ever yours,
Dorothy

1. John Steinbeck, *The Wayward Bus* (New York: Viking Press, 1947), book-of-the-month, Mar. 1947.
2. See Letter 141, note 1.
3. Harry Scherman.

147. To Upton Sinclair
December 4, 1946
Arlington, Vermont

Dear Mr. Sinclair:

Your letter, very welcome, and the enclosed from Mr. Huebsch,[1] greeted me as I return from a family visit to my daughter in Maine.

You are right, of course, I should have spoken about *The Jungle* in my remarks in "I wish I'd written that."[2] It is a perfect example of fiction written from the point of view of the inarticulate wage-earner. Is, in fact, the acknowledged classic example.

But even if I had remembered to speak of it with the admiration I feel for the book, I think I would have said that it is not exactly what I mean by a book about *industrial* workers, since it does not deal with people who serve and tend machines, whose earning-a-living occupation has the strange non-human, non-organic, non-living quality of all-powerful steel machinery.

You are very good to ask Mr. Huebsch to send me a copy of *The Jungle,* and since I don't happen to own a copy, the shelves in my work-study will be the richer for it. A new edition,[3] too, I notice. That's glory, for a still-living author. But you have plenty of that article, now!

With thanks for your letter and every good wish,
Faithfully yours,
Dorothy Canfield Fisher

1. B. W. Huebsch (1876?–1964), American publisher, was founder of B. W. Huebsch Publishing Co. and editor-in-chief and vice-president of the Viking Press.
2. Upton Sinclair, *The Jungle* (New York: Doubleday & Page, 1906). DCF selected a passage from Alex Comfort's *The Power House* (1945) for inclusion in *I Wish I'd Written That,* ed. Eugene J. Woods (New York: McGraw-Hill, 1946). Sinclair chose passages on social justice from John Ruskin and Isaiah for the volume comprised of favorite writings nominated by thirty-three authors.
3. Two editions of *The Jungle* were published in 1946, one as a Harper Modern Classic, the other by Viking.

148. *To Willa Cather*
[April (20?) 1947][1]
Arlington, Vermont

Dear dear Willa:

I was just sitting down to write you when your letter came in—feeling that you must be told the sad news that our dear Stella, Jim's wife, is dead. Jim just telephoned me from Miami. They had one of their peaceful sunny winters there, in their lovely home. They had started to drive to the restaurant where they were to have dinner. Stella died in the car. Instantly. Like a candle blown out.

Almost the instant after these words had reached my ear as soon as I had caught one breath after the shock, I remembered that Stella's mother, her Aunt Phebe, and her beloved brother, had died of the same trouble—with their hearts. But in no such instant peace as Stella. They had lingered on for many months, in a distressing state of mental deterioration, as the blood slowly failed to find its way to the brain. Stella had been distracted with pity and horror to see the condition into which Charlie Elliott, so soberly steady and intelligent, had fallen before death finally took him. It had been a nightmare for her—the thought that she too might die in that way. When Jim can recover a little from the shock, he will not fail to remember this, and to be thankful for Stella that she was spared this terrible ordeal.

I can't imagine, literally, what he will do, poor Jim, nor how he will be able to organize his life without this life companion—fifty years they had shared, together in the closest intimacy. He will come to us of course when he first comes north. But I doubt if he will be able to stay anywhere, long.

His sons (the oldest is forty-seven years old—does it seem possible) went at once by plane to Miami, to be with their father and drive him north. I imagine they will start very soon. Jim said over the telephone, that his one wish was to get back to Vermont as soon as that was possible. Stella was just past seventy. Jim is seventy-three and not well, himself, having had a phlebitis, last autumn, in one leg, which has never been completely cured.

Yes, I remember very well that visit to Houseman,[2] now that you remind me of it. Let me set down, as I write, what comes into my head about it. It may give you a detail or two more. You and Isabelle,[3] back from Ludlow, had secured Houseman's address—out in some rather drab London suburb, as I remember it. As we went out together, I remember your saying how odd it was that nobody knew a thing about him, personally. This was of course long before the Houseman cult. I remember your saying "We may find that he is a blacksmith, for all we know."

At the house, the landlady received us with a cordiality which struck me as a

little odd, and called up the stairs (no, went up the stairs) to tell Houseman—
as we asked her to say that "some American young ladies had come to see
him."

He came running down the stairs, looking very cordial and welcoming—
and was greatly surprised to find that we were not some young-lady-cousins of
his from Canada, who were expected any minute. (This explained the landlady's cordiality.)

But he was courteous, said with a neutral, British pleasantness that he would
be glad to have us go upstairs to his study. That was a plain, rather threadbare room, I remember, with boarding-houseish cheap furniture—not ram-
shackle, but not a bit good, and badly needing some wax and rubbing. On the
floor was what was then called in England, an "oil cloth" what we called (I
think even then) linoleum. Rather thin. A rug or two, also thin, and somewhat
crumpled up. I remember thinking, as I took in these details, and looked at the
thin, ascetic-looking scholar with his straggly moustache, that the whole setting and the man himself were just what scholars had always had and been,
from medieval times down to Nebraska University.

I find I don't remember much about the conversation at first. I don't think
I took part in it, considering myself just taken along with you and Isabelle
(who had a perfectly good reason, in just having been to Ludlow) just because
you were kind and knew I'd be interested. You and Isabelle were, I think,
speaking about Ludlow, the castle, the country-side, the people in a way which
I found very interesting.

But presently Houseman turned to me, in the well-bred way which carefully brought up people have, (so I thought) noticing that I was being rather
left out, and not realizing that that was what I had expected and found natural. He asked me, "And have you too been to Ludlow?" I said I'd had no such
luck, but had been in the British Museum, slugging away at manuscripts. He
asked another question, about my subject, and hearing that it was Romance
languages, asked if I had been studying in Paris? I said yes, I had, with old
Paul Meyer,[4] of the École des Hautes Études. He showed interest, asked if I
had ever heard of the old-French Mss. which Paul Meyer had unearthed in the
Bodleian. I said sure I had, I had been reading it with him. He asked some
other questions—evidently knowing a lot about the whole subject of reading
manuscripts, and I happened to mention that I had done some work on pre-
classic Latin. (You know I've always had a perverse, slate-pencil-eating interest in pure linguistics.) This was evidently his subject, and he held forth at
length.

I remember feeling very uncomfortable and thinking, "This is terrible. Must
be boring Willa and Isabelle to death." I was rather bored myself, having enough
of that sort of talk in my student associations. But that was in the period when

young ladies were taught that the prime virtue for them, socially was to talk brightly about whatever seemed to interest the man who was conversing with them. And anyhow I was youthfully inept about managing conversation, and couldn't seem to think of any way to get off that absurd topic—absurd, because it had nothing to do with the purpose of our going.

But I really felt very uneasy, about what seemed bad manners on my part, and after we had gone, and were sitting on the top of a bus, going back to our lodgings, and I saw you were weeping, my heart was simply broken because I thought I had spoiled the whole occasion for you. But, generously, warm-heartedly, you relieved me by assuring me that your feeling had nothing to do with anything I had done during the visit. I thought it then (and still think it) characteristically great-hearted of you not to have minded.

With all my love, dear old comrade,
Your devoted,
Dorothy

[Handwritten written in left margin of page one] Yes, Houseman was Professor of Latin at London University then (I got an *impression* that he sort of apologized for being there rather than at Oxford or Cambridge.) I think his specialty was early Latin, and Latin linguistics not literature—but am not sure, I find.

---

1. Date: Cather's letter requesting details of the visit to Housman is dated Apr. 17, 1947. DCF would have had to send her response on or about Apr. 20 for Cather to have read it before her death on Apr. 24.
    2. The trip to visit Housman, whom DCF and Cather greatly admired (see Letter 2), occurred in 1902, while Cather was traveling in Europe, and DCF was studying at the Sorbonne.
    3. Isabelle McClung (1877–1938), friend of Cather's (see Letter 4, note 2).
    4. Paul Meyer, DCF's professor in Old French, is profiled in *Raw Material*.

149. *To Reginald L. Cook*
June 18, 1947
[Arlington, Vermont][1]

Dear Professor Cook:
    Yes, July 14, Monday will do very well for me. And I to speak in the evening, as before?[2] I assume so, and will start from here in time to be with you for supper, at six unless you send other suggestions.
    Have you thought at all what you would like me to talk about? What would you think of a talk with some such title as "Writing Fables," or "Narratives for

Children." I have been writing a series of stories for an English text-book series for children in our American public-schools,[3] from the pre-school age kindergarten child, up to (so far) the fifth grade. If I can venture to pronounce so great a name as Tolstoy's, in connection with an enterprise of my own, I'd like to remind you that Tolstoy wrote a series of "moral" stories for children to read in schools.[4] Mine aren't moral—not in that sense, but are intended to enlarge the horizon of the children's imagination, fancy, and social sense. Well no, they are intended first of all to be lively tales to hold the children's attention, and they have been tried out on many children in many schools to test this quality. Any other intention is by implication alone, quite in the background.

I think an interesting hour's talk could be made out of some of the material and the background for it. All the real problems of writing narration are involved, of course.

How does that idea strike you?

With good greetings,
Faithfully yours
Dorothy Canfield Fisher

---

1. Place: implied.

2. DCF is responding to an invitation to address the Bread Loaf School of English in Middlebury, Vermont, which Cook directed.

3. See Letter 134, note 4.

4. Count Leo (Lev) Nikolayevich Tolstoy (1828–1910), Russian novelist. Tolstoy wrote a series of graded readers comprised mostly of material from his *New ABC Book* (1875). His interest in the project grew out of the experimental school he established for the children of the serfs on his estate. The readers were recommended by the Ministry of Education and were widely used.

150. To Thomas Dinesen
June 21, 1947
Arlington, Vermont

My dear Mr. Dinesen:

I can't find words to tell you what your letter meant to me, in which you informed me of the death of my beloved friend, your Aunt Mary.[1] I'm close to seventy now myself, and hence naturally am of the age when there are many deaths in my close circle. Since my dear Jimmy's death I have heard a veritable roll-call of much cherished names, of those dear to me from whom I will never hear again. My lifelong intimate in France,[2] a French friend who was as close as any sister could be to me, died just before the liberation of France. She and our Jimmy almost at the same time.

Yet the death of "my dear Mary," as I always thought of her, has a different quality for me. You see, I had heard a false report that she had died during the war—a Norwegian clergyman whom I saw occasionally had heard through Danish friends that she had died during the German occupation of Denmark. Your Aunt Mary and I thought after we did come together again by letter, that perhaps he was thinking of your mother's death.

So that my dear Mary had really seemed to come back to me from death when I began to hear from her again after the war. And, for me, to know her was more a spiritual experience of golden value, than just a human acquaintanceship. I think I wrote your sister Karen once—or was it of your mother?— that I sometimes felt on closer and more intimate terms with your aunt than I would have been if I had lived next door. Our having practically no material everyday things in common, what we did have in common, which was enormous, and of inestimable value to me—was a spiritual and moral attitude towards life. I think I have never had in all my long life a relationship so beautifully pure and clear from any trivialities as that which has made one of the great lights of the later years of my life—Mary Westenholz' sharing of her life experience with me. I have never known a more beautiful nature than hers, and my contact with it came at a time of terrible doubt of anybody's nature which now envelopes all the globe in apprehension and anxiety.

So that the thought of her does not now come to me with the sorrow which usually hangs like a pall over those who have recently lost a dearly loved friend by death, but with a sort of exaltation. I'm not a religious person as she was,— part of our comparison of our interpretations of life turned on this big difference between us. But I certainly do not feel that she has died—not for me, at any rate.

Thank you so much for taking the time to write me in detail about her last illness. It is a very great comfort to me to know that she did not suffer and that she had been in bed for only two days. When I last heard from her she was having an attack of jaundice, and you must have by this time a letter from me to her in which I begged for more news of her health. But she wrote as always, her handwriting clear and firm—much better than mine—and her mind in its usual radiant sincerity. So that I was not really anxious about her.

Won't you remember me warmly to her old servant Anna, whom I must have seen on my one brief visit to Folehave. I too have a very old servant who has been with me for many years and to whom I am greatly devoted.

It gives me the greatest happiness to know that you and your wife may come to this new world, for I had hoped sometime—in spite of her age—to see your Aunt Mary. I shall certainly hope to see you both here in Arlington for a visit long enough for us to have some real talks together. I feel we have a great deal in common, and in these days whatever people have in common who live in different lands, should be shared, I think, as part of the preparation for the new kind of global life which perhaps—if men of good will are successful—lies before us. I shall look forward to this visit with more pleasure than I can put into words.

Now I wonder if I could ask you to send me some little thing which your Aunt Mary owned and used, which I could keep and use myself as a link to her. Your mother, years ago when I was first able to do something for your sister Tania's books, sent me a piece of her own handwork—a lovely piece of embroidery which has been one of my great treasures ever since.

Is there some small object among my dear Mary's household goods which she used every day or looked at every day, which would not be too much trouble for you to send me. It would be a comfort to me to touch and handle or to look at something which had been part of her daily life.

With warm friendly greetings to you and so many thanks for your letter,

Faithfully yours,

---

1. See Blixen entry in Notable Recipients.
2. Céline Sibut, see entry in Notable Recipients.

151. To Reginald L. Cook
June 30, 1947
Arlington, Vermont

Dear Professor Cook:

You are right, I am sure; although as always I deplore with sadness the assumption that women only, never men, see the importance of the development of personality in young people and children and understand the vital bearing on this development of what is read by those who, in a few years will be American voting citizens. They will be, also, the book-buying (or not-buying) public and their attitude towards reading, taught them by the general atmosphere about them in their youth, will determine to a considerable extent, the attitude of American readers towards their reading.

So I withdraw the suggestion about fable-writing.

Here is another idea, presented for your consideration. I am working on a book to be called "Vermont Tradition." It is intended solely for adult readers (hence to be taken seriously by men). It will not be in the least a factual history of the state—no need of another one of those, but is rather a sort of interpretation of the facts as passed on in local, oral tradition.

In your last letter you say the Bread Loaf School audience would be interested in the "technique of method, the possibilities in the use of material." Would you consider (I do) that under that heading would come some talk about the possibilities in the use of the material for history which is lying all about us, but not yet poured into the set mould of the professional historian's treatment?

I would perhaps read a chapter or two of what I have written and then comment on it, along these lines.

Just let me know, will you, how this strikes you as a possibility. If you think something else might be better, do say the word, and I'll suggest something else.

Sincerely yours
Dorothy Canfield Fisher

152. To Bernardine K. Scherman
January 21, 1948
[Arlington, Vermont]¹

Dear Bernardine:

I've been sitting in my usual winter-evening corner in the study, by the open fire in the Franklin stove, which is lighted in October and never goes out till May. The heavy curtains are drawn to help shut out the below-zero cold, our road is so heaped with snow that nobody could get up to us from the outside world. It was just the time to reach for your short-story anthology,² with my conscience clear about not working, for I can't go on with reading a huge book by Laski,³ because the proofs are badly printed and hard on the eyes, and Harry's trying to get a better set of galleys to me.

It has been such a grand evening that now I jump up and come to the type-writer to tap down for you in my own bad amateur typing, some of my appreciation of this book. It's given me a couple of hours of such rich delight in the art of fiction as seldom comes to anybody who has been reading as many years as I. Gracious! how long *have* I been reading stories? I'll soon be sixty-nine years old, and I think it must have been when I was twelve, in Paris with my mother, that I first read Balzac's "Passion in the Desert"—fifty-seven years ago. I've never read it since, have scarcely thought of it, but will you believe it, the impression made on me was so great that I found I still remember some of the exact turns of phrase, remembered too—and *felt again*—in bodily fibre, the singularly sensuous quality of the story, could hear the formidable reverberations of the panther's purring, felt under my hand again that ominously stone-hard skull, under the soft thick fur.

I can't remember how old I was—fifteen maybe—when I first read *The*

Death of Ivan Ilyich, and burst into tears of agonized emotion over what I still think one of the most moving passages in literature, at the end, after the appalling three-day-long scream, when "he rolled forward into the hole, and there at the end was some sort of light"—and then that bold, masterly use of new modern material in the comparison to what sometimes happens in a train going through a tunnel, when all at once you see that you are going the other way from what you thought. At least, as I remembered it, it was while the train was going through a tunnel. In the more than fifty years since, I've never gone through a tunnel in a train without remembering that soaring moment of inner vision. I see to my surprise that your English translator[4] doesn't put in any tunnel. I read the story in a French translation, the only way Tolstoy was generally available as long ago as when I was in my teens.

Well, didn't I once again, cringe under those terrible screams, and once again feel the tears on my cheeks as the dying man realized that he had, all the time, been going in the other direction from what he had feared. What a genius! Like Beethoven, like Michel-Angelo, how he can pass the sword through your vitals with one stroke.

Well, then I wiped my eyes and turned back to read your foreword and found I had been doing exactly what you wanted the reader of the book to do—to be *moved* by what you offer him.

I think that foreword is a wonderfully fine piece. Because of its understanding, not just because of its brilliance—"today's popular success can wear as thin as Ravel's *Bolero,*" there's a whole essay of aesthetic criticism amusingly compressed into that short phrase. And "It is a song, not a symphony." I can't make out whether *you* say that, or Bliss Perry.[5] A gold medal should be hung on whichever!

I particularly like the simple, graceful, unpontifical tone of the foreword. It must have been difficult to strike that easy, unforced note, to make so natural, so personal and so attractive a gesture of invitation to accompany your swinging open of those great doors.

Heavens! what an amount of work you have done on this, just plain grinding desk work, not to speak of the intricate effort of selection, omission, good judgment, and the writing of the introductory pieces about each writer. Many thanks for what you say about my work.[6] It not only pleased me greatly—who wouldn't be pleased!—but seemed to me penetrating. I mean you pointing out that the simplest human material (like the old Vermont lore in which I am soaked to my marrow) if it is fully known by an author, even of only moderate talents if an honest reporter, in all the time-sequence of many years of contact with it, and has been deeply reflected on, has a special quality of depth and meaning—I won't look back over that sentence, pretty sure that it fell over its grammatical feet. But you can, I know, see what I mean. It is what you meant.

I mustn't give the impression that I read, as I turned over the pages only the great classics—and the older ones. I turned very soon to Eudora Welty, whose work gives me an enchanted pleasure, like something simply delicious to eat. By good luck I had never read "The Petrified Man"[7] before, so it had all the joy of freshness added to the other joys she gives. I revelled in it. The conversation of those nit-wit women in the beautician's parlor—really Daumier[8] never did anything more telling in the way of an exhibition of human idiocy.

I tried a mystery story[9] too, the one about the mezzo-tint of the old house, which is a lulu—at least the first part, which is absolutely hair-raising. I thought the explanation at the end rather flat. But maybe that's the accepted tradition in that literary genre. I've read very little of it. And the Saki story[10] is a scream, one loud hilarious scream.

Well, I've had a good time, as you can see, and now gloat over the many pages of the collection, with cheerful anticipations of more evenings like this one.

With admiring affection, always
Dorothy

---

1. Place: implied.

2. *A Treasury of Short Stories,* ed. Bernardine Kielty (New York: Simon & Schuster, 1947), book-of-the-month dividend, 1947.

3. Harold Joseph Laski, *The American Democracy: A Commentary and an Interpretation* (New York: Viking, 1948).

4. Constance Garrett, translator.

5. Refers to a quote by Bliss Perry in the anthology's "Foreword": "[The short story] may be the merest sketch of a face, a comic attitude, a tragic incident: it may be a lovely dream, a horrid nightmare, or a page of words that haunt us like music." Kielty adds, "It is a song, not a symphony."

6. The anthology includes DCF's "Sex Education," originally published in the *Yale Review* 35 (Dec. 1945): 252–64, and reprinted in *Four-Square* (1949) and *A Harvest of Stories* (1956). In an introductory note, Scherman writes of DCF: "Though she often writes of Vermonters, her work is in no way 'regional,' because Vermont, as she presents it, is not limited to local talk and customs. Her country people, with their independent ideas, might as easily be Norwegians (to whom she often compares them) or Scots or French peasants. She has lived many years in France, and besides French, which she speaks fluently, she knows Danish, German, Spanish, and Italian. It is this knowledge and understanding of the peoples of many nations that add another dimension to her plain Vermont characters and to her thoughtful stories, so simple on the surface, of the why and how of their lives."

7. Welty's "The Petrified Man" was originally published in her first book, *A Curtain of Green* (New York: Harcourt, Brace, 1941).

8. Honoré Daumier (1808–1879), French sculptor, Impressionist painter, caricaturist.

9. "The Red-Headed League" by Sir Arthur Conan Doyle.

10. "The Open Window." Saki is the pseudonym of the British short story writer Hugh Munro (1870–1916).

153. *To Harry Scherman*
April 9 [1948][1]
[Arlington, Vermont][2]

Dear Harry:

I have always kept in touch with the Sergeant in Jimmy's outfit, in the Philippines, and once in a while get a letter from him, about things in general. In his last letter he made a comment on *The Naked and the Dead,*[3] which I think you might be interested in. He was five years in the Army as a private and then non-com. A Minnesota man by birth. Now living in California.

"I read *The Naked and the Dead,* and was more than a little disappointed. Where the author imagined he could find *one* short platoon of soldiers who were all such unmitigated screwballs is beyond me. In five years service in the army, I met my share of candidates for such a "Section Eight" but it's the first time I ever heard of them being *all* incorporated in of all things an I and R platoon. He managed to bring in the profanity that seems to follow the service but he eliminated every bit of the imagination and color that the dogface expressed in his adjectives and reduced to a mere monotony of vulgarity."

That's what I felt about that now much praised novel. But of course what an elderly woman living in Vermont thinks and what is thought by an ex-sergeant of five years experience, are two different things. I was encouraged to have my opinion backed up by somebody who really has the background to know, at least, about the probability of the facts cited. What's an I and R platoon[4] I wonder?

Ever yours
Dorothy Canfield Fisher

---

1. Date: publication date of Norman Mailer's *The Naked and the Dead* (New York: Rinehart, 1948).
2. Place: implied.
3. See note 1.
4. "I and R" stands for Intelligence and Reconnaissance.

154. *To Albert L. Guerard*
May 22, 1948
Arlington, Vermont

My dear Professor Guerard:

I have been an admirer of yours for so many years that it makes me happy to have this personal contact with you through your warm-hearted letter[1] to

Miss Connolly of the Book-of-the-Month Club organization. I prize your letter highly—as one of the most worthwhile rewards for the often thankless job of book reviewing—and I am making it one of the papers which I send up to the University of Vermont in Burlington. That is our State university, and they are making a collection of papers of mine which may possibly interest future students of the period. Their idea is not a bad one I think, not to wait until an author has been dead twenty or thirty years, and his children and grandchildren have lost most of his papers—for who nowadays with families moving around all the time could possibly keep a mass of papers together?—but to collect them while the author is still alive. Most of them will not be of any interest to anybody, perhaps none of them will be. But no harm is done in placing them in a fire-proof building instead of in a trunk under the eaves in the attic.[2]

So that is what I am doing with an occasional paper which I highly prize. And that is where your letter is going, as one of such highly prized papers.

With friendly greetings,
Faithfully yours,
Dorothy Canfield Fisher

---

1. In a May 4, 1948, letter, Guerard thanks DCF for her favorable mention of his autobiography, *Personal Equation* (1948) in the *Book-of-the-Month Club News*.
2. DCF began donating her papers to the University of Vermont in 1953.

155. To John P. Marquand
September 19 [1948][1]
Arlington, Vermont

Dear John:

I sit down to write you about my impressions of *Midnight Lace*[2] without knowing, for fair, exactly what they are. I read it last night, and there's no doubt about it, with that quick turning over of the next page to see what happens, that can be produced only by a man who knows how to tell a story. I really was wondering whether this middle-western Becky Sharp[3] could pull off her con game or not. And it took me all the evening to read it, so that I went to bed on the ending.

But this morning, I wonder if there is anything in it *except* skill in narration? No novelist will ever fail to give that particular gift its full share of admiration. But is it enough?

Of course there is, in the book, also, a very complete reconstruction of a middle-western prairie town of that period—complete as any of the recent historical studies, as to customs, costumes, moral standards, house-furnishings and all the rest. (Apologies for the extraordinary typing. I am writing you without waiting for the arrival of a secretary to make it ship-shape on the page.)

Is *this* enough, or rather are these two things enough to put it into class A quality?[4] For the narration is oddly old-fashioned and literal and also inept (it seems to me) in the ending. All the portentous hints about the awful past back of Dolly are realized of course by the actual facts as revealed in the very last— revealed but not really realized. I doubt if you can lay down before the reader such a brief, factual, statement of a life most people haven't the least idea about, and get the emotionally complete reaction needed for the place in this story of that fact. Doesn't it—for all its awfulness—but awfulness not really presented, and rather unimaginable in details to most readers—sound like sort of a flatness, to have that page or so of literal statement turn out to be revelation about which we have had horrid-sounding hints flung out from the first page, almost? This is not a rhetorical question, I really don't know.

And of course the ending is no conclusion, psychologically considered. It is just an accident and really who would think a modern writer would construct a story which turns entirely on somebody's overhearing a conversation? And the husband and wife are just the same as they always were, and I don't feel that we have sufficient indications of what's going to happen to them, from what has happened? Do you?

But of course it *is* what the French call *attachant* narration—you do want to know what is going to happen on the next page, right through. And that's a cardinal virtue in any novel.

As you can see, I'm thinking aloud and wavering from side to side. I think there's time, isn't there, before the meeting for me to get your impression of the book. I'll be here, almost any time, reachable by telephone—67, ring 6, Arlington—always about half-past eight in the morning, and generally at half-past twelve noon. Hastily, always with comradely good greetings

Dorothy

---

1. Date: publication date of MacKinlay Kantor's *Midnight Lace* (New York: Random House, 1948).
   2. See note 1.
   3. Becky Sharp is the protagonist of William Makepeace Thackeray's *Vanity Fair* (1847).
   4. Books under consideration by the BOMC were graded as A, B, or C early in the reviewing process. *Midnight Lace* was not selected as a book-of-the-month.

156. To Harry Scherman
October 8, 1948
Arlington, Vermont

Dear Harry:

I'm no *great* admirer of the Sinclair Lewis fiction, as you may have observed; and I took *The God-Seeker*[1] up as with the tongs. Well sir, believe it or not, it sounds to me as though S. Lewis has finally become objective enough to write with some shadings, with some qualifications and in-between tones in his characterizations. There is some mellowness in the book, no subtlety, no fine accuracy of touch,—you wouldn't expect that from this author—but infinitely less of the grotesque black-and-white cartoon than in any book of his.[2]

I don't know whether this novel will be as popular and sensational as most of the Lewis novels, but I bet it will be vastly more cherished and believed in.

I haven't read it all yet, but report on it when I've gone through about a third of the book, that I like it very much and would be glad to send it out, unless something very queer happens in the pages I haven't read. I'll go on with it at once and report on the whole by—well, Monday probably.[3] But I'm quite sure enough now that it is a sound, vivid and (to me anyhow) extremely interesting piece of fictional reconstruction of the settlement of Minnesota, which we should certainly send out.

Ever yours
Dorothy

---

1. *The God-Seeker* (New York: Random House, 1949). The novel was not selected as a book-of-the-month.
2. See Letter 43, note 3; Letter 62, note 4; and Letter 79, note 1 for further comment on Lewis's fiction.
3. The next Monday fell on Oct. 11.

157. To Harry Scherman
October 25, 1948
Arlington, Vermont

Dear Harry:

John and I have been feverishly reading the Dos Passos book,[1] comparing notes, talking it over, discussing—and here's the general impression, set hastily down, for there's only barely time to catch the last mail out. Just now, as John left me to write this, while he went out to see a man come to see about digging a well for a house of ours, down the hill, he summed it up "Tell Harry it's like a well-arranged shop-window, makes you think it's better than it is. When you look it over to see if you want to buy anything shown, you see you don't."

It is, as the first readers said, a roman à clef—even to us, who don't know Washington gossip at all, many characters are recognizable, as being pictures of Justice Frankfurter,[2] or Henry Wallace,[3] or some equally prominent official. And probably for those in the know, everybody in the book can be tagged with a real name. This element is not—for this book—just a literary curiosity. It must be taken into account in trying to appraise the value of the story. For, if you *didn't* guess, easily, who the different characters are, you wouldn't be interested in them. Dos Passos assumes, apparently, that you know who the original is, and hence that he won't need to do more than tell you a little about his mannerisms, looks, and something with a looking-through-the-keyhole quality of confidentialness about his private life. He certainly does not tell you anything about his people, below the surface, counting (I assume) on your supplying all that from having already read a lot in the newspapers about him. This seems to be proved (for me) by some characters whom I *don't* recognize. They are nothing but names on the page, floating in and out of the interminable cocktail drinking, gossiping *talk* which fills the book. There is one character who, I suppose, has not a conspicuous political original—the daughter of a college professor of history, a well-educated, soft-headed young woman, who has various love-affairs in the course of the book and commits suicide at the end. As far as creative fiction goes, she is a failure—a newspaper reporter's idea of a heroine in a novel.

Now I've said the worst, I think, that can be brought against the book. In its favor is Dos Passos' skill as a writer. He is certainly one of our most gifted journalists. Every time a scene is to be presented to the reader—a trip to the South to see how the New Deal farm measures are really working, or a picket line of brash young communistic radicals picketing the White House and getting shunted off by a good-natured, smiling policeman,—well, it's *excellent,* as good as anybody need ask for.

And the occasional pages of general comment, à la Whitman-category, are also well done, once in a while grandiloquent, but mostly really eloquent.

The real personal emotion of the book is, I should say, a detestation of Henry Wallace. The general abstract theme is disillusion that when the war began, the Administration dropped all its hopes for improving the common lot, and focussed on war—with a shrewd eye to votes. Here's a typical passage—"That's undoubtedly the position the isolationists are taking," he said coldly. "In my opinion the President has determined to let nothing stand in the way of defense production and immediate assistance to Russia."

"Nothing except politics," Tyler said.

Will the book be successful? Yes I should think so. Readers usually love guessing at the originals of characters in a roman a clef. That's sure fire. And the writing is of the best journalistic quality.

It really does not amount to much. But I don't feel (except for the Whitman-like rhetoric of those occasional pages of the author's comments on the times) that Dos Passos makes any claim that it is anything so much.

I'd think it would be all right to take it, as a well-written journalist's picture of war-time Washington. But I wouldn't feel the least bit disappointed if we didn't send it out.

Hastily, always yours
Dorothy

---

1. John Dos Passos, *The Grand Design* (Boston: Houghton Mifflin, 1949). The novel was not selected as a book-of-the-month. It was republished with *Adventures of a Young Man* (1939) and *Number One* (1943) as the final part of a trilogy entitled *District of Columbia* (1952).

2. Felix Frankfurter (1882–1965), associate justice of the U.S. Supreme Court (1939–1962). He is the model for the character named Judge Oppenheim.

3. Henry Agard Wallace (1888–1965), vice-president of the U.S. (1941–1945) under Franklin Delano Roosevelt, editor of the *New Republic* (1946–1947), Progressive party candidate for president (1948). He is the model for the character named Walker Watson.

158. To Anzia Yezierska
January 10, 1949
Arlington, Vermont

Dear Miss Yezierska:

Having seen my cluttered work-study, as you used to, during your stay in Arlington and on occasional visits to me here, I'm sure you will not be surprised—only smile at poor old Mrs. Fisher's inability to keep her papers in order!—when I tell you that your letter of the 10th has been somehow snowed under. I couldn't find it! And since I had no address to which to write, and couldn't think of anybody who might know it, I've been really *concerned,* for fear I couldn't answer it—and then how ungracious and unfriendly you would think this old Vermonter.

But just now, going through a big pile of accumulated (and alas! unanswered) letters, there to my relief I see your familiar handwriting. So I sit right down to let you know that your letter is here, and that I will be very glad to see you, on any of my Book-of-the-Month Club trips to New York. I'm usually at the Commodore Hotel, which is convenient for everybody arriving on the New York Central railroad, for one doesn't need to hire a cab or a porter, but can just walk through the Grand Central waiting-room to the hotel—like a termite, entirely underground.

But before I see you, I ought to tell you in case you may not have heard this tragic news, that our dear Jimmy was killed in the war. You remember him, I am sure, and probably felt how intimately beloved he was to both his parents. His death has broken our lives—our inner lives—utterly, although we try to go forward for the years which are left to us, with courage, and as usually as we can.

Jimmy had gone to the Harvard Medical School, had become a doctor, had three years of experience as an intern, in the Boston hospitals, and volunteered for service in the Army Medical Corps. After training in this country, he volunteered again for active service in the Orient, and was one of the very first Americans who landed on the Philippines when the war went into that front. The papers I send with this, tell you the rest of the story.

I still cannot speak of him—or even write—without uncontrollable weeping. The sorrow grows no less with the passage of time—although the element of shock has worn away in the almost four years since the news came to us.

My dear husband—you will remember the tender affection which united father and son—was terribly shaken by this blow. He has had a severe coronary thrombosis, after which for some ten weeks he lay between life and death, and has never—of course—recovered his normal strength.

But he exercises to the full his great self-control and intelligent self-discipline, in limiting his efforts to what the doctor thinks possible for his now limited vitality, and has for ten years served the children of Vermont, acting in their interest on the State Board of Education of Vermont.

I too have been devoting myself to education and young people, as I am now working very hard on the local School Board here.

I thought you ought to know that we have been going through black waters of affliction since we last saw you.

I'll let you know when, during one of my trips to New York for the Book-of-the-Month Club, I'll have a free time for a visit with you. Perhaps you could come to have breakfast with me at the hotel. That is often my only free hour.

With every good wish,
Faithfully yours,
Dorothy Canfield Fisher

159. To David _____
[January 17, 1949][1]
[Arlington, Vermont][2]

Dear David:

Well, it is not only between East Arlington and Arlington that the mails run slowly. Here's a letter from you dated January 13 which doesn't reach me for four days—it's now the 17th.

Well, I'm glad to get it, anyhow, and I hasten to say yes sure I should say I am in the Van Waters case[3]—with both feet, and shouting. I was one of the first to prepare a statement about my opinion of her work, last summer when all this misery began to show its head. But Miriam had been expecting for a couple of years before that. One of the main difficulties is patronage. As soon as the State government got into politicians' hands, they began sending people out to Framingham, looking for jobs—utterly unsuited—rough and tough customers, but with a politicians' backing. Miriam would have none of this, and stood up for the protection of her charges. This is infuriating to all politicians. Furthermore, the real question at issue, is the treatment of all people in prisons or reformatories. This is a back-wash of the wave of reaction—away from the feeling that [what] we want to do for them is to make decent citizens of them, as far as possible, back to the older idea that what we want (and need and must do) in their case is to PUNISH them. We ran into that here in Arlington, in an odd way—I don't know if I ever happened to tell you and Dorcas about it. Old Mr. Pollard, who ran our library for a good many years, was beside himself at the "softness" with which the library board treated people who kept books beyond the regular allowed time. What we wanted in such cases, was to get the book back, and still keep the reader involved as a patron of the library. What Mr. Pollard clamored for was JUSTICE, by which he meant, as many people mean, *suffering* for people who have broken a rule, whether it makes them break more rules or not. He used to say, glaring around helplessly, at the good-natured easy-going Library Board, who had said "Oh, I'll just step into her house and ask her for the book. She's probably forgotten all about it, yes, in spite of your post-card reminders. You know, her youngest child has been pretty sick lately." Mr. Pollard used to roar "But there is a PRINCIPLE involved. You don't seem to realize it is not just getting the book back. She must be made to feel that she has broken a rule." We used to go around and around, inside the tiny teaspoon of the Arlington Library, on a matter which has universal significance. So—how often it happens that from a tiny event, well understood, a light is cast on something vastly bigger, when the Van Waters trouble began, I could see that not *all* of her enemies are the corrupt politicians. Some of them are the Old Guard of Old Testament ways of thinking. But mostly it is just plain corruption—they want the enormous chances for easy money which they'd have if they had the ordering of the tons of supplies needed in such big institutions, and they want the vote-patronage that would come if they could put in ignorant people of their own choice, to bully the inmates. I'm so glad you and Dorcas are in on it. I'm a member of the Friends of Framingham Reformatory—a regular Association and think you two ought to be.

Yes, sure, of course, I know Oldtown Folks, Poganuck People[4]—lots of them. They were all of them around me in the Brick House in Arlington, much more highly esteemed by my grandfather's generation than Mrs. Stowe's other. I'm honored to have you think my work like hers—honest, unpretentious, New Englandism.

Affectionate greetings to you both from
D.C.F.

———

1. Date: chronology of the "Van Waters case."
2. Place: implied.
3. Miriam Van Waters (1887–1974), American penal reformer and social worker. Van Waters was superintendent of the Massachusetts State Reformatory for Women at Framingham from 1931 to 1957. She emphasized rehabilitation over punishment and granted prisoners liberal privileges: special education and clubs, pay for work, and permission to keep pets. A legislative investigation was launched in 1948 to examine charges of "lax" conditions at the institution, and Van Waters was ordered to return to the rules of 1923. With support from prominent figures, including DCF and Eleanor Roosevelt, Van Waters defended her methods, but in Dec. 1948 it was announced that she would be fired when Governor-Elect Paul A. Dever took office the following month. After her firing, Gov. Dever appointed a commission to re-examine the case, and Van Waters was exonerated in Mar. 1949. She was reinstated and served as superintendent for eight more years.
4. *Oldtown Folks* (Boston: Fields, Osgood, 1869) and *Poganuck People: Their Loves and Lives* (New York: Fords, Howard & Hulbert, 1878) are novels by American author Harriet Beecher Stowe (1811–1896).

160. To Rosemary Benét
March 2, 1949
Arlington, Vermont

Dear Rosemary:

I have just read with the closest attention and interest your report on *Death of a Salesman*.[1] And I write to ask you a question your answer to which would really be useful to me, in thinking about that moving play.

It is this: am I being too cold and dam-yankeeish a Vermonter to feel startled by the complete omission in the author's presentation of the situation, of the obvious fact that Willy was a very poor salesman indeed, and that if he had been a carpenter or professor of Latin or a grocery man or a banker or an athletic coach with the same idea about how to do his work, he would have come to the same ignominious and tragic end. For if he had tried to earn his living in any kind of work, by not doing the work but being genial, he would have been a failure. I can't understand the author's making his hero enough of a success *in New England* to have lasted up to his 60th year as a salesman. For he must have dealt with business men and women, and I never in all my life met a New England business man who didn't turn to ice, when anybody tried to sell him something by turning on the charm, not by claiming (and proving, if he was successful) that the product he had to sell was more worth buying than that of some other salesman. Yankees often listen tolerantly to a man with Willy's temperament making a speech, for he is often fluent and amusing. But they don't vote for him. And they don't buy from him.

And I don't believe this is restricted to New England. There have been salesmen in the circle of my acquaintance of course they are so numerous we all know some. I never knew one who was succeeding, who wasn't deeply interested in the thing he was selling, often tiresomely so. But no where in the play does Willy seem to have the least real interest in stockings. In fact a good many first-night comments on it, of people who had not read the play, include a passing reference to the fact that it wasn't very clear what the hero had been selling. I never saw a business which would have kept such a poor excuse as a salesman as Willy on for a year, let alone thirty years.

This odd lack of connection with reality seems to me basic, makes the premises of the whole play false to me. *Am I exaggerating?* Either the premises are true, in which case, the resultant life would have been different. Or else they are false. How does this seem to you.

Of course, Willy's encouraging his sons' stealing of a commercially saleable product like building material from the house being constructed, and the theft of the expensive basket-ball show, it seems to me, a personality which *could* not have succeeded in any calling in life. If he was as dishonest as that, it would have shown in his own actions, he would soon have been distrusted by his business associates, and could not have gone on. That too seems to me just phony—premises which, if true, would have quickly led to consequences quite other than those the author shows.

Now I can't be the only person who has noticed this lack of organic connection between premises set up by the author, and what the author claims were the conclusions from them. Nobody else has said a word about this. I don't go to the theater often—perhaps a play is allowed a much wider gap than a novel between cause and obvious effect? Maybe theatrical license is large enough to cover such a gap?

Send a line or two down to me, Friday, will you, which I can read before we have the discussion at the meeting of the Committee of Selection. Does this play seem "sound" to you, as a novel must be sound to be seriously considered as a work of art?

You *said* you didn't mind sudden response to one of your reports. Here is one.

Ever yours
Dorothy Canfield Fisher

———

1. Arthur Miller, *Death of a Salesman* (New York: Viking, 1949), book-of-the-month, July 1949 (with *Father of the Bride* by Edward Streeter).

161. *To Sarah Cleghorn*
July 7, 1949
[Arlington, Vermont]¹

Dear Sally:

Your letter began at 7:30 on Sunday morning, June 26th, has been on my desk for several days as you can see by the date. I too often rise early, sometimes as early as 4:30, because I find the fresh cool of the early morning the best time for me to get anything done. Unfortunately I now find with the steady lessening of vitality which comes to all of us in our age group, that if I get work done at that end of the day, I can't get any done in the afternoon. No other end to the candle to burn I find.

I was very much interested to hear about your visit to the zoo. I haven't been in one in more years than I could set down. The last time I think was when I took the children to the zoo in Paris towards the very end of the first World War. Food was so short at that time, and nobody had any coal for keeping tropical animals warm, that the zoo was very much depleted. But since the children didn't know any different kind of a zoo they didn't notice the absence of many of the animals usually found.

My recollection of that last visit was this:—in the monkey room there were very few monkeys left, and they were huddled on their perches under heavy woolen shawls which they held closely around themselves exactly like old ladies. Looking at them reflectively while the children exclaimed and threw them peanuts or whatever we had in those days, I thought (the Russian Revolution was fresh in everybody's mind then, and the White Russian refugees were [I] think in Paris) that they represented the last of a leisure class kept on from a past habit of society, but now on their way out—as the present socialistic society of great Britain shows. When I read in the newspapers that a Duke is selling the vegetables in his garden in the market nearest his castle, in England because he can't get money any other way, I remember those monkeys!

I have called up Mrs. Wyman whose room will be free any time (I gather from what she said) during the first half of August. So feel free to come along whenever the spirit moves you to come along from Susan's. I am so glad that you are going to see that dear sister of yours.

Now as to the second half of your letter, "the radiant cloud of knowing about peace." It is as you say a mystic's spiritual condition. And as such I think it is wholly individual with each person. That is each person has his own kind of radiant cloud.

Do you remember as far back as when we were working on that book to-gether up in Thetford,[2] that you wrote a passage about the difference between our way of undertaking to wash out dark spots of gloom or discouragement or dreariness or guilt in our lives. You said, as I remember the passage, (I haven't seen the book in many years) that Dorothy's way was to consider each spot, what had caused it, analyzed the process which had brought it there on the kitchen floor so to speak, and then to try first to clean up the spot and then to avoid the process which had brought it there. While your natural instinctive way of managing was to pour over the whole of the kitchen floor a great flood of prayer, contemplation, and spiritual faith and radiance. I am not quoting exactly but something like that. I was quite struck, I remember, with your power of analysis in so clearly stating the difference between our way of com-batting evil.

Well, I think we still have that marked difference. Your method of approach-ing the problem of preventing war, or doing your share toward preventing war, is to flood the area in which you are with a hatred of war in general, and a love for peace in general, without analysis of the economic and political causes which lie back of the recurrent almost helpless compulsion to war. Your feeling is that if people wished for peace ardently enough they would not make war.

I think that is a beautiful way to approach the problem and to work for peace.

But it is not my way. My way is to read incessantly and to study as pro-foundly as my brains and education allow me the economic problems—well, say of colonialism, so that when the occasion occurs as it does practically every day of my life in conversation with this or that person, for putting in a word for the treatment of the problem of colonialism which, in my estimation, will help remove one of the causes of war, I will be able to speak the right word. My experience has been that in my big correspondence, letters from people from all over you know, and in the flood of visitors who come and go in this house, hardly one letter or conversation goes by without some mention of what seems to me the root of war in racial prejudice or economic stupidity or greed. My method is to keep myself alert to see such mention, and to perceive their some-times remote but I think very actual connection with the compulsion towards war which often seems so mysterious, and to strike what blow I can at the root. A good deal of the talk about peace and about the need for waging peace and avoiding war, seems to me too general—that is as if one would say to someone very sick with typhoid fever that if he would just flood his being with the will to be healthy he would rise from his bed. But, I am absolutely sure that I am wrong. I am sure that your method provides an immense impulsion towards peace which my method does not at all. But I am also sure that my method fills in, gaps left by your beautiful wave of passion for peace. I feel the passion for peace. I think as ardently as you do, just as one feels the ardent wish for the recovery of the sick person.

So I don't really see that we could work together on this problem and I don't think we need to. I think you are doing a wonderful work in all these various approaches to libraries and to people to whom you write.

You know, you must know because I keep speaking of it more and more often as I get older, that my observation of the human scene leads me to a greater and greater estimation of the importance of variety of approach for all problems, because there is such a variety of personality. My mother used to quote me an old folk saying on which she was brought up and which I must have passed on to you, as I pass on to you practically all that it is in my mind, about what was said by the different church bells as they rang for Sunday morning. The Baptist bells, she said called out "Total immersion! Total im-mersion!" The Episcopalian bells rang out "Apostolic Succession! Apostolic Succession!" But the Methodist bells rang out "There's room for all!" I have that feeling about the approach to the fight for peace.

Now I've told you how your "concern" impresses me. It's your turn to write me what you think of my reaction to it. Good news from your namesake Sally. She and Paul and that menagerie of all-aged children reached Wyoming safely and happily!

So much love always,

---

1. Place: implied.
2. *Fellow Captains* (1916).

162. *To John P. Marquand*

August 11, 1949

[Arlington, Vermont][1]

Dear John:

Agreed, absolutely on "Curtain Time."[2] Doesn't amount to a whoop. Let's leave it out.

Yes, I too am anxious to talk over the Vermont Symposium with you. Maybe we can steal a little time during the meeting. Probably the others won't mind— in fact, the only one who wasn't in Vermont won't be there, so we can have an all-around discussion.

At the last round-table meeting, Friday afternoon, I put in an appearance— having said I would. I hadn't heard Mr. Aldridge[3] hold forth before, and was I startled by his reading a prepared statement (which took one full half-hour out of the time of the meeting) stating his convictions about the decadence, degeneracy etc. of the modern novel and his ideas of the reasons for it. Cowley, Geizmar, Burlingame[4] and somebody else whose name my deaf ears didn't catch, were there. I waited and waited for one of them to pick up the ball. But either they were worn out (as I gather from your letter they might well be, by Mr. Aldridge's having repeated this so often—this was the first time for me, you see) or maybe they thought as older men, they would have to be courteous to a young man, or perhaps they felt they were guests at the Symposium—well anyhow, none of them said a word of what was sizzling hot within me. So by and by, I took an axe in one hand, a hatchet in the other and a knife between my teeth and sailed in. No courtesy is needed between an old woman and a young man, and my foot was on my native heath, and I wasn't under obligation to anybody—quite the contrary—for having invited me to Vermont.

The *Burlington Free Press*, reporting on this discussion group, said that after Mrs. Fisher began, the "discussion was a slugfest." To my great pleasure Burlingame, Cowley, and Geizmar immediately seconded what I said—evidently had been wanting to say it themselves. Mr. Aldridge kept that poker face blank solemnity—I thought I was saying something new to him, but I see from your letter that I was only repeating what you, Burlingame et al. had already said. Well, it came with evident freshness from me, since I hadn't been there.

Kip[5] spoke very well I thought, plain, practical (but erudite in his singularly unobtrusive way) discussion of how book-reviewing is really done in the actual literary world.

Everybody said you spoke admirably, said what evidently needed to be said, with force and point and held the audience's attention without a quaver. But I hear that the loud-speaker contraption didn't work for Henry Canby[6] and that people couldn't hear him—could hardly see him, behind the big rostrum. I'm sorry, for I gather he spoke in defense or explanation, rather, of well run book-clubs.

Lots and lots of people came, more and more as the week went on. Every-body seemed stimulated, argumentative, stirred up over fiction-writing—which is all to the good.

Ever yours
Dorothy

What a prince of a man George Merck[7] is!

---

1. Place: no reason to doubt Arlington.
2. Lloyd R. Morris, *Curtain Time: The Story of the American Theater* (New York: Random House, 1953).
3. John W. Aldridge (b. 1922), American educator and literary critic. Aldridge was a lecturer (1948–1950) and Assistant Professor of English (1950–1955) at the University of Vermont.
4. Malcolm Cowley (1898–1989), American poet and editor of many works by major American writers. Maxwell Geismar (1909–1979), American literary critic and editor. Roger Burlingame (1900–1967), American author, editor, and literary critic.
5. Clifton Fadiman.
6. See Letter 79, note 2.
7. George Merck (1894–1957), American business executive. Chairman of the Board of Merck and Co., a chemical and pharmaceutical manufacturing firm in Rahway, N. J. Merck and Marquand first met as classmates at Harvard University.

163. *To Bennett Cerf*
December 23, 1949
Arlington, Vermont

Dear Bennett:

I return the four contracts signed, but with a change in them.[1] I've marked out that typed in material, saying that an advance payment is to be made on signing of the contract, and left it that all the advance payment is to be made when the Mss. is delivered to the publisher.

It may sound foolish to a seasoned publisher like you, that a seasoned writer, like me, can still object to that clause. But I do. I've never taken any payment in advance of doing any work—couldn't bear the idea of getting money for something I haven't done yet. Especially such a chancey piece of work as writing a book.

For, there again, seasoned though I am, with more books back of me than I can remember the titles of, I never take on a new one without butterflies in the stomach, like a singer going out on the platform for a solo.

This really isn't so idiotic as it sounds—the point is that each new book is a creative piece of work, which depends on that complex and mysterious entity known as one's personality. I never have in all these years, been stopped by any book I've undertaken. But who knows whether this one will be the exception.

It would make me nervous,—I wouldn't be able to sleep well o' nights—if, before I had written a word, I accepted payment. So just let this elderly author have her Vermontish way, and put off any advance payment till you have the script in your hands.

Everything else fine—and I'm really (although throwing inward fits of nervousness) delighted with the assignment, which catches me exactly between jobs, with the last of the twelve-year-old stories done for those public-school readers[2] of which I told you, and before I start (again) on a book about Vermont for which I am under contract with Little Brown and Co.[3]

With every good wish for this season of good wishes—may the New Year prove kinder than we fear (in our darker moments) and may this series of yours turn out to be the success which, to me, seems inevitable.

Ever yours,

---

1. Cerf had asked DCF to write the first two "Landmark Books," an American History series for young adults. The books, *Paul Revere and the Minutemen* and *Our Independence and the Constitution,* were published by Random House the following year.

2. *The Crabtree-Canfield Basic Readers* (see Letter 134, note 4).

3. *Vermont Tradition* (1953).

— *Part 6* —

Letters, 1950–1958

164. To Harry Scherman
February 1 [1950][1]
[New York, New York][2]

Dear Harry:

I get out of bed to write you this brief note because it has just occurred to me that possibly Merle or Bob Haas may chance to speak to you about what the oculist told me this afternoon. Merle is inclined to take medical authorities rather more seriously and literally than I. I was going to wait till I reached home and write you legibly on the typewriter but, remembering that Merle was in the office and heard what Dr. Paton said, I write you now.

Nothing at all drastic or melodramatic. My eyes are in no danger of losing their vision or going back on me seriously, but he does think I should give up all "pressure reading," that is, professional reading which has to be done by a dead-line date. I said I *was* talking it over with you, that it was a rather complex proposition for you to find replacements for your old readers, and would take time, so I had thought I'd plan to get along through this year, but make it the last year. He shook his head and said he didn't think I ought to wait a year.

Now if Merle hadn't happened to come in and hear this, I wouldn't have mentioned it to you. For a specialist is somebody to *consult* (so I think) rather than to obey, as if he were an officer giving a command. He did *not* seem especially concerned about my eyes; from what he said, I gather that there is no real danger in using them reasonably and prudently a little while longer. *And that's what I mean to do.*

Of course not if any fireworks symptoms show themselves. I'll be sensible. But I am morally sure from the general tone of the consultation that there isn't the slightest need for haste. What he said confirmed my own opinion that my stopping time isn't far off. But as you know, I'd had that opinion before I went to him.

It's not that I don't feel confidence in him. I liked him very much and thought all that he had to say was sensible and well-informed. I just don't think that opinion meant quite so much as Merle seemed to think, wasn't even intended as anything so decisive.

Oh, Harry how I wish *I* had something to dedicate to you on your birthday! My heart was full when I heard today was your birthday.

A thousand blessings on you from
Your devoted
Dorothy

---

1. Date: reference to DCF's last year on the Committee of Selection. She retired in 1951.
2. Place: letterhead, Commodore Hotel, New York.

165. *To Walter Collins O'Kane*
April 26, 1950
[Arlington, Vermont][1]

Dear Walter:

It's a beautiful book[2]—as far as my ailing eyes (very troublesome just now) have permitted me to look at it. I don't see how anything could be better— what a wonderful range you have, of human climates in which you are at home! I don't know anyone who has a wider.

Would your publisher like me, perhaps, to write something they might be able to use as a part of their publicity for this splendid example of bridge- making between different human groups. I never read anything, I think, which gave me such a sound, satisfactory feeling of understanding the Indian way of life in its general outlines.

Usually I have shied off from such attempts, because of their self-conscious- ness, artiness, and (it has seemed to me) extreme colors. This makes the Hopis sound really like members of our human family—not low-caste dark-skinned folks, nor yet demi-gods, with the ability to solve all human problems by their divinations of depths below the grasp of our limited white brains (this of course is the D.H. Lawrence attitude towards Indians.)

Thanks so much for letting me have a copy of this grand book.

Ever yours
Dorothy

---

1. Place: no reason to doubt Arlington.
2. *Sun in the Sky* (Norman: University of Oklahoma Press, 1950).

166. *To David E. Scherman*
July 6 [1950][1]
[Arlington, Vermont][2]

Dear Mr. Scherman:

No, your Uncle Harry hadn't mentioned to me this very interesting assign- ment given you by *Life*.[3] But that is no sign he's not interested. We never have an instant's time in the cram-packed-with discussion meeting of the Commit- tee of Selection of the Book-of-the-Month Club, for any personal exchanges. It's a little like trying to pass personal news along in the middle of a group of people running to catch a train in the Grand Central.

Now I do know about it, I'm much interested, as Willa Cather was a classmate of my brother's in the University of Nebraska,[4] and an old friend of mine. I'm so glad her memory is to be celebrated in the way I know you'll do it.

Yes, I remember Mrs. Bennett[5] very well, and remember the little talk we had here in Vermont. She must think I *am* an old lady if she thinks I might have forgotten her. But come to think of it, she doesn't perhaps know that I have had several long talks here with Professor E. K. Brown of the English Department of the University of Chicago,[6] who is gathering material for a life of Willa Cather— commissioned to do so, I believe, or anyhow authorized to do so, by Willa's literary executor, Miss Edith Lewis[7] and her publisher, Alfred Knopf. Professor Brown has seen everybody and read everything imaginable in connection with this assignment, and has often mentioned Mrs. Bennett to me, as one of the people who has a great deal of Willa's record in her youth.

As to the poem of Heine, yes, I did have it, as Willa translated it, many years ago.[8] But I think I must have sent it to the University of Vermont, in Burlington where the library is making a collection of my papers and letters. At any rate I don't lay my hands on it here in Arlington.

But I can give you the name and address of two old gentlemen who knew Willa years ago when she was teaching high school in Pittsburgh. One is Mr. George Gerwig, 38 Orchard Road, Wheeling, West Virginia; the other is Mr. George Seibel, Carnegie Free Library of Allegheny, Pittsburgh. Mr. Gerwig, as I remember it was the person who got Willa's first job for her in Pittsburgh— as headline writer on a local newspaper—no, as editor in a little magazine somebody was trying to print there. They are both pretty old, as Willa would have been herself if she had lived. My brother is now 76 and he was in her class at the University of Nebraska. And I can't be sure that they would remember the episode of Willa's translating the Heine poem. (It was the Christmas poem which begins:

> *Die heil'gen Kön'ge aus Morgenland*
> *Siefrugen in jedem Stadtchen*

if you want to look it up.) It was in Mr. Seibel's house that she thought of doing it. We were there for Christmas Eve, and Mr. Seibel (a German, of very literate tastes) pulled his Heine out of the bookcase to read it to us, Willa was greatly taken with it, and borrowed the book to translate it. And got it published and *paid for*—quite an event in the early years of a writer!

Cordially yours
Dorothy Canfield Fisher

Mrs. Bennett may remember that the person in charge of that collection of my papers at the University of Vermont, is Mrs. Sumner Willard, U.V.M., Burlington, Vermont.

Why don't you get in touch with Professor Brown at the University of Chicago. He might have interesting suggestions.

---

1. Date: publication date of David Scherman's article "Willa Cather Country" in *Life* 30 (Mar. 19, 1951): 112–23.
2. Place: stated.
3. See note 1.
4. DCF's brother Jim and Cather attended the University of Nebraska from 1891 to 1895 (see Letter 84, note 9).
5. Mildred Bennett (1909–1989), author of critical works on Willa Cather, including *The World of Willa Cather* (1951), which she was researching in 1950.
6. Edward Killoran Brown (1905–1951), American educator and literary critic, author of *Willa Cather: A Critical Biography* (completed by Léon Edel, 1953).
7. Edith Lewis (1882–1972) Cather's housemate (1908–1947) (see Letter 3, note 4).
8. Cather's translation of the Heine poem was published in the *Home Monthly* (Dec. 1896). DCF wrote about the Christmas Eve with Seibel in "Novelist Recalls Christmas in Blue-and-Gold Pittsburgh," *New York Herald Tribune* (Dec. 21, 1947):42.

167. *To Harry Scherman*
July 13, 1950
Arlington, Vermont

Dear Harry:

Have you (I dare say you have) seen this paragraph?[1] Because it is proof of what I have felt all my life, that Boswell's *Life of Johnson* is enormously overestimated by professors of English Literature, and really is a bore to most people (as it certainly was to me). I send it along to you before the next meeting. I'll hardly venture there, for fear of tramping too viciously on Henry's and Chris' toes, to say what I really think about this newly discovered *Boswell's Journal*.[2] I don't think it any more ostensibly outspoken about sex than many other books we have all read, both for the Book-of-the-Month Club and just in general, in 18th century and in 20th century English. Certainly it is not any more clinical-frank about sex than many other English books of its time— *Tristram Shandy*[3] for instance. Although that comparison is not an exact one for *Tristram Shandy* is really often very funny, and penetrating, while the Boswell is just dismally mediocre (seems to me).

I think it terribly dull. The last 30 pages after Dr. Johnson comes in are the only ones in all that pile which have anything to say—and we have already had a good deal of that in the original Boswell's *Johnson*.

I have read Chris' introduction with its whoop-it-up, unquestioning acceptance of the tradition that what happened in that special circle in London and

England at that time, is somehow, of importance to history, to literature, to the understanding of human nature. And I feel just like the child in the Hans Christian Andersen story of "The Emperor's New Clothes" listening with open-mouthed astonishment to people praising to the sky something which his own eyes tell him is not there at all.

In that period of history, England seems to me (and to everybody else I ever heard of except some English people and American professors in college English Departments) at the lowest ebb—unimaginably corrupt, financially and politically (a good thing for us Americans or we never would have staggered through to a victorious end of our Revolution). It was in the trough of the wave as to literature with a mighty period before it and coming after it, and really just about bankrupt as to creative thought, scholarship, and art. This is at a time when France and Germany were rich with real, sure-enough giants of the intellect, real master artists, whose thought and work had a lasting influence on the development of the human spirit.

About the years of this ebb-tide of civilization in England, we already know all we need to know, through lots of writers—Smollett, Sterne, Goldsmith (minor) and *Fielding*! (major). They knew how to write, although none of them except Fielding was of first-rate ability. They are still readable today. They have wit, taste, zest. They give a complete picture of the times to the last button. Boswell's *Life of Johnson* adds something to this, gives a picture of a British oddity (Was Dr. Johnson anything more than this?) but half of it would do as well as the whole bulk.

To add to that, *more* Boswell saying tiresomelessly over and over what has already been told to us in other books, about a period of no importance anyhow, and about a shallow-natured, trivial-minded man—

Well, I didn't mean to let go quite so energetically. But I'll send it to you anyhow because I don't want to say anything like this at the meeting. It really wouldn't be decently courteous to do so, to an ex-professor of English like Henry,[4] and somebody like Chris who has a strong and perfectly natural family tradition (the old colonial tradition) that whatever is British, is by definition, of importance to Americans, although we stopped being British colonials some 170 years ago.

What I hope is that the others will just decide early in the discussion that the Boswell *Journal* will not do, for one and another reason. Then I won't have to say a word of my feeling that any more Boswell than the world already has can't possibly interest anybody but History-of-English-Literature fans like Chris or professors of English like Henry. Except for the mystery-story quirk of the way it has been hidden all these years and just come to light.[5] A very mildly interesting item it seems to me.

I am waiting with the liveliest interest for more news of the Seversky book.[6]

I think John Marquand is right that the Korean mix-up whatever it is, takes the shine off Seversky's main theme.

Ever yours,

[Handwritten] P.S. Now this is Monday morning—July 17. This letter comes back from the typist's desk, and, since I've seen Meredith Wood and his wife, I want to add a postscript. I don't know when I had been more pleased and satisfied, than to see my John so whole-heartedly liking Woodie! John is no push-over you know, in the matter of personal likings. He just delighted in Meredith's honesty, unassuming intelligence, warm-heartedness—general attractiveness. We both thought Helen Wood a joy, too.

So, yesterday, when Meredith came over to the house for a quiet talk, John sat in with us, and shared my touched and moved appreciation of what he said about a pension, for these latest years of my life. We consider that it is a real gift—something extra—your generosity. And do we appreciate it! But we'll never be able to suggest, even tentatively, any sum. We don't know nearly enough about the business end of things. But later on for that. Both John and I spoke out to Meredith as we would to you, that is, without any reservations, about anything—exactly what was in our hearts, as if you'd been there. As one so seldom, in life, ever can. He'll tell you.

With such appreciation
Dorothy

---

1. Newspaper article enclosed: "There have been many lists of the best books—the ten best, the 100 best, etc. What about a list of the ten most boring? Editor Fon W. Boardman, Jr., of *Pleasures of Publishing,* a Columbia University Press trade letter, thought it might be fun to make one. He polled several hundred U.S. librarians, editors, authors, reviewers, and school-teachers, asking them to send him a list of the ten classics that have bored most people most. Last week Boardman announced the results.

The ten that led all the rest: Bunyan's *Pilgrim's Progress,* Melville's *Moby Dick,* Milton's *Paradise Lost,* Spenser's *Faerie Queene,* Boswell's *Life of Samuel Johnson,* Richardson's *Pamela,* Eliot's *Silas Marner,* Scott's *Ivanhoe,* Cervantes' *Don Quixote,* Goethe's *Faust.* "

2. *Boswell's London Journal, 1762–1763,* with an "Introduction" by Christopher Morley, ed. Frederick A. Pottle (New York: McGraw-Hill, 1950), book-of-the-month dividend, 1951.

3. Novel (1760, 1767) by English author Laurence Sterne.

4. Canby taught English at Yale University from 1900 to 1916.

5. Morley's "Introduction" details the journal's discovery by Prof. Claude C. Abbott at Lord Clinton's Fettercairn House in the early 1930s, the lawsuit over its ownership, and its eventual purchase by Yale University in 1949.

6. Alexander P. De Seversky, *Air Power: Key to Survival* (New York: Simon & Schuster, 1950).

168. To Anzia Yezierska
August 15, 1950
Arlington, Vermont

Dear Miss Yezierska:

At last I have managed in various ways by being read aloud and by reading a little at a time to read your autobiography,[1] in spite of the wretched condition of my eyes.

It has given me much pleasure and interest, as you must have known it would. It really is like a visit with you such as we used to have down in your little house or here. I have many memories of you here, place-memories connected with times when we talked things over together. One of them is of a sunny, late winter afternoon, when we were sitting together on the sofa in my little living-room and looked out of the window at the blue line of the mountains on the other side of the valley. I don't remember what we said at all at that time, but I remember the pleasantest feeling of comradeship.

I hope you won't mind that I have let several people in Arlington read the proof sheets of your book while I was slowly going through it. They will see it anyhow when it is printed and I couldn't see that it would do any harm to let them see something of this advance copy. They were immensely interested in it, astonished by your Hollywood experience so far outside anything that any of us have ever had the slightest contact with, delighted with your ironic and vivid treatment of WPA days, and very much touched, as I was, by your objective, reasonable and kind account of your stay in Arlington, at least we take it to be your stay in Arlington and I am pretty sure you mean it for that.

We all think that in that you have shown the most remarkable capacity for impersonal, good judgement on something in which you were a major character.

And that is rather unusual. Ever so many other people, of course, have come to Arlington, trying to live here, some of them have settled down and become a part of our community, working and living with us here, and others have found as you did that it was not the right soil for their deepest tap-roots, and have gone away. I don't know anybody who has been so kind and understanding and appreciative as you.

This whole question of the establishment of people from quite a different culture in a society new to them, is of especial interest now as Mr. Auden says in his fine introduction. For the whole idea of "One-World" in which we put our hopes these forlorn days, is that it may be possible to make such adjustments, for everybody is doing it more or less.

Nobody has really studied seriously and objectively the difficulties in the way of it. But I have for a great many years been collecting in my memory instances of success or failure in this kind of adjustment to a new and different culture. One of them was an experience which my brother and his wife had in going across the Gibraltar Straits from Spain to Morocco. They had been travelling in Spain, had been told that Morocco was an interesting country to visit, had bought their tickets, made their reservation for two weeks' stay there. They took the ship across the Straits and landed in Morocco in the morning, and by the end of the first day they had been so alarmed, almost terrified by the look of active, burning hatred which was turned on them by every Moham-medan in Morocco that they took the ship back to Spain that night, feeling themselves so unwelcome, unwanted and detested, that they said they wouldn't be able to digest their food if they stayed. That is an extreme example of course. But one about which I really knew. My brother and his wife were middle-aged, sensible, not very imaginative people who hadn't had the slightest idea of dislike felt for Christians by Moslems, so they can hardly have made this up beforehand.

At the other extreme is the case of several French people I know who have been so unhappy in the fixed, formal society of France that arriving in Amer-ica where everything is so much more fluid, they felt an immense relief, plunged into activity here and have become such Americans that you can't tell them from the native-born.

In between of course there are all kinds of shades of adjustment. Among the Hitler-exiles, there were those both in the first Italian anti-fascist group and in the later anti-nazi group who were dismayed by American life. They didn't like (and don't like still) American food or manners or way of travelling, our houses or our clothes or shops. The fact that they can't get their meals at the same hours as in the older home makes them acutely unhappy. And these are by no means thoughtless people or trivial ones. Some people seem so devotedly attached to the exact daily routine of their lives that it disturbs them to the very roots of their being when that is changed.

There are others like Professor Salvemini[2] who has taught for fifteen years in Harvard, who seem to be rooted spiritually in a soil of thought and spirit so deep and so universal that it doesn't make any difference where they live. He was well over fifty when he escaped from Italy to come to this country yet he was not shocked and dismayed by all the differences in American life but con-tinued on his intellectual work as historian of the Middle Ages. It has been really inspiring to me to see how tranquilly he has withstood transplantation, because for him it really wasn't transplantation at all, he still lived on in the scholar's and thinker's world without noticing that he had been geographically separated from the old soil.

Now when all this is so important to us, such a study as yours which although brief is poignant and vivid, is of real value as well as of real interest to us all.

Here in Arlington, in this tiny corner of the great world which comes so closely under our observation I have watched the people who have come in

from outside and I think I can make a generalization (inaccurate as all generalizations are but with some truth in it) that the people who come here to work
here to earn their living here, never have any difficulty in adjusting themselves
and being accepted without any special thought by the people who live here. I
think the point is that everybody who lives here has to work hard for his living.
Somebody who comes in from outside who doesn't seem to be working for his
living is alien to them *for that reason* rather than for any reasons of race or religion. It is a kind of social and economic difference I think, rather than as it
appears, a reticent reserve about outsiders.

For instance, I knew a man from Philadelphia who came here as a house
painter. He lived here about twelve years before he died, and when I went to
his funeral I found that people who had just had their attention called by the
obituary notices to the fact that he came from Philadelphia, were genuinely
surprised to find that he had not always been an Arlington man. He had been
wholly accepted because he was engaged in earning his living in a way that
seemed familiar to all of here. And some of the so-called city people who have
come in, if they start working actively with Arlington people in projects for the
general welfare like the Library or for the public schools, or in work for our
young people's recreation—they too seem to be taken in with no sense of odd-
ness, although some of them are quite odd in person and very different from
our own Vermonters. What do you think of that theory of mine, I wonder?

Certainly your treatment of Arlington, your feeling so deeply that these
hills are not your hills, and these skies not your skies, is perfectly intelligible to
any of us here—for we are terribly rooted people as you know, and I think any
one of us would die of homesickness if transplanted to live say, in an Italian or
German village. In fact I am lost in admiration of the moral courage of the
people who do come to America, because they have to, and somehow manage
to strike root here, even if not tap-roots.

I mustn't close this long letter without telling you that the people here who
have seen your book are not only deeply interested in the story of your life
which is like a fairy story to them of strangeness, but also touched to see your
appreciation of their intention to be kind—no matter whether they were awkward in showing it.

With every good wish for the success of the book,
Faithfully and cordially yours,
Dorothy Canfield Fisher

[Handwritten] I am sending you, in another package a collection of stories of
mine, of which one "A New Pioneer"[3] shows that I quite understand and share
your feeling about the American "Thanksgiving Day."

1. *Red Ribbon on a White Horse,* with an "Introduction" by W. H. Auden (New York: Scribner's, 1950).

2. Gaetano Salvemini (1873–1957), Italian historian and educator, professor of history at Harvard University.

3. DCF's "Thanksgiving Day" is included in *Nothing Ever Happens and How It Does* (1940) and published as "A New Pioneer" in *Something Old, Something New* (1949).

169. To Bernardine K. Scherman
December 22, 1950
[Arlington, Vermont]¹

Dearest Bernardine:

John swung me down from the train (it was two hours late and had to wait on a siding in Arlington, for the south-bound train to come through) with an exclamation of relief to see me whole, and Dr. Russell² came charging up to the house, as soon as he heard the train come in, to see how I had survived. Both were agreeably surprised to find me in such fine spirits, so happy over a happy, happy experience.

Dr. Russell took blood-pressure, pulse, temperature, all the medical goings-on, and certified that the trip had done me no harm whatever. I told him quite the contrary—that it had charged the old battery to a higher current. And then we sat by the fire, and the old lady told the two old gentlemen all about it—even to delivering (to their shouts of appreciation) a spirited liver-punch, from the toes, with all I had!

What a wonderful achievement such a day is. It's seldom, seldom, seldom, that in the tough and resistant stuff of actual life, one can live through something which will be flawless in the memory. In an art, you can revise, retouch, take out the wrong notes,—in something lived, it is as it is, and can't be no iser, as the railroad foreman used to say.

What material for long quiet hours of reflection and living-over at the three in the morning meditation. Last night, at that hour, I started at the beginning, when I stepped into your beautiful apartment home, and lived through every minute of it all,—which was, because of the special quality of the occasion, fixed on my mind and memory, in every detail. What pictures—that exquisite cat with his rare, significant lines, sitting by that strangely beautiful old do-funny—pitcher was it?—from Egypt—you and your beautiful grown-up daughter going off together to the opera, in such amity and warmth of comradeship as hardly ever happens between mother and grown-up daughter—Harry's dear face at the gate to my train as I went away—and all those friendly, animated, *vital* people at that wonderful party. It's like a great album of pictures. I'm set for years of three-o'clock wakefulness!

Also—to be mundane, I ate (by doctor's permission) for my supper last night, creamed chicken and rice, had pea soup, and ate the insides of an Alsatian cream pie, our Marguerite's masterpiece—and suffered no untowards effects.

With this news, I leave you, with a great hug of admiration and affection.

Your devoted Dorothy

[Handwritten] I'm so glad you are going to take that African trip. You're going to take me with you, you know, as part of your baggage.

---

1. Place: implied.
2. George A. Russell (1880–1968), Arlington physician, model for "The Family Doctor," one of Norman Rockwell's well-known paintings. He is referred to in the "Preliminary Remarks" to *Vermont Tradition*.

170. To Clifton Fadiman
January 6, 1951
[Arlington, Vermont][1]

Dear Kip:

The only trouble with that comforting, hearts-solace you sent for Christmas,[2] is—where to keep it!

In spite of all I can do, my study, meant for a work-room, is the gathering place of all the family, town and country, or so it seems to me at times. People waiting for me to finish a telephone call, or get a batch of dictated letters signed, roam around, pick up books, look at everything. And I'd hate to have a casual eye light on your inscription which means so much to me.

But I don't want to put it away safely. For then I wouldn't have it at hand to take up and read, as I've done so many times since it came, and will do, over and over—read again the serene sadness you have set down—I mean "serene" the way one thinks of the heart-broken confession of sin in the Bach Mass *Miserere Nobis*—[3]

Well, what I have done is to tuck it under the upper left-hand corner of my blotter. But suppose I get suddenly killed in an automobile accident. Those few words written on the fly-leaf mean far too much to me to have them part of the "Canfield collection" of papers, at the University of Vermont library, for a cataloguer to list alphabetically and leave to students to finger over,—students too young to understand *anything*!

How would this do? If you do hear of my sudden death, you or Annalee[4] write to my executor to say I had requested you to ask for the return of the

Christmas booklet in the down-stairs study. If I die before my husband, never mind. It'll be all right. He'll know what I want done. After considerably more than forty years of marriage, we have between us one of those supra-sensory communication systems so much more accurate than words.

Thanks for the note about the children's books.[5] I meant to ask your opinion (of the two both of you) about one detail of the manner of presentation of the material for children. But that can wait till I see you again. May that be soon! And on an occasion less confusing and agitating than that Christmas party. Not that I didn't appreciate the great good fortune that party brought me to see your wife's diamond-bright and pearl-soft dark eyes. What a joy to see a woman (or man) with the ability to love writ large in the expression— most precious, I think, of all human gifts!

Affectionate greetings to you both
Dorothy

As to that precious inscription, you must have learned that in the world of the heart and spirit, the same law holds as in the world of physics—action and reaction are, by definition, equal each to the other. If you have received, so— oh Kip, so have you given!

---

1. Place: implied.

2. Fadiman sent DCF a copy of a fable about world government entitled *The Last Christmas* (printed privately).

3. Bach's *Mass in B Minor.*

4. Fadiman's wife.

5. DCF's children's books, *Paul Revere and the Minute Men* and *Our Independence and the Constitution,* were published the previous year.

171. *To James Thurber*
March 28, 1951
[Arlington, Vermont][1]

Dear Mr. Thurber:

Your letter of the 19th comes in today, of the most extreme interest to me, as all your letters have been.

I have time now for only one item—I'm trying to catch the last mail out from our country post office—in answer to what you say about Henry James. You say that "I insist James drew on music and painting and the theatre for his best effects." And I think I should pass on to you some information I had not long ago before he died, two or three years ago, from Henry James, Jr., William James's son, the nephew of the novelist. He and his wife had a summer home just over the mountain from our valley, and I often saw him.

I was reading that very fine book about the James family, and fell to wondering how it was that so highly cultivated a family circle never had in their letters, journals, and books anything to say about music. How could they, I wondered, have lived for years at a time in parts of Europe which were musical centers and never mention ever having gone to a concert or heard a note played or sung. The Jameses seem, now, like "history people" and it was only after some meditation on the subject that it occurred to me that one of them was still alive and my neighbor here. So I wrote him (Henry James, Jr.) putting my question to him. He answered with quite a long letter in which he said that as far as he could remember none of the family had any ear for music, could not tell one tune from another, never went to a concert, never had any music in their home.

I just thought I ought to send you this item so that if you go on discussing the matter with Professor Coffin[2] you will not forget that Henry James, the novelist, could hardly have drawn on music for some of his best effects. Restrict yourself to painting and the theatre and you'll be on firm ground I think.

By the way I believe that Professor Coffin perhaps has something in objecting to your full quotation of the Runaway Incident.[3]

Hastily, always faithfully yours
Dorothy Canfield Fisher

[Handwritten] I write almost as slowly and rewrite just about as much as you do. It's comforting to me to learn I'm not the only one who struggles so.

---

1. Place: implied.
2. Charles Monroe Coffin (b. 1904), professor of English at Kenyon College (Ohio), author of *John Donne and the New Philosophy* (New York: Columbia University Press, 1937).
3. In "Man With a Pipe," *New Yorker* (Aug. 25, 1951), an essay on Ohio State English professor Joseph Russell Taylor, Thurber quoted a long passage about a runaway horse cab from Taylor's book *Composition in Narration*. The essay reappeared in the collection *The Thurber Album;* Coffin commented negatively on the full quotation of the passage after reading Thurber's essay in typescript.

172. To James Thurber
April 17, 1951
[Arlington, Vermont][1]

Dear Mr. Thurber:

Your letter of the 13th is here, and although I don't happen to have a secretary available, and my own typing is typical of those who learned to use the machine many years before anybody had invented a "system" for using it accurately and hence is sometimes hard to read, I must lose no time in saying I am appreciative of your sympathy about the appearance of my name on some list of Americans accused of Communist leanings. I didn't know it had so appeared, but it doesn't surprise me at all, for I have been on every such list, it seems to me, since William Allen White and I appeared together on the Red Network list.

He was one of my father's devoted old students,[2] and a close friend of our family, so that he shared fully with me his amusement at seeing his name in such a connection. Amusement in his case, personally, for he liked nothing better than a fight on such a matter. But, like you, indignation, too, for those who are put into real danger by such accusations.

From my great-grandmother on down, each generation of the Canfields has been obnoxious to the ultra-conservatives, and very much honored to be so. When your letter came in, I looked in my files to see if I still had (I don't "keep things"—there are so many of them, we wouldn't be able to get into the house if we kept things) an article written by a Negro writer, who lives in Vermont, "up north" that is, near the Canada line, as we say, to the intense amusement of Southern visitors. For a wonder it had not disappeared, and I send it along to you as the best explanation I know for the venom with which I have always been, off and on, assailed. My father was an ardent and very vocal free-trader— in States where the Republican party was the Colossus of Rhodes astride all the world,[3] so he always caught it, too. And that invitation to Booker Washington, when he was President of O.S.U. was the final affront to Ohio standards which set the pack on him so fiercely that he couldn't stay.[4]

Of course, I have also done as much as I possibly could with limited resources (financial and of vitality) for refugee children in this country, and that too apparently riles up the McCarthys and the Winchells.[5] Winchell devoted some space to me last summer, observing in a phrase so characteristic that it was funny "I don't say that Mrs. Fisher is a Communist, or ever has been a Communist, but she certainly is on all the lists of subversives-organizations our Congressmen have," etc. etc. etc.

All right about the M.A. and Joe Taylor.[6] You're right, it is not at all important. I just got a qualm of self-doubt about the detail.

Well, it's nice to know that if I do get put in jail for sending medicine to sick children in China or something, that you can be counted on to come and hand me a basket of food through the window.

I hope you're having a *good* time in Bermuda—the New England spring is being absurdly bad this year.

Ever yours
Dorothy Canfield Fisher

1. Place: implied.

2. DCF's father taught White at the University of Kansas (see Letter 70, note 5).

3. The Colossus was a massive statue of Apollo said to span the harbor of Rhodes so that ships sailed through its legs at the harbor's entrance.

4. See Letter 118, note 2.

5. Joseph R. McCarthy (1908–1957), U.S. Senator from Wisconsin (1947–1957). Noted for his accusations against many individuals for subversive activities and links to the Communist party. Walter Winchell (1897–1972), American journalist. Columnist for the *New York Daily Mirror* (1929–1963); he also appeared on radio and television. Noted for opinionated style of reporting.

6. In a letter of Mar. 8, 1951, DCF said she doubted whether OSU professor Joseph Taylor held an M.A. Thurber said Taylor received the degree from Columbia University.

173. To Merle Haas
November 10, 1951
[Arlington, Vermont][1]

Dearest Merle:

Reading over, once again that admirable little monograph, statement, pamphlet, whatever you want to call it, about Breughel, which you so casually dropped on my desk, I wonder if I have ever told you how fine I think it. I don't know at all, do you I wonder? who the Professor Agnes M. Rindge of Vassar, is who understands Breughel so well. Is she a "professor of Art?" Is there such a thing? Anyhow, I like her ideas and I am glad you happened to notice it and thought of me, when you happened to see it.

I had something else on my mind, I wanted to tell you, when I started this— oh yes, a letter from a friend in Paris who had seen Rivers[2] and his wife, and who was chiefly struck by his wife's advanced state of pregnancy, apparently very visible indeed.

And I wanted too to let you know that I have at last heard that Dr. Hindemeyer (they spell it Hintemeyer I notice probably don't get it right) has been to see Marguerite Fischbacher,[3] is in touch with her son André, who is a government doctor in Morocco, now back for a leave of absence, and together they seem to be planning for a stay of a month or so *dans une clinique de Bellevue,* where she can get treatment she needs, chiefly the opportunity to try to regain a more normal command of her muscles on the side which is not paralyzed.

Do you know where Bellevue is? It's right spang next town to Sèvres—in sight, fairly, an easy walk. Think of there having been a *clinique* which can be considered suitable by Dr. Hindemeyer, so near to Marguerite all this time! For months and months, my guarded and then more and more pressing suggestions that *something* be done, other than wait on her, hand and foot, day and night, met with silence, and then defeatist astonishment at the very idea, and then alarm at the idea, which would be "dangerous" so some of their doctor friends thought—and all the time a *clinique* where she might be helped in sight of the house in Sèvres. Beats all.

I've just had a telephone talk with Mrs. Weaver, who says they are all in fine shape and very happy here, and Lea[4] is in Boston, visiting some friends, after having been back to her surgeon who certifies her as 100% all right, after the operation. Very good news, my goodness! I have just risen from my fifteen-minutes allowed reading time, with a smile over a statement of Henry Canby's or maybe Henry James, in Henry Canby's comments on *The Bostonians.*[5] Seems the theory is (maybe James himself said this but I gather it was Henry's idea—that's the trouble with this fifteen-minute reading period, you can't get into all the corners and find out every detail) that James wrote with such savage satire of the Boston reforming women, who (idiots that they were) "wanted to make the world a better place to live in," because he thought that they were engaged in destroying the "sentiment of sex." Is *that* a joke! As if anything could! And this fear lest the "sentiment of sex" be diminished, from a man who, as far as the eye can see, never had a bit of it. Something like the Pope telling the world in all the modern languages all about what the relations between husband and wife should be.

Do you remember the ancient story about the high school teacher who gave a little physiology (of digestion) to his freshman class and the next morning one of the girl students brought a note from her mother reading "I don't want you to tell Lottie all this about her insides. First off, 'taint decent, and then it will turn her against her vittles." As if anything could.

We've had a beautiful beautiful fall of snow here, which we all enjoyed as you enjoy a Mozart quartet, it was that kind of snow, not the Wagnerian kind. I wish you and Bob could sometime manage to be here in snowtimes, long enough to get the good beauty of it. How you would both paint! Dot and Chuck Canfield[6] have been at the brick-farm-house again, and, to my surprise, it turns out that this is the first time that Dot has ever seen the valley in snow-time. Again to my surprise, she was simply enchanted with it—never had dreamed how white snow can be when not dirty—if you get me.

Lots of love, always, to all of you from your devoted Dorothy

---

1. Place: implied.

2. Haywood Bill Rivers (b. 1922), African-American artist.

3. Marguerite Fischbacher, a French friend of DCF's. In 1917 she took over the Braille press Fisher established in Paris for the war blind. DCF arranged for her to host Robert Frost's daughter Marjorie in Paris in 1928.

4. Probably Lea Ehrich, an Arlington artist who designed the cover of *Memories of My Home Town* (1957).

5. Canby's comments on Henry James are contained in *Turn West, Turn East* (Boston: Houghton Mifflin, 1951).

6. Charles (Chuck) Canfield was the son of DCF's brother James. Dot was his wife.

174. *To Christopher Morley*
November 19, 1951
[Arlington, Vermont][1]

Well, my dear old comrade-at-arms, Harry sent me your letter to read, with the good news of your having been to a meeting again, with champagne to celebrate. I'm glad to know they celebrated the occasion. If I'd been there when you came in, triumphing over calamity,[2] not even my venerable years would have prevented my jumping from the chair I sat in to give you a real Jenny-welcome.

But your letter was so exactly you, undiminished, that it is almost as good as having seen you come in. I'll sleep better nights, now I've seen you quite yourself, within, no matter what hampering limitations have been loaded on you from without. I've been so deeply concerned (you brought up as a Friend know what concern means) about you and so eager, and yet afraid, to learn how *you* are, not your troubled right hand and side, but your spirit.

Now I know, it is all right, what it always has been—calamity has not got you down.

Do you remember—but how would you?—once in that dreadful time after my dear lost son's death, when I was struggling to breathe, just to stay alive, when you said something kind and tender to my misery, that I tried to quote you, the rough old ballad, by which I was living in those days, "Ffight on, ffight on, my men" he said,

> I'm wounded sore, but I am not slaine.
> I'll just lie down and bleed awhile
> And then I'll rise and fight againe"[3]

That wound is still a sore one, it still gushes out great gouts of pain at—at so many things, at the look of the horizon just before twilight comes because that was once a joy we shared, at a line of a Goethe poem because we read it together.

Many years ago, when my children were still young, I saw my dear, quiet Quaker father-in-law standing out in the June sunshine trimming a hedge. I always loved him, and went over to stand near him. He stopped his work, bared his white head for a moment to the summer sun, and said, musingly "It was forty years ago today that Willie died." (That was the first child, the little boy who died at five, before my husband was born.) He went on, as if he were thinking aloud, "If I had known then, what I was to suffer from sorrow, I do not think I would have wished to live."

It frightened me. I went to look up my own little boy and took him into my arms.

But the old man who had so suffered that he could almost not bear it, did not die from that sorrow. I often reach my hand back over the years to take his wrinkled old hand in mine—old and wrinkled now, too. He was wounded sore, but he was not slaine.

And neither are you,—hallelujah!

Ffight on, ffight on—

With love
Your Dorothy

---

1. Place: no reason to doubt Arlington.
2. In 1951 Morley suffered the first of three incapacitory strokes that all but ended his writing career.
3. See Letter 136, note 2.

175. *To Eleanor Roosevelt*
May 2, 1952
[Arlington, Vermont][1]

Dear Mrs. Roosevelt:

Knowing what a superhuman lot of work you get through in your busy days, I try to keep my occasional letters to you as few and brief as possible. So I haven't written you to thank you for the splendid great mass of material which, at your request, the United Nations office sent to me in connection with my effort to make accessible to young people the Universal Declaration of Human Rights.[2] They sent up a bushel-basket-full (so to speak) of the big bound volumes of reports on the minutes of the meetings when the thirty Articles were discussed; as well as all sorts of other material useful and indeed indispensable for my work.

I've spent most of the winter on the comments for youngsters, (between eleven and fourteen years of age). It was a difficult assignment. In all my long years of writing, I never took on one which seemed to me more important, or harder to manage, than to turn into concrete, simple, understandable language, the beautifully accurate abstract and legal words of the Articles.

But I do not regret an hour of the many I spent on this effort. It was an honor to have the opportunity to help the younger generation grasp the noble meaning of the great Declaration.

The typescript of my work was tried out in school classrooms with children from eleven to fourteen, both in rural communities and in a big city (Brooklyn). It was also submitted to the members of the Department of the United Nations specially concerned. They went over the text very attentively and made many helpful (although mostly small and verbal) suggestions.

Now, I'm sending a set of the galley proofs to you, with the—well, the *hope,* both from the publishers (McGraw Hill and Company) and the author, that after looking it over you might feel moved to write a preface of a few lines, to start it off.

Don't do it, if this seems a last-straw burden. I will quite understand if you don't feel that you can add it to all you have already taken on. Who could understand better than I, for I am often overwhelmed by "small" requests which, coming on top of each other, are very much last-straws.

But we will very much hope that you may feel you can give the incalculably great help of your name to this effort to make intelligible to young people (both in English-speaking and other countries, for there are plans to have it appear in several translations) the general idea of each one of those magnificent Articles, to the preparation of which you gave so much of your vitality.

With—as always—affectionately proud and admiring appreciative good wishes

1. Place: no reason to doubt Arlington.
2. See Roosevelt entry in Notable Recipients.

176. *To Roy Jansen*
November 7, 1952
[Arlington, Vermont][1]

Dear Mr. Jansen:

Your letter of the 4th, just in, interests me because of the feature you are doing for newspapers, and because it was as a reporter that we had a meeting in Pittsburgh. That must have been quite a long time ago, as I remember it.

I have no special recommendations to offer because I don't see that mass action can be taken by those past the age of 65 any more than by any other age group. Within the group all men and women have their individual tastes, needs, and standards. You would have to be familiar with each individual case before it would be safe to offer any advice that would have any value.

It seems to me a mistake to think of people past 65 as a certain kind of human being, instead of as varying individuals—varying quite as widely in all directions as they did before they reached that age.

The story is told about a questionnaire sent out to the students in several women's colleges some thirty years ago dealing with social standards. One of the questions asked was whether the student thought it was all right for a girl to kiss a boy good night when he brought her home from a date. One group of answers were to the effect that of course it was all right, times had changed from grandma's day, and so had social standards, and this was just a good example of progress. Another group were firmly against such liberties and thought boys should not even feel that they might ask for such a privilege. There was just one other answer—and that girl got the highest mark for it— two words, "*That depends.*"

Well, I feel that way about people over 65. It all depends on the sort of people they have grown to be in their life before that age, and no blanket generalizations can really be valuable as advice.

With cordial good greetings and all friendly wishes for the success of your feature with the newspapers,

Dorothy Canfield Fisher

------

1. Place: implied.

177. To Bernardine K. Scherman
January 5, 1953
[Arlington, Vermont][1]

Dearest Bernardine:

You will probably give a shout of protest when I say that I am sending you this account of the state of Kenya because you are my "African expert." But honestly it is true,—you have been there, and recently, and judging by your letters (you know Harry gave me the great pleasure and interest of reading some of them) you did get to some extent the feel of the place—at least the feel of the places where you were, what the white folks were like, what the colored people seemed like.

That is, of course just one hundred per cent more than I know about it. I am deeply, painfully interested in what's going on in Africa from the dreadful state of things in South Africa with the Boers[2] to the dreadful state of things in Kenya (apparently) with the British,[3] with the Belgian colony so rich in uranium, described to me by some old French friends whose daughter (a friend of my Sally) is married to a French forester in the French Kameroun,[4] and who has visited the Belgian African region and described it as ultra prosperous *for the whites,*—nothing but Rolls-Royces etc., very scarifying to her feelings because the French Kameroun is, she reports, very poor, with no pickings for anybody, black or white, and *why* should Belgium have the luck to have uranium discovered under their soil. And of course there is the Gold Coast[5] and Liberia where some kind of a door to the future seems open,—as not in these other places.

Well, although I take the liveliest interest in all this, such an astonishing development for anybody brought up on African missionaries as the sole whites, as I was, and as was that old lady who wrote the memoirs of her life as a child in central Africa, do you remember? I sent you that as to "my African expert" and I send this casual article. Take a look at it, don't try to answer this letter, just the next time I see you (may it be soon) tell me how Kenya looked to you. I *have* one other "authority," Isak Dinesen in *Out of Africa*. But she is as old as I am, almost, and was then, when she wrote the book, in love with a member of the British aristocracy, and liked her black people all right, but only if they were *hers*. So I doubt if she'd have an idea in her head about all this.

Maybe the real reason I'm writing you is to try to let you know what an enormous lift your remarks about *Vermont Tradition* in the *News* gave to both John and me. I have labored so long and so hard on that book, always with the spectre at my shoulder of a reader who couldn't see what it was to him! Your generous words are the first comment I've had—and they do calm my troubled spirit! I never *had* such a prepublication lift before—never needed it so much either!

Thousands of thanks and much love, always
Dorothy

---

1. Place: no reason to doubt Arlington.

2. In 1952 the 300th anniversary of the landing of the first Dutch colonists in South Africa was marked by public protests against apartheid laws. The government reacted with even stricter regulations on the freedom of non-whites.

3. A state of emergency was in effect in Kenya from 1952 to 1960 due to the violent struggle between the British and Africans.

4. The British and French Cameroons in west-central Africa were divided (1960–1961) between Cameroon and Nigeria.

5. Gold Coast was a former British colony in coastal West Africa, now part of Ghana.

178. To John P. Marquand
January 5, 1954
Arlington, Vermont

Dear John:

It won't surprise you, I am sure, to have me write you that you have been often and often in my mind during this illness of mine.[1] Not only because you

also are still feeling the devitalizing effects of another kind of serious illness—
or as my doctor calls this cerebral hemorrhage of mine—"accident." No, it is
because I have been for weeks on the point of writing you some sage advice—
and now find myself, the tables turned, in a situation where that advice applies
to me—and what a different face it wears!

I'm not quite enough older than you to be of your mother's generation, but
plenty old enough to be one of your aunts, and it was an aunt-like counsel I
meant to send to you. A good sound one, too, just as appropriate now as when
it hung on the tip of my pen, ready to pass on to you. It's this:—You have
written of feeling really disheartened as you recover from that thrombosis,[2] by
the slowness with which your general vitality return—or doesn't return. No
pep, you write, no invention welling up from its mysterious springs, to go on
with that novel[3] left unfinished on your writing table when your heart gave
way—none of the literally compulsive *interest* in the characters and their doings
which is the only motive an author can have, powerful enough to make him go
through the anguish of writing, and which only an author knows about or can
believe in.

I've felt for you, heaven knows, I've understood how it must make you suffer, but I've been wanting to write you to have more patience about the resto-
ration of that inner writer's-life without which nobody can do creative work.
That inner world is so great that it needs all the vitality a human being can
have, focused intently—every fiber beating with as organic a unity as the pulse
on which our bodily life depends.

And that requires all the bodily life to be intact. When, only a month after
your heart had had that very rough jolt, you wrote that you'd already "tried to
go on" with the unfinished novel and were shocked and dismayed to find that
you seemed to have no invention, no real initiative, I was surprised at your
lack of philosophical poise. And now how I share it!

It is really almost a comic situation I find myself in, or would be if it weren't
so exasperating. For I am now in that very same slough of despond, prostrate
in a lack of vitality that astonishes me. It is as though somebody had turned on
the faucet and gone away and all of my own strength had just leaked out leaving me empty.

But now every time I feel with panic that wretched inner vacuum, I am
brought up sharply by the recollection of what I have been meaning to write
you—namely, just to *wait,* to allow the passage of time and the process of nature to do that mysterious healing which the passage of time has accomplished
so often in my observation, in everybody's observation.

That, dear John, is the sententious sage, aunt-like good counsel I was going
to send you.

But not now, not now. I have none to spare for you. I need it all myself.

And, anyhow, so much time has passed since I last heard from you, probably you have moved forward to normal writing-activity, and can hardly remember when you were not interested in what happened or was going to happen to the characters in your new novel.

Certainly that's the heart-felt hope of your devoted

Dorothy

---

1. In Dec. 1953 DCF suffered a cerebral hemorrhage which left one side of her body paralyzed.

2. Marquand suffered a coronary attack in mid-July 1953.

3. Marquand was working on *Sincerely, Willis Wayde* (Boston: Little, Brown, 1955).

179. To Christopher Morley
April 12, 1954
[Arlington, Vermont][1]

Dear Chris:

Here we are in April, and I have never put away in my files your letter of February 3rd—it was more than just a letter, it was a true bulletin of news from the inner life, such as seldom gets put into an envelope. Mostly when something dramatic is going on within—as now for you and me—one lives in solitude. The outer voices have no resonance. One waves a hand to recognize the friendly intention (something to be thankful for) but the words don't come through.

But yours was an inner voice. And it certainly has rung in my ears ever since. When I now—as I do, of course—wake at that dark three in the morning and wonder if I am still alive or not, I start my wheels moving again with an admiring smile to see you valiantly drinking your saucepan of hot milk to keep those inner wheels from slowing down altogether.

I do hope that your inner news is more quiet by this time, with fewer of those deadly hours of wakefulness before dawn. On the whole, my own news bulletin is quiet. I've had no later attacks from the one in December,[2] my left hand is still partly paralyzed, but I "manage"—and without pitying myself too much, living as I do among men who earn their livings dangerously in forests and pastures, who lose fingers by axe or drill press or saw and stoically go on working without them. I can, too.

And like your "weeks of blissful ease," I savor with intensity the joys of unhurried leisure, such as I have never known before, for books and music—sometimes exasperated by thin places which I just now perceive in the texture of masterpieces I used to idolize; some other times exhilarated to inner shouting joy by depths and loveliness and meanings which till now I never had sense enough fully to see. John, dear John, reads aloud to me a good deal. We share this new leisure as we have always shared life.

And memories. I am much older than you, I think, and realize that I am truly venerable, as the memories come floating up, some from long ago, of my father, my mother, of the passionate joy and active games which so brightly colored my little girlhood, of the deeply loved Morgan colt given me when I was 12, which I myself broke and trained (badly) to ride. What a crazy thing for my elders to allow! I'd never dream of letting a child of that age handle an unbroken young horse.

But not all those vivid memories are remote. In many of these sudden gusts from the past, it is my lost son who is there beside me, on woodland path or upland field, trotting with the then-living collie dog so like the now-living collie always at my heels.

For years after my son's death I dreamed of him often and in those dreams he was there vividly and naturally alive and I had no idea that he had died. But little by little, that blessed unawareness in sleep of what had happened was worn away by the abrasion of long waking hours filled with sorrow. And in the end, even in dreams, I knew, or almost knew, with pain that what I was dreaming was not true. And when that happened, the dreams stopped. Now, he comes back in what I know are memories, not reality, but so bright that their joy makes sorrow only a shadow, not all there is.

And I have another old woman's joy—my grandchildren, four of them, and their mother—all five seem about the same age to my antiquity. They are like fireworks of vitality, racing forward into life, discovering, exclaiming, arguing, alive to the last fiber, full of excited tales of what they are doing—new themselves, hence all that happens to them is new. "Granny, I can play three waltzes in the song on my trumpet." "Granny, we are making a terrarium at school. Granny, do you know what a terrarium is?" "I'm editing the high school magazine, and I can't get over how the kids who try to write always follow the party line! Make a guess at what they think is in style in writing nowadays, and that's what they do! Why can't they write what they feel like writing!"

The oldest of this brood, now 19, is going to spend next winter at college in England (by an interesting exchange arrangement with her American college) and I can hardly wait to see what she makes out of these experiences.

And of course the children who come in and out of my life are not only my grandchildren—children who live near us here—the dears!—who come in with tiny sprigs of the first arbutus, and for a chance to report their latest marks at school and what the new puppy is like. Or perhaps six-foot boys or tall girls back from college who (so it seems to me) were last week concerned about the puppy, reporting Phi Beta Kappa won or troubles with freshman classes, or that they are engaged, or expect alas! soon to be drafted into the army.

I find I can hardly tell the difference anymore between this youth and the bright, flashing, living brooks I cross on my slow woodland walks. I get the same impression from both of them of ever-new, ever-renewed life.

There, that's my news bulletin—of what's going on within. Little, really nothing—to report of what is visible physically—a quiet, old country woman, deaf, with dimmed eyes, partially paralyzed, going slowly along the paths where she used to outrace her own children.

She sends you her comradely affection as always.

Dorothy

---

1. Place: implied.
2. See Letter 178, note 1.

180. To Granville Hicks
July 5, 1954
[Arlington, Vermont][1]

Dear Mr. Hicks:

I am very much honored that you remembered my interest in your Grafton library project[2]—one of the most daring and courageous efforts I've ever seen carried out in the kind of background very familiar to you and to me. It's wonderful to know how well you have carried it through to within hailing distance of a complete achievement. I read this program of your this year's celebration with much pride in what you Grafton people have been doing.

Now at this point let me tell you a story about Joel Spingarn[3]—you may remember him, one of the most brilliant men ever connected with Columbia. He went to live in the country in a little town not far from Poughkeepsie, in Dutchess County. We used to go to see them there once in a while, and were very much impressed by the wonderful impression which he made on daily life in that rural region. Under his auspices a "farmer's reunion" was established where every year after the crops were in, farmers came together on some big fields near Spingarn's house for—well, for a good time of all sorts—comparison of notes on crops that year, square dancing, plowing contests, community sings and what not. Hundreds and hundreds of farm families used to assemble there for two days of the best possible community gathering.

One day I exclaimed to him "I think it is almost miraculous what you have succeeded in doing here. What is your secret I wonder." He answered, poker faced and grave, "It's perfectly simple. All that's needed is cooperation. And I furnish the cooperation."

You probably know this story about somebody else, for it's an old one, but you can imagine that it came to my mind as I turned over the chronicle of Grafton's achievement in this catalog.[4]

I was very much an invalid when I found I couldn't go to be with you and I'm no less of one now, having become very much a stay-at-home—a situation not to be pitied but very enjoyable I find in some ways. And if, as you say, you and Mrs. Hicks recover sufficiently from your big job of cooperating I'll be hoping to have a call from you later on in the summer.

Appreciatively yours
Dorothy Canfield Fisher

---

1. Place: implied.
2. See Hicks entry in Notable Recipients.
3. Joel Spingarn (1875–1939), American poet and critic. Spingarn was a founder and literary advisor of Harcourt, Brace, and Co. (1919–1932), a founder (1909) and chair of the board of directors of the NAACP (1913–1919), and later treasurer (1919–1930) and president (1930–1939) of that organization.
4. See note 1.

181. *To Louise [Hieatt] Forscher*
November 18, 1955
[Arlington, Vermont][1]

Dear Mrs. Hieatt:
I have kept your letter before my eyes, ever since it came in. For it is a real treasure. You seem to me very much like a spiritual daughter, added to my flesh-and-blood daughter (she also was a Swarthmore graduate, only long before you).[2]

The generous impulse which sent you to your desk to write to me so appreciatively of that novel of mine[3] has resulted in a very great deal of pleasure to an old author, now a little nearer eighty than seventy and retired from active life.

I don't go out in public anymore, but I very well remember that graduation address which I gave for your class,[4] because its subject was one which has recurred to me so many times in the years I have been observing and commenting on the life offered to women of your kind and mine and my daughter's by our country in these years. I'm very much struck by the fact that although

America offers us a life astonishingly safe from most disastrous dangers, it plunges us into another danger which is devilishly insidious because it falls so imperceptibly about us as we live—and that is the danger of becoming held and mastered by triviality. The little things of life, of no real importance, but which have to be "seen to" by American home makers, is like a blanket smothering out the fine and great potential qualities in every one of us. I was always taking advantage of being asked to speak to young Americans to warn them of this danger, and as I remember it I spoke ardently on that theme at Swarthmore that day. It's wonderful that you remember my being there. That doesn't often happen to seniors on the last day of their college life. The older generation person set to give them the last wave of the hand hardly seems actual or real to them—if I remember my own college life.

And of course I am deeply touched that Matey[5] said something to you, for as you guessed, I was the person who was saying it of course and to have an echo of that long ago call of mine come back to me now is a golden reward for the years of very strenuous struggle with my own limitations involved in my writing.

With heart-felt thanks for your letter,

Faithfully yours,
Dorothy Canfield Fisher

[Handwritten] How I *wish* my eyes were not dimming so that I must dictate my letters! I can't get used to the remoteness of that way of answering letters which have deeply moved me, as your daughterly note did—for it made you seem a spiritual daughter of mine—blessings on you!

---

1. Place: implied.
2. Sally Fisher graduated from Swarthmore College in 1930.
3. *The Deepening Stream* (1930).
4. DCF spoke to the graduating class of Swarthmore in Feb. 1944 (see Forscher entry in Notable Recipients).
5. Matey Gilbert, female protagonist of *The Deepening Stream*.

182. *To Francis Steegmuller*
March 21, 1956
[Arlington, Vermont][1]

Dear Mr. Steegmuller:

Now I sit down to write you about La Fontaine,[2] I feel abashed at the idea that I might have something of interest to you in my head, accomplished as you are in the field of literary history involved. I'll make my letter reasonably short, at least, not to bother you too much.

Here's my notion: Ever since I was a little girl in school in France, nearly seventy years ago, I have inwardly protested against the current conception of La Fontaine as an apostle of the meanly "prudent" way of life, the narrow exponent of thrift and caution and servile bowing to constituted authority. I used to feel—indeed have always felt—that the readers of his fables read into them their own cautious opinions.

La Fontaine's own personal life was wildly at variance with prudence, thrift, eager subservience to authority,—it seems to me it casts a light upon his work which comes from quite another direction. Since he is—anybody with half a literary eye in his head can not but see this—a writer of the first rank, I have always felt that it would be worthwhile to look into this phenomenon of misinterpretation.

Since my youth, two elements have come into human experience which would, I feel, help to give to La Fontaine the look which really sees what is before it. The first of these elements is the awareness (since Freud) of the unconscious or partially unconscious in human action. The other element is the painful observation of the ruses necessary under a dictatorship to express opinions contrary to those enforced by military and police power. We have seen French plays written in protest against the German occupation, but so composed that the censor was powerless to punish the author. Isak Dinesen wrote a fine novel to pillory the German military occupation of Denmark;[3] her meaning perfectly plain to the wide general public but so ingeniously expressed that the German censor could not object.

With these two factors in mind, and (also in mind as you certainly have to the last detail) the overwhelmingly prevalent social atmosphere of the court and nation under Louis XIV, the "Fable of the Dog and the Wolf" seems to me a powerful protest against the attitude enforced by the king on the nobles of his time. The joyful ending of it when the wolf sets off in a free racing run, *et court encore,* always opened to me the door out of the smothering social subservience of the court, so well known to La Fontaine. Even that threadbare old "Crow and Fox" which I suppose every French child has had to learn by heart takes on a new meaning in this light—or does to me. Was there any other way to protest against the insanely constant flattery which was by accepted convention troweled out on the king. "The Ant and the Grasshopper"—why should it be assumed as it generally is, even by—especially by ordinary French readers—that so desperately improvident a singing *cigale*[4] as La Fontaine should have wished to set up the callously unaesthetic Ant as a model of conduct.

I have written this book in my mind so many times that, now the faucet has been opened, I find it hard to shut it. But this is enough. If there is anything in my idea for you, you will have seen it from these few references.

There are two immediate causes for my thus emerging with the idea of a subtle book about the court of Louis XIV and one of the subtlest and most skillful writers in France. Last summer a favorite French god-daughter of mine, made the great effort to leave her fine husband and five children and come and make me a visit here in Vermont. In the course of the rushing talk between us to make up for a long separation, she happened to say, "I detest the philosophy of La Fontaine but sometimes it almost seems that taking precautions and prudence are really wise." I did not take any of the precious brief time we had together to cry out what I felt for the hundredth time in my life, "What in the world makes you think that is the *personal* philosophy of La Fontaine!" But I thought it.

The second reason for my speaking up is the appearance of your book on *La Grande Demoiselle,*[5] which showed you to have such a masterly grasp of the life, court, century around La Fontaine. I don't know anybody else who could give expression to an idea which has been in my mind for so many years.

With every good wish,
Faithfully yours,
Dorothy Canfield Fisher

---

1. Place: implied.
2. Jean de La Fontaine (1621–1695), French poet and fabulist, author of *Fables* 1668, 1678, 1693. DCF refers to his fable of the grasshopper and the ant in the "Prologue" to *A Harvest of Stories:* "When I first read that fable, a little nine-year-old in a French classroom, did I admire the prudent responsible ant? Not at all. I was revolted by his self-righteous cruelty. I still am" (xx).
3. *The Angelic Avengers* (see Letter 144, note 1).
4. Cicada.
5. *La Grande Mademoiselle* (London: Hamish Hamilton, 1956).

183. To Karen Blixen
August 14, 1956
[Arlington, Vermont][1]

My dear Tania:
What an electrifying presence yours always is! Just after a long period when I have felt so sadly anxious about your health, from the occasional news-bulletin passed along by your brother Tom, suddenly comes this wonderful collection of typescripts of your lately written, powerful and beautiful stories,[2] as new-minted as though they were the first ever to flow from your pen.

Mr. and Mrs. Haas have been here for their usual summer month spent in their Vermont home, and my husband and I have had the very great pleasure of hearing Mr. Haas read them aloud—for my eyes dimming more and more rapidly in these later-seventy years of my old age, permit almost no reading to myself.

What memorable seances these reading-aloud evenings have been! What strong currents of emotion, admiration, vividly stimulated thought we have enjoyed in that open and free interchange of impressions only possible between old friends who have for years shared life intimately in all confidence.

Our common impression is of astonished relief that, the terrible weeks and months of illness[3] have not in the slightest degree lowered or diminished the extraordinary brightness and clarity with which your literary flame burns. There is really little to write you except that a general shock of admiring, appreciative joy in your great literary gift, which has so survived your health difficulties.

Of course, some of the tales struck us all as more perfect than others. My husband and I both were quite carried away by "A Country Tale" which has enough pure beauty, power and forward narrative movement to fit out a long novel. The social implications of that story, implications unspoken but so exquisitely sounding as overtones, make the story, so we felt, as truly *great* a piece of work as you have ever done. At the other end of the gamut we put "The Cardinal's Third Story" which, fine as it is, appealed to us least. "The Blank Page" is a brilliant tour de force and more significant than a brief tour de force has any right (literally speaking) to be. "The Cardinal's First Story" is very fine, and "Converse at Night in Copenhagen" has passages of description as startlingly fine as ever were written—old-Copenhagen streets on a rainy night—that is so beautifully written that it seems to glow and gleam on the page.

As you see, my "comment" is mostly exclamatory admiration—sent to you with much happy relief that you are, evidently, making such a recovery as we hardly hoped for.

With affectionate good wishes,
Dorothy Canfield Fisher

---

1. Place: implied.

2. *Last Tales* (New York: Random House, 1957).

3. In Jan. 1956 Blixen underwent major stomach surgery for the removal of ulcers, an operation from which she never completely recovered.

184. To Albert L. Guerard
January 30, 1957
[Arlington, Vermont][1]

Dear Professor Guerard:

Your letter is here, rejoicing me by your friendly, appreciative, and keenly understanding comments on my collection of short stories.[2] Both my husband and I are very glad you mention particularly the double interpretation possible in the case of the story called "The Saint of the Old Seminary."[3]

You should just see the number of letters that have come in from readers about that story (for it has been republished in a good many other publications, since the *Yale Review* first printed it) asking me about that same double interpretation. "*Which* one is the *real* one?" such letters ask. And my answer always is "What do you mean, 'real'?"

That story was written after a prolonged, close reading of a biography by a very pious author, of the great Saint Teresa of Ávila, a scrutiny which revealed more, I thought, than the pious author meant to put in. At that time I was living in the little Basque fishing village of Guethary and in close touch with Bayonne friends from whom I learned of the filthy old slum tenement called "The Old Seminary," and with whom I visited it several times.

My husband and I are having a wonderful time reading aloud your book about the classical ideal,[4] and last night had a celebration with fireworks and bonfires over the chapter about the Encyclopaedists. Of course! We knew it was going to be exactly to our taste, but we really did not foresee the strikingly brilliant, and yet wonderfully sane and balanced treatment you would give those great favorites of ours. How I admire your discriminating, *fair* statement about Rousseau,[5] for I am one of the people who feel an involuntary, almost physical repulsion for Rousseau.

One sentence in your letter is bringing down on you another book of mine—*Vermont Tradition.* You speak of your little granddaughter looking up at a severe face of an Eastern Massachusetts worthy and saying with a rebelliousness which rejoices my heart, "You're not the boss of *me.* " You say casually of the dark old portrait, that it is of one of the people "like those you describe" in my stories of old-time Vermonters, and I cried out "No, no, *no, not* that and thought I must send you my *Vermont Tradition.*

I found so much more historical tradition involved in that delicious child story than you know, or could be expected to know, that I am moved to pass along to you—for (I hope) reading aloud to your wife—a historical, social and economic study I wrote some five or six years ago, on the subject of the very great differences between the 17th century tradition of Eastern Massachusetts and the New Haven part of Connecticut, and the 18th century tradition of

Vermont. Our state was settled in 1764, by Western Massachusetts and Western Connecticut people, all of them younger-generationers of communities which had never been Puritan in spirit. They were children of the Great Enlightenment and consciously so. The local lending library of our small (1400 inhabitants) town of Arlington was organized, quite formally with a written constitution in 1803. One clause of this constitution stated that at no time was more than one 36th part of the money in hand (and you can imagine how little cash was at that time in possession of a small community of farmers in a narrow valley of the Green Mountains) to be spent on "books of divinity." Not a volume of sermons has ever stood on its shelves. And, in the very first books purchased was an edition of Gibbon's *Decline and Fall of the Roman Empire*[6]— a book which was anathema to Eastern Massachusetts, clergy-dominated communities.

You may be smiling (many Americans do who live in the widely spacious West and Middle West) at the idea of a marked difference in local traditions between one section and another of New England, (the whole of which looks so small on the map of our immense American United States).

But since you are Albert Guerard, I think you may be interested in the story of the historical reasons back of such a marked difference in social ideals and traditions. So the rather formidably thick *Vermont Tradition* will go across the continent to you as soon as I can get, over snowy roads, to the town of Manchester to the north of Arlington where there is—astonishingly, for a small mountain town—an excellent bookstore. The mail package with the book about Vermont ideals may cross, perhaps in Nebraska or Arizona, your *History of World Literature*[7]—a quaint idea don't you think?

With every comradely and most admiring greeting,

Dorothy Canfield Fisher

---

1. Place: implied.

2. *A Harvest of Stories* (1956).

3. "The Saint of the Old Seminary" was originally published in the *Delineator* 118 (Jan. 1931): 8–9 and is included in *Basque People* (1931) and *A Harvest of Stories* (1956). The double interpretation centers on the character Tomasina, who as a young woman was responsible for a man's death and spent the rest of her life in self-inflicted penance for it.

4. *France in the Classical Age: The Life and Death of an Ideal* (New York: Scribner's, 1928). Reprint. (New York: Braziller, 1956).

5. Jean-Jacques Rousseau (1712–1778), French philosopher and author. Guerard writes of him: "We find it exceedingly difficult to entertain any great reverence for the man Rousseau, for his thought, and even for much of his art: yet he can not be eliminated from the world's history any more than Napoleon. We find him at the head of all the great tendencies in the nineteenth century: religious revival, democracy, romanticism, socialism. He is as ardently combated today, in France and America, as when he was alive: and we do not fight the dead" (277).

6. English historian Edward Gibbon's (1737–1794) *Decline and Fall of the Roman Empire* (six vols., 1776–1788) presents a negative view of Christianity.

7. *Preface to World Literature* (New York: Holt, 1940).

185. *To Merle and Robert Haas*
February 13, 1957
[Arlington, Vermont][1]

Dear Merle and Bob:

About a year ago a very nice person, a writer, (Mrs.) Elizabeth Yates, McGrael,[2] whose books for older young people have taken several national prizes, and whom I have known for some time, came to see me to ask if I would be willing to have her write my biography.

You know I have never been willing to have that written, because I don't like the trivialities of personal talk. She explained, however,—and this disarmed John and I completely, that what she wanted to do was to write a book to bring out the universal themes which I have tried to express in my books. That sounded good. I think I've told you about this already, a little, with this much explanation.

She's getting along, has some kind of a first draft done of about half of the book, and passing through New York this month some time, she would like to go to see you for half an hour's talk.

You can imagine that what I am now doing is to write you to ask you *if* the opportunity offers and *if* it seems natural, to try to back up what John and I feel, that is, that she has a tendency, perhaps inevitable, to give too much space and attention to my various efforts to be a good citizen and useful to the country in practical matters, rather than to my efforts to express in fiction more universal ideas.

I suppose it is much easier to write about actions than about fiction,—at any rate John feels quite strongly, and I agree with him, that she is, in spite of what we thought she meant to do, and what I think she thought she meant to do (for she is a very honest person) saying too much about actual material actions and activities of mine, and giving too little space to the novels and short stories.

If she telephones you when she goes through New York, and if you do see her for a while, and if the occasion presents itself, just give a push in the direction of more careful reading of the novels and short stories and more space given to considering them, than kind activities.

All well here, Jim in Florida and Jack in North Carolina report peaceful winters being had—ours is a lovely one, this February being really an ideal winter month—except that there isn't quite enough snow. But that wonderfully pure, stimulating winter air, still and sunlit! Nobody could ask for better.

With a heart full of affection always
Your Dorothy

[Handwritten] Mrs. William McGrael, of Peterborough, New Hampshire. Dutton publishes her books. She has won several national prizes for books for High-School-age young Americans. Amos Fortune is one, Prudence Crandall is another.[3]

  1. Place: implied.
  2. Elizabeth Yates McGreal (b. 1905), American author. McGreal's *Amos Fortune, Free Man* (New York: Dutton, 1950) won the Newbery Medal and the William Allen White Children's Book Award. DCF wrote the "Foreword" to her *Prudence Crandall, Woman of Courage* (New York: Dutton, 1955). The biography, *Pebble in a Pool,* was published in 1958.
  3. See note 2.

186. To Albert L. Guerard
March 7, 1957
[Arlington, Vermont][1]

My dear Professor Guerard:
    You are fortunate in that this is an especially busy time for me, with the typescripts just being put together for a new piece of writing going out to the publisher.[2] I've been far too busy to write you, and am now temporarily far too low in vitality to begin to say what I'd like to about your book on world literature.[3] If I began, there'd be no end to it! [Handwritten: "I'm new to the art (is it an art?) of dictating into a machine instead of writing what I mean to say. This incredibly confused paragraph [shows?] that if I had not been so much occupied with my own work, I'd have bothered you by far too many many letters because you have been much in my thoughts."]
    We are reading it, a little at a time, my husband and I, because we like it so much,—as you sip a liqueur. I've *never* seen any really intelligent discussion of translations before, it seems to me, and as I have struggled with translation from the Italian several times in my laborious past, and as my daughter has made a couple of excellent, serious translations from the French within the last few years, the subject is fresh in my mind. I also think it a very important subject,—and in that, I am running against the Anglo-Saxon literary current apparently. For it is so poorly paid and so little recognized that I am surprised that they can get *any*body to take on translating, anybody competent, that is.
    The long translation of the Papini *Life of Christ*[4] (which I didn't like—just

not to my "taste" at all) was wished on to me by a chance remark of mine in a book review of a translation of a d'Annunzio short story.[5] The *Yale Review,* I think it was, sent me the translation asking me to make a comment on it. I was really shocked by it, by the bad quality of the translation, and said so, in my review. Here's an example, in a description of a small Italian town street scene, the translator set down "At this point, the ostentation came out of the church and went down the street." I said with some heat that if American publishers were not going to provide better translations than that, they would do well not to publish any translations at all.

That was a risky remark. Two days later, Alfred Harcourt of Harcourt, Brace and Company drove up in person, to our little mountain home, with a big, thick Italian book in his hand and asked me to translate it. I looked at it, and exclaimed, recoiling in alarm, "Who, *me*? I don't like Papini anyhow, and I have all my schedule made out for a couple of years ahead of me." Alfred Harcourt (he was a classmate of my husband's in Columbia hence an old friend of the family) said, "Aha! you see, that's what happens to publishers,—they can't get people who are competent, to translate." This was a challenge which I couldn't leave unanswered, and I took the book on. What an unrewarding and endlessly long task *that* was!

Last evening was a celebration for both my husband and me with your chapter on taste. I think that's one of the most brilliantly written statements you ever made—and that's a superlative.

But now I set that down, it makes me remember something I've been meaning to write ever since your letter came in about the absurdly small publication your brilliant and discriminating essays have received in American magazines. Something had been in my mind for some time about that, and I pass it along to you for what it is worth—perhaps not much. I've long been an admirer of your work, and have talked a great deal about your books to my circle of friends, and loaned your books. I think I have some idea what the point is— your illustrations are quite naturally, drawn from your French training, not exclusively, but more than the Anglo-Saxon acquaintance with French literature will bear. For instance, in this very chapter we admire so much, you fall back again as you have so many other times on Descartes,[6] with a mention of Pascal.[7] I think it just isn't safe to assume that, even when American readers *know* those names, that they have anything like the richly clustering association of ideas with them which you have, and which English-speaking people have with such a name as Thackeray or Milton or any other of the great masters writing in English. I noticed, for instance, that at the end of that very fine essay on the Algerian situation which I admired so much, you quoted Bossuet.[8] But in English imaginations, that name does not roll sonorously or thunder or lightening as the very mention of it does in French.

Perhaps I have thought of this because my husband often says that I do very much the same thing with my music in my novels:—that is, assume that my readers are going to feel the same sort of associations which I have, with music. For me, the high point, crisis and turning point of *Seasoned Timber* is the beautifully fortifying spiritual message brought to a man sorely tried in daily life, by hearing first the tramp! tramp! tramp! of the chorus in the *St. John Passion* to the words "We have no King but Caesar."[9] And the heavy and apparently triumphant materialism of this blunt, brutal credo swept away by the soaring-up of the chorus, *In Meines Herzens Grunde*[10] after it. My husband has pointed out to me, reasonably enough, that I can hardly expect the meaning of such a passage in a novel for American readers, to be the same for other people as for someone very familiar with Bach. I know he's right but I went ahead and left it in.

Already, you see, this letter is longer than I meant it to be. And we are only in the middle of your fine book. More later and always affectionate and comradely greetings,

from your Vermont admirer
Dorothy Canfield Fisher

---

1. Place: implied.
2. *Memories of Arlington, Vermont* (1957).
3. See Letter 184, note 7.
4. Giovanni Papini, *Life of Christ,* trans. Dorothy Canfield Fisher (1923).
5. DCF reviewed Gabriele D'Annunzio's *Tales of My Native Town,* trans. Rafael Mantellini (New York: Doubleday, Page, 1920) in the *Yale Review* 10 (Apr. 1921): 664–67.
6. René Descartes (1596–1650), French mathematician and philosopher.
7. Blaise Pascal (1623–1662), French mathematician and philosopher.
8. Jacques Bengine Bousset (1627–1704), French theologian and orator.
9. See Letter 113, note 3.
10. Translation from German: "From the bottom of my heart."

187. To Mary C. Jane
September 3, 1957
[Arlington, Vermont][1]

My dearest Mary:

You can't imagine how good your letter sounded to me, for I have now moved into another and very difficult (to me) phase of this strange attack from which I've been suffering since the first of April. You know what it was, an embolism pressing on the brain, creating the strangest ideas and emotions. Nothing to do with me personally yet seeming to come from my inner self. It is the most disturbing experience I've ever had in my life and I should think it would be for almost anybody. Well, the doctors kept telling me that the embolism would be absorbed, and I think now it has for I have some memory, coherence, and so forth, and am perfectly well physically. But now the question is how to get back to work, and for me of course work means writing. I was right in the middle of a book for young people when this fell on me like a thunderbolt, and I haven't been myself enough since then to think of it.[2] But now I think of it and find myself almost unable to put two ideas together. I haven't put things together, you see, all these months when I've been, so to speak, struggling to keep my head above water.

The idea of the book is an interesting one, I think. It was for McGraw-Hill, very good publishers for young people. The book was to be called "Beacon Lights from the Past," and it was to [be] memorable doings or sayings of people in the past who sort of set an example for us. But nothing from the battlefield. That's going to be the novelty of the book. For instance I want to have Nichols' exclamation to his men when they saw the Spanish warships careening over and the men jumping into the water and his men began to cheer, "Don't cheer, men. The poor devils are dying." It seems to me that is a real turning point, the first breakthrough of a man trained to war who suddenly saw what war is. It is often quoted but I don't think with enough significance given to it. But will I be able now in this strange confusion of mind in which I come back to my work to bring that out. That is the trouble and it throws me into a sort of nervous panic at the thought of it. Think of me with sympathy, won't you my dear girl, and send me occasionally a word of sympathy, for I love your letters. The letter you wrote my daughter when all this began was a great delight to her. And somehow I must bring myself together to go on with that work for I was right in the middle of it.

I want also to bring out Robert E. Lee's use of the period of his life after his defeat. That ought to be a good lesson for me. Most of us don't know anything about him after he rode away from Appomattox in his fresh grey uniform with its red silk sash. What he did then was to refuse all offers to set him up in some handsome style living, for he hadn't a penny, but turned to a very poor Virginia college to which he devoted himself, raising funds to keep it going, supervising the curriculum, getting students to come.[3] It seems to me that is a real lesson in defeat, and since defeat comes to all of us some time or another, I think that is a good thing to set down for our young people.

Well, that is the sort of thing I'm just aching to set down on paper, but will I be able to? For my brain is still pretty disorganized. I suppose this kind of a shock you can't pass off as you can a physical shock. The brain centers seem somewhat disturbed, even yet.

Well, remember me and write me one of your good letters once in a while, and above all tell me what you are doing. Your life has always been so constructive and active, it does me good to hear about it. I think of you with thanksgiving for what you have helped me with, all these years, and hope you will keep on with an occasional letter.

With love and admiration and appreciation
Dorothy Canfield Fisher

———
1. Place: no reason to doubt Arlington.
2. Published posthumously as *And Long Remember.*
3. After the Civil War, Lee became president of Washington College (now Washington and Lee University) in Lexington, Virginia.

188. To Karen Blixen
November 12, 1957
[Arlington, Vermont][1]

My dear Tania:

I have now just recently seen a photograph of you which, in spite of being printed in a newspaper seemed to me to show your strange and unusual beauty as much as print in a book shows—almost like a special glow—the strange and unique beauty of your words. How we in this small old home on the side of a Vermont mountain did enjoy, this summer, the reading aloud to us in typescript of these "Last Tales!" That was last June,[2] I think, but I am now infirm with too many years and the confusion of brain centers which fell on me with that cerebral accident (as the doctors call all such physical and material disarrangement of brain-centers) so that I am never sure of the conventional measures of time. I was (as always with your writing) quite carried away into your special vision of life and the world. It was a great comfort and reassurance to me that old and infirm as I am, I can still feel the benediction of great admiration of wonderful gifts!

And now your book (printed) comes in with the lovely photograph of your house, prefaced to the eye by a wonderful big bush bursting out in an explosion of roses. I never saw a more attractive photograph of your lovely home. How glad I am to set it on my desk (that desk so unused in these long months of half-life for me) and revel in it.

Thank you so much dearest Tania for somehow crossing the Atlantic with your personality—although you have been so terribly ill,[3] so your brother has written me—as living as ever.

I shall ask one of my readers aloud (for my eyes are dimming so rapidly, I can no longer read to myself even my most personal letters) to read the *Last*

Tales aloud, as the world moves forward into the darkness of a northern-climate winter which you Dinesens must know as well as Vermonters do.

With affection and great admiration from your ancient, distant

Dorothy

---

1. Place: implied.
2. DCF seems to have meant June 1956 (see Letter 183, which mentions the typescript of *Last Tales*).
3. See Letter 183, note 3.

189. To Robert Haas

September 16, 1958

[Arlington, Vermont][1]

Dear Bob:

Helen Congdon[2] is here today, reading me the excellent book on the Naval Academy which you so kindly sent to Ethel Hard, and she has just come across an explanation of that apparently idiotic hazing of the Plebes by the upper-classmen. The purpose given is that "keeping a mass of unrelated information in mind ready for recitation is supposed to teach the Plebe to think accurately and quickly under pressure." So I see some reasonable ground for hazing is given at Annapolis, as I hope so much some reasonable ground is given to the American young men for the instant obedience exacted from them by our American army. And the statement is also made that Plebes were formerly sometimes "beaten, humiliated and even tortured as a part of hazing." So, as I surmised, it is now much milder.

There is one other statement on which I would like verification and don't know how to get it. The statement is made that "no applicant is barred because of race, color, or religion." Of course, in the midst of the present segregation turmoil the question now comes to my mind, is this statement really justified? Has Annapolis ever received and given a chance at its training to any colored man? How can I find out the answer to this question? You'd think it would be simple just to write the Superintendent and ask him this, but all Americans have grown so suspicious of the publicity agents of our institutions that I am a little afraid that if I wrote on my own letterhead and signed my own name to the inquiry my name might be recognized as someone who might, through publishing the answer, "make trouble." Annapolis is rather far to the south and we all know how adept southern heads of schools have become in denying constitutional rights to education to colored children. In view of the present situation I don't feel that I am being unreasonable—for once in my life—in trying to suggest a way to get the truth about this matter in an answer on which I can rely. Poor Bob, you are the person in the big American world in whom I feel I can have complete trust so I turn to you to ask, did you ever hear of a colored graduate of the Naval Academy? I know the Army is now really honest-to-goodness not reserved for the white race and I think I know that there have been colored graduates of West Point, but I never happened to hear about Annapolis.

Thanks so much for any suggestion you can make, and apologies for continuing to be a troublesome correspondent to you who have so many other things on your mind.

Affectionately yours,
D.C.F.

---

1. Place: implied.
2. DCF's secretary.

Bibliography

Note: Dorothy Canfield Fisher published fiction under her maiden name (with the exception of her only play, *Tourists Accomodated*) and nonfiction under the name Dorothy Canfield Fisher (with the exception of her dissertation). Fisher published hundreds of stories and articles in various periodicals, a complete bibliography of which is currently being compiled and which will appear separate from this volume due to its length. Primary sources are listed chronologically; secondary works are organized alphabetically.

Primary Sources

Fiction

Gunhild. New York: Henry Holt, 1907.

The Squirrel-Cage. New York: Henry Holt, 1912.

Hillsboro People. New York: Henry Holt, 1915.

The Bent Twig. New York: Henry Holt, 1915. Cutchogue, N. Y.: Buccaneer Books, 1981.

The Real Motive. New York: Henry Holt, 1916.

Fellow Captains (with Sarah N. Cleghorn). New York: Henry Holt, 1916.

Understood Betsy. New York: Henry Holt, 1917. New York: Dell, 1987.

Home Fires in France. New York: Henry Holt, 1918.

The Day of Glory. New York: Henry Holt, 1919.

The Brimming Cup. New York: Harcourt, Brace, 1921. New York: Virago, 1987.

Rough-Hewn. New York: Harcourt, Brace, 1922.

Raw Material. New York: Harcourt, Brace, 1923.

The Home-Maker. New York: Harcourt, Brace, 1924. Chicago: Academy Chicago, 1983.

Made-to-Order Stories. New York: Harcourt, Brace, 1925.

Her Son's Wife. New York: Harcourt, Brace, 1926. New York: Virago, 1987.

The Deepening Stream. New York: Harcourt, Brace, 1930.

Basque People. New York: Harcourt, Brace, 1931.

Bonfire. New York: Harcourt, Brace, 1933.

Tourists Accomodated. New York: Harcourt, Brace, 1934.

Fables for Parents. New York: Harcourt, Brace, 1937.

Seasoned Timber. New York: Harcourt, Brace, 1939.

Four-Square. New York: Harcourt, Brace, 1949. Reprint. Salem, N. H.: Ayer Publishers.

A Harvest of Stories. New York: Harcourt, Brace, 1956.

Nonfiction

Corneille and Racine in England. 1904. Reprint. New York: AMS Press.

A Montessori Mother. New York: Henry Holt, 1912.

A Montessori Manual. Chicago: Richardson, 1913.

Mothers and Children. New York: Henry Holt, 1914.

Self-Reliance. New York: Bobbs-Merrill, 1916.

Life of Christ by Giovanni Papini. Trans. Dorothy Canfield Fisher. New York: Harcourt, Brace, 1923.

Why Stop Learning? New York: Harcourt, Brace, 1927.

Work: What It Has Meant to Men through the Ages by Adriano Tilgher. Trans. Dorothy Canfield Fisher. New York: Harcourt, Brace, 1932. Salem, N. H.: Ayer Publishers, 1977.

Nothing Ever Happens and How It Does (with Sarah N. Cleghorn). Boston: Beacon Press, 1940.

Tell Me A Story. Lincoln, Nebraska: University Publishing, 1940.

Our Young Folks. New York: Harcourt, Brace, 1943.

American Portraits. New York: Henry Holt, 1946.

"Novelist Remembers Blue-and-Gold Christmas in Pittsburgh." *New York Herald Tribune* December 21, 1947: 42.

Our Independence and the Constitution. New York: Random House, 1950. New York: Random House, 1964.

Paul Revere and the Minute Men. New York: Random House, 1950.

A Fair World for All. New York: Whittlesey House, 1952.

Vermont Tradition. Boston: Little, Brown, 1953. Marietta, Ga.: Cherokee Books, 1987.

Memories of Arlington, Vermont. New York: Duell, Sloan, and Pearce, 1957.

And Long Remember. New York: Whittlesey House, 1959.

What Mothers Should Know about the Montessori Method of Education. New York: American Institute of Psychology, 1985.

Selected Introductions by Dorothy Canfield Fisher

Kent, Rockwell. *Wilderness*. New York: G.P. Putnam's Sons, 1920.

Dinesen, Isak. *Seven Gothic Tales*. New York: Smith & Haas, 1934.

Wright, Richard. *Black Boy*. New York: Harper & Brothers, 1940.

———. *Native Son*. New York: Harper & Brothers, 1940.

Tolstoy, Leo. *What Men Live By*. Trans. Louise and Aylmer Maude. New York: Pantheon, 1943.

Zoff, Otto. *They Shall Inherit the Earth.* Trans. Garrison. New York: John Day, 1943.

Guptill, Arthur. *Norman Rockwell, Illustrator.* New York: Watson-Guptill, 1946.

Secondary Sources

Apthorp, Elaine Sargent. "The Artist at the Family Reunion: Visions of the Creative Life in the Narrative Technique of Willa Cather, Sarah Orne Jewett, Mary Wilkins Freeman, and Dorothy Canfield Fisher." Ph.D. diss. University of California–Berkeley, 1986.

Biddle, Arthur W. and Paul A. Eschholz, eds. *The Literature of Vermont: A Sampler.* Hanover, N.H.: University Press of New England, 1973.

Boynton, Percy H. "Two New England Regionalists." *College English* 1 (January 1940): 291–99.

Brooks, Van Wyck, Archibald MacLeish, and Thornton Wilder. "Letter to the Editor on Detroit's Ban of *To Have and Have Not.*" *Nation* 147 (July 23, 1938): 96.

Bruccoli, Matthew J., ed. *Selected Letters of John O'Hara.* New York: Random House, 1978.

Bynner, Witter. *Prose Pieces: The Works of Witter Bynner.* Edited by James Kraft. New York: Farrar, 1979.

Cather, Willa. "The Profile." *McClure's Magazine* 29 (June 1907): 135–40.

———. *The Troll Garden.* 1905. Edited by James Woodress. Lincoln: University of Nebraska Press, 1983.

Cleghorn, Sarah. *Threescore.* New York: Smith & Haas, 1936.

Firebaugh, Joseph J. "Dorothy Canfield and the Moral Bent." *Educational Forum* 15 (March 1951): 283–94.

Hackett, Alice Payne. *Seventy Years of Best Sellers, 1895–1965.* New York: R. R. Bowker, 1967.

Humphrey, Zephine. "Dorothy Canfield." *Woman's Citizen* 10 (January 1926): 13–14, 36.

Kutner, Nanette. "If You Worked for Dorothy Canfield Fisher." *Good Housekeeping* 117 (November 1943): 41, 196.

Lee, Charles. *The Hidden Public: The Story of the Book-of-the-Month Club.* New York: Doubleday, 1958.

Lovering, Joseph P. "The Contribution of Dorothy Canfield Fisher to the Development of Realism in the American Novel." Ph.D. diss. University of Ottawa, 1956.

———. "The Friendship of Willa Cather and Dorothy Canfield." *Vermont History* 48 (1980): 144–55.

Luccock, Halford E. *Contemporary American Literature and Religion.* Chicago: Willett, Clark, 1934.

Madigan, Mark J. *Dorothy Canfield Fisher.* New York: Twayne Publishers, forthcoming.

————. "Profile: Dorothy Canfield Fisher." *Legacy: A Journal of American Women Writers* 9, issue 1 (1992): 49–58

————. "'This allegation we repudiate!': An Unpublished Poem by Dorothy Canfield Fisher." *Vermont History News* 41 (March-April 1990): 35–36.

————. "Willa Cather and Dorothy Canfield Fisher: A Literary Correspondence." Master's thesis, University of Vermont, 1987.

————. "Willa Cather and Dorothy Canfield Fisher: Rift, Reconciliation, and *One of Ours.*" In *Cather Studies,* edited by Susan J. Rosowski, vol. 1. Lincoln: University of Nebraska Press, 1990.

————. "Willa Cather's Commentary on Three Novels by Dorothy Canfield Fisher." *American Notes & Queries* 3 (January 1990): 13–15.

Mann, Dorothea Lawrence. "Dorothy Canfield: The Little Vermonter." *Bookman* 65 (August 1927): 695–701.

McCallister, Lois. "Dorothy Canfield Fisher: A Critical Study." Ph.D. diss. Case Western Reserve University, 1969.

Overton, Grant. *The Women Who Make Our Novels.* Freeport, N. Y.: Books for Libraries Press, 1967 (pp. 61–74).

Phelps, William Lyon. "Dorothy Canfield Fisher." *English Journal* 22 (January 1933): 1–8.

Pottle, Frederick A. "Catharsis." *Yale Review* 40 (January 1951): 621–41.

Price, Alan. "Writing Home from the Front: Edith Wharton and Dorothy Canfield Fisher Present Wartime France to the United States." *Edith Wharton Newsletter* 5 (Fall 1988): 1–5.

Quinn, Athur Hobson. *American Fiction: An Historical and Critical Survey.* New York: Appleton-Century-Crofts, 1936 (pp. 706–14).

Radway, Janice. "The Book-of-the-Month Club and the General Reader: On the Uses of 'Serious' Fiction." *Critical Inquiry* 14 (Spring 1988): 516–38.

Rahn, Suzanne. "Empowering the Child: Rediscovering Dorothy Canfield's *Made-to-Order Stories.*" *The Lion and the Unicorn: A Critical Journal of Children's Literature* 13 (December 1989): 109–30.

Reynolds, Paul R. *The Middle Man: The Adventures of a Literary Agent.* New York: William Morrow, 1972.

Rubin, Joan Shelley. *The Making of Middlebrow Culture.* Chapel Hill: University of North Carolina Press, 1992.

Schroeter, Joan G. "Crisis, Conflict, and Constituting the Self: A Lacanian Reading of *The Deepening Stream.*" *Colby Quarterly* 27 (September 1991): 148–60.

Silverman, Al, ed. *The Book-of-the-Month: Sixty Years of Books in American Life.* Boston: Little, Brown, 1986.

Smith, Bradford. "Dorothy Canfield Fisher." *Atlantic Monthly* 204 (August 1959): 73–77.

———. "Dorothy Canfield Fisher: A Presence among Us." *Saturday Review* 41 (November 29, 1958): 13–14.

"The Squirrel Cage." *Progressive Woman* (July 1912).

"The Squirrel Cage." *San Francisco Call* (June 2, 1912).

Starr, Louis M. "An Interview with Dorothy Canfield Fisher." *Columbia University Oral History Collection,* 1956.

Thaddeus, Janice. "The Metamorphosis of Richard Wright's *Black Boy.*" *American Literature* 57 (May 1985): 199–214.

Turnbull, Andrew, ed. *The Letters of F. Scott Fitzgerald.* New York: Scribner's, 1963.

Wagenknecht, Edward. *Cavalcade of the American Novel.* New York: Holt, Rinehart, Winston, 1952 (pp. 294–99).

Warfel, Harry R. *American Novelists of Today.* New York: American Book Co., 1951 (pp. 79–81).

Washington, Ida H. *Dorothy Canfield Fisher: A Biography.* Shelburne, Vt.: New England Press, 1982.

———. "Isak Dinesen and Dorothy Canfield: The Importance of a Helping Hand." *Continental, Latin and Francophone Women Writers.* Edited by Eunice Myers and Ginette Adamson. Lanham, Maryland: University Press of America, 1987.

White, William Allen. "The Other Side of Main Street." *Collier's Weekly* 68 (July 30, 1921): 7–8, 18–19.

Williams, Blanche Colton. *Our Short Story Writers.* New York: Moffat, Yard, 1920 (pp. 41–54).

Wright, Richard. *Early Works.* Edited by Arnold Rampersad. New York: Library of America, 1991.

Wyckoff, Elizabeth. "Dorothy Canfield: A Neglected Best Seller." *Bookman* 74 (1931): 40–44.

Yates, Elizabeth. *Pebble in a Pool.* Brattleboro, Vt.: Stephen Greene Press, 1958.

Calendar of Letters

Copy-Text Key

ALS = Autograph Letter Signed
CCTL = Carbon Copy Typed Letter
PTL = Published text of letter, original unlocated
TLS = Typed Letter Signed

1900–1908

1. Louis Wiley	Mar. 10 [1900]	ALS: 2 pp.; NRU
2. Curtis Hidden Page	Dec. 31, 1903	ALS: 4 pp.; NNU-F
3. Willa Cather	[Jan. 1, 1905]	ALS: 4 pp.; VtU
4. Willa Cather	Jan. 9, 1905	ALS: 1 p.; VtU
5. Willa Cather	Jan. 19, 1905	ALS: 1 p.; VtU
6. Family	July 30, 1905	ALS: 8 pp.; VtU
7. John O'Hara Cosgrave	[Late 1905 or 1906]	ALS: 3 pp.; ViU
8. Céline Sibut	May 11, 1906	ALS: 6 pp.; VtU
9. John O'Hara Cosgrave	Sept. 17, 1906	ALS: 3 pp.; ViU
10. Céline Sibut	May 15, 1908	ALS: 1 p.; VtU

1912–1919

11. Paul Reynolds	Nov. 3, 1912	TLS: 2 pp.; NNC
12. Paul Reynolds	June 21, 1913	TLS: 2 pp.; NNC
13. Paul Reynolds	Mar. 31 [1915]	TLS: 2 pp.; NNC
14. Henry Holt	[Sept. 14, 1915]	ALS: 4 pp.; NjP
15. Alfred Harcourt	[Nov. or Dec. (1915?)]	TLS: 1 p.; VtU
16. Robert Frost	Jan. 14, 1916	ALS: 4 pp.; NhD
17. Alfred Harcourt	Feb. 3, 1916	TLS: 2 pp.; VtU
18. Sarah Cleghorn	Mar. 4, 1916	TLS: 2 pp.; VtU
19. Louise Pound	[Mar. 13, 1916]	ALS: 4 pp.; NcD
20. Henry Kitchell Webster	Mar. 16, 1916	TLS: 2 pp.; ICN
21. Henry Kitchell Webster	Mar. 26, 1916	TLS: 1 p.; ICN
22. Louise Pound	Apr. 2, 1916	ALS: 3 pp.; NcD

23. Paul Reynolds	Apr. 26, 1916	TLS: 2 pp.; NNC
24. Louise Pound	May 16, 1916	ALS: 4 pp.; NcD
25. William Lyon Phelps	Aug. 3, 1916	ALS: 6 pp.; CtY
26. Scudder Klyce	Sept. 5, 1916	TLS: 2 pp.; DLC
27. Sarah Cleghorn	Dec. 28 [1916]	ALS: 2 pp.; VtU
28. Louise Pound	Feb. 14, 1917	TLS: 2 pp.; NcD
29. Sarah Cleghorn	Mar. 3, 1917	TLS: 3 pp.; VtU
30. Scudder Klyce	Apr. 3, 1917	TLS: 3 pp.; DLC
31. John S. Phillips	May 12, 1917	TLS: 1 p.; InU
32. Sarah Cleghorn	Sept. 5 [1917]	TLS: 2 pp.; VtU
33. Scudder Klyce	Oct. 27, 1917	ALS: 3 pp.; DLC
34. "Folks"	Mar. 23 [1918]	TLS: 1 p.; VtU
35. Sarah Cleghorn	Apr. 8 [1918]	TLS: 4 pp.; VtU
36. Amelia Reynolds	July 31 [1918]	TLS: 1 p.; NNC
37. James Hulme Canfield	Nov. 23 [1918]	TLS: 2 pp.; VtU
38. Paul Reynolds	Jan. 9, 1919	TLS: 2 pp.; NNC

1920–1929

39. Alfred Harcourt	Jan. 28, 1920	TLS: 1 p.; VtU
40. Louise Pound	Jan. 28, 1920	TLS: 2 pp.; NbHi
41. Paul Reynolds	Feb. 6 [1920]	TLS: 2 pp.; NNC
42. Paul Reynolds	Oct. 22 [1920]	TLS: 2 pp.; NNC
43. Alfred Harcourt	Nov. 10 [1920]	TLS: 2 pp.; VtU
44. William Lyon Phelps	Nov. 10, 1920	TLS: 4 pp.; CtY
45. W. E. B. Du Bois	Jan. 3, 1921	TLS: 1 p.; MU-Ar
46. Alfred Harcourt	Apr. 6 [1921]	TLS: 2 pp.; VtU
47. Julia Collier Harris	Apr. 13, 1921	ALS: 5 pp.; MNS
48. Scudder Klyce	Nov. 16, 1922	TLS: 1 p.; DLC
49. Julia Collier Harris	Dec. 8 [1922]	TLS: 3 pp.; MNS
50. Elizabeth Jackson	Feb. 25 [1923]	TLS: 2 pp.; VtU
51. Julia Collier Harris	Mar. 9 [1923?]	TLS: 2 pp.; MNS
52. Paul D. Moody	May 31, 1923	TLS: 2 pp.; VtMiM
53. Elizabeth Jackson	June 14 [1923]	TLS: 2 pp.; VtU
54. Elizabeth Sessums	Aug. 16 [1923]	TLS: 2 pp.; ViLRM
55. William Lyon Phelps	Nov. 1 [1923]	TLS: 2 pp.; CtY
56. Paul Reynolds	Nov. 20, 1923	TLS: 1 p.; NNC
57. Alfred Harcourt	Mar. 12, 1924	TLS: 2 pp.; VtU
58. Alfred Harcourt	June 7, 1924	TLS: 2 pp.; VtU
59. Edith F. Wyatt	Sept. 21, 1924	TLS: 1 p.; ICN
60. Paul Reynolds	Sept. 29, 1924	TLS: 2 pp.; NNC

61. Alfred Harcourt	Oct. 4, 1924	TLS: 3 pp.; VtU
62. Alfred Harcourt	Mar. 11, 1925	TLS: 1 p.; VtU
63. Paul Reynolds	Mar. 28 [1925]	TLS: 1 p.; NNC
64. H. Robinson Shipherd	July 10 [1925]	TLS: 1 p.; ViU
65. Alfred Harcourt	Sept. 28 [1925]	TLS: 1 p.; VtU
66. Alfred Harcourt	Nov. 27 [1925]	TLS: 2 pp.; VtU
67. Paul Reynolds	Feb. 11, 1926	TLS: 2 pp.; NNC
68. Julia Collier Harris	Aug. 16, 1926	TLS: 1 p.; MNS
69. James Weldon Johnson	[1927]	ALS: 3 pp.; CtY
70. Julia Collier Harris	Mar. 21 [1927?]	TLS: 1 p.; MNS
71. Alfred Knopf	Aug. 15 [1927]	TLS: 1 p.; NNAL
72. Robert Frost	[1928]	ALS: 2 pp.; NhD
73. Scudder Klyce	Jan. 6, 1929	ALS: 2 pp.; DLC
74. Robert Frost	[Oct. 7, 1929]	TLS: 1 p.; NhD
75. Alfred Harcourt	Dec. 12 [1929]	TLS: 1 p.; VtU

1930–1939

76. Elinor Frost	Sept. 15 [1930]	ALS: 4 pp.; NhD
77. Paul Reynolds	Nov. 3 [1930]	TLS: 1 p.; NNC
78. Pearl Buck	Nov. 7 [1930]	ALS: 4 pp.; ViLRM
79. Elinor Frost	Nov. 10 [1930]	TLS: 2 pp.; NhD
80. Fred Lewis Pattee	Nov. 24, 1930	TLS: 1 p.; PSt
81. Merle Haas	Dec. 14 [1930]	TLS: 2 pp.; VtU
82. Merle Haas	[1931?]	TLS: 2 pp.; VtU
83. Margaret Sanger	Oct. 4, 1931	CCTL: 1 p.; VtU
84. Ruth Suckow	Oct. 8 [1931]	TLS: 2 pp.; IaU
85. Paul Reynolds	Jan. 29, 1932	TLS: 2 pp.; NNC
86. Merle Haas	[Feb. or Mar. 1932]	TLS: 3 pp.; VtU
87. Paul Reynolds	Feb. 25 [1932]	TLS: 3 pp.; NNC
88. Alfred Harcourt	Mar. 1 [1932?]	TLS: 1 p.; VtU
89. George Palmer Putnam	Mar. 22 [1932]	CCTL: 2 pp.; MBU
90. Paul Reynolds	Mar. 28 [1932]	TLS: 2 pp.; NNC
91. Anzia Yezierska	Mar. 31, 1932	TLS: 3 pp.; MBU
92. André Maurois	Apr. 7, 1932	CCTL: 2 pp.; VtU
93. Thomas Dinesen	Aug. 12, 1932	CCTL: 1 p.; RLC
94. Paul Reynolds	Dec. 5, 1932	TLS: 1 p.; NNC
95. Paul Reynolds	[Mid-Dec. 1932]	ALS: 2 pp.; NNC
96. Paul Reynolds	[Jan. (19?) 1933]	ALS: 2 pp.; NNC
97. Merle Haas	[Apr. (1933?)]	TLS: 1 p.; VtU
98. Karen Blixen	Apr. 30, 1933	CCTL: 2 pp.; RLC

99. Alfred Harcourt	May 3 [1933]	TLS: 1 p.; VtU
100. Alfred Harcourt	Oct. 5, 1933	TLS: 1 p.; VtU
101. Harry and Bernardine K. Scherman	[1934]	ALS: 8 pp.; NNC
102. Ruth Suckow	Oct. 7 [1934]	TLS: 2 pp.; IaU
103. Bernard De Voto	Sept. 29, 1935	ALS: 4 pp.; CSt
104. Robert Haas	Feb. 22 [1936?]	TLS: 2 pp.; VtU
105. Paul Reynolds	[Oct. (8?) 1936]	TLS: 2 pp.; NNC
106. Mrs. Haven	Apr. 5, 1937	TLS: 1 p.; MNS
107. Bernardine K. Scherman	[1938]	TLS: 3 pp.; NNC
108. Mary C. Jane	Feb. 7, 1938	TLS: 3 pp.; MCJ
109. Franklin Folsom	June 23, 1938	TLS: 1 p.; CU
110. Robert Haas	Aug. 10 [1938]	TLS: 2 pp.; VtU
111. Arthur H. Quinn	Sept. 5, 1938	CCTL: 3 pp.; VtU
112. Ruth Suckow	Jan. 7, 1939	TLS: 2 pp.; IaU
113. Bernardine K. Scherman	[Dec. 1939]	ALS: 5 pp.; NNC

1940–1949

114. Willa Cather	Oct. 9, 1940	ALS: 3 pp.; HCS
115. Eva Robin	Mar. 15, 1941	TLS: 1 p.; CLU
116. Mary C. Jane	July 16, 1941	TLS: 3 pp.; MCJ
117. Carlton F. Wells	Mar. 30, 1942	TLS: 1 p.; CLU
118. Pearl Buck	July 20, 1942	TLS: 1 p.; VtU
119. Robert Frost	Sept. 12, 1942	TLS: 2 pp.; NhD
120. Robert Haas	Oct. 6, 1942	TLS: 1 p.; VtU
121. Paul Reynolds	[Oct. (7?) 1942]	TLS: 1 p.; NNC
122. Christopher Morley	[1943]	ALS: 3 pp.; TxU
123. Albert Einstein	Feb. 20, 1943	CCTL: 1 p.; VtU
124. Pearl Buck	June 22, 1943	CCTL: 2 pp.; VtU
125. E. B. White	Aug. 25, 1943	CCTL: 5 pp.; VtU
126. Pearl Buck	Aug. 26, 1943	CCTL: 4 pp.; VtU
127. Otelia C. C. Connor	May 16, 1944	TLS: 1 p.; NcU
128. Richard Wright	July 1, 1944	TLS: 3 pp.; CtY
129. Richard Wright	July 12, 1944	TLS: 4 pp.; CtY
130. Richard Wright	July 21 [1944]	ALS: 4 pp.; CtY
131. Richard Wright	July 23 [1944]	ALS: 4 pp.; CtY
132. Harry Scherman	July 27, 1944	TLS: 2 pp.; VtU
133. Richard Wright	Aug. 23 [1944]	TLS: 2 pp.; CtY
134. Anna P. Broomell	Sept. 8, 1944	CCTL: 2 pp.; VtU
135. Zephine Humphrey	Jan. 10, 1945	CCTL: 1 p.; VtU

136. Christopher Morley	Apr. 18, 1945	ALS: 1 p.; TxU
137. Robert Frost	June 8, 1945	CCTL: 1 p.; VtU
138. Frederick A. Pottle	Aug. 22, 1945	CCTL: 3 pp.; VtU
139. J. W. Lane	Nov. 3, 1945	TLS: 1 p.; VtU
140. Zephine Humphrey	Dec. 18, 1945	CCTL: 1 p.; VtU
141. Mrs. M_____	[1946]	PTL: Silverman
142. Margaret Mead	Jan. 3, 1946	CCTL: 2 pp.; VtU
143. Christopher Morley	Jan. 11, 1946	CCTL: 2 pp.; VtU
144. Robert Haas	Apr. 16, 1946	CCTL: 2 pp.; VtU
145. Raymond Holden	Nov. 16, 1946	TLS: 2 pp.; NhD
146. Meredith Wood	Nov. 16, 1946	TLS: 2 pp.; VtU
147. Upton Sinclair	Dec. 4, 1946	TLS: 1 p.; InU
148. Willa Cather	[Apr. (20?) 1947]	TLS: 2 pp.; VtU
149. Reginald L. Cook	June 18, 1947	TLS: 1 p.; VtMiM
150. Thomas Dinesen	June 21, 1947	CCTL: 2 pp.; VtU
151. Reginald L. Cook	June 30, 1947	TLS: 1 p.; VtMiM
152. Bernardine K. Scherman	Jan. 21, 1948	TLS: 2 pp.; NNC
153. Harry Scherman	Apr. 9 [1948]	TLS: 1 p.; VtU
154. Albert L. Guerard	May 22, 1948	TLS: 1 p.; CSt
155. John P. Marquand	Sept. 19 [1948]	TLS: 2 pp.; VtU
156. Harry Scherman	Oct. 8, 1948	TLS: 1 p.; VtU
157. Harry Scherman	Oct. 25, 1948	TLS: 2 pp.; VtU
158. Anzia Yezierska	Jan. 10, 1949	TLS: 2 pp.; MBU
159. David _____	[Jan. 17, 1949]	TLS: 2 pp.; MCR
160. Rosemary Benét	Mar. 2, 1949	TLS: 2 pp.; CtY
161. Sarah Cleghorn	July 7, 1949	CCTL: 2 pp.; VtU
162. John P. Marquand	Aug. 11, 1949	TLS: 2 pp.; VtU
163. Bennett Cerf	Dec. 23, 1949	CCTL: 1 p.; VtU

1950–1958

164. Harry Scherman	Feb. 1 [1950]	ALS: 4 pp.; NNC
165. Walter Collins O'Kane	Apr. 26, 1950	TLS: 2 pp.; OKU
166. David E. Scherman	July 6 [1950]	TLS: 2 pp.; VtU
167. Harry Scherman	July 13, 1950	TLS: 3 pp.; NNC
168. Anzia Yezierska	Aug. 15, 1950	TLS: 3 pp.; MBU
169. Bernardine K. Scherman	Dec. 22, 1950	TLS: 2 pp.; NNC
170. Clifton Fadiman	Jan. 6, 1951	ALS: 4 pp.; CF
171. James Thurber	Mar. 28, 1951	TLS: 2 pp.; OSU
172. James Thurber	Apr. 17, 1951	TLS: 2 pp.; OSU
173. Merle Haas	Nov. 10, 1951	TLS: 3 pp.; VtU

174. Christopher Morley	Nov. 19, 1951	TLS: 1 p.; TxU
175. Eleanor Roosevelt	May 2, 1952	CCTL: 1 p.; VtU
176. Roy Jansen	Nov. 7, 1952	TLS: 2 pp.; P
177. Bernardine K. Scherman	Jan. 5, 1953	TLS: 2 pp.; NNC
178. John P. Marquand	Jan. 5, 1954	TLS: 3 pp.; MH
179. Christopher Morley	Apr. 12, 1954	TLS: 2 pp.; TxU
180. Granville Hicks	July 5, 1954	TLS: 2 pp.; NSyU
181. Louise (Hieatt) Forscher	Nov. 18, 1955	TLS: 2 pp.; LHF
182. Francis Steegmuller	Mar. 21, 1956	TLS: 2 pp.; NNC
183. Karen Blixen	Aug. 14, 1956	TLS: 1 p.; RLC
184. Albert L. Guerard	Jan. 30, 1957	TLS: 2 pp.; CSt
185. Merle and Robert Haas	Feb. 13, 1957	TLS: 2 pp.; VtU
186. Albert L. Guerard	Mar. 7, 1957	TLS: 2 pp.; CSt
187. Mary C. Jane	Sept. 3, 1957	TLS: 3 pp.; MCJ
188. Karen Blixen	Nov. 12, 1957	TLS: 2 pp.; RLC
189. Robert Haas	Sept. 16, 1958	TLS: 2 pp.; VtU

Location Key: Libraries and Personal Collections

CF	Clifton Fadiman, Captiva Island, Fla.
CLU	Department of Special Collections, University Research Library, University of California, Los Angeles.
CSt	Bernard De Voto Papers; Albert Guerard Papers, Department of Special Collections, Stanford University, Stanford, Calif.
CtY	Collection of American Literature, Beinecke Rare Book and Manuscript Library, Yale University, New Haven, Conn.
CU	Bancroft Library, University of California, Berkeley.
DLC	Library of Congress, Washington, D.C.
HCS	Helen Cather Southwick, Pittsburgh, Pa.
IaU	University of Iowa Libraries, Iowa City.
ICN	Henry Kitchell Webster Papers; Edith Franklin Wyatt Papers, Newberry Library, Chicago, Ill.
InU	Lilly Library, Indiana University, Bloomington.
LHF	Louise (Hieatt) Forscher, Bedford, N. Y.
MBU	Mugar Memorial Library, Boston University, Boston, Mass.
MCJ	Mary C. Jane, Newcastle, Me.
MCR	Dr. Miriam Van Waters Papers, Schlesinger Library, Radcliffe College, Cambridge, Mass.
MH	Houghton Library, Harvard University, Cambridge, Mass.
MNS	Sophia Smith Collection, Smith College, Northampton, Mass.
MUAr	Special Collections Department, University Library, University of Massachusetts, Amherst.

NbHi	Louise Pound Papers, Nebraska State Historical Society
NcD	Louise Pound Papers, Manuscript Department, Duke University Library, Durham, N. C.
NcU	Southern Historical Collection, Library of the University of North Carolina at Chapel Hill.
NhD	Dartmouth College Library, Hanover, N. H.
NjP	Princeton University Library, Princeton, N. J.
NNAL	Archives of the American Academy and Institute of Arts and Letters, New York, N. Y.
NNC	Paul R. Reynolds Papers; Harry and Bernardine Scherman Papers; Francis Steegmuller Papers, Rare Book and Manuscript Library, Columbia University, New York, N. Y.
NNU-F	Fales Library, New York University, New York, N. Y.
NRU	Louis Wiley Papers, Department of Rare Books and Special Collections, University of Rochester Library, Rochester, N. Y.
NSyU	Granville Hicks Papers, George Arents Research Library for Special Collections, Syracuse University, Syracuse, N. Y.
OkU	Western History Collections, University of Oklahoma Libraries, Norman.
OU	Division of Rare Books and Manuscripts, Ohio State University Libraries, Columbus.
P	State Library of Pennsylvania, Harrisburg.
PSt	Penn State University Libraries, University Park.
RLC	Royal Library, Copenhagen, Denmark
TxU	Harry Ransom Humanities Research Center, University of Texas at Austin.
ViLRM	Lipscomb Library, Randolph-Macon Woman's College, Lynchburg, Va.
ViU	Dorothy Canfield Fisher Collection, Manuscripts Division, Clifton Waller Barrett Library, University of Virginia Library, Charlottesville.
VtMiM	Special Collections Department, Abernethy Library, Middlebury College, Middlebury, Vt.
VtU	Special Collections Department, Bailey/Howe Library, University of Vermont, Burlington

Institutional Holders of Letters Not Represented in This Edition

(Alphabetized by state)
University of Southern California, Los Angeles.
Henry E. Huntington Library, San Marino, Calif.

University of Delaware, Newark, Del.
Loyola University, Chicago, Ill.
Knox College, Galesburg, Ind.
DePauw University, Greencastle, Ind.
New England Historic Genealogical Society, Boston, Mass.
Baker Library, Harvard University, Cambridge, Mass.
Mount Holyoke College, South Hadley, Mass.
Williams College, Williamstown, Mass.
Colby College, Waterville, Me.
Michigan Historical Collections, Ann Arbor.
Minneapolis Public Library, Minneapolis, Minn.
University of Minnesota, Minneapolis, Center for Children's Books
University of Minnesota, Social Welfare History Archives
Vassar College, Poughkeepsie, N. Y.
Pack Memorial Library, Asheville, N. C.
University of Oregon, Eugene.
Allegheny College, Meadville, Pa.
Temple University, Philadelphia, Pa.
University of Pennsylvania, Philadelphia.
Texas Christian University, Fort Worth.
Martha Canfield Memorial Library, Russell Vermontiana Collection, Arlington, Vt.
Vermont Historical Society, Montpelier.

Notable Recipients

(Letter numbers follow in parentheses.)

Benét, Rosemary (Carr) (1897–1962). American poet and translator, wife of Stephen Vincent Benét. She was an editor for the BOMC while DCF was a member of the Selection Committee. Her translations of French include stories by Colette. (160)

Blixen, Karen (1885–1962). Danish author who wrote under the pseudonym Isak Dinesen. DCF was instrumental in arranging the American publication of Blixen's first book, *Seven Gothic Tales*. Blixen's brother, Thomas Dinesen, who knew of DCF's friendship with one of their aunts, sent a copy of the manuscript to Arlington. DCF's initial attempts to find a publisher were unsuccessful, but she later showed the stories to her friend Robert Haas of Random House, who praised them highly. *Seven Gothic Tales,* published by Random House in 1934, was a book-of-the-month, as were Blixen's *Out of Africa* in 1938, *Winter's Tales* in 1943, *Angelic Avengers* in 1947, and *Shadows on the Grass* in 1961. (98, 183, 188)

Broomell, Anna Petit. Broomell edited *The Children's Story Caravan* (Philadelphia: Lippincott, 1935) and *The Friendly Story Caravan* (Philadelphia: Lippincott, 1945), for which DCF wrote introductions. (134)

Buck, Pearl S[ydenstricker] (1892–1973). American author. Buck's second book, *The Good Earth* (Pulitzer Prize, 1931), became a book-of-the-month upon DCF's strong recommendation. Buck's works were chosen six times by the club, more than that of any other author during DCF's tenure as judge. In 1938 she became the first American woman to win the Nobel Prize for Literature. (78, 118, 124, 126)

Cather, Willa (1873–1947). American author. DCF and Cather first met at the University of Nebraska, where Cather was a student and DCF's father was chancellor in 1891. In ensuing years, the two authors relied upon each other for literary advice, sympathy, and friendship. (3, 4, 5, 114, 148)

Cerf, Bennett (1898–1971). American publisher and editor. Cerf formed Random House publishers with Donald S. Klopfer in 1927, of which he was president (1927–1965) and chairman of the board (1965–1970). In 1949 he asked DCF to write the first two titles for "Landmark Books," an American History series for young adults. The books, *Paul Revere and the Minutemen* and *Our Independence and the Constitution* were published in 1950. (163)

Cleghorn, Sarah N. (1876–1959). American poet. The friendship between DCF and Cleghorn, who lived in nearby Manchester, Vermont was close; Cleghorn was the godmother of DCF's daughter, who was named Sarah after her. A pacifist and Socialist whom Robert Frost once referred to as "saintly," she collaborated with DCF on *Fellow Captains* (1916) and *Nothing Ever Happens and How It Does* (1940). (18, 27, 29, 32, 35, 161)

Cook, Reginald L. (1903–1984). American educator and literary critic. Cook taught American literature at Middlebury College (Vermont) from 1929 to 1969 and was director of the allied Bread Loaf School of English (1946–1964), where DCF lectured on several occasions. He is the author of *The Dimensions of Robert Frost* (1958) and *Robert Frost: A Living Voice* (1974) and studies of Emerson and Thoreau. (149, 151)

Cosgrave, John O'Hara (1864–1947). American editor and journalist. Cofounder and editor of the *Wave* and later editor of the *New York World Sunday Magazine* (1912–1927), Cosgrave was editor of *Everybody's Magazine* (1900–1911), which published several of DCF's stories. (7, 9)

De Voto, Bernard (1897–1955). American author, critic, and educator. Noted for his critical studies of Mark Twain and for his history of the Western fur trade, *Across the Wide Missouri* (Pulitzer Prize, 1947), De Voto was Professor of English at Harvard University and Northwestern University. (103)

Dinesen, Isak. See Blixen, Karen.

Dinesen, Thomas (b. 1891). Brother of Danish author Karen Blixen. His *My Sister, Isak Dinesen* (1975) tells of his family's friendly relations with DCF. (93)

Du Bois, W[illiam] E[dward] B[urghardt] (1868–1963). American author, educator, and sociologist. The author of *The Souls of Black Folk* (1903), Du Bois was a founder of the National Association for the Advancement of Colored People (1909) and editor of the *Crisis* (1910–1934), to which DCF was a contributor. DCF was also a judge for the Spingarn Medal (1926) and a member of the Advisory Board for the Du Bois Literary Prize (1931). (45)

Einstein, Albert (1879–1955). German-born theoretical physicist. Einstein was on the faculty of the Institute for Advanced Study at Princeton (1933–1945). The Institute's director, Frank Aydelotte, was associated with DCF through their work for the Women's International League for Peace and Freedom. (123)

Fadiman, Clifton (b. 1904). American literary critic, editor, translator, and radio and television personality. Fadiman is the author of several collections of essays and criticism, including *Party of One: The Selected Writings of Clifton Fadiman* (1955), *Appreciations: Essays* (1962), and *Enter, Conversing* (1962), books for children, and introductions to books by Wharton, Melville, Sinclair Lewis, Stendhal, and Conrad. He was book editor of the *New Yorker* (1933–

1943) and host of radio and television programs: "Information, Please!" (1938–1943), "Conversation" (1954–1957), and "Quiz Kids." In 1944 he joined the BOMC Committee of Selection. (170)

Folsom, Franklin (b. 1907). American author. In addition to his writing of children's books, Folsom served as secretary of the League of American Writers (1937–1942), which urged DCF to denounce the ban on Hemingway's *To Have and Have Not* (1938). (109)

Forscher, Louise (Hieatt). American educator. Forscher has taught college-level English for many years, chiefly at the University of Connecticut. DCF spoke at her graduation from Swarthmore College in 1944, leaving the distinct physical impression of being "a very small woman in a voluminous academic gown." Forscher read *Made-to-Order Stories* and *Understood Betsy* as a child and *Mothers and Children* as a parent. She wrote to DCF in appreciation of *The Deepening Stream* after the Swarthmore commencement. (181)

Frost, Elinor (1874–1938). Wife of poet Robert Frost. His first book of poems, *A Boy's Will* (1913), is dedicated to her. Frost credited his wife's understanding and encouragement for allowing him to write for twenty years until he won recognition. Many of his poems attest to Elinor's importance in his life and work. (76, 79)

Frost, Robert (1874–1964). American poet. Frost, a four-time Pulitzer Prize–winner, wrote an introduction to Sarah Cleghorn's autobiography, *Three-score,* in which he wrote of DCF, Zephine Humphrey, and Cleghorn: "One of these is wise and a novelist, one is a mystic and an essayist, and the third is saintly and a poet." In December 1915, DCF met Frost in Boston at a dramatization of his narrative dialogues. She had advised her publisher, Henry Holt, to print an American edition of Frost's *North of Boston* one year earlier. When the Frosts searched for a farm in Vermont, DCF offered them free board, which they accepted, and showed them the property they eventually bought in South Shaftsbury (halfway between Arlington and Bennington). *A Further Range* (1936) was the first of Frost's books to be selected by the BOMC. In an obituary for DCF, Frost wrote: "Dorothy Canfield was the great lady of Vermont, just as someone else we all admire might be called the great lady of the United States. But there was more to it than just that. . . . There was nothing she was happier in than storytelling in prose and speech unless it was doing good to everybody and anybody." (16, 72, 74, 119, 137)

Guerard, Albert Léon (1880–1959). Franco-American historian, critic, and educator. Guerard wrote more than twenty books concerned with biography, autobiography, and history. His work ranges from studies of France and its people to comparative literature to religious thought. In his autobiography, *Personal Equation* (1948), he wrote, "Thinking has been my pleasure, my business and my dignity" (9). Guerard taught at several U.S. universities, including Stanford, where he was Professor of English (1925–1946). (154, 184, 186)

Haas, Merle (1896?–1985). American translator. She is best known for her translations of French author Laurent de Brunhoff's "Babar" books for children. Married to publisher Robert K. Haas. (81, 82, 86, 97, 173, 185)

Haas, Robert K. (1890?–1964). American publisher. Haas was a cofounder and president of the BOMC (1926–1931). In 1932 he founded the publishing firm of Harrison Smith and Robert Haas, which merged with Random House in 1936. The Haases were summer neighbors and friends of the Fishers. (104, 110, 120, 144, 185, 189)

Harcourt, Alfred (1881–1954). American publisher. Harcourt, who was John Fisher's roommate at Columbia University, became DCF's publisher when he left Henry Holt to form his own firm with Donald Brace in 1920. He published all of her fiction from that date on, and the two families cultivated an enduring friendship. (15, 17, 39, 43, 46, 57, 58, 61, 62, 65, 66, 75, 88, 99, 100)

Harris, Julia Collier (b. 1875). American author and journalist. In the 1920s, Julia and her husband, Julian LaRose Harris (1875–1963), edited the daily *Enquirer Sun* (Columbus, Ga.), which waged a vigorous campaign against the Ku Klux Klan. In *Rope and Faggot,* a history of lynching, Walter White has written of the Harrises and the *Enquirer Sun,* ". . . in the face of advertisers' boycotts, loss of great percentages of readers and other financial difficulties, to say nothing of the actual threats against their lives, [the newspaper] has militantly and brilliantly fought lynching. . . . It fought the Klan when that movement absolutely dominated the state of Georgia and when even the Governor was a Klansman." Julian, son of author Joel Chandler Harris, was awarded a Pulitzer Prize (1926) for the effort. In addition to editorial work, Julia wrote magazine articles on travel and art and books on her father-in-law. (47, 49, 51, 68, 70)

Hicks, Granville (1901–1977). American author and critic. A member of the Communist party in the 1930s, Hicks is best known for *The Great Tradition* (1933), a Marxist interpretation of American literature. In 1932 he moved to Grafton, N. Y., the subject of *Small Town* (1946). His autobiography, *Part of the Truth* (1965), details the building of the Grafton Library by the townspeople over several years. The project was funded in large part by a Fourth of July celebration and sale of a corresponding souvenir program. (180)

Holden, Raymond (1894–1972). American author and literary executive. Holden is the author of novels, poetry, and children's books, including *Famous Scientific Expeditions* (1955), which has been translated into several languages. He worked for the BOMC as an editor and personnel director (1939–1951) during DCF's tenure on the Selection Committee. Holden was a noted friend of Robert Frost's. (145)

Holt, Henry (1840–1926). American author and publisher. Holt published DCF's work from 1907 to 1919 and was a longtime friend of her father, James Hulme Canfield. (14)

Humphrey, Zephine (Fahnestock) (1874–1956). American author. Humphrey wrote novels, including *Grail Fire* (1917), and travel books which were well received in the 1930s: *Green Mountains to Sierras* (1936), *Cactus Forest* (1938), and *Allo Goodby* (1940). She lived in Dorset, Vermont, and formed a lasting friendship with her neighbors, DCF and Sarah Cleghorn, to whom she was introduced by her publisher Henry Holt in 1908. Cleghorn reports in her autobiography, *Threescore,* that she and Humphrey often read and commented on DCF's works-in-progress. (See also note on Robert Frost.) (135, 140)

Jane, Mary C[hilds] (b. 1909). American author. Jane wrote many mystery books for children, one per year from 1955 to 1970, all published by Lippincott. Her *Ghost Rock Mystery* (1967) was awarded the Boys Club of America Gold Medal. (108, 116, 187)

Jansen, Roy (1890–1975). American journalist. Jansen wrote for the *Pittsburgh Sun-Telegraph* and *Pittsburgh Post Gazette* and was best known for his daily column for the Pittsburgh Medical Society, which was syndicated in over one hundred papers. (176)

Johnson, James Weldon (1871–1938). American author and educator. Author of *The Autobiography of an Ex-Colored Man* (1912), *God's Trombones* (1927), and numerous songs including "Lift Every Voice and Sing" (1899, with his brother John Rosamond Johnson), Johnson was a recipient of the Spingarn Medal (1925). He was executive secretary of the NAACP (1920–1930) and was appointed Professor of Creative Literature at Fisk University in 1930. (69)

Klyce, Scudder (1879–1933). American author and scientist. Klyce's works include: *Universe* (1921), *Sins of Science* (1925), *Dewey's Suppressed Psychology* (1928), and *Outline of Basic Mathematics* (1932). (26, 30, 33, 48, 73)

Knopf, Alfred A. (1892–1984). American publisher. Called "the perfect publisher" by H. L. Mencken, Knopf published over five thousand books, including the work of sixteen Nobel Prize winners. DCF's friend Willa Cather enjoyed a long, fruitful association with Knopf. (71)

Marquand, J[ohn] P[hillips] (1893–1960). American author. After first gaining notoriety for his *Saturday Evening Post* stories featuring Mr. Moto, the Japanese detective, Marquand published many novels, including the Pulitzer Prize–winning *The Late George Apley* (1937), a study of New England and New York upper-class manners. He joined DCF on the BOMC Selection Committee following the death of Heywood Broun in 1939, and remained until his own death in 1960. (155, 162, 178)

Maurois, André (pseud. of Emile Salomon Wilhelm Herzog) (1885–1967). French author. Among Maurois's biographies, essays, histories, and novels are *Climats* (1928), *Le Cercle de Famille* (1932), and *Private Universe* (trans. 1932). (92)

Mead, Margaret (1901–1978). American anthropologist. Known as a popular and controversial speaker on social issues, Mead was long associated with

the American Museum of Natural History, first as assistant curator of eth-
nology (1926) and then as curator (1964–1969). Her major works include *Coming of Age in Samoa* (1928), *Male and Female* (1949), and *Childhood in Contemporary
Cultures* (1955, with Martha Wolfstein). (142)

Moody, Paul D. (1879–1947). American minister and educator. Moody
was president of Middlebury College (Vermont) from 1921 to 1942. (52)

Morley, Christopher (1890–1957). American author. An influential columnist for the *Saturday Review of Literature* (1924–1941), Morley wrote more
than fifty books, many of them novels, including *Where the Blue Begins* (1922)
and *Kitty Foyle* (1939). His essays are collected in *Shandygaff* (1918), *Mince Pie*
(1919), and *Forty-Four Essays* (1925), and his verse is collected in his *Poems* (1929).
A member of the first BOMC Selection Committee with DCF, he retired in
1954. (122, 136, 143, 174, 179)

O'Kane, Walter Collins (b. 1877). American author and entomolgist.
O'Kane was the author of books on New Hampshire's White Mountains (1925),
Vermont's Green Mountains (1926), and New York's Adirondack Mountains
(1928), in addition to works on the southwest, *Sun in the Sky* (1950) and *The
Hopis: Portrait of a Desert People* (1953). (165)

Page, Curtis Hidden (1870–1946). American educator and poet. Page
taught English and other languages at Harvard, Columbia, and Northwestern
universities before joining the faculty of Dartmouth College in 1911, where he
was Professor of English until his retirement. He translated many works of the
French poets, wrote a history of Japanese poetry, and served several terms in
the New Hampshire Legislature. (2)

Pattee, F[red] L[ewis] (1863–1950). American educator and literary critic.
As a professor at Penn State in the 1890s, Pattee led the movement to have
American literature included as a major subject in U.S. colleges. He was a
member of the Bread Loaf School of English faculty from 1924 to 1936, where
he worked with DCF. He is the author of *History of American Literature Since 1870*
(1915), *Century Readings of American Literature* (1919, rev. 1922, 1926, 1932) and
The New American Literature 1890–1930 (1930). (80)

Phelps, William Lyon (1865–1943). American educator and literary critic.
Phelps was Professor of English at Yale University (1892–1933) and a friendly
critic of DCF's work. His *Selected Readings from Much Loved Books* (1940) contains a three-page excerpt from *Her Son's Wife,* of which he wrote: " 'Her Son's
Wife' is Dorothy Canfield's masterpiece and it is also *a* masterpiece. It is a
profound, subtle analysis of human character and human life and a very remarkable book. I predict that it will win the Pulitzer Prize for 1926. It deserves
it." (25, 44, 55)

Phillips, John S[anborn] (1862–1949). American publisher. Phillips founded
McClure's Magazine with S. S. McClure in 1893, and the Phillips Publishing

Co. in 1906, the same year he started *American Magazine*. In addition to DCF, he published many popular authors in the *American,* including Finley Peter Dunne, Lincoln Steffens, Ida Tarbell, and William Allen White. (31)

Pottle, Frederick A. (1897–1987). American educator and literary critic. Appointed Sterling Professor of English at Yale University in 1944, Pottle is best known for his work on the private papers of eighteenth-century biographer James Boswell. Boswell's recognition as a major biographer is widely credited to Pottle's scholarship, among which is the best-selling edition of *Boswell's London Journal 1762–1763.* (See letter 167, July 13, 1950.) (138)

Pound, Louise (1872–1958). American educator and folklorist. After taking a Ph.D. at Heidelberg University, Pound was a Professor of English at the University of Nebraska, specializing in American speech and folklore. As an undergraduate at Nebraska she was a classmate of Willa Cather and a friend of the younger DCF, whose father was chancellor of the university from 1891 to 1895. Pound was the first woman president of the Modern Language Association. (19, 22, 24, 28, 40)

Putnam, George P[almer] (1887–1950). American publisher. G. P. Putnam's Sons published many of Anzia Yezierska's books, including *All I Could Never Be* (1932), which DCF read in manuscript. In 1931 Putnam married Amelia Earhart; he edited her book *Last Flight* (1938). (89)

Quinn, Arthur H[obson] (1875–1960). American educator and literary critic. Quinn was Professor of English at the University of Pennsylvania for many years and author of *A History of American Drama* (3 vols. 1923, 1927) and a biography of Poe (1941) among other critical works. His *American Fiction* (1936) discusses DCF's work. (111)

Reynolds, Amelia. Wife of literary agent Paul R. Reynolds, Sr. (36)

Reynolds, Paul R[evere], Sr. (1864–1944). American literary agent. Reynolds founded Paul R. Reynolds & Son in 1893, one of the first literary agencies in America. He began a long, profitable business relationship as DCF's agent in 1912. During the depression he was able to sell the serial rights to Fisher's novel *Bonfire* (1933) for thirty thousand dollars. Reynolds's other clients included Stephen Crane, G. B. Shaw, Leo Tolstoy, and Joseph Conrad. (11, 12, 13, 23, 38, 41, 42, 56, 60, 63, 67, 77, 85, 87, 90, 94, 95, 96, 105, 121)

Roosevelt, Eleanor (1884–1962). American author, diplomat, political figure, and wife of U.S. President Franklin D. Roosevelt. While chair of the United Nations Committee on Human Rights, Roosevelt helped draft and secure adoption of the Universal Declaration of Human Rights in 1948. DCF's *A Fair World for All* (1952), with an "Introduction" by Roosevelt, explains the Declaration in plain terms for young people. Roosevelt once cited DCF's "Petunias—That's for Remembrance" as her favorite short story and in 1958 called the author one of the ten most influential women in America. (175)

Sanger, Margaret (1883–1966). Founder of the American birth control movement. Sanger was founder and first president of the American Birth Control League (1921–1928) and author of *What Every Mother Should Know* (1917) among other books on the subject of birth control. (83)

Scherman, Bernardine Kielty (1890–1973). American author and editor. A director and reader for the BOMC, which was founded by her husband Harry, Scherman was associate editor of *Story* magazine and wrote a book review column, "Under Cover," for the *Ladies' Home Journal* for many years. She wrote several books, of which the most popular was the autobiographical *The Girl from Fitchburg* (1964). (101, 107, 113, 152, 169, 177)

Scherman, David E[dward] (b. 1916). American magazine editor and photographer. A staff photographer for *Life* (1939–1947), Scherman was later associate editor (1947–1966) and senior editor (1966–1972) of that magazine. He was also a contributor to newspapers and the author of *Literary England* (1944) and *Literary America* (with his wife Rosemarie Redlich Scherman, 1951) and editor of *The Best of Life* (1973). (166)

Scherman, Harry (1887–1969). American publisher and literary executive. Previously associated with Charles and Albert Boni in establishing the Little Leather Library Corporation, Scherman founded the BOMC with Robert K. Haas and Maxwell Sackheim in 1926. The monthly selections were chosen by a Selection Committee, which originally consisted of DCF, Heywood Broun, Henry Seidel Canby, Christopher Morley, and William Allen White. (101, 132, 153, 156, 157, 164, 167)

Sibut, Céline (1870?–1944). A teacher in the Paris public school system for many years. Fisher met Céline at the turn of the century, during one of her first trips to France. Although separated by great distance, they maintained a lifelong friendship nonetheless. (8, 10)

Sinclair, Upton (1878–1968). American author and political activist. Sinclair's *The Jungle* (1906), a depiction of the working conditions in Chicago's meat packing houses at the time, is his best-known work. He wrote more than one hundred books, many of which reflect his socialist political philosophy, including *King Coal* (1917) and *OIL!* (1927). (147)

Steegmuller, Francis (b. 1906). American author and literary critic. Among Steegmuller's biographies, criticism, and novels are *La Grande Mademoiselle* (1956) and *Cocteau* (1970). His highly acclaimed *Letters of Gustave Flaubert* was published in 1980. (182)

Suckow, Ruth (1892–1960). American author. Suckow's novels and stories, including *Iowa Interiors* (1926), *Cora* (1929), *The Folks* (1934), and *New Hope* (1942), emphasize the setting and character of the Midwest, especially her home state of Iowa. She spent the summer of 1936 near DCF at Robert Frost's farm in Vermont. In 1929 she married author Ferner Nuhn. (84, 102, 112)

Thurber, James (1894–1961). American artist and author. From the 1920s on, Thurber was associated with the *New Yorker,* to which he contributed essays, stories, and drawings noted for their humor and graceful style. In 1951 he wrote for the *New Yorker* a series of biographical sketches of Ohio State University professors. He wrote to DCF, who had attended the school from 1895 to 1899 and whose father was the university's chancellor during that period, for her recollections of professors Joseph Russell Taylor, Joseph V. Denney, and William L. Graves. In the "Foreword" to *The Thurber Album* (1952), in which the essays were collected, Thurber wrote: "One of the most pleasant results of the writing of *The Thurber Album* has been the letters that I received from Mrs. Dorothy Canfield Fisher. If nothing else had come of it all, these letters would have amply repaid me for my efforts." (171, 172)

Webster, Henry Kitchell (1875–1932). American author. Webster's stories were in great demand by popular magazines in the 1910s and 1920s. Webster was one of fourteen American authors, including DCF, who wrote a chapter of the collaborative novel *The Sturdy Oak* (1919), proceeds from which were donated to the Woman's Suffrage Movement. (20, 21)

Wells, Carlton F. American educator. Wells was Professor of English at the University of Michigan. With Arno L. Bader, he co-edited *Essays for Our Time* (1947), which includes DCF's "Supply and Demand." (117)

White, E[lwyn] B[rooks] (1899–1985). American author and critic. Associated from the 1920s with the *New Yorker,* White was asked to join the BOMC Selection Committee, following the death of William Allen White in 1943. When he declined (despite DCF's Aug. 25, 1943 letter asking him to reconsider), Clifton Fadiman was chosen to fill the position. Selections from White's writings are gathered in *The Wild Flag* (1946) and *The Points of My Compass* (1962); he also revised William Strunk, Jr.'s *The Elements of Style* (1959). (125)

Wiley, Louis (1896–1935). American newspaper executive. Wiley joined the *New York Times* in 1896 and became business manager in 1906, a position he held until his death. (1)

Wood, Meredith (1896–1974). American publisher. Wood joined the BOMC in 1929 as treasurer and executive vice-president, succeeded Harry Scherman as president in 1950, and remained a BOMC director after his retirement in 1960. (146)

Wright, Richard (1908–1960). American author. In addition to *Native Son* (1940) and *Black Boy* (1945), which were books-of-the-month, Wright's major works include *Uncle Tom's Children* (1938), *12 Million Black Voices* (1941), *The Outsider* (1953), *The Long Dream* (1958), and *Eight Men* (1961). (128, 129, 130, 131, 133)

Wyatt, Edith F. (1873–1958). A noted friend of William Dean Howells', Wyatt wrote the novels *Everyone His Own Way* (1901), *True Love* (1903), and *The Invisible Gods* (1923). (59)

Yezierska, Anzia (1883–1970). American author. Yezierska, a factory worker and domestic servant before becoming a writer, is best known for her novels and stories about New York City's Russian-immigrant Jews, including *Hungry Hearts* (1920), *Children of Loneliness* (1923) and *Bread Givers* (1925). In 1931 she moved from New York to Arlington to be near DCF, whose writing she greatly admired. Her experiences during her one-and-a-half years in Vermont are recounted in her autobiographical novel *Red Ribbon on a White Horse* (1950). (See also note on George P. Putnam.) (91, 158, 168)

Index

For a list of Dorothy Canfield Fisher's letters to individuals, see Notable Recipients.

Aldridge, John, 10, 282
Allen, Fred, 165
Andersen, Hans Christian, 16, 29; "The Emperor's New Clothes," 291
Aswell, Edward, 231, 235
Auden, W. H., 293
Aydelotte, Frank, 219

Bach, Johann Sebastian, 21, 204, 297, 322
Baker, Newton, 199, 225
Balzac, Honoré de, 15, 175; "Passion in the Desert," 266
Baray, Henry, 48
Batchelder, Mildred, 113, 114
Beecher, Henry Ward, 19, 214
Beethoven, Ludwig van, 19, 196, 255, 267
Belloc, Hillaire: *Cromwell*, 187
Bennett, Mildred, 289
Blixen, Karen (Isak Dinesen), 5, 15, 18, 177, 178, 255, 264, 265; *Angelic Avengers*, 255; *Last Tales*, 316, 324; *Out of Africa*, 190, 200, 307; *Seven Gothic Tales*, 10, 18, 176–78, 187, 188, 199; *Winter's Tales*, 216–17
Book-of-the-Month Club, 5–6, 15, 16, 18, 129, 161, 174, 185, 186, 209–10, 215, 216, 221–26, 231, 234, 235, 236, 238, 247, 249, 251, 257, 258, 270, 271, 274, 275, 279, 287, 288, 290
Bossuet, Jacques, 321
Boswell, James: *Life of Samuel Johnson*, 16, 17, 290–91; *London Journal, 1762–1763*, 17, 290–91
Breughel, Pieter (the elder), 301
Brooks, Van Wyck, 17, 198
Broun, Heywood, 5, 226
Brown, E. K., 289, 290
Brown, John, 19, 214
Brush, Katharine: *The Red-Headed Woman*, 167
Buck, John Lossing, 154; *Chinese Farm Economy*, 154
Buck, Pearl S., 5, 8, 10, 15, 18, 19; *American*

Unity and Asia, 215; *The Exile*, 221; *The Fighting Angel*, 221; *The Good Earth*, 18
Budd, Ralph, 225
Burlingame, Roger, 282
Burnett, Frances Hodgson: *The Secret Garden*, 55
Burnett, Whit, 243
Bynner, Witter: "Autobiography in the Shape of a Book Review," 13

Caine, Hall, 44
Canby, Henry Seidel, 5, 154, 209, 223, 238, 249, 282, 290, 291, 302; *Turn West, Turn East*, 303
Canfield, Charles (nephew), 302
Canfield, Dot, 302
Canfield, Flavia (mother), 1, 28, 30, 56, 86, 87, 130, 134, 151
Canfield, James (brother), 1, 47, 49, 57, 63, 162, 260, 290, 294, 319
Canfield, James Hulme (father), 1, 27, 28, 30, 128, 134, 214, 300
Canfield, Mattie (paternal aunt), 63
Canfield, Nat (cousin), 155
Canfield, Phebe (maternal aunt), 30
Canfield, Stella (sister-in-law), 57, 63, 260, 294
Cannan, Gilbert, 44
Cather, Willa, 6, 11, 15, 158, 288, 289; *Death Comes for the Archbishop*, 129; "The Fear That Walks by Noonday" (with Dorothy Canfield Fisher), 11, 162, 168; *One of Ours*, 13; "The Profile," 12–13, 26–29; *Sapphira and the Slave Girl*, 209; *Shadows on the Rock*, 162; *The Troll Garden*, 12, 13
Cerf, Bennett, 14
Cerqua, Ida, 46
Cleghorn, Carl, 60, 75
Cleghorn, Dalton, 75
Cleghorn, Fanny, 75
Cleghorn, Sarah, 7, 9, 11, 57, 58, 98, 185, 192, 197, 240, 248; "Comrade Jesus,"

162; *Fellow Captains*, 65, 281; *Portraits and Protests*, 66; *The Spinster*, 60; *Threescore*, 195; "War Journal of a Pacifist," 73
Coffin, Charles Monroe, 299
Congdon, Helen, 7, 324
Conrad, Joseph, 189
Corelli, Marie, 44
Corneille, Pierre, 2
Coughlin, Charles Edward, 219
Cowley, Malcolm, 282
Cullinan, Elizabeth, 7

Dana, John Cotton, 134
D'Annunzio, Gabriele, 321
Daumier, Honoré, 268
Descartes, René, 321
De Seversky, Alexander: *Air Power*, 291
Dinesen, Isak. *See* Blixen, Karen
Dinesen, Thomas, 176, 315
Dos Passos, John: *The Grand Design*, 17, 272–74
Doyle, Arthur Conan: "The Red-Headed League," 268
Dreiser, Theodore, 236, 237
Du Bois, W. E. B., 19
Dunne, Finley Peter, 128

Edwards, Harry Stillwell, 15, 127; *AEneas Africanus*, 127–28
Ehrich, Lea, 302
Eliot, George: *Middlemarch*, 1
Elliott, Charlie, 260
Emerson, Ralph Waldo, 237; "Brahma," 77

Fadiman, Annalee, 297
Fadiman, Clifton, 5, 226, 249, 283
Fahnestock, Wallace, 75, 181, 182
Farrar, John, 161, 185
Faulkner, William, 6
Fielding, Henry, 291
Fischbacher, Marguerite, 301
Fisher, Dorothy Canfield: works of, "An American Citizen," 19, 96; *American Portraits*, 257; *And Long Remember*, 5, 324; *Basque People*, 5; "The Bedquilt," 13, 246; *The Bent Twig*, 4, 19, 43, 46, 47, 81, 197; *Bonfire*, 5, 15, 135, 164, 167, 171, 178, 181, 183, 196, 200–202; *The Brimming Cup*, 3, 4, 6, 14, 15, 19, 81, 88, 90, 91, 95, 96, 98, 112, 113, 130; "Conqueror," 79; *Corneille and Racine*, 68; *Crabtree-Canfield Basic Readers*, 241, 284; *The Day of Glory*, 4; *The Deepening Stream*, 1, 5, 13, 134, 151, 156,

158, 163, 200, 313; *Elementary Composition*, 33; *Fables for Parents*, 5, 177, 197; "Fairfax Hunter," 19, 108; "The Fear That Walks by Noonday" (with Willa Cather), 11, 163, 168; *Fellow Captains* (with Sarah Cleghorn), 65, 281; "Flint and Fire," 121; "The Forgotten Mother," 195; *Four-Square*, 5; "Goblin Gold," 35; "A Good Fight and the Faith Kept," 78; "The Great Refusal," 50; *Gunhild*, 3, 32, 35; *A Harvest of Stories*, 5, 318; "Hats," 78; *Her Son's Wife*, 5, 6, 14, 32, 73, 116, 119, 120, 123, 156, 163; *Hillsboro People*, 42, 43, 46, 47; "Holy Week in Spain," 25; *Home Fires in France*, 4, 66, 78, 79, 80; *The Home-Maker*, 3, 4, 6, 7, 19, 103, 108, 114, 115, 117–18, 119, 122, 131, 163; "How 'Flint and Fire' Started and Grew," 85, 121; "How to Combat Racism," 229; "In the Campo Santo," 41; "The Knot-Hole," 5, 217, 239; "The Last of the Garrison," 35; "Lo, the Poor Introvert," 166; *Made-to-Order Stories*, 112–14, 117, 118, 120, 122, 151; *Memories of Arlington, Vermont*, 322; *A Montessori Manual*, 19, 40; *A Montessori Mother*, 2, 19, 40, 59; "The Moran Scandal," 184; "Motes, Beams, and Foreigners," 153, 159; *Mothers and Children*, 9, 19, 40, 53, 59, 60; "A New Pioneer," 295; "Novelist Recalls Christmas in Blue-and-Gold Pittsburgh," 290; *Our Independence and the Constitution*, 284, 298; *Our Young Folks*, 230, 252; *Paul Revere and the Minutemen*, 284, 298; "The Poet and the Scullery Maid," 30; *Raw Material*, 109, 262; *The Real Motive*, 46, 79; "Robert Frost: A Neighbor of Mine," 156; *Rough-Hewn*, 9, 90, 100, 101, 103, 123, 162; "The Saint of the Old Seminary," 317; *Seasoned Timber*, 5, 13, 15, 191, 194, 197, 203, 204, 209, 211–12, 322; "Sex Education," 268; "Shall I Marry a Farmer?," 125; *The Squirrel Cage*, 3, 47, 51, 81; "Thanksgiving Day," 295; *Understood Betsy*, 19, 40, 56, 74; "Undine's Revenge," 42; *Vermont Tradition*, 2, 92, 265, 284, 307, 317–18; "Vignettes from Life at the Rear," 65; "A Warning," 42; *Why Stop Learning?*, 2, 19, 134
Fisher, Esther (sister-in-law), 61
Fisher, Irving: *How to Live*, 67
Fisher, James (son), 4, 7, 8, 32, 34, 43, 47, 56, 57, 64, 68, 71, 73, 74, 75, 76, 79, 81,

112, 113, 114, 119, 120, 151, 184, 185, 187, 253–54, 263, 269, 275

Fisher, John (husband), 2, 4, 7, 9, 34–36, 42, 46, 47, 48–49, 54, 56, 60, 61, 62, 64, 68, 70, 74, 75, 85, 86, 91, 94, 96, 97, 101, 112, 113, 119, 120, 134, 154, 155, 162, 164, 170, 174, 183, 186, 254, 292, 296, 307, 308, 310, 319, 320, 321

Fisher, Sally (daughter), 4, 7, 8, 39, 45, 47, 56, 64, 68, 70, 71–73, 74, 75, 77, 80, 85, 113, 114, 118, 151, 155, 165, 187, 204, 281, 306, 313

Fisher, William (father-in-law), 34, 103, 158, 303

Fitzgerald, F. Scott, 6

Flexner, Abraham, 166

Flexner, Eleanor, 166

Foerster, Norman, 163

Frankfurter, Felix, 273

Freud, Sigmund, 54, 196, 314

Frost, Elinor, 46, 85, 91, 133, 162, 256

Frost, Irma, 216

Frost, Lesley, 151, 216

Frost, Marjorie, 151, 302

Frost, Prescott, 243

Frost, Robert, 15, 85, 91, 102, 132, 151, 154, 159, 162, 244, 256; *A Masque of Reason*, 243; *North of Boston*, 46; *The Witness Tree*, 215

Gale, Zona, 95

Geismar, Maxwell, 282

Gerwig, George, 289

Gibbon, Edward: *Decline and Fall of the Roman Empire*, 318

Gill, Eric: *Autobiography*, 241–42

Gilman, Charlotte Perkins, 53

Glasgow, Ellen, 44

Gleed, Dorothy, 32

Gleed, James Willis, 60

Gobineau, Joseph Arthur, 19, 111

Goethe, Johann Wolfgang von, 303

Goldsmith, Oliver, 291

Guerard, Albert L., 1; *France in the Classical Age*, 318; *Preface to World Literature*, 319

Haas, Merle, 189, 190, 193, 199, 287, 315

Haas, Priscilla, 188, 189, 190

Haas, Robert, 18, 157, 158, 159, 165, 177, 179, 180, 199, 255, 287, 302, 315, 316

Halle, Samuel H., 107

Harcourt, Alfred, 2, 5, 9, 19, 65, 70, 77, 94, 155, 321

Harcourt, Ellen, 113, 117, 168, 182

Harcourt, Hastings, 85, 118, 134, 168

Harcourt, Sue, 47, 85, 90, 96

Hard, Ethel, 325

Hard, Margaret, 132, 243

Hard, Walter, 132

Harris, Joel Chandler, 15; "Uncle Remus," 99, 100, 128

Harris, Julia, 9, 15, 19

Harrison, Sydnor, 44

Hazlitt, William, 75

Hegel, Georg Friedrich Wilhelm, 234

Heine, Heinrich, 289

Hemingway, Ernest, 6; *To Have and Have Not*, 17, 198

Herbert, George: "Vertue," 204

Herrick, Robert, 44

Hill, Francis, 28

Hindus, Maurice, 185, 187

Hitler, Adolf, 197, 212, 228

Holden, Raymond: *Selected Poems*, 257

Holt, Henry, 70

Holt, Roland, 47

Holt, Winnifred, 62

Horace, 92

Housman, A. E., 13, 25, 260–62; "A Shropshire Lad," 26

Howells, William Dean, 60; *An Imperative Duty*, 66

Huebsch, B. W., 259

Humphrey, Zephine, 75–76, 132, 133; *A Book of New England*, 249; *Grail Fire*, 66

Hunt, Henry Alexander, 96

Hutchins, Robert Maynard, 225

Ibsen, Henrik: *An Enemy of the People*, 29

Ilin, M.: *The Russian Primer*, 210

James, Henry, 10, 298–99; *The Bostonians*, 302

James, Henry, Jr., 298–99

James, William, 245, 246, 298

"Johnie Armstrong" (ballad), 243, 303

Johnson, George, 225

Johnson, James Weldon, 19; *God's Trombones*, 10, 126–27

Johnson, Owen: *Making Money*, 51

Johnson, Samuel, 290–91

Joslyn, Carl Smith, 200

Kantor, MacKinlay: *Midnight Lace*, 270–71

Kaufman, Enit: *American Portraits*, 241

Kent, Laura, 73

Kent, Rockwell: *Salamina*, 183
Kerfoot, J. P., 46
Kipling, Rudyard, 54, 214
Klyce, Scudder: *Dewey's Suppressed Psychology*, 131
Knopf, Alfred, 161, 178, 289
Knox, Jack, 96, 181, 193, 216

LaBatt, Lillian, 243
La Fontaine, Jean de, 15, 313–15
Lane, Gertrude Battles, 88, 116, 120, 123, 134, 163–64, 166–67, 170, 190–91
La Rochefoucauld, François de, 232
Laski, Harold: *American Democracy*, 268
Lathrop, Dorothy, 119
Lawrence, D. H., 17, 188, 288
Lee, Robert E., 323
Lewis, Edith, 27, 289
Lewis, May, 62
Lewis, Sinclair, 17, 156, 237; *Arrowsmith*, 5, 119; *The God-Seeker*, 272; *Main Street*, 4, 91, 152–53
Lindbergh, Charles, 212
Lippman, Walter: *U.S. Foreign Policy*, 229
Little, Frank, 71
Lovering, Joseph P., 6

McCarthy, Joseph, 300
McClung, Isabelle, 11, 12, 13, 28, 260, 261
McClure, S. S., 13
MacLeish, Archibald, 17, 198
Mailer, Norman: *The Naked and the Dead*, 17, 269
Mann, Dorothea, 61, 62, 63, 114
Markel, Lester, 217
Marquand, John P., 5, 226, 249, 292; *Sincerely, Willis Wayde*, 309
Maurois, André: *Le Cercle de Famille*, 174; *A Private Universe*, 174
Mead, Margaret, 19; "What Women Want," 253
Mears, Clif, 180
Mears, Nettie, 180
Medicis, Marie de, 80
Mencken, H. L., 236
Merck, George, 283
Meyer, Frank, 165
Meyer, Paul, 261
Michelangelo, 267
Miller, Arthur: *Death of a Salesman*, 17, 277–79
Milton, John, 321; *Comus*, 78
Moffett, Anne, 117
Montessori, Maria, 2, 19, 39, 72

Moody, William Vaughn, 102
Moore, Annie Carroll, 122
Morley, Christopher, 5, 8, 17, 223, 249, 290, 291
Morris, Lloyd R.: *Curtain Time*, 282
Mozart, Wolfgang Amadeus, 19, 302
Munro, Hugh (Saki): "The Open Window," 268
Mussolini, Benito, 197

Nuhn, Ferner, 163, 186, 203

Ober, Harold, 249
O'Hara, John: *Appointment in Samarra*, 16
O'Kane, Walter Collins: *Sun in the Sky*, 288
Oppenheim, Bertha, 132
Osborne, Evelyn, 11–13, 27, 28
Overton, Grant, 130

Page, Curtis Hidden, 14, 25
Pangborn, H. L.: "The Cry of the Children," 119
Papini, Giovanni, 321; *Life of Christ*, 2, 4, 320–21
Parsons, Alice Beal, 166
Pascal, Blaise, 321
Pattee, Fred Lewis, 159
Peach, Arthur W., 131
Perry, Bliss, 267
Pestalozzi, Johann Henrich, 91
Phelps, William Lyon, 5, 14, 15, 76, 92, 154
Porter, Gene Stratton, 44
Pottle, Frederick: "Catharsis," 244–46
Pound, Louise, 10
Pound, Roscoe, 50
Putnam, G. P., 13

Racine, Jean, 2
Rampersad, Arnold: *Richard Wright: Early Works*, 19, 233
Ravel, Maurice, 267
Reynolds, Amelia, 87, 89
Reynolds, Paul, 4, 8, 9, 14, 15, 19, 77, 78, 96, 113, 159, 165, 168
Reynolds, Paul Revere, Jr., 168, 239
Rindge, Agnes, 301
Rivers, Haywood Bill, 301
Robeson, Paul, 233
Roderick, Virginia, 50, 51, 81
Ronsard, Pierre de, 26
Roosevelt, Eleanor, 2; *Universal Declaration of Human Rights*, 304–5
Rousseau, Jean Jacques, 317

Rowell, Chester, 225
Russell, George, 296

Saki. *See* Munro, Hugh
Salter, Katharine, 219
Salvemini, Gaetano, 294
Santayana, George, 17, 218; *Persons and Places*, 218
Scherman, Bernardine K., 8; *A Treasury of Short Stories*, 266–68
Scherman, Harry, 8, 17, 18, 183, 192, 193, 194, 221, 223–25, 238, 258, 288, 303, 306
Scott, John Paul, 204, 281
Sedgwick, Anne, 95
Sedgwick, Ellery, 30, 31, 50
Seibel, George, 289
Shakespeare, William, 15, 123, 127
Shipherd, H. Robinson: *Americans All*, 121; *The Fine Art of Writing for Those Who Teach It*, 121
Sibut, Céline, 4, 48
Silone, Ignazio: *Bread and Wine*, 190
Simpson, Mary J., 126
Sinclair, Upton: *The Jungle*, 259
Skinner, John S., 156
Smith, Bradford, 7
Smith, Pauline, 105
Smollett, Tobias, 291
Soskin, William, 249
Spingarn, Joel, 311
Steegmuller, Francis: *La Grande Mademoiselle*, 315
Steinbeck, John: *The Moon Is Down*, 213; *The Wayward Bus*, 17, 257–59
Sterne, Laurence, 291; *Tristram Shandy*, 290
Stowe, Harriet Beecher: *Oldtown Folks*, 277; *Poganuck People*, 277
Suckow, Ruth, 7, 10; *Children and Other People*, 163; *The Folks*, 185; "Hollywood Gods and Goddesses," 203; *New Hope*, 204; "What Have I?," 203
Sunday, William Ashley, 165

Taylor, Helen, 19
Taylor, Joseph, 300
Tchaikovsky, Peter Ilich, 19, 197
Thackeray, William Makepeace, 321; *Vanity Fair*, 271
Thaddeus, Janice: "The Metamorphosis of Richard Wright's *Black Boy*," 19, 233
Thomas, Calvin, 31
Thomas, Paul, 31
Thoreau, Henry David, 237

Tilgher, Adriano: *Work: What It Has Meant to Men through the Ages*, 2
Tolstoy, Leo, 15, 263; "The Death of Ivan Ilyich," 267

Undset, Sigrid: *The Wild Orchid*, 162

Valtin, Jan: *Out of the Night*, 210
Van Waters, Miriam, 276–77
Vermeer, Jan, 186

Wagenknecht, Edward: *The Cavalcade of the American Novel*, 6
Wagner, Richard, 302
Wakeman, Frederick: *The Hucksters*, 250–52, 257–58
Wallace, Henry Agard, 273
Walsh, Richard, 229
Washington, Booker T., 19, 214, 300
Washington, Ida H., 1, 2, 4, 6
Watson, Thomas E., 127
Webster, Doris, 117
Webster, Henry Kitchell, 7, 9; *The Real Adventure*, 51–52
Wells, H. G., 52, 53, 161; *The Passionate Friends*, 52; *The Wife of Sir Isaac Harmon*, 52
Welty, Eudora, 15; "The Petrified Man," 268
West, Harmon, 173
Westenholz, Mary, 176, 254–55, 263–65
Wharton, Edith, 90; *The Age of Innocence*, 95
Wheeler, Howard Duryce, 81
White, William Allen, 4, 5, 223, 300
Whitman, Walt, 273, 274
Wiggam, Albert Edward, 111
Wilde, Oscar: "The Ballad of Redding Gaol," 255
Wilder, Thornton, 17, 198
Wiley, Louis, 14
Willard, Sumner, 289
Wilson, Woodrow, 64
Winchell, Walter, 300
Woll, Matthew, 225
Wood, Helen, 292
Wood, Meredith, 231, 292
Woods, Eugene J.: *I Wish I'd Written That*, 259
Woodward, Helen: *Through Many Windows*, 126
Woolf, Virginia: *A Room of One's Own*, 9
Wright, Harold Bell, 44

Wright, Richard, 6, 15, 18, 19, 237, 238; *American Hunger*, 233; *Black Boy*, 18, 231–39, 247–48; *Native Son*, 18, 231, 234
Wyman, Edith, 189
Wyman, Harold, 189

Yates, Elizabeth, 319; *Amos Fortune*, 320; *Pebble in a Pool*, 6, 320; *Prudence Crandall*, 320

Yaukey, Grace Sydenstricker: *The Exile's Daughter*, 220–21
Yezierska, Anzia, 7; *All I Could Never Be*, 11, 13, 169, 171–74; *Red Ribbon on a White Horse*, 293–96
Young, Owen D., 199, 225

Zimmermann, Arthur, 64